34

m

Application of Classification Techniques in Business, Banking and Finance

CONTEMPORARY STUDIES IN ECONOMIC AND FINANCIAL ANALYSIS, Volume 3

CONTEMPORARY STUDIES IN ECONOMIC AND FINANCIAL ANALYSIS

An International Series of Monographs

Series Editors: **Edward I. Altman and Ingo Walter**
Graduate School of Business Administration, New York University

Volume 1. **DYNAMICS OF FORECASTING FINANCIAL CYCLES: Theory, Technique and Implementation**
Lacy H. Hunt, II, *Fidelcor Inc. and the Fidelity Bank*

Volume 2. **COMPOSITE RESERVE ASSETS IN THE INTERNATIONAL MONETARY SYSTEM**
Jacob S. Dreyer, *Office of Monetary Research, U.S. Treasury*

Volume 3. **APPLICATION OF CLASSIFICATION TECHNIQUES IN BUSINESS, BANKING AND FINANCE**
Edward I. Altman, *Graduate School of Business Administration, New York University,* Robert B. Avery, *Graduate School of Industrial Administration, Carnegie-Mellon University,* Robert A. Eisenbeis, *Federal Deposit Insurance Corporation,* and Joseph F. Sinkey, Jr., *College of Business Administration, University of Georgia*

Volume 4. **PROBLEM AND FAILED INSITUTIONS IN THE COMMERCIAL BANKING INDUSTRY**
Joseph F. Sinkey, Jr., *College of Business Administration, University of Georgia*

Volume 5. **A NEW LOOK AT PORTFOLIO MANAGEMENT**
David M. Ahlers, *Graduate School of Business and Public Administration, Cornell University*

Volume 6. **MULTINATIONAL ELECTRONIC COMPANIES AND NATIONAL ECONOMIC POLICES**
Edmond Sciberras, *Science Policy Research Unit, University of Sussex*

Volume 7. **VENEZUELAN ECONOMIC DEVELOPMENT: A Politico-Economic Analysis**
Loring Allen, *University of Missouri, St. Louis*

Volume 8. **ENVIRONMENT, PLANNING AND THE MULTINATIONAL CORPORATION**
Thomas N. Gladwin, *New York University*

Volume 9. **FOREIGN DIRECT INVESTMENT, INDUSTRIALIZATION AND SOCIAL CHANGE**
Stephen J. Kobrin, *Sloan School of Management, Massachusetts Institute of Technology*

Volume 10. **IMPLICATIONS OF REGULATION ON BANK EXPANSION: A Simulation Analysis**
George S. Oldfield, Jr., *Graduate School of Business and Public Administration, Cornell University*

Volume 11. **IMPORT SUBSTITUTION, TRADE AND DEVELOPMENT**
Jaleel Ahmad, *Concordia University, Sir George Williams Campus*

Volume 12. **CORPORATE GROWTH AND COMMON STOCK RISK**
David R. Fewings, *McGill University*

Volume 13. **CAPITAL MARKET EQUILIBRIUM AND CORPORATE FINANCIAL DECISIONS**
Richard C. Stapleton, *Manchester Business and New York University,* and M.G. Subrahmanyam, *Indian Institute of Management and New York University*

Volume 14. **IMPENDING CHANGES FOR SECURITIES MARKETS: What Role for the Exchanges?**
Ernest Bloch and Robert A. Schwartz, *Graduate School of Business Administration, New York University*

Volume 15. **INDUSTRIAL INNOVATION AND INTERNATIONAL TRADING PERFORMANCE**
William B. Walker, *Science Policy Research Unit, University of Sussex*

Volume 16. **FINANCIAL POLICY, INFLATION AND ECONOMIC DEVELOPMENT: The Mexican Experience**
John K. Thompson, *Mellon Bank, N.A.*

Volume 17. **CORPORATE LIQUIDITY MANAGEMENT**
Michel Levasseur, *Centre d'Enseignement Superieur des Affaires, Jouy-en-Josas, France*

Volume 18. **STABILIZATION OF INTERNATIONAL COMMODITY MARKETS**
Paul Hallwood, *University of Aberdeen*

Volume 19. **PROBLEMS IN EUROPEAN CORPORATE FINANCE: Text and Cases**
Michel Schlosser, *Centre d'Enseignement Superieur des Affaires, Jouy-en-Josas, France*

Volume 20. **THE MULTINATIONAL ENTERPRISE: International Investment and Host-Country Impacts**
Thomas G. Parry, *School of Ecomomics, University of New South Wales*

Volume 21. **POLICY RESPONSES TO RESOURCES DEPLETION: The Case of Mercury**
Nigel Roxburgh, *Management Studies Division, The Economist Intelligence Unit, Ltd.*

Volume 22. **THE INTERNATIONAL MONEY MARKET: An Assessment of Forecasting Techniques and Market Efficiency**
Richard M. Levich, *Graduate School of Business Administration, New York University*

Volume 23. **TRANSNATIONAL CONGLOMERATES AND THE ECONOMICS OF DEPENDENT DEVELOPMENT: A Case Study of the International Electrial Oligopoly and Brazil's Electrical Industry**
Richard Newfarmer, *University of Notre Dame*

Volume 24. **THE POLITICAL ECONOMY OF ENVIRONMENTAL PROTECTION**
Horst Siebert, *University of Mannheim,* and Ariane Berthoin Antal, *International Institute for Environment and Society, Science Center, Berlin*

Volume 25. **BIDDING AND OIL LEASES**
James B. Ramsey, *New York University*

Volume 26. **THE ECONOMICS OF EXPLORATION FOR ENERGY RESOURCES**
James B. Ramsey, *New York University*

Volume 27. **TECHNOLOGY TRANSFER TO DEVELOPING COUNTRIES: The Case of the Fertilizer Industry**
Subrata Ghatak, *University of Leicester and University of Guelph*

Volume 28. **MULTINATIONALS: Bank and Corporation Relationships**
Olivier Pastre, *Universite Paris-Nord*

Volume 29. **THE PRIMARY MARKET FOR MUNICIPAL DEBT: Bidding Rules and Cost of Long-Term Borrowing**
G.O. Bierwag, *University of Oregon*

Volume 30. **EFFICIENCY IN THE MUNICIPAL BOND MARKET: The Use of Tax Exempt Financing for "Private" Purposes**
George G. Kaufman, *Loyola University of Chicago*

Volume 31. **FOREIGN INVESTMENT AND TECHNOLOGY TRANSFER: The Tire Industry in Latin America**
Peter West, *Caracus, Venezuela*

Volume 32. **DIMENSIONS OF ENERGY ECONOMICS**
Noel D. Uri, *Catholic University of America*

Volume 33. **INDIGENIZATION AND ECONOMIC DEVELOPMENT: The Nigerian Experience**
Nicholas Balabkins, *Lehigh University*

Volume 34. **INTERNATIONAL FINANCIAL MANAGEMENT: Problems, Issues, and Experiences**
John S. Oh, *Portland State University*

Volume 35. **PURCHASING POWER PARITY AND EXCHANGE RATES: Theory, Evidence and Relevance**
Lawrence H. Officer, *Michigan State University*

Volume 36. **FINANCIAL REPORTING RULES AND CORPORATE DECISIONS: A Study of Public Policy**
Bertrand Horwitz, *State University of New York-Binghamton* and Richard Kolodny, *University of Maryland*

Volume 37. **CONSUMER EMANCIPATION AND ECONOMIC DEVELOPMENT**
Hans B. Thorelli, *Villa Serbelloni, Bellagio and Indiana University* and Gerald D. Sentell, *NIDA, Bangkok and the University of Tennessee*

Volume 38. **INSURING NUCLEAR POWER: Liability, Safety and Economic Efficiency**
William C. Wood, *Owen Graduate School of Management, Vanderbilt University*

Volume 39. **NEW DIMENSIONS IN PUBLIC UTILITY PRICING**
Noel D. Uri, *Catholic University of America*

Volume 40. **ECONOMIC DECISIONS UNDER INFLATION: The Impact of Accounting Measurement Error**
Stephen M. Cross, *College of the Holy Cross*

This volume is dedicated to:

Elaine Altman and Gregory Alain

Mary Ellen Avery, David and Mark

Marilyn Eisenbeis, Mark and Jill

Mr. and Mrs. Joseph Sinkey, Sr.

Application of Classification Techniques in Business, Banking and Finance

by EDWARD I. ALTMAN
Graduate School of Business Administration
New York University

ROBERT B. AVERY
Graduate School of Industrial Administration
Carnegie-Mellon University

ROBERT A. EISENBEIS
Division of Research and Statistics
Board of Governors of the
Federal Reserve System

JOSEPH F. SINKEY, JR.
College of Business Administration
University of Georgia

JAI PRESS INC.
Greenwich, Connecticut

Library of Congress Cataloging in Publication Data
Main entry under title:

Application of classification techniques in business, banking, and finance.

(Contemporary studies in economic and financial analysis; v. 3)
Bibliography: p.
Includes indexes.
1. Commercial statistics. 2. Finance—Statistical methods. I. Altman, Edward I., 1941- . II. Title: Classification techniques in business, banking, and finance. III. Series.
HF1017.A65 332'.028 76-5759
ISBN 0-89232-004-4 AACR2

36 Sherwood Place
Greenwich, Connecticut 06830

ISBN NUMBER: 0-89232-004-4
Library of Congress Catalog Card Number: 76-5759
Manufactured in the United States of America

CONTENTS

List of Figures *xiii*
List of Tables *xv*
Preface *xix*

I. Two-Group Classification Techniques: Conceptual Issues **1**
Introduction 1
Linear Probability Model 3
Introduction—Least Square 3
Heteroskedastic Adjustment 5
The Linear Probability Model 7
Constrained Estimation 8
Example—Director Interlocks I 11
Probit and Logit Analysis 13
Introduction 13
The Probit Model 14
The Logit Model 16
Probit/Logit Models and Probabilistic Choice 18
Parameter Estimation—Many Observations per Cell 23
Parameter Estimation—Individual Data 27
Example—Director Interlocks II 31
Discriminant Analysis 33
Introduction 33
Classification Probabilities 34
Classification—Group Assignment 39
Significance Tests and Examinations of Group Overlaps 42
Discriminant Functions 47
Example—Director Interlocks III 52
Appendix 54
Maximum Likelihood Estimation 54

II. Multigroup Classification Techniques: Conceptual Issues **59**
Introduction 59
Regression, Probit, and Logit—Multiple Choice 60
Introduction 60
Ordered Multiple Choice 61
The Ordered Logistic Model 62
The Ordered Probit Model 66
Unordered Multiple Choice 68
Multinominal Logit Model 70
Probabilistic Choice 73
Multinominal Logit—Parameter Estimation 76
Multinominal Probit Model 80
Sequential Models 82
Multiple Discriminant Analysis 84
Introduction 84
Classification Probabilities 85
Classification—Group Assignments 88
Significance Tests 91
Discriminant Functions 96
Special Topics 101
Nonrandom Sampling 101
Model Selection—Goodness of Fit 104
Model Selection—Theoretical Considerations 109
Example—Director Interlocks IV 112

III. Discriminant Analysis Application Problems **119**
Introduction 119
Violation of the Assumptions of the Discriminant Analysis Model 120
Multivariate Normality 120
Unequal Group Covariance Matrices 126
The Definitions of the Groups 129
The Relative Significances of Individual Variables 135
Reduction of Dimensionality and Elimination of Insignificant Variables 144
Variable Selection Methods 145
Elimination of Discriminant Functions 148
Specification of Classification Schemes 150
The Selection of the Appropriate A Priori Probabilities and Costs 150
Assessment of Classification Error Rates 153

Time-Series Applications 158
Summary and Conclusions 160

IV. Credit Scoring Applications 167
Introduction 167
The Methodology of Credit Scoring Models 168
Review of Credit Scoring Models 172
Methodological and Statistical Problems in Credit Scoring Models 189
Distribution of the Variables 190
Equal versus Unequal Covariances 191
The Role of Individual Variables 191
Problems in the Definitions of the Groups 192
Use of Inappropriate A Priori Probabilities and Costs of Misclassification 193
Estimation of Classification Error Rates 194
Selection of Analysis Samples 194
Time-Series Problems 196
Summary and Conclusions 196

V. The Application of Statistical Classification Methods to Bond Quality Ratings 199
Introduction 199
Statistical Bond Rating Analysis 201
Evolution of Statistical Techniques 202
Multiple Regression Analysis Studies 203
Discriminant Analysis Studies 205
Logit Analysis 210
How Accurate Have Statistical Bond Rating Studies Been? 211
Rating Replication Results—Can They Be Improved? 214
Statistical Methodology 215
Industry Effects 215
Bond Rating—A Subjective Process 216
Mixed Bond Ratings—An Observed Phenomenon 217
Conclusion 218
Appendix A 220
Appendix B 224

VI. Statistical Classification Models Applied to Common Stock Analysis **227**
Introduction 227
Common Stock Investment Category Classification 228
Common Stock Price and Earnings Performance Classification 232
Price-Earnings (P-E) Ratios 232
Price Volatility Classification 235
Earnings Classification 236
Discrimination Based on Accounting Information and Common Stock Returns Performance 237
Collinearity and Multivariate Normality 240
Sample Properties and Estimation Results 241
Capital Structure Decisions and Classification Techniques 242
Debt versus Equity 242
Convertible Debt Characteristics: Debt or Equity 243
Share Repurchase 244
Summary and Conclusion 246
Appendix 248

VII. Failure–Prediction Models for Nonfinancial Firms **255**
Introduction 255
Models for Predicting Business Failures: Why, What, How, and for Whom 255
Why Predict Business Failures? 255
What Business Failure to Predict? 256
How to Predict Business Failures 257
For Whom the Prediction Tolls 257
A Decade of Failure Prediction: Beaver (1967) to Altman (1977) 257
Beaver (1967) 258
Altman (1968) to (1977) 262
Altman's Critics 270
Zeta Analysis 272
Altman, Haldeman and Narayana (1977) 272
Seven Other Models 277
Blum's Failing Company Model (1974) 277
Deakin (1972) 280
Libby (1975) 283

Deakin (1977) 286
Edmister (1972) 289
Elam (1975) 292
Wilcox (1971a), (1971b), (1973), and (1976) 295
Epilogue 300
Appendix 303

VIII. Early-Warning Systems for Financial Institutions 307
Introduction 307
The Financial Environment in the 1980s 308
The Concept of an Early-Warning System 308
Information Available for Identifying Banks with Financial Difficulties 309
Early Warning and Bank Supervisory Issues 310
FDIC Studies 312
Meyer and Pifer (1970) 312
Sinkey (1974–1979) 315
Population Predictions: National Banks 325
The Outlier Approach 326
The Failed-Bank Approach 328
Critique of FDIC Research 332
Federal Reserve Bank of New York Studies 333
Introduction: Martin (1977) 333
The National Bank Surveillance System 339
Introduction 339
The Components of NBSS 339
The NBSS Outlier or Peer-Group Approach 340
Summary and Conclusions 344
Critique 344
Federal Reserve Studies 345
Hanweck (1977a, b) 345
The Simulation Model 345
The Failure-Prediction Model 346
Other Studies 348
Introduction 348
Santomero and Vinso (1977) 349
Pettway (1980) 354
Shick and Sherman (1980) 356
Pettway and Sinkey (1980) 356
Altman (1977) 357

Collins (1980) 361
Altman and Loris (1976) 361
Epilogue on Early-Warning Systems 364
Appendix 367
References 373
Author Index 405
Subject Index 413

List of Figures

Chapter I

1.	The Linear Probability Model	8
2.	Biased OLS Slopes	9
3.	Biased Quadratic Programming Slopes	10
4.	Probit Probability Model	15
5.	Standard Normal and Logistic Cumulative Distribution Functions	17
6.	Standard Normal and Logistic Density Function	17
7.	Standard Extreme Value Density Functions	22
8.	Quadratic Classification	41
9.	Linear Classification	42
10.	Reduced Space Transformation	51

Chapter II

1.	Classification Cutoffs	113

Chapter VII

1.	The Relationship Between EBIT and SLTA	265

Chapter VIII

1.	The Distribution of S & V's Safety Index	351

List of Tables

Chapter I

1. Variable Statistics 12

Chapter II

1. Horse Race Model 106
2. Predicted Probabilities Director Interlocks 114
3. Model Fits 116

Chapter III

1. Classification Results—Iris Data 130
2. Expected Group Overlap—Iris Data 130
3. Criteria for Determining the Importance of Variables 137
4. Significance of the Roots in the Security Analysis Problem 148
5. Comparison of One- and Two-Dimensional Linear Classification Results—Security Analysis Problem 149
6. Equal and Unequal *A Priori* Quadratic Classification Results—Business Loan Study 152
7. Error Estimation Methods for Two-Group Equal Covariances Case 155

Chapter IV

1. Consumer Loan Studies 173
2. Commercial and Business Loan Studies 182

Chapter V

1. Comparison of Empirical Results: Corporate Bond Rating Models 213
2. Identical Rating Changes by Moody's and S&P on Public Utility Bonds, Summary Data on Comparative Timing (1960–1970) 217
3. Number of Times and Duration That One Rating Agency's Change in Bond Rating Leads the Other (Public Utility Bonds, 1960–1979) 219

Chapter VII

1. The Twenty Largest U.S. Bankruptcies 256
2. Means and F-Statistics One Year Prior to Bankruptcy 264
3. Z-Scores: Best and Worst Performers 268
4. Stock Prices: Best and Worst Z-Scores 268
5. Type-I Errors: ZETA Model versus Altman's 1968 Model 275
6. Blum's Validation-Sample Classification Results 279
7. Failed and Nonfailed Firms: Means of Cash Flow, Net Income and Total Debt 282
8. Loan Officers' Predictive Accuracy (60 Firms) 285
9. Deakin's Classification Results 286
10. Deakin's Follow-up Analysis 287
11. Capitalized Leases: Bankrupt and Nonbankrupt Firms 293
12. Elam's Financial Ratios 294
13. Wilcox's Classification Results 299
14. W. T. Grant's Gambler's–Ruin Score 299

Chapter VIII

1. Meyer and Pifer's Zero-One Registration Results: One Year Prior to Failure 314
2. Problem Banks, 1968 IV—1976 II 317
3. Means and Standard Deviations of Selected Variables for Problem and Nonproblem Banks 321
4. Quadratic Classification Results 322
5. Classification Results 325
6. Prediction of Problem National Banks 326
7. Group Means 326
8. Large Banks and the Predictability of NCR 332
9. Hanweck's Group Means and t-Statistics One Year before Failure 348

10. Hanweck's Estimated Probit Function 348
11. Bank Capital: More or Less? 352
12. Pettway's Sample of Failed Banks 355
13. Altman's Lachenbruch Validation Tests for SLAs 359
14. Altman's Composite-Rating Scheme for SLAs 360

Preface

The application of statistical techniques to classification problems in business, banking, and finance has increased dramatically over the last decade or so. Indeed, the pragmatic implementation of these techniques in certain areas of both private and public enterprises have become accepted and important in the operation of these entities. This book is primarily concerned with classification techniques, one of the major "families" of statistical analysis, and with the conceptual and practical issues underlying their usage. The presentation emphasizes the major advantages and disadvantages of alternative classification techniques including ordinary least squares as a linear probability function, probit, tobit, and logit analyses and several forms of discriminant analyses.

This book is divided into two main sections. Section A (3 chapters) explores the conceptual and theoretical aspects of alternative classification methodologies and lays the groundwork for the applications described in Section B (5 chapters). Five distinct applied areas in business, banking, and finance are explored in detail. The subject areas are (1) credit scoring, (2) fixed-income-security ratings, (3) common-stock analysis, (4) failure classification of nonfinancial institutions and (5) early warning and detection of problems in financial institutions. Each chapter focuses upon the major classification research in a particular area with commentary regarding the strengths and weaknesses of the studies reviewed. Particular emphasis is placed upon the proper application of statistical procedures to significant and current issues in the focal areas. A better understanding of the underlying economic, behavioral, and financial processes is an important aspect of the overall analysis.

The book is written for both academic and professional audiences. We have attempted to present material so that it will be useful to students, researchers, and managers who have worked, or are planning to work, with statistical classification techniques and who would like to learn more about the potential benefits and pitfalls in their utilization. One does not have to be trained as a statistician to plan and implement a careful study of a classification problem (i.e., one involving assigning sample observations to distinct groups). There is considerable opportunity to learn from the mistakes and successes of past studies. Our objective has been to provide (1) a strong foundation to understand classification analysis (2) constructive commentary on the research analyzed, and in some areas (3) ideas and guidelines for future successful research.

Depending upon the background of the reader, the book can be examined in different sequences. For example, one who is proficient with the concepts and utility of statistical classification techniques might skim over the material in Section A to determine if it is in conformity with his/her own thinking. In contrast, the reader who is unfamiliar with these techniques should read Section A more carefully. Regardless of one's background, however, the chapters in Section B are quite independent from one another and can be read in any sequence. The material in these chapters reflects both the personal experience of the authors in applying these techniques and the insights gained from a careful analysis of other relevant works.

As a point of information for the readers, the writing work load was distributed as follows: Chapters I and II were written by Robert Avery, Chapters III and IV by Robert Eisenbeis, Chapters V and VI by Edward Altman and Chapters VII and VIII by Joseph Sinkey. Because we have exchanged ideas and comments on various drafts of our chapters, we share responsibility for any errors of omission and/or commission.

Although the book has been in the works for several years, we have attempted to present the most up-to-date material. We are most appreciative of JAI Press for being patient with us over the long process of writing a book with four authors.

Edward I. Altman
Robert B. Avery
Robert A. Eisenbeis
Joseph F. Sinkey, Jr.

Chapter I

Two-Group Classification Techniques: Conceptual Issues

INTRODUCTION

The first three chapters of this book have a significantly different emphasis from the last five. Our concern in this chapter and the two that follow is with statistics and estimation technique. Our purpose is to provide the statistical groundwork for the application issues discussed later in the book. We will make some attempt to link statistical concerns with substantive and modeling issues. However, most of these linkages are left to the application chapters.

Although the models that we will be presenting in these chapters vary quite substantially in their assumptions, structure, and in the statistical techniques used to estimate their parameters, they all have a common bond. In each case the model links a set of "independent" variables to a "dependent" variable that can take on only discrete values. These can be values for units such as groups, classes, or cells. The dependent variable could be ordered or unordered. For example, the dependent variable might be college major—economics, finance, or other—three unranked groups. Alternatively the dependent variable might have an implied ordering, such as bond ratings or Michelin restaurant rating. The critical difference that sets these problems off from conventional models with continuous dependent variables is the fact that the dependent variable cannot be ranked with a cardinal scale. Thus we are concerned with problems where we want to predict student's college major but are unable (or unwilling) to assign a cardinal ranking to "majors." We cannot say whether economics is a "better" major than finance; or even if we could, we are unwilling to say how much better.

Examples of discrete dependent variables are numerous in finance. Firm bankruptcy, loan default, bond ratings, public–private ownership, and loan classifications are all examples of "grouped" dependent variables of interest in finance. Given such a dependent variable, the researcher is generally interested in predicting the "value" of the dependent variable given values of certain independent variables. For example, we might believe that key financial ratios are accurate indicators of firm bankruptcy, or we might try to link firm characteristics to bond ratings. The objective of the first three chapters of this book will be to present a number of model forms that could be used to link the independent and dependent variables and to show how these models could be estimated. The model forms will be quite general, accommodating lines of causality running from the independent to dependent variables or vice versa.

In this chapter, we concern ourselves with two-group problems—problems where the dependent variable can take on only two values. Sometimes referred to as dichotomous, 0–1, or two-choice problems, these encompass instances where the dependent variable is a yes/no, bankrupt/nonbankrupt, buy/don't buy variable. We consider four different models for this kind of problem: (1) linear probability model (regression); (2) probit model; (3) logit model; and (4) discriminant analysis model. We discuss each of these models in turn, focusing both on the assumptions and underpinnings of the model and on estimation issues. We also use a running example to illustrate an actual application of the models.

In Chapter II, we consider problems where the dependent variable can take on more than two values. Sometimes referred to as polytomous, multigroup, or multiple-choice models, these include problems where the dependent variable is both unordered or ordered (ordinally). We consider the multi-group extensions of the probit, logit, regression, and discriminant analysis models. We also include a discussion of how to choose among models both on a theoretical, substantive basis and by the "fit of the data." We also deal briefly with the issue of stratified sampling.

For the probit and logit models, we discuss both applied and theoretical issues simultaneously in Chapters I and II. However, since discriminant analysis has been used so extensively in finance, we limit our discussion in Chapters I and II primarily to theoretical issues and devote an entire chapter, Chapter III, to applications. We provide an extensive survey of practical empirical issues, drawing not only from finance but other areas as well.

Although some areas may be somewhat technical and burdensome reading for the casual user, we have tried to make these chapters readable for persons with a basic knowledge of multivariate statistics. A good understanding of regression should be sufficient.

LINEAR PROBABILITY MODEL

Introduction—Least Squares

By far the most common empirical model form used in economics and finance is the linear regression model. Both because of its understandability and ease of use, the regression framework is particularly attractive. It is natural, therefore, to seek ways of casting binary dependent variable models as regressions. Suppose, for example, that firm bankruptcy is modeled as follows.

Let y be a dependent variable that takes on only two values:

$$y_n = \begin{cases} 1 & \text{if the } n\text{th firm goes bankrupt} \\ 0 & \text{otherwise} \end{cases}$$

Consider a sample of N firms where we postulate the model

$$y_n = \alpha + \beta X_n + \varepsilon_n \qquad n = 1, \ldots, N \tag{1.1}$$

where X_n is the firm's debt/equity ratio, α and β are unknown coefficients, and ε_n an unknown error. With the exception of the particular nature of the dependent variable, this is the classical linear regression model. We have chosen a simplified case with only one explanatory variable; however, the model is easily generalized to m independent variables:

$$X_n'\beta = \sum_{i=1}^{m} x_n^{(i)} \beta^{(i)}$$

In the classical framework we require certain conditions on the errors to hold. In particular, that

1. $E(\varepsilon_n|X) = 0$: the expectation of the error term given X is zero. This condition covers both the case where X is fixed and X is random.
2. $E(\varepsilon_n^2|X) = \sigma^2$: the variance of each error is identical.
3. $E(\varepsilon_n\varepsilon_{n'}|X) = 0$ where $n \neq n'$: the covariance of the errors of different observations is zero.

Under these conditions, the common method of estimating the parameters α and β is to compute the least squares coefficients,

$$\hat{\beta} = \frac{\sum_{n=1}^{N} (X_n - \bar{X})(y_n - \bar{y})}{\sum_{n=1}^{N} (X_n - \bar{X})^2}$$

$$\hat{\alpha} = \bar{y} - \hat{\beta}\bar{X}$$

where $\bar{X}$ and $\bar{y}$ are the sample means of X and y. If Condition 1 holds, then the least squares coefficients will be *unbiased*: the expectation of the coefficients will be the true parameters. With certain general restrictions on how the independent variable is drawn, Condition 1 also implies that the coefficients will be *consistent*: they converge to the true parameters with probability one as the sample size goes to infinity. If Conditions 2 and 3 also hold true, the least squares coefficients will be "best" or "efficient" in that they have the *smallest variance* of the general class of linear unbiased estimators.

Let us return to the bankruptcy model (1.1) and ask whether it meets the conditions of the classical linear regression model. Consider the expectation of the random variable y_n given X_n. Define P_n as the *ex-ante* probability of the nth firm going bankrupt given the firm's debt/equity ratio. Since the variable y_n can take on only two values, we can describe its entire probability distribution

$$y_n = \begin{cases} 1 & \text{with probability } P_n \\ 0 & \text{with probability } 1 - P_n \end{cases}$$

which implies

$$E(y_n|X_n) = 1 \cdot (P_n) + 0 \cdot (1 - P_n)$$
$$= P_n$$

Thus, P_n can also be interpreted as the expectation of y_n given X_n. However, we can also take the expectation of both sides of Eq. (1.1)

$$E(y_n|X_n) = \alpha + \beta X_n + E(\varepsilon_n|X_n) \tag{1.2}$$

If we assume that $E(\varepsilon_n|X_n) = 0$ to satisfy Condition 1, it implies that

$$E(y_n|X_n) = \alpha + \beta X_n$$

or

$$P_n = \alpha + \beta X_n$$

Thus the assumption that the errors have an expectation of zero implies that we can interpret the regression equation as describing the probability of bankruptcy given the debt/equity ratio. Thus the probability of bankruptcy will be a linear function of the debt/equity ratio, which has led Eq. (1.1) to be referred to as the *linear probability model.*

We can flip this argument around and show that the assumption that $P_n = \alpha + \beta X_n$ implies that the errors will have an expectation of zero. Given X_n, y_n is a Bernoulli random variable that can take on only two values. Obviously, ε_n will also have only two possible values. Specifically, given X_n, the distribution of ε_n is

	ε_n	*Probability*
$y_n = 1$	$1 - (\alpha + \beta X_n)$	P_n
$y_n = 0$	$-(\alpha + \beta X_n)$	$1 - P_n$

If we assume $P_n = \alpha + \beta X_n$, we can solve for the expectation of ε_n

$$\begin{aligned} E(\varepsilon_n|X_n) &= (1 - \alpha - \beta X_n)P_n + (-\alpha - \beta X_n)(1 - P_n) \\ &= (1 - \alpha - \beta X_n)(\alpha + \beta X_n) - (\alpha + \beta X_n)(1 - \alpha - \beta X_n) \\ &= 0 \end{aligned}$$

Thus, if Eq. (1.1) is a linear probability model, then the errors will satisfy the conditions for least squares coefficients to be unbiased and in general consistent, despite the fact that ε_n can take on only two distinct values.

Heteroskedastic Adjustment

Although Condition 1 of the classical linear regression model holds for the linear probability model, in general, Condition 2 will be violated. We can solve for the variance of ε_n as

$$\begin{aligned} E(\varepsilon_n^2|X_n) &= (1 - \alpha - \beta X_n)^2 P_n + (-\alpha - \beta X_n)^2(1 - P_n) \\ &= (1 - \alpha - \beta X_n)^2(\alpha + \beta X_n) + (\alpha + \beta X_n)^2(1 - \alpha - \beta X_n) \\ &= (1 - \alpha - \beta X_n)(\alpha + \beta X_n) \\ &= P_n(1 - P_n) \end{aligned}$$

Thus, the variance of ε_n will depend on the value of P_n. Since P_n will be expected to vary across observations, this suggests that the error variances will be heteroskedastic and not constant. Even though least squares coefficients will be unbiased, they will not be efficient, hence minimum variance.

One effect of the violation of the assumption of homoskedastic errors (Condition 2) is that the standard errors estimated for the ordinary least squares (OLS) coefficients and shown on computer printouts will be *biased.* Furthermore, the direction (high or low) of bias is uncertain. Thus, even if one ignores the fact that the binary regression errors are heteroskedastic and computes the OLS coefficients, the standard errors and functions of the standard errors, such as *t*-statistics, should not be used.

The standard fix-up for heteroskedastic problems is weighted or generalized least squares (GLS). If P_n were known and Condition 3 holds, we could weight each observation by the square root of the error variance and perform OLS on the transformed observations. Thus we fit

$$[P_n(1 - P_n)]^{1/2}y_n = [P_n(1 - P_n)]^{1/2}(\alpha + \beta X_n) + [P_n(1 - P_n)]^{1/2}\varepsilon_n \quad (1.3)$$

The resulting GLS coefficients will be unbiased, in general consistent, and most importantly, efficient.

In practice, we are unlikely to actually know P_n (particularly since P_n depends on the unknown α and β). This suggests an approximate procedure sometimes called "modified GLS" (see Goldberger, 1964). The first step is to run the model OLS (ignoring the heteroskedasticity), computing coefficients $\hat{\alpha}$ and $\hat{\beta}$. Since these estimates are consistent, they can be used to calculate consistent estimates of the probabilities (see McGillivray, 1970)

$$\hat{P}_n = \hat{\alpha} + \hat{\beta}X_n$$

We note, as an interesting algebraic characteristic of OLS, that the mean of the estimated $\hat{P}_n$'s will be identical to the fraction of the sample where $y_n = 1$. We then weight observations by the estimated probabilities, fitting

$$[\hat{P}_n(1 - \hat{P}_n)]^{1/2}y_n = [\hat{P}_n(1 - \hat{P}_n)]^{1/2}(\alpha + \beta X_n) + [\hat{P}_n(1 - \hat{P}_n)]^{1/2}\varepsilon_n \quad (1.4)$$

with OLS. Because we are using estimated P_n's, we can no longer unambiguously claim that the modified GLS coefficients are more efficient than OLS. We can show that asymptotically in large samples the modified GLS coefficients will be more efficient. However, this may not be the case in small samples.

As with all modified GLS problems, there is disagreement as to when the gains to GLS outweigh the costs. The asymptotic properties of modified GLS argue strongly for its use when samples are large. It will also be the case that descriptive statistics such as *t*-statistics and coefficient standard errors computed for OLS computer packages will be incorrect without the heteroskedastic adjustment. However, there are particular problems with binary regression that argue against the heteroskedastic adjustment. The variance term $P_n(1 - P_n)$ is smallest for observations with probabilities close to one or zero. Thus by weighting by the inverse of the variance, the heteroskedastic adjustment tends to place excessive weight on extreme observations. It is also more likely to amplify problems of model misspecification. For these reasons, some authors, such as Domencich and McFadden (1975), recommend the unweighted OLS procedure over the heteroskedastic adjustment.

It is often mistakenly believed that regression errors must be normal for OLS coefficient estimators to have desirable properties. This, of course, is not true; however, nonnormal errors may cause problems in the use of statistical tests. When sample sizes are small, the Bernoulli form of the binary regression errors suggest caution in the use of normal-based statistics (such as regression F and coefficient t-statistics). However, with larger samples, such tests could be justified on asymptotic central-limit theorem grounds (see Warner, 1963 and Goodman, 1976).

The Linear Probability Model

A serious weakness of the linear probability model is the possibility that for some observations, $\alpha + \beta X_n$ may be outside the zero–one interval. This can cause problems for several reasons. First, our interpretation of $\alpha + \beta X_n$ is the *ex-ante* probability of bankruptcy given X_n. Clearly a probability that is negative or greater than one has no meaning. Secondly, a value $\alpha + \beta X_n$ greater than one or less than zero must imply a violation of the assumption of zero-expectation errors necessary for least squares estimation. For example, both possible values of ε_n are positive if $\alpha + \beta X_n$ is negative, thus it cannot have an expectation of zero. For these reasons, the linear probability model is usually modified in the following way:

$$P_n = \begin{cases} 0 & \text{if } \alpha + \beta X_n \leq 0 \\ \alpha + \beta X_n & \text{if } 0 < \alpha + \beta X_n < 1 \\ 1 & \text{if } 1 \leq \alpha + \beta X_n \end{cases}$$

Thus the probability is linear in X_n only for the bounded zero–one region. Above a certain value of X, the probability of bankruptcy is assumed to be one. Similarly the probability is assumed to be zero for all X below a certain value. This model is depicted graphically in Figure I.1. Note that the probability is linear in X only between the bounds $-\alpha/\beta$ and $(1 - \alpha)/\beta$.

The alteration of the linear probability model created by the end bounds should not affect the properties of least squares estimates if we are willing to assume that X is drawn only from the interval $-\alpha/\beta$ to $(1 - \alpha)/\beta$. Note that this is not necessarily an unreasonable assumption. For example, the debt/equity variable we have used in our running example might naturally be bounded by construction. Note, however, that even if the "true" probabilities are restricted to the zero–one in-

Figure I.1. The Linear Probability Model

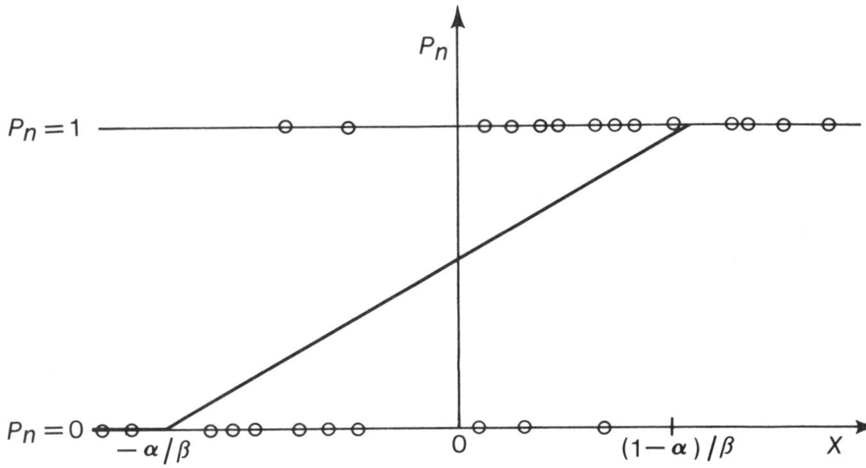

terval, it is possible that estimated probabilities will not be. If we are concerned only with prediction, one possibility would be to set extreme predicted probabilities to either zero or one. However, this may not set well with the view that no events can be predicted with the absolute certainty implied by zero or one probabilities. In fact, it may even be the case that the sample contains observations that directly contradict the certainty prediction.

Another problem generated by estimated probabilities outside the zero–one interval is the possibility of inadmissible weights for the heteroskedastic adjustment. Extreme predicted probabilities from the first stage will imply negative variances: $\hat{P}_n(1 - \hat{P}_n) < 0$; hence, negative weights. There are several possible solutions to this problem. One possibility is to drop any such observations. Alternatively, we could assign them an arbitrary weight. For example, Smith and Cicchetti (1972) ran Monte Carlo studies comparing three different weighting schemes for observations with negative estimated variances: (1) setting $\hat{P}_n$ to .5; (2) using the absolute value of the estimated variances; and (3) setting $\hat{P}_n$ to .98 or .02. Unfortunately, their study did not yield unambiguous evidence as to which method is best.

Constrained Estimation

We should emphasize that as long as the X variable is restricted to the range where the "true probability" ($\alpha + \beta X_n$) lies between zero and one, least squares coefficient estimates will still be unbiased and consistent. This will be the case even if some predicted probabilities calculated from the estimated coefficients $\hat{\alpha}$ and $\hat{\beta}$ happen to lie outside the interval. If extreme predicted probabilities are unacceptable, however, it is possible to estimate Eq. (1.1) by least squares but subject to the constraint that

$$0 \leqslant \hat{\alpha} + \hat{\beta}X_n \leqslant 1$$

for all observations in the sample. Obviously, if all predicted probabilities are within the zero–one interval for the unrestricted OLS coefficients, then the constraint is irrelevant. Otherwise, the estimation procedure can be expressed as a quadratic programming problem and solved by a straightforward algorithm. This heuristic will produce estimates that are consistent but will be biased in small samples. The direction of the bias will be to underestimate the steepness of the slope. Domencich and McFadden (1975) argue that on a mean-squared error basis, the inequality constrained coefficients are likely to be preferable to OLS estimates. However, they are also considerably more difficult and costly to compute (if OLS violates the constraints), and more sensitive to specification error.

The estimation problem changes significantly if we believe that the "true probability" of some sample observations is in fact zero or one. In this case, OLS estimates will generally be biased. This is illustrated by Figure I.2. Note that the estimated regression slope coefficient underestimates the slope of the true linear probability model.

An alternative estimation procedure would be to take explicit account of the boundary conditions. Again formulating the procedure as a quadratic programming problem, we minimize

$$\sum(y_n - \hat{P}_n)^2$$

Figure I.2. Biased OLS Slopes

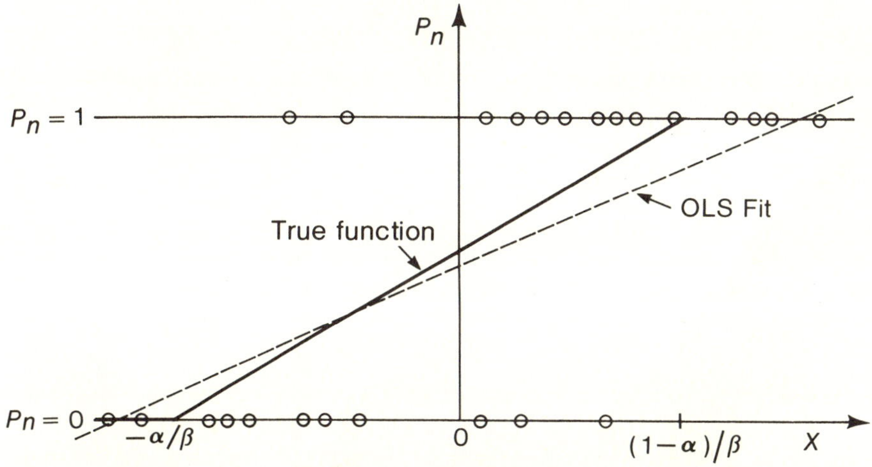

where

$$\hat{P}_n = \begin{cases} 0 & \text{if } \hat{\alpha} + \hat{\beta}X_n \leq 0 \\ \hat{\alpha} + \hat{\beta}X_n & \text{if } 0 < \hat{\alpha} + \hat{\beta}X_n < 1 \\ 1 & \text{if } \hat{\alpha} + \hat{\beta}X_n \geq 1 \end{cases}$$

To insure model consistency, we might require that

$$\hat{P}_n \neq 1 \text{ if } y_n = 0$$

and

$$\hat{P}_n \neq 0 \text{ if } y_n = 1$$

This procedure will yield consistent coefficient estimates, although they will be biased in small samples. If all observations near the interval upper bound happen to be ones, or to be zeros near the lower bound, then the quadratic programming coefficients will systematically overestimate the slope. This is illustrated by Figure I.3. As with the quadratic programming problem we discussed earlier, this procedure is likely to be expensive and difficult to use. There may also be serious objections to the underlying assumption that some observations can be predicted with absolute certainty.

It is clear from the above discussion that there are no clear-cut rules to use in estimating the linear probability model. Arguments can be made for the use of each of the methods we have proposed—OLS,

Figure I.3. Biased Quadratic Programming Slopes

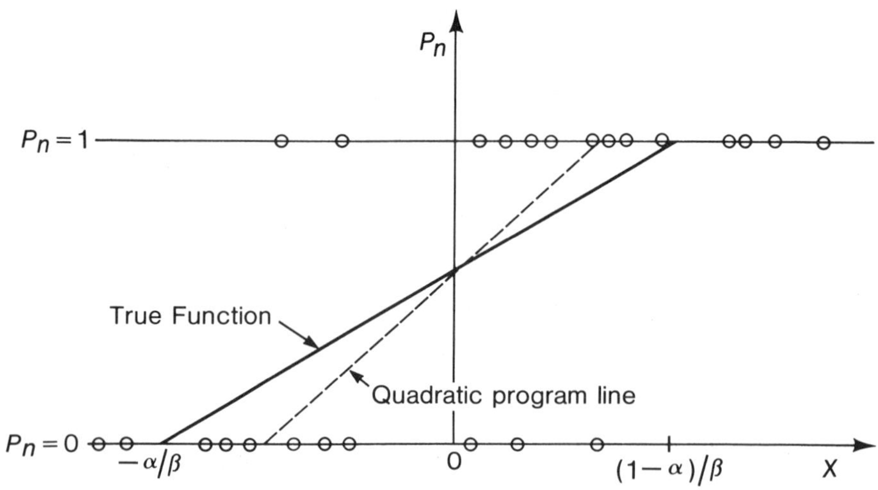

heteroskedastic weighting, and the two quadratic programming procedures. Similarly, each technique has drawbacks that argue against its use. We have restricted our discussion to the choice of an estimation technique given a linear probability model. Clearly, however, we are often making decisions not only on estimation technique, but model form as well.

Example—Director Interlocks I

The example we present in this section will also be used later to illustrate the probit, logit, and discriminant analysis models. Our objective is to highlight the use of each of these models on an identical problem. In each case, the data will be the same, with only the technique varying.

Our example is drawn from two recent studies by Eisenbeis and McCall (1971,1978). The objective of these studies was to investigate the relationship between director interlocks of commercial and mutual savings banks and bank performance. Prior to 1971, New Hampshire mutual savings banks were permitted to share housing and/or directors and own stock in New Hampshire commercial banks. The question of interest was whether such affiliations would affect the performance of the commercial banks. Specifically, Eisenbeis and McCall examined whether a commercial bank's affiliation status could be predicted on the basis of its participation in the principal product markets of mutuals—time and savings deposits and residential mortgages. We examine this issue with a linear probability model. The model is

$$A = \alpha + \beta_1 \mathrm{TSD} + \beta_2 \mathrm{RL} + \varepsilon$$

where

$$A = \begin{cases} 1 & \text{if commercial bank is affiliated with a mutual} \\ 0 & \text{if it is not} \end{cases}$$

$$\mathrm{TSD} = \frac{\text{Total Savings and IPC Time Deposits}}{\text{Total Savings and IPC Time and IPC Demand Deposits}}$$

$$\mathrm{RL} = \frac{\text{Total Conventional Residential Real Estate Loans}}{\text{Total Loans and Gross Discounts}}$$

Data were drawn from the 38 New Hampshire commercial banks used in both Eisenbeis and McCall studies, with variables measured as of 1968. A complete listing of the observations is given in Chapter II as part of a comparison of models. Table I.1 shows variable means broken down by the 24 affiliated and 14 nonaffiliated banks in the study. The

Table I.1. Variable Statistics

	Number	*Mean*	*Standard Deviation*
Affiliated – TSD	24	.291	.275
Affiliated – RL	24	.113	.127
Nonaffiliated – TSD	14	.674	.094
Nonaffiliated – RL	14	.312	.189

model was first estimated by ordinary least squares with no adjustment for heteroskedasticity. The estimation results are (we list standard errors in parentheses despite the fact that because of heteroskedasticity they will be biased)

$$\underset{}{A} = \underset{(.109)}{1.111} - \underset{(.27)}{.827}\,\text{TSD} - \underset{(.43)}{.656}\,\text{RL}$$

$$R^2 = .447$$

The mean predicted value of A was .632, which, as it should be, is identical to the actual fraction of the sample that is affiliated. Using .5 as a cutoff, the model predicts 19 of the 24 affiliated banks correctly (predicted probability $\geqslant .5$) and 10 of the 14 unaffiliated banks (predicted probability $< .5$).

The model was reestimated correcting for heteroskedasticity. Predicted probabilities $\hat{P}$ were formed using the OLS coefficient estimates and used to compute the heteroskedastic weightings, $[\hat{P}(1 - \hat{P})]^{1/2}$. Nine banks, all affiliated, had predicted probabilities larger than 1 (notice that this occurs if TSD and RL are both 0). These observations were arbitrarily assigned $\hat{P}$'s of .98 in computing weights. Results for the heteroskedastic regression are (standard errors in parentheses)

$$A = \underset{(.085)}{1.153} - \underset{(.23)}{.862}\,\text{TSD} - \underset{(.36)}{.724}\,\text{RL}$$

The mean predicted probability was .646, with classification predictions identical to the OLS model.

Coefficients from both regression models can be interpreted directly as partials. Thus, for example, if TSD is .5 instead of .4 holding RL constant, the likelihood that the bank would be affiliated would fall by .086. However, since we have not assumed a specific line of causality, we cannot assume that a change of .1 in TSD would *cause* a .086 decline in the probability that a bank would be affiliated; only that .1 changes in TSD are associated with .086 changes in the likelihood of affiliation.

PROBIT AND LOGIT ANALYSIS

Introduction

As we argued in the previous section, there is nothing inherently wrong with the linear probability model. Indeed, if the probability of an event occurring is truly linear in X, the use of any other model would be inappropriate. However, many of the conceptual and computational problems of the linear probability model mentioned in the previous section have prompted researchers to search for alternative specifications. Of particular concern was the possibility that the linear regression version of the linear probability model can lead to "probability" predictions below zero or larger than one. A natural response would be to seek out transformations that would restrict probability predictions to the zero–one interval. Particularly desirable transformations would be those where, unlike the linear probability model, probabilities are never actually equal to zero or one. This is consistent with the view that even for extreme outliers, no event can be predicted with the absolute certainty implied by a probability of one or zero.

Put in the context of the bankruptcy model presented in the previous section, y_n is defined as a dependent variable that takes on only two values

$$y_n = \begin{cases} 1 & \text{if the } n\text{th firm goes bankrupt} \\ 0 & \text{otherwise} \end{cases}$$

We want to model the conditional probability of bankruptcy (or conditional expectation of y_n) as a function of the firm's debt equity ratio X_n

$$P_n = E(y_n|X_n) = F(X_n)$$

with P_n restricted to the zero–one interval. One transformation that meets this requirement but that we will not pursue in great detail is the Gompertz curve (the Gompit model),

$$F(X_n) = \alpha\beta^{X_n} \qquad 0<\beta<1$$

Another set of transformations are the so-called "angular transformations," including

$$\begin{aligned} F(X_n) &= 1/2 + (1/\pi)\arctan(\alpha + \beta X_n) \\ F(X_n) &= \tanh(\alpha + \beta X_n)/2 \qquad (1.5) \\ F(X_n) &= [1 + \sin(\alpha + \beta X_n)]/2 \qquad \pi/2 \leq \alpha + \beta X_n \leq \pi/2 \end{aligned}$$

Another class of transformations that restrict P_n to the zero–one interval and that have the added attraction of being monotonically increasing (or decreasing) in X_n are *cumulative distribution functions,* or

$$F(X_n) = \int_{-\infty}^{\alpha+\beta X_n} f(z)dz$$

where $F(\ )$ is a cumulative distribution function and $f(z)$ the density function for a given probability function. There are of course a large number of possible cumulative distribution functions. The linear probability model, for example, can be viewed as the cumulative distribution function of the uniform distribution defined over the interval $[-\alpha/\beta, (1 - \alpha)/\beta]$. As another example, the arctangent transformation given in Eq. (1.5) is the cumulative distribution function for the Cauchy distribution. However, in this section we shall focus on only two cumulative distribution functions, the standard normal and the logistic. We do this not because other functions are uninteresting, but because of features of the normal and logistic functions that make them particularly attractive.

The Probit Model

Suppose we believe that the probability of bankruptcy, given a firm's debt–equity ratio X_n, is given by

$$P_n = F(\alpha + \beta X_n)$$

where $F(\alpha + \beta X_n)$ is the *cumulative standard normal distribution function*

$$F(\alpha + \beta X_n) = \int_{-\infty}^{\alpha+\beta X_n} f(z)dz \qquad (1.6a)$$

with

$$f(z) = [1/(2\pi)]^{1/2} \exp(-z^2/2) \qquad (1.6b)$$

as the standard normal density function (mean 0 and variance 1). Then bankruptcy is determined by what we call a *probit probability model,* or, as it is sometimes called, *normit.* For simplicity we are assuming a simple linear function of X_n as the argument of the cumulative normal. However, the model is easily generalized for a vector of variables X_n, i.e.,

$$P_n = \int_{-\infty}^{X_n'\beta} f(z)dz$$

The probit model has been used since the days of Bliss (1934), primarily in the physical sciences. Finney (1971), for example, describes the application of the probit model to the effect of drug doses on the probability of animal death. Cox (1970) also describes similar biological applications. Probit, however, was not used by social scientists until Tobin (1955). Not until very recently has its use become widespread, and to date, applications in finance have been few.

We can make several comparisons of the probit and linear probability models. For one, the probit probability P_n is constrained to the zero–one interval and becomes asymptotic to these values as X_n goes to ∞ and $-\infty$. The distribution of P_n is illustrated by Figure I.4. The "sigmoid" shape of the distribution function is approximately linear in its middle range. However, it differs substantially in the tails from the linear probability model shown in Figure I.1. Another difference is that the partial derivative of the conditional probability of bankruptcy with respect to X_n (or change in the probability for a given change in X_n) is no longer constant, i.e.,

$$\begin{aligned} \frac{\partial P_n}{\partial X_n} &= f(\alpha + \beta X_n)\beta \\ &= [1/(2\pi)^{1/2}] \exp\left[\frac{-(\alpha + \beta X_n)^2}{2}\right]\beta \end{aligned} \tag{1.7}$$

The partial thus depends upon the probability and is smallest in the tails and largest at $P_n = .5$. This is not necessarily an undesirable feature, because it is reasonable to think that a given change in the debt–equity ratio will have a smaller effect on firms with either very high or very low probabilities.

The fact that they cannot be directly interpreted as partials suggests that the parameters α and β are less informative than the coefficients

Figure I.4. Probit Probability Model

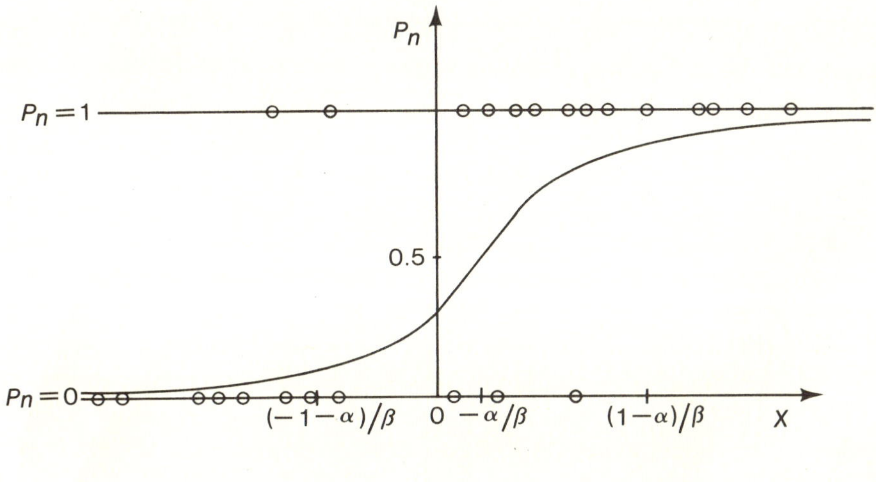

are in regression models. In the case of a vector of X characteristics, we can interpret relative variable coefficients as relative partials. However, their absolute scale is not meaningful. This is illustrated by the arbitrary scaling inherent in the use of the standard normal distribution function. We could just as easily have said that P_n was equal to the cumulative distribution

$$P_n = F^*(\alpha^* + \beta X_n^*) = \int_{-\infty}^{\alpha^* + \beta^* X_n} f(z)dz$$

where

$$f(z) = [1/(2\pi\sigma)^{1/2}] \exp\left[-\frac{1}{2}\left(\frac{Z - \mu}{\sigma}\right)^2 \right]$$

with μ and σ preset parameters. However, this model is identical to the probit model with the standard cumulative normal distribution and

$$\alpha = \frac{\alpha^* - \mu}{\sigma}$$

$$\beta = \beta^*/\sigma$$

While the probit model is an attractive alternative to the linear probability model, we shall demonstrate later that it presents several computational difficulties in estimation. This led to early interest in the less complex, but very similar, cumulative logistic function.

The Logit Model

Consider a model identical to the probit model in that $P_n = F(\alpha + \beta X_n)$, but where $F(\alpha + \beta X_n)$ is equal to the *cumulative standard logistic function*

$$\begin{aligned} F(\alpha + \beta X_n) &= \int_{-\infty}^{\alpha + \beta X_n} f(z)dz \\ &= \frac{1}{[1 + \exp(-\alpha - \beta X_n)]} \end{aligned} \tag{1.8a}$$

with $f(z)$, the standard logistic (or sech^2) density function, equal to

$$f(z) = \frac{\exp(z)}{[1 + \exp(z)]^2} \tag{1.8b}$$

This model was termed by Berkson (1944) as the *logit probability model.* The distribution and density functions of the standard logistic are very similar in shape to the standard normal distribution, as illustrated by Figures I.5 and I.6. Like the normal distribution, the standard logistic

Figure I.5. Standard Normal and Logistic Cumulative Distribution Functions

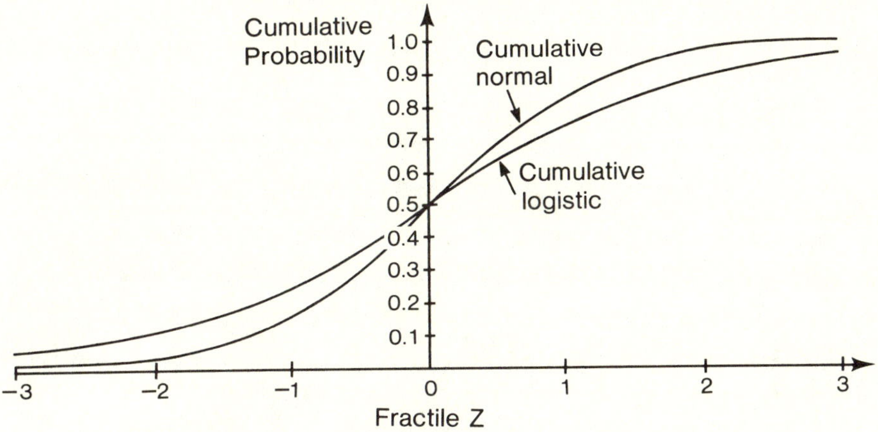

distribution is symmetric with mean, mode, and median at zero. However, it has a variance of 3.29 and a standard deviation of 1.81, compared to a variance and a standard deviation of 1 for the standard normal distribution. Thus, as shown in Figures I.5 and I.6, the logistic distribution has more mass shifted to the tails.

Another difference between the normal and logistic distributions is that unlike the normal distribution, the logistic distribution has a "closed form" expression for its cumulative distribution. As we shall show later, this makes the logistic distribution considerably more tractable computationally. In other respects, the logit model is quite similar to the

Figure I.6. Standard Normal and Logistic Density Functions

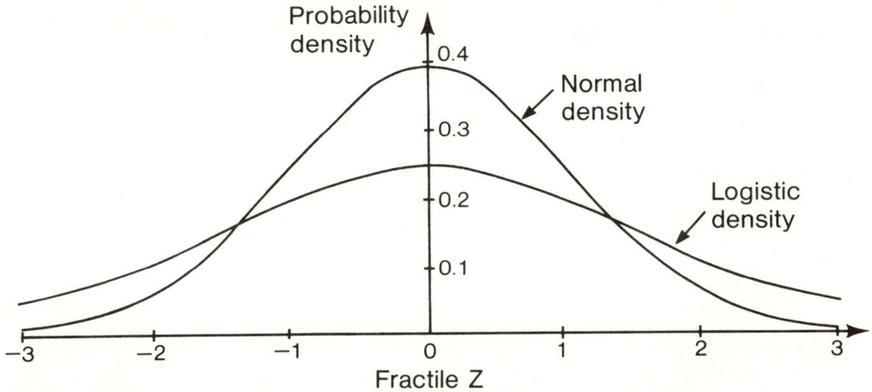

probit model. Both imply probabilities of .5 when $\alpha + \beta X_n = 0$. Partial derivatives of the logit conditional probability with respect to X_n are also dependent upon P_n, i.e.,

$$\begin{aligned}\frac{\partial P_n}{\partial X_n} &= f(\alpha + \beta X_n)\beta \\ &= P_n[1 - P_n]\beta\end{aligned} \tag{1.9}$$

Again, this will be smallest in the tails. Like the probit model, the absolute magnitudes of the parameters α and β are not terribly meaningful. Note, however, that since the standard logit has a standard deviation of 1.8, we would expect that, *ceteris paribus,* logit parameters would be 1.8 times smaller in absolute magnitude than those of a comparable probit model.

Probit/Logit Models and Probabilistic Choice

We have suggested that the probit and logit models may be attractive transformations to use in modeling problems, such as bankruptcy, where the dependent variable can take on only two values. We have justified their use in part because the transformation is monotonic, bounded in the zero–one interval, and asymptotic to zero or one in the tails. For many problems we may not need any more justification than this. However, there are many other transformations that offer similar properties. There is also the troublesome problem of a meaningful interpretation of the model parameters. This has generated attempts to justify the probit and logit models on less arbitrary grounds (e.g., McFadden, 1974a). This discussion has focused on constructing underlying structural equations that give rise to probit or logit probability models.

One commonly used specification is to assume that there is a relationship between the binary dependent variable y_n and an index function of a vector of independent variables $I(X_n)$. X_n could be just one variable, as in our bankruptcy example, or a vector of m characteristics. To make our results more general, let us assume that X_n is indeed a vector of many variables

$$X_n = (x_n^{(1)}, \ldots, x_n^{(m)})'$$

The index is assumed to be a linear function of the x's

$$I(X_n) = X_n'\beta = \sum_{i=1}^{m} x_n^{(i)}\,\beta^{(i)} \tag{1.10a}$$

Note that if one of the variables is always equal to 1, the linear weighting can include a constant term. The dependent variable is assumed to be determined by

$$y_n = \begin{cases} 1 & \text{if } I(X_n) \geq \varepsilon_n \\ 0 & \text{if } I(X_n) < \varepsilon_n \end{cases} \tag{1.10b}$$

where ε_n is a stochastic, unobserved, error term that is normally distributed $N(0,1)$ in the probit model, or distributed as a standard logistic (or sech^2) in the logit model. Note that this specification implies that $E(y_n|X_n)$ will be given by either the probit model, [Eq. (1.6)] or the logit model [Eq. (1.8)]. The index $I(X_n)$ could be thought of as a "predisposition for y," given the independent variables. The ε_n's might be viewed as random thresholds where, if the predisposition exceeds the threshold, the event occurs. Martin (1977), for example, in building a model to predict bank failure, views the index as a measure of a bank's vulnerability to failure. The stochastic term is thought of as a "tolerance for vulnerability." Thus, banks are assumed to fail whenever their vulnerability exceeds their tolerance. Other problems that fit this framework would be drug tests, where $I(X_n)$ measures dosage and ε_n measures an individual's tolerance. Another would be a job search model, where $I(X_n)$ measures reservation wage and ε_n random wage offers. Each of these problems could be modeled as a probit or logit, the models differing only in their assumptions about the distribution of ε_n. This also suggests a more concrete interpretation of the parameter vector β, as weights of the index function. Note, however, that since neither ε_n nor $I(X_n)$ are directly observed, their scale is arbitrary.

Many past and potential applications of probit/logit models in the social sciences involve problems of individual choice behavior: for example, Kohn, Manski, and Mundel (1976) investigate student selection of commuting versus noncommuting colleges; Pindyck and Rubenfeld (1976) discuss voting behavior in yes/no elections; Poirier (1977) models the decision to purchase a home; McFadden (1976b) investigates choice of transportation mode; Hotz (1980) examines fertility behavior. In each case, the observed dependent variable could be viewed as a choice among two alternatives. Since y_n represents an explicit choice by a decision maker, a number of researchers, particularly McFadden (1974a, 1978, 1980a), argue that the choice should be modeled as the end product of individual utility maximization. In particular, the observed choice selection should be assumed to always have a higher utility (satisfaction, reward, etc.) or expected utility than the rejected alternative. McFadden (1974a) develops this principle and shows how it can give rise to a logit or probit model specification. Since this is potentially an important behavioral rationale of the logit or probit models, these arguments deserve further attention.

Suppose the nth decision maker is faced with a choice between two alternatives, say, voting Democrat or Republican, or buying a Chevy or a Ford. Furthermore, assume that he observes data on the characteristics of the choices (X_1, X_2, ε_1, ε_2) and that the utility of each choice is given by a function,

$$\begin{aligned} U_{1n} &= U_{1n}(X_{1n},\varepsilon_{1n}) \\ U_{2n} &= U_{2n}(X_{2n},\varepsilon_{2n}) \end{aligned} \qquad (1.11a)$$

The decision maker is assumed to *always* choose the alternative with the highest utility. However, given *only* the values of X_1 and X_2, utility *may appear* to be random in that it can be decomposed into stochastic and nonstochastic components. Thus, linearizing the utility function

$$\begin{aligned} U_{1n} &= X_{1n}'\beta_1 + \varepsilon_{1n} \\ U_{2n} &= X_{2n}'\beta_2 + \varepsilon_{2n} \end{aligned} \qquad (1.11b)$$

where ε_{1n} and ε_{2n} are zero mean stochastic errors independent of X_{1n} and X_{2n}, and β_1 and β_2 are vectors of fixed weights. ε_{1n} and ε_{2n} might be interpreted as "left-out variables," unobserved by the econometrician but known to the decision maker. Alternatively, the utility function itself might be viewed as random. For example, if the parameters β_1 and β_2 are not individual specific, but signify the parameters of a "representative" or "average" individual, the error terms might arise from interpersonal variation in taste as in a "random coefficients model" (see Hausman and Wise, 1978). The utility function might also be truly random in the sense that the decision maker's state of mind varies from situation to situation (a view traceable to Luce, 1959).

Regardless of the origin of the error terms, the decision maker is assumed to observe them prior to making his decision. Thus choice 1 occurs if

$$X_{1n}'\beta_1 + \varepsilon_{1n} > X_{2n}'\beta_2 + \varepsilon_{2n}$$

or

$$X_{1n}'\beta_1 - X_{2n}'\beta_2 > \varepsilon_{2n} - \varepsilon_{1n}$$

Choice 2 occurs if

$$X_{1n}'\beta_1 - X_{2n}'\beta_2 < \varepsilon_{2n} - \varepsilon_{1n}$$

Suppose that we assume that ε_{1n} and ε_{2n} are bivariate normal, each with mean 0, variances σ_1^2 and σ_2^2, and covariance σ_{12}, then $\varepsilon_n^* = \varepsilon_{2n} - \varepsilon_{1n}$ is also normal with mean 0 and variance $\sigma_*^2 = \sigma_1^2 + \sigma_2^2 - 2\sigma_1\sigma_2$. Then the probability of choice 1 given X_{1n} and X_{2n} can be expressed as

$$P(\text{choice } 1|X_{1n},X_{2n}) = \int_{-\infty}^{X_{1n}'\beta_1 - X_{2n}'\beta_2} f(\varepsilon_n^*)d\varepsilon_n^* \qquad (1.12)$$

where $f(\varepsilon_n^*)$ is the normal density of ε_n^*. If we normalize by the scalar term σ_*, then choice probabilities reduce to the probit model

$$P(\text{choice } 1|X_{1n},X_{2n}) = \int_{-\infty}^{(X_{1n}'\beta_1 - X_{2n}'\beta_2)/\sigma_*} f(z)dz$$

where $f(z)$ is the standard normal density.

Thus, the assumption that utility errors are normal yields a reduced form probit model for choice probabilities. This may give us a clearer interpretation for the probit coefficients. $(X_{1n}'\beta_1 - X_{2n}'\beta_2)$ might be interpreted as an index measuring the individual's net preference for choice 1 over choice 2 given the nonstochastic components of utility. As it should, this index is increasing in the utility of choice 1, $X_{1n}'\beta_1$, and decreasing in the utility of choice 2. It also allows us to directly interpret the coefficient on any variable that appears in only X_1 or X_2 as a parameter of the utility function. However, only the net effect can be measured for variables appearing in both equations.

In deriving a probit probability model from choice equations, we used the property of the normal distribution that linear combinations of normal variables will themselves generally be normal. This property, however, holds for few other distributions, which might imply that normality of the utility errors is a needed assumption in deriving closed form expressions for the probabilities. Of particular interest for our purposes is whether there exists a plausible distribution for the underlying utility errors that yields logistic reduced forms. McFadden (1974a) shows that indeed there is such a distribution. He proves that if ε_{1n} and ε_{2n} of Eq. (1.11) are identically and independently distributed with the standard extreme value cumulative distribution

$$\text{Prob}(\varepsilon < T) = \exp[-\exp(-T)] \tag{1.13a}$$

with density

$$f(\varepsilon) = \exp(-\varepsilon) - \exp[-\exp(-\varepsilon)] \tag{1.13b}$$

then the probability of choice 1 given X_1 and X_2 is

$$P(\text{choice } 1|X_{1n},X_{2n}) = \frac{\exp(X_{1n}'\beta_1)}{\exp(X_{1n}'\beta_1) + \exp(X_{2n}'\beta_2)} = \frac{1}{1 + \exp(X_{2n}'\beta_2 - X_{1n}'\beta_1)} \tag{1.14}$$

or the logit model. The extreme value (distribution of the largest extreme) distribution is also called the Gnedenko or double exponential distribution. It is asymmetric, skewed to the right, with mode 0, mean .58, and variance 1.65, as illustrated in Figure I.7. Given these assumptions, parameters of the logit model can be interpreted in the

Figure I.7. Standard Extreme Value Density Function

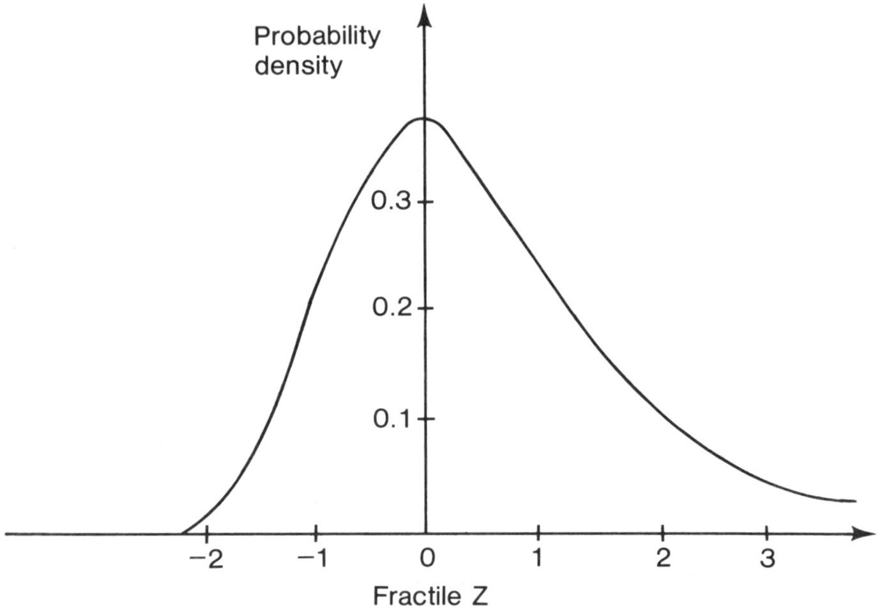

same manner as the probit model. Again, utility function parameters will be identified only for those variables that appear only in one equation.

One difference between the extreme value and normal assumptions is that we had to assume that ε_{1n} and ε_{2n} were both independent and identically distributed to derive the logit model. This is not likely to cause great concern in the two-choice model; however, later when we discuss the multi-choice logit model, we will see that it is quite a restrictive assumption.

The choice behavior analysis most clearly applies to selections by individual utility-maximizing decision makers. Before leaving this area, however, let us suggest how it might be applied to problems lacking a specific decision maker. Consider, for example, our problem of bankruptcy. Suppose that we believe that firm bankruptcy occurs when the present value of firm liabilities L exceeds the present value of firm assets A. Furthermore, assume that A and L are unobserved, but determined by the equations,

$$L_n = X'_{1n}\beta_1 + \varepsilon_{1n}$$

$$A_n = X'_{2n}\beta_2 + \varepsilon_{2n}$$

where ε_1 and ε_2 are stochastic errors either normally or extreme-value distributed. This specification then implies that the probability of bankruptcy, given X_1 and X_2, will be given by a probit or logit model.

Parameter Estimation—Many Observations per Cell

We have not yet addressed the problem of parameter estimation in the probit/logit models. Since the dependent variable is a nonlinear function of the X's, parameter estimation may not be straightforward. Recognizing this problem, pioneers working in this area sought out ways to easily obtain parameter estimates. An outgrowth of this search is a relatively simple method of estimation developed by Berkson (1951) and generalized by Theil (1969, 1970). The "Berkson–Theil" method applies to the logit model and requires that repeated draws on y be observed for each value of X. This restriction is quite reasonable for many studies in the physical sciences, where data are generated in an experimental setting. Experiments often consist of repeated trials, holding generally discrete independent variables constant. In the social sciences, however, this requirement may be too restrictive. Most social science data are likely to be continuous, where observations differ both in dependent and independent variable values. Particularly in models with many continuous independent variables, as also is common, it would be very unlikely to have natural repeated trials with the X's held constant.

There is, however, a class of social science problems where data can be viewed as the product of repeated trials with fixed X. Researchers often use data where the dependent variable is an aggregate measure of individual choices or an aggregate rate: for example, births per thousand people; bond defaults per year; loans granted per applicant; human mortality rates; fraction of high school seniors going to college. Researchers may want to relate the value of the dependent variable to characteristics of area, if observations are aggregated spatially, or of time period, if aggregated temporally. If area-wide independent variables are considered measures of "representative" or "mean" taste, these problems could be viewed as repeated micro zero–one trials.

The Berkson–Theil method is derived as follows. Assume for the nth observation that the conditional probability P_n is given by the cumulative logistic

$$P_n = 1/[1 + \exp(-X_n'\beta)]$$

Then

$$\exp(-X_n'\beta) = (1 - P_n)/P_n$$

Hence

$$\exp(X_n'\beta) = P_n/(1 - P_n)$$

Taking logs of both sides

$$X_n'\beta = \ln[P_n/(1 - P_n)] \tag{1.15}$$

This relationship holds for *one* observation. Suppose that we have data on R_n repeated trials on y given X_n, and let r_n be the number of times $y = 1$ for a given X_n. Clearly, the expectation of the fraction of the sample where $y = 1$, $\tilde{P}_n = r_n/R_n$, is equal to P_n. Domencich and McFadden (1975) show that by a Taylor expansion the following expression approximately holds

$$\ln[\tilde{P}_n/(1 - \tilde{P}_n)] = \ln[P_n/(1 - P_n)] + \tilde{\varepsilon}_n \tag{1.16a}$$

Hence

$$\ln[\tilde{P}_n/(1 - \tilde{P}_n)] = X_n'\beta + \tilde{\varepsilon}_n \tag{1.16b}$$

where $\tilde{\varepsilon}_n$ is a zero mean, normally distributed, random variable. This implies that what Berkson (1951) defined as the sample log-odds or "logit,"

$$\ln[\tilde{P}_n/(1 - \tilde{P}_n)] = \ln[r_n/(R_n - r_n)], \tag{1.17}$$

is approximately equal to $X_n'\beta$ plus a random error. Given a sample with sufficient variation in the X's and repeated trials for each X_n, Berkson (1951) shows that an estimate of β can be obtained by applying OLS to Eq. (1.16b). These estimates will be consistent in that they will converge in probability to β as the number of repetitions given X_n is made arbitrarily large. Under these circumstances, the Berkson–Theil coefficients have properties asymptotically equivalent to the maximum likelihood estimates described in the next section.

There are a number of variations of the Berkson–Theil procedure that have been proposed by various authors as improvements of the basic procedure. Several of these proposals are briefly described below.

McFadden (1974a) and Cox (1970) argue that the rate of convergence of the estimators to their large sample values can be improved by slightly altering the sample log-odds and fitting the equation

$$\ln[(r_n + 1/2)/(R_n - r_n + 1/2)] = X_n'\beta + \tilde{\varepsilon}_n \tag{1.18}$$

instead of Eq. (1.16).

Another proposed improvement is based on the fact that $\tilde{\varepsilon}_n$ in Eq. (1.16) will have an approximate variance of $1/[R_nP_n(1 - P_n)]$. Thus, the large sample properties of the estimates of β could be improved by fitting the weighted least squares equation

$$w_n\ln[\tilde{P}_n/(1 - \tilde{P}_n)] = w_nX_n'\beta + \tilde{\varepsilon}_n \tag{1.19}$$

where

$$w_n = [R_n P_n(1 - P_n)]^{1/2}$$

Estimates of the weights can be calculated in two ways. The actual sample proportions $\tilde{P}_n$ could be used as estimates of each P_n, allowing Eq. (1.19) to be estimated in one pass. Alternatively, Eq. (1.16) can be fitted, with coefficient estimates $\hat{\beta}$, (which are consistent, even though errors are heteroskedastic) and used to compute estimates of $\hat{P}_n$, i.e.,

$$\hat{P}_n = 1/[1 + \exp(-X_n'\hat{\beta})]$$

The latter procedure is similar to the two-pass heteroskedastic adjustment proposed for the linear probability model.

Finally, the adjusted log-odds and heteroskedastic improvements could be combined by fitting the equation

$$w_n \ln[(r_n + 1/2)/(R_n - r_n + 1/2)] = w_n X_n'\beta + \tilde{\varepsilon}_n \qquad (1.20)$$

where

$$w_n = [R_n(r_n + 1)(R_n - r_n + 1)/(R_n + 1)(R_n + 2)]^{1/2}$$

The fact that the logit model implies that the error variance of Eq. (1.16) will depend on the coefficient vector β suggests a simple specification test for the model. The actual sample variances of the $\tilde{\varepsilon}_n$'s could be compared with the predicted variances inplied by the weights given in Eq. (1.19). Given a sample of size N, this test could be done formally, using what Berkson (1955) termed the "logit χ^2,"

$$\sum_{n=1}^{N} R_n\tilde{P}_n(1 - \tilde{P}_n)\{\ln[\tilde{P}_n/(1 - \tilde{P}_n)] - X_n'\hat{\beta}\}^2 \sim \chi^2\,(N - m) \qquad (1.21)$$

which is asymptotically distributed as a chi-square with $N - m$ (m being the dimension of β) degrees of freedom when the model is true. $\hat{\beta}$ can be calculated from either Eq. (1.16) or Eq. (1.19). Notice that the numerator of the test statistic is the squared residual of Eq. (1.16). An extreme value of the test statistic would cast doubt on the validity of the model.

The test statistic given in Eq. (1.21) is approximately the same as the conventional multinomial statistic

$$\sum_{n=1}^{N} R_n(\tilde{P}_n - \hat{P}_n)^2/[\hat{P}_n(1 - \hat{P}_n)] \sim \chi^2\,(N - m) \qquad (1.22)$$

which is also asymptotically distributed as a chi-square with $N - m$ degrees of freedom when the model is true. The form of the chi-square statistic gives rise to yet another variation of the Berkson–Theil estimation procedure termed "minimum chi-square." Berkson (1955) proposed the estimator $\tilde{\beta}$, which minimizes Eq. (1.22), where

$$\hat{P}_n = 1/[1 + \exp(-X_n'\tilde{\beta})]$$

Unfortunately, computation of this estimator will generally require iterative methods, restricting its usefulness relative to the Berkson–Theil regression estimators. Notice that the estimator that minimizes the "logit χ^2" [Eq. (1.21)] is the weighted least squares estimator of Eq. (1.19). Although they have the same large sample properties, they will generally differ from the "minimum chi-square" estimators, which minimize Eq. (1.22).

Domencich and McFadden (1975) argue that the Berkson–Theil regression procedure will generally yield good parameter estimates even when there are only a moderate number of repetitions for each X. [McFadden (1974a) suggests that as a rule-of-thumb both r_n and $R_n - r_n$ should be $\geqslant 5$.] This is particularly true when probabilities are close to .5. Observations with probabilities close to zero or one may require substantially more repetitions. There are, however, two potentially serious problems with the method. The first is that there may be some observations where all repetitions of y_n either equal zero or one. In this case, the sample logit will be undefined. Theil (1970) suggests removing these observations and perhaps other observations with a very small number of repetitions.

A second and more serious drawback to the Berkson–Theil method is the fact that it requires repetitions for fixed X. Since many data do not come in this form, researchers have tried to approximate the Berkson–Theil requirement by grouping observations in cells created by categorizing continuous independent variables. For example, the debt–equity variable used in our bankruptcy example might be broken into four categories, (0–.5; .5–1; 1–2; 2+), with firms assigned to the cell covering their debt/equity ratio. A Berkson–Theil regression could then be run, using the cell means to represent the X value for each of the four observations. Unfortunately, this type of arbitrary grouping generally creates an errors-in-variables problem that biases the estimated coefficients toward zero. Domencich and McFadden (1975), however, report on a Monte Carlo experiment that suggests that the Berkson–Theil method may provide desirable estimates even in the presence of the errors-in-variables effect. Even where the errors-in-variables problem may be potentially serious, researchers will have to balance the potential bias against the computational ease of the method.

We have discussed Berkson–Theil estimation only for the logit model. This is primarily because of the simple closed form expression for the sample logit in Eq. (1.17). All of our discussion, however, could have applied equally well to the probit model. However, the dependent variable for each of the regressions would be the sample "probit" $F^{-1}(\tilde{P}_n)$

where F^{-1} is the inverse cumulative standard normal distribution function [i.e., $F^{-1}(.5) = 0$]. F^{-1} does not have a simple closed form solution but can be approximated by

$$F^{-1}(\tilde{P}_n) = t - \frac{2.30753 + .27061t}{1 + .99229t + .04481t^2} \tag{1.23}$$

where

$$t = [-\ln(\tilde{P}_n)]^{1/2}$$

for $0 < \tilde{P}_n \leq .5$. For $\tilde{P}_n > .5$, $t = [-\ln(1 - \tilde{P}_n)]^{1/2}$ and the sign of $F^{-1}(\tilde{P}_n)$ is reversed. This procedure has also been called "normit." In fact, technically the term "probit" has been used to refer to $F^{-1}(\tilde{P}_n) + 5$, the "plus five" term added to insure that the probit was always positive (see Nerlove and Press, 1973). It is not clear what this adds.

Berkson (1955) and Zellner and Lee (1965) show that, like the logit model, the probit regression can also be adjusted for heteroskedasticity in the errors. They show that the appropriate weights corresponding to w_n in Eq. (1.19) are

$$w_n = \left[\frac{R_n f(P_n)^2}{P_n(1 - P_n)}\right]^{1/2} \tag{1.24}$$

where

$$f(P_n) = [1/(2\pi)^{1/2}] \exp\left(-\frac{1}{2}P_n^{\,2}\right)$$

If sample weights $\tilde{P}_n$ are used to estimate P_n, weighted least squares is equivalent to minimizing what Berkson termed the "normit χ^2,"

$$\sum_{n=1}^{N} \frac{R_n f(\tilde{P}_n)^2}{\tilde{P}_n(1 - \tilde{P}_n)} [F^{-1}(\tilde{P}_n) - X_n'\hat{\beta}]^2 \sim \chi^2\,(N - m) \tag{1.25}$$

with respect to $\hat{\beta}$. This statistic is distributed asymptotically as a chi-square with $N - m$ degrees of freedom when the model is true.

Finally, the Berkson–Theil procedure could also be applied to other probability transformation models. For example, if P_n is given by the arctangent transformation in Eq. (1.5), the inverse function corresponding to Eq. (1.23) is $F^{-1}(\tilde{P}_n) = \tan[\pi(\tilde{P}_n - 1/2)]$.

Parameter Estimation—Individual Data

Many dichotomous dependent variable problems in finance and the social sciences are unlikely to have the data form required for the Berkson–Theil procedure. Instead of multiple repetitions for each fixed

X in many data sets, there is only one choice observed for each draw on the independent variables. One proposal for dealing with individual data is a nonlinear least squares procedure offered by Walker and Duncan (1967). Their procedure is based on a Taylor series expansion similar to Eq. (1.16), except that the dependent variable is 0 or 1. Unfortunately, their procedure involves an iterative solution. A similar but better known approach is *maximum likelihood* (ML) estimation. This procedure also does not require repetitions and can be adapted to both the logit and probit models. Under very general conditions this method can be used to compute estimates that have the desirable properties of consistency, asymptotic efficiency, and asymptotic normality. The disadvantage of the method is that it involves substantially more computational costs than the regression procedures, generally requiring iterative solutions to nonlinear equations. In this subsection we shall discuss the application of ML methods to the logit and probit models, focusing on problems involving data without repetition. Because we shall not go into details on maximum likelihood estimation, a short summary is provided in the Appendix for readers unfamiliar with the procedure.

Although the maximum likelihood procedure can be applied to both the logit and probit models, we focus first on the logit case. Assume that we have a *random* sample of N observations, where for the nth observation we observe *one* dependent variable y_n, which has a value zero or one, and a vector of m independent variables X_n. Using the bankruptcy problem as an example, y_n might represent failure (1) or nonfailure (0) of a firm, and X_n might represent characteristics of the firm. We assume that the sample consists of N_1 observations, denoted X_{1n}, where $y_n = 1$, and N_0 observations, denoted X_{0n} where $y_n = 0$, with $N_1 + N_0 = N$. Note that since we have specified a random sample from the entire population, N_1 and N_0 are themselves random. As shown by many authors (e.g., Cox, 1970; McFadden, 1974a), the log of the probability of observing a given sample is

$$\ln L = \sum_{n=1}^{N_1} \ln(P_n) + \sum_{n=1}^{N_0} \ln(1 - P_n) \tag{1.26}$$

where P_n, the probability $y_n = 1$ given X_n, has the form

$$P_n = 1/[1 + \exp(-X_n'\beta)]$$

We call $\ln L$ the *log-likelihood function.* Substituting for P_n in Eq. (1.26) and rearranging terms, $\ln L$ can be rewritten as

$$\ln L = \sum_{n=1}^{N_1} \ln\left[\frac{\exp(X_{1n}'\beta)}{1 + \exp(X_{1n}'\beta)}\right] + \sum_{n=1}^{N_0} \ln\left[\frac{1}{1 + \exp(X_{0n}'\beta)}\right] \tag{1.27}$$

$$= \sum_{n=1}^{N_1} \{X_{1n}'\beta - \ln[1 + \exp(X_{1n}'\beta)]\} - \sum_{n=1}^{N_0} \ln[1 + \exp(X_{0n}'\beta)]$$

The ML estimators of β will be the vector $\hat{\beta}$, which, when substituted into Eq. (1.27), yields the highest sample log-likelihood. One way to solve for these estimators is to differentiate Eq. (1.27) with respect to β and find the estimators $\hat{\beta}$, which set the derivatives to zero, i.e.,

$$\frac{\partial \ln L}{\partial \beta} = \sum_{n=1}^{N_1} \left[1 - \frac{\exp(X_{1n}'\hat{\beta})}{1 + \exp(X_{1n}'\hat{\beta})}\right] X_{1n} - \sum_{n=1}^{N_0} \left[\frac{\exp(X_{0n}'\hat{\beta})}{1 + \exp(X_{0n}'\hat{\beta})}\right] X_{0n} = 0 \quad (1.28)$$

Defining $\hat{P}_n = 1/[1 + \exp(-X_n\hat{\beta})]$ as the predicted probability that $y_n = 1$ given X_n, the first order conditions [Eq. (1.28),] can be expressed as

$$\sum_{n=1}^{N_1} (1 - \hat{P}_n)X_{1n} = \sum_{n=1}^{N_0} \hat{P}_n X_{0n} \quad (1.29)$$

If the X_n vector contains a constant, the first order condition Eq. (1.29) applied to the intercept implies that

$$N_1 = \left(\sum_{n=1}^{N_1} \hat{P}_n + \sum_{n=1}^{N_0} \hat{P}_n\right)/N \quad (1.30)$$

Thus, if predicted probabilities are calculated from the ML estimators, the mean predicted probability will be identical to the actual fraction of the sample where $y_n = 1$. This is similar to the condition that the mean of the predicted y's is identical to the mean of the dependent variable in an OLS regression. If the X variables contain any dummy variables (for example, a 0–1 variable, which is one only if a firm has a particular attribute such as being located in the Northeast), the first order conditions also imply that the mean predicted probability for the identified subgroup (i.e., firms in the Northeast) will be identical to the actual fraction of that subgroup where $y_n = 1$.

The second order condition for a maximum requires that the matrix

$$\frac{\partial^2 \ln L}{\partial \beta \partial \beta'} = -\sum_{n=1}^{N_1} \hat{P}_n(1 - \hat{P}_n)X_{1n}X_{1n}' - \sum_{n=1}^{N_0} \hat{P}_n(1 - \hat{P}_n)X_{0n}X_{0n}' \quad (1.31)$$

be negative definite. If the X's are not collinear, this condition will be met for any coefficient vector, implying that $\ln L$ is globally concave and will have a unique maximum when the first order conditions hold.

Given the strict concavity of the log-likelihood function, the nonlinear first order conditions can be solved for the ML estimators by a variety of iterative techniques [see Goldfeld and Quant (1972) for a survey of these techniques]. Once attained, ML estimators will be consistent, with smaller large sample (asymptotic) variance than any other estimator, and asymptotically normal. Their covariance matrix can be estimated by the inverse of the negative of the matrix of second derivatives

$$S(\hat{\beta}) = \left[\sum_{n=1}^{N_1} \hat{P}_n(1 - \hat{P}_n)X_{1n}X_{1n}' + \sum_{n=1}^{N_0} \hat{P}_n(1 - \hat{P}_n)X_{0n}X_{0n}' \right]^{-1}$$

which can be used for standard errors or hypothesis testing.

Maximum likelihood estimation of the probit model proceeds in an almost identical manner to the logit case (see Tobin, 1955 or Finney, 1971). Again assuming a random sample from the population of size N_1 where $y_n = 1$ and N_0 where $y_n = 0$, the sample log-likelihood is

$$\ln L = \sum_{n=1}^{N_1} \ln(P_n) + \sum_{n=1}^{N_0} \ln(1 - P_n) \tag{1.32}$$

where, defining

$$f(X_n'\beta) = [1/(2\pi)^{1/2}]\exp[-(1/2)(X_n'\beta)^2] \qquad \text{(Standard Normal Density)}$$

$$F(X_n'\beta) = \int_{-\infty}^{X_n'\beta} f(z)dz \qquad \text{(Standard Cumulative Normal)}$$

then

$$P_n = F(X_n'\beta)$$

First order conditions for $\hat{\beta}$ to maximize $\ln L$ are that

$$\frac{\partial \ln L}{\partial \beta} = \sum_{n=1}^{N_1} \frac{f(X_{1n}'\hat{\beta})}{F(X_{1n}'\hat{\beta})} X_{1n} - \sum_{n=1}^{N_0} \frac{f(X_{0n}'\hat{\beta})}{[1 - F(X_{0n}'\hat{\beta})]} X_{0n} = 0 \tag{1.33}$$

Notice that unlike the logit model, the mean predicted probability will no longer be required to equal the actual sample fraction where $y_n = 1$ (although it is likely to be close). The second order condition for the probit model is that

$$\begin{aligned} \frac{\partial^2 \ln L}{\partial \beta \partial \beta'} = & \sum_{n=1}^{N_1} \left[\frac{-f(X_{1n}'\hat{\beta})}{F(X_{1n}'\hat{\beta})} X_{1n}'\hat{\beta} - \frac{f(X_{1n}'\hat{\beta})^2}{F(X_{1n}'\hat{\beta})^2} \right] X_{1n}X_{1n}' \\ & + \sum_{n=1}^{N_0} \left[\frac{f(X_{0n}'\hat{\beta})}{[1 - F(X_{0n}'\hat{\beta})]} X_{0n}'\hat{\beta} - \frac{f(X_{0n}'\hat{\beta})^2}{[1 - F(X_{0n}'\hat{\beta})]^2} \right] X_{0n}X_{0n}' \end{aligned} \tag{1.34}$$

be negative definite. Note that like the logit model, the second order condition will hold for any coefficient vector. Hence $\ln L$ will be globally concave (see Haberman, 1974.) The inverse of the negative of the matrix of second derivatives in Eq. (1.34) may again be used for estimation of standard errors of the coefficients and for hypothesis tests.

We have had reasonable success in computing maximum likelihood estimators of both the probit and logit models, even with sample sizes as large as 2000 and with 40 variables. The iterative procedure we've used usually converges quite rapidly, particularly for the logit model. Several words of caution, however, should be added. There are several situations where the logit and probit models will be unestimable. The first arises when there exists a linear combination of the X's, say $X_n'b$, which perfectly classifies each of the sample observations, i.e., $X_n'b$ will be greater than some constant α for all observations where $y_n = 1$, and less than α for all observations where $y_n = 0$. This situation will of course arise if any single variable is a perfect classifier. Thus, there must be some overlap in the range of every X variable for the two sample groups where $y_n = 1$ and $y_n = 0$. Another unestimable situation arises if $y_n = 1$ or $y_n = 0$ for all observations for a subgroup defined by a dummy independent variable (e.g., all firms in the Northeast are bankrupt when Northeast location is indicated by a dummy variable). Conditions for an unestimable model will usually be signaled by an excessive number of iterations with no convergence, or signs that coefficients are being driven to $+\infty$ or $-\infty$.

Example—Director Interlocks II

The example we present to illustrate the probit and logit models is the same one used to illustrate the linear probability model. The problem is discussed in detail in the section "Director Interlocks I"; briefly, we want to examine whether the affiliation status

$$A = \begin{cases} 1 & \text{if commercial bank is affiliated with a mutual} \\ 0 & \text{if it is not} \end{cases}$$

of 38 New Hampshire commercial banks can be predicted on the basis of two variables:

$$\text{TSD} = \frac{\text{Total Savings and IPC Time Deposits}}{\text{Total Savings and IPC Time and IPC Demand Deposits}}$$

$$\text{RL} = \frac{\text{Total Conventional Residential Real Estate Loans}}{\text{Total Loans and Gross Discounts}}$$

The problem is first examined as a logit model with individual data. The model was estimated using a maximum-likelihood nonlinear Davidon–Fletcher–Powell algorithm (see Goldfeld and Quant, 1972), utilizing a linear probability model for coefficient starting values. The estimated coefficients maximize the log-likelihood function

$$\ln L = \sum_{A=1} \ln(\hat{P}) + \sum_{A=0} \ln(1 - \hat{P})$$

where

$$\hat{P} = [1 + \exp(\alpha + \beta_1\text{TSD} + \beta_2\text{RL})]^{-1}$$

The coefficients that maximize the log-likelihood function are (standard errors in parentheses)

$$\hat{\alpha} = 5.51 \qquad \hat{\beta}_1 = -7.89 \qquad \hat{\beta}_2 = -3.18$$
$$(2.17) \qquad\qquad (3.58) \qquad\qquad (2.95)$$

ln of the likelihood function = −14.0

The mean predicted value of $\hat{P}$ for the sample was .632, which is identical (as it should be) to the actual fraction of the sample that is affiliated. Using a predicted probability of .5 as a cutoff, the model predicted 20 of the 24 affiliated banks and 10 of the 14 unaffiliated banks correctly.

Maximum likelihood estimation of the probit model coefficients proceeds in an almost identical fashion. Again using a Davidon–Fletcher–Powell iterative algorithm, we find the coefficients that maximize the log-likelihood function

$$\ln L = \sum_{A=1} \ln(\hat{P}) + \sum_{A=0} \ln(1 - \hat{P})$$

where

$$\hat{P} = \int_{-\infty}^{\alpha + \beta_1\text{TSD} + \beta_2\text{RL}} [1/(2\pi)^{1/2}] \exp[-(1/2)z^2]dz$$

The coefficients (with standard errors in parentheses) that maximize the probit log-likelihood are

$$\hat{\alpha} = 3.25 \qquad \hat{\beta}_1 = -4.62 \qquad \hat{\beta}_2 = -1.97$$
$$(1.27) \qquad\qquad (2.11) \qquad\qquad (1.80)$$

ln of the likelihood function = −13.9

The mean predicted value of $\hat{P}$ for the sample was .635 (this does not necessarily have to equal the sample fraction). Classification predictions were identical to the logit model.

Interpretation of the individual estimated parameters must be done with care. As noted earlier in this section, the scale of the coefficients depends upon a normalization. Since the logistic model has a scaling factor (standard deviation of the error) 1.81 times the probit, we would expect coefficients to be 1.81 times larger. Notice that if we divide each of the estimated logit coefficients by 1.81, we obtain

$$\hat{\alpha} = 3.04 \qquad \hat{\beta}_1 = -4.36 \qquad \hat{\beta}_2 = -1.76$$

which are roughly comparable to the probit model.

It is also important to remember that coefficients cannot be directly interpretable as partials, as the partial will depend upon the probability. Recall that for the logit model

$$\frac{\partial P}{\partial X_i} = P(1 - P)\beta_i$$

and for the probit model

$$\frac{\partial P}{\partial X_i} = [1/(2\pi)^{1/2}] \exp[-(\alpha + \beta_1 TSD + \beta_2 RL)^2/2]\beta_i$$

In reporting results, it may often be useful to calculate these predicted changes in the probability for a given change in the independent variables, evaluated at different points. For example, we would predict the following changes in the probability of affiliation for a .01 rise in TSD and RL evaluated at $P = .25$ and $P = .5$.

	TSD		*RL*	
	logit	*probit*	*logit*	*probit*
$P = .25$	−.0145	−.0144	−.0059	−.0062
$P = .5$	−.0197	−.0184	−.0080	−.0079

DISCRIMINANT ANALYSIS

Introduction

The 0–1 regression, probit, and logit models discussed in the previous two sections evolved from the traditional regression model. In all three cases we postulate a line of causality running from exogenously determined X variables and stochastic errors ε to a random variable Y, which takes on only two discrete values. We assume that this relationship is deterministic in that if we knew the X's and ε's, we could solve for Y. In all three cases we are interested in estimating the conditional expectation of Y (or probability of an event) given X. The estimated coefficients are unknown parameters of this expectation function.

The model that we will discuss in this section—the discriminant analysis model—arose from an entirely different tradition. Dating from the work of R.A. Fisher (1936), discriminant analysis evolved as a variant and multivariate extension of univariate analysis of variance techniques. More so than the regression tradition, the application of analysis of variance has been primarily to descriptive and inferential questions and often not concerned with specific causal flows. It is generally concerned with comparisons of the distribution of one or more variables across different groups or populations. In particular, discriminant analysis assumes known, identifiable, mutually exclusive groups. A sample of observations is drawn from each group, where each observation is described by measurements on a set of variables. By making assumptions about how the variables are distributed within each group, one can address such issues as (1) testing for differences in variable mean vectors and/or covariance structures across groups and (2) constructing schemes to estimate *ex-ante* probabilities of group membership for future observations given only information on the independent variables.

The presentation of discriminant analysis seen in most textbooks (e.g., Tatsuoka, 1971; Anderson, 1958; Overall and Klett, 1972; Green, 1978; Cooley and Lownes, 1971; Eisenbeis and Avery, 1972) begins with a discussion of hypothesis testing leading to a discussion of the problems of classification and prediction. In order to clearly demonstrate both the commonalities as well as the differences between discriminant analysis and regression, probit, and logit, we shall deviate from the standard format, reverse this order, and discuss classification first. We do this hoping not to confuse readers already familiar with discriminant analysis.

The discussion in this section will focus on developing the theory of discriminant analysis. Because this technique has been used so often in finance, we will discuss problems in the application of the technique separately in Chapter III.

Classification Probabilities

Using the example of firm bankruptcy, consider the following model of the differences between two discrete populations. Let there be two identifiable populations representing bankrupt and nonbankrupt firms. Let population (group) membership be represented by the variable y where

$$y_n = \begin{cases} 2 & \text{if the } n\text{th firm is bankrupt (group 2)} \\ 1 & \text{otherwise (group 1)} \end{cases}$$

Furthermore, assume that each firm is also characterized by measurements on m independent variables X. For the nth observation, we represent X as an m length column vector

$$X_n = (x_n^{(1)}, x_n^{(2)}, \ldots, x_n^{(m)})'$$

These may be variables such as the debt/equity ratio, retained earnings, firm size, or other financial variables whose distribution is thought to be related to bankruptcy. Within each group, we assume the X variables are distributed with a *multivariate normal* distribution. Thus, the X variables of nonbankrupt firms are distributed

$$X_n \sim N(\mu_1, \Sigma_1) \qquad \text{given } y_n = 1$$

and for bankrupt firms,

$$X_n \sim N(\mu_2, \Sigma_2) \qquad \text{given } y_n = 2$$

where μ_1 and μ_2 are m length mean vectors and Σ_1 and Σ_2 are $(m \times m)$ variance–covariance (dispersion) matrices.

Although they may lead to similar predictions, the assumptions of the discriminant analysis model are markedly different from those of the regression, probit, and logit models discussed earlier. For the regression, probit, and logit models we assumed an explicit causal flow, where exogenous variables X and stochastic errors ε determined group membership. Thus, bankruptcy was an endogenous variable determined by an explicit structural model. For the discriminant analysis model, the groups are taken as given. Then, given group membership, the distribution of the X variables is determined. As we shall argue later in this section, these conditions may be consistent with a number of structural models. However, there is an inference that the causal flow is from group membership to the X's.

In our discussion of the regression, probit, and logit models, our first concern was parameter estimation, because it was clear that this would be necessary for any application of the model. Given parameter estimates with desirable properties, we could discuss application issues such as prediction and classification. Unfortunately, the construction of a discriminant analysis model cannot proceed in a similar fashion, as there is no explicit model to estimate. Instead we must start by specifying the specific objective of a problem (such as prediction or classification), which in turn will imply the need to estimate particular parameters.

Perhaps the most common objective of the problems mentioned in this book is the prediction of group membership given information only on the X variables. This might take two forms. We might only be interested in predicting the "most likely" group. Alternatively, we might be interested in computing explicit probabilities of group membership. In either case, we presume the existence of well-defined groups and deal only with the problem of deciding how to classify as yet unknown observations. This should be distinguished from the related but different taxonomic problem, which involves establishing the system of groups. Alternative techniques such as cluster analysis (see Tryon and Bailey, 1970), which we do not discuss, can be used to address the taxonomic problem. Since knowledge of the probabilities could be trivially used to compute "most likely," let us consider this problem first.

Put in the context of the bankruptcy problem, our objective is to predict the relative probability that a form with an observed debt/equity ratio was drawn from the bankrupt or nonbankrupt group. Since explicit causality is not assumed to run from the X's to group membership, we are not trying to predict whether that firm will go bankrupt. Rather, we are trying to infer which group it was that generated that observation. The concept has often been referred to as the concept of "resemblance" rather than probability. We try to construct a scheme that will assign probabilities to observations of unknown group membership on the basis of which of the two populations the observation "resembles" the most. We measure "resemblance" by how the values of the m variables for the observation compare with samples drawn from each group where group membership is known. Differences between probability and resemblance will be discussed in more detail in Chapter II.

The concept of resemblance has a traditional interpretation as a Bayesian posterior on group membership given values of the m variables for an observation with unknown group membership. In fact, the discriminant analysis classification scheme that we outline in this section is a standard Bayes procedure as shown in textbooks such as Anderson (1958) or DeGroot (1970). As with all Bayesian procedures, posterior probabilities for each unknown observation are constructed from likelihood functions for each group. These are derived as follows for the discriminant analysis model.

Assume that we observe characteristics of the nth firm X_n. The likelihood that a firm of those characteristics would be generated if the prevailing group were nonbankrupt firms is the multivariate normal density

$$f_1(X_n) = [1/(2\pi|\Sigma_1|)^{1/2}] \exp[-(X_n - \mu_1)'\Sigma_1^{-1} (X_n - \mu_1)/2] \quad (1.35a)$$

Similarly, the likelihood of observing X_n given the generating group is bankrupt firms is

$$f_2(X_n) = [1/(2\pi|\Sigma_2|)^{1/2}] \exp[-(X_n - \mu_2)'\Sigma_2^{-1} (X_n - \mu_2)/2] \quad (1.35b)$$

Classification probabilities and rules are constructed in an intuitively appealing fashion by comparison of the two group likelihood functions. However, unless the two groups are the same size (not just samples, but the population), the likelihood must be weighted before they can be compared.

Define π_1, as the *a priori* probability of an observation being drawn from group 1, and π_2 as the *a priori* probability of an observation being drawn from group 2. We can think of π_1 and π_2 as the relative likelihoods of the two groups, given no information about X characteristics. Alternatively, they can be interpreted as the relative sizes of the two populations.

Probabilities of group membership are computed from ratios of the weighted likelihood functions:

$$P(\text{group } 1|X_n) = \frac{\pi_1 f_1(X_n)}{\pi_1 f_1(X_n) + \pi_2 f_2(X_n)}$$
$$P(\text{group } 2|X_n) = \frac{\pi_2 f_2(X_n)}{\pi_1 f_1(X_n) + \pi_2 f_2(X_n)} \tag{1.36}$$

Computing group membership from the formulas in Eq. (1.35) is often called "*quadratic classification.*" This follows from the fact that the likelihood functions $f_i(X_n)$ are quadratic functions of the X's. If m is large (i.e., we observe a large number of characteristics for each firm) then the likelihoods may be expensive to compute.

We have assumed that the variance–covariance matrix of each group was different. However, the complexity of computing group membership probabilities can be substantially reduced by assuming group variance structures are the same, i.e.,

$$\Sigma = \Sigma_1 = \Sigma_2$$

Using the probability of Group 1 as an example

$$P(\text{group } 1|X_n) = \frac{\pi_1 f_1(X_n)}{\pi_1 f_1(X_n) + \pi_2 f_2(X_n)}$$
$$= \left[1 + \frac{\pi_2 f_2(X_n)}{\pi_1 f_1(X_n)}\right]^{-1}$$

The ratio of group likelihoods can be simplified

$$\frac{\pi_2 f_2(X_n)}{\pi_1 f_1(X_n)} = \frac{\pi_2\{(2\pi|\Sigma|)^{-1/2}\exp[-(1/2)(X_n - \mu_2)'\Sigma^{-1}(X_n - \mu_2)]\}}{\pi_1\{(2\pi|\Sigma|)^{-1/2}\exp[-(1/2)(X_n - \mu_1)'\Sigma^{-1}(X_n - \mu_1)]\}}$$
$$= (\pi_2/\pi_1)\exp\{-(1/2)[(X_n - \mu_2)'\Sigma^{-1}(X_n - \mu_2)$$
$$- (X_n - \mu_1)'\Sigma^{-1}(X_n - \mu_1)]\}$$
$$= (\pi_2/\pi_1)\exp\{-(1/2)[(X_n'\Sigma^{-1}X_n - \mu_2'\Sigma^{-1}X_n$$
$$- X_n'\Sigma^{-1}\mu_2$$
$$+ \mu_2'\Sigma^{-1}\mu_2 - X_n'\Sigma^{-1}X_n + \mu_1'\Sigma^{-1}X_n$$
$$+ X_n'\Sigma^{-1}\mu_1 - \mu_1'\Sigma^{-1}\mu_1]\}$$
$$= (\pi_2/\pi_1)\exp[X_n'\Sigma^{-1}(\mu_2 - \mu_1)$$
$$- (1/2)(\mu_2 + \mu_1)'\Sigma^{-1}(\mu_2 - \mu_1)]$$

Define the vector, $\gamma = \Sigma^{-1}(\mu_1 - \mu_2)$, and the scalar $\alpha = (1/2)(\mu_1 + \mu_2)'\gamma$.

The vector γ is often referred to as weights of the population *discriminant function,* and the inner product $X_n'\gamma$ referred to as the discriminant function or *discriminant score* for a particular observation. These concepts will be discussed in more detail later in this section. We note that the probabilities of group membership can now be calculated from exponential transformations of linear functions of X_n

$$P(\text{group } 1|X_n) = [1 + (\pi_2/\pi_1)\exp(-X_n'\gamma + \alpha)]^{-1} \tag{1.37}$$

$$P(\text{group } 2|X_n) = [1 + (\pi_1/\pi_2)\exp(X_n'\gamma - \alpha)]^{-1}$$

This has led classification under the assumption of equal group covariance matrices to be referred to as "*linear classification.*" Note that if groups have equal *a priori* probabilities, the probabilities of group membership have exactly the same form as the logit model. This fact, noted by many (see Nerlove and Press, 1973), is particularly interesting given the fact that the discriminant analysis and logit models appear to be based on entirely different assumptions. It also suggests that if the assumptions of the discriminant analysis model are true, and *a priori* probabilities are equal, then the parameters γ and α will be proportional to the logit parameters and the logit model will also be applicable. Note, however, that this argument cannot be reversed. If the logit assumptions hold, but the X's are not multivariate normally distributed in groups, then the discriminant analysis model will not be applicable.

Thus far we have assumed that the population parameters $\{\mu_1,\mu_2,\Sigma_1,\Sigma_2\}$ are known exactly. As a practical matter, however, this is rarely the case. More realistically, assume a random sample of firms of size $N_1 + N_2 = N$, where N_1 are *known* to be nonfailed and N_2 are *known* to be bankrupt firms. Defining X_{1n} as observations from group 1 and X_{2n} as observations from group 2, many authors dating from Fisher (1936) suggest computing sample estimates of the mean vectors,

$$\hat{\mu}_1 = \bar{X}_1 = \sum_{n=1}^{N_1} X_{1n}/N_1$$

$$\hat{\mu}_2 = \bar{X}_2 = \sum_{n=1}^{N_2} X_{2n}/N_2$$

and group covariance matrices,

$$\hat{\Sigma}_1 = S_1 = \sum_{n=1}^{N_1} (X_{1n} - \bar{X}_1)(X_{1n} - \bar{X}_1)'/(N_1 - 1)$$

$$\hat{\Sigma}_2 = S_2 = \sum_{n=1}^{N_2} (X_{2n} - \bar{X}_2)(X_{2n} - \bar{X}_2)'/(N_2 - 1)$$

which are substituted for the parameters of Eq. (1.35) in computing estimates of group probabilities. If linear classification is desired

$$\hat{\Sigma} = S = \frac{\sum_{n=1}^{N_1} (X_{1n} - \bar{X}_1)(X_{1n} - \bar{X}_1)' + \sum_{n=1}^{N_2} (X_{2n} - \bar{X}_2)(X_{2n} - \bar{X}_2)'}{N - 2}$$

which is commonly referred to as the "within-groups" variance–covariance matrix can be used as an estimate of Σ in computing probabilities from Eq. (1.37).

These estimates are standard maximum likelihood estimators and clearly will be consistent. Thus, probability estimates will also be consistent. As is generally the case, small sample properties are less certain; however, intuition does not suggest clear alternatives.

The previous discussion assumes known *a priori* probabilities. There may, however, be cases where the researcher cannot assign prior probabilities to the two groups. If the data sample is a random draw from the entire population, then the sample ratio N_1/N_2 could be used as a consistent estimate of π_1/π_2. However, in cases where the sample is random within groups but not between groups, N_1/N_2 will generally not be consistent for π_1/π_2. For example, in the bankruptcy problem, researchers might sample virtually all failed firms, but only a small fraction of nonbankrupt ones. In this case, the *a priori* probabilities could not be computed from sample ratios. It is not uncommon in cases like this to see researchers ignore the *a priori* probabilities, often just assuming that they are equal. In such a situation, the computed probabilities may bear no relation to the "true" probabilities and in fact they may be highly misleading. Consider, for example, the bankruptcy model and assume an observation where $f_1(X_n) = f_2(X_n)$. Thus, if we assumed equal *a priori* probabilities we would compute probabilities of .5 for each group. However, in reality there are far more nonfailed firms than failed firms, say 99 to 1. Using 99 to 1 as the "true" *a priori* probabilities would yield a probability of .99 that the firm would not fail, a far cry from .5.

Classification—Group Assignment

The researcher's objective may not be to assign observation-specific group probabilities, but rather to derive classification assignment rules that can classify observations into one group or the other given their X characteristics. Given the previous discussion on computing group probabilities, it might seem logical to assign observations to the group with the highest predicted probability. This, in fact, is often what is done. However, we can also consider more general problems; in particular, problems where there may be explicit costs of misclassification.

Suppose, for example, the researcher perceives costs of misclassification of $C(1/2)$ and $C(2/1)$, where $C(i/j)$ is the cost of classifying an observation as group i when it truly belongs to group j. Furthermore, assume we wish to construct a classification scheme that will minimize expected costs from misclassification for a random draw of the population. Defining G_1 as the region of the X space where observations would be classified as group 1 and G_2 as the region where observations would be classified as group 2, the expected loss for a particular classification scheme is

$$L = \int_{X_n \in G_1} C(1|2)\pi_2 f_2(X_n)dx_n + \int_{X_n \in G_2} C(2|1)\pi_1 f_1(X_n)dx_n \quad (1.38)$$

Anderson (1958) shows the classification rule for minimizing this loss function.

Rule 1. Assign an observation with characteristics X_n to group 1 if

$$\frac{f_1(X_n)}{f_2(X_n)} \geqslant \frac{C(1|2)\pi_2}{C(2|1)\pi_1}$$

and to group 2 otherwise.

Notice that if the costs of misclassification are equal, i.e., $C(1|2) = C(2|1)$, then the classification rule is identical to assigning observations to the group with the highest probability as given in Eq. (1.36). Those familiar with Bayesian procedures will notice that Rule 1 is the general Bayes solution to the classification problem.

If group covariance matrices are not equal, i.e., $\Sigma_1 \neq \Sigma_2$, Rule 1 can be expressed as a quadratic function.

Rule 2. Assign an observation with characteristics X_n to group 1 if

$$X_n'(\Sigma_1^{-1} - \Sigma_2^{-1})X_n - 2(\mu_1'\Sigma_1^{-1} - \mu_2'\Sigma_2^{-1})X_n + \mu_1'\Sigma_1^{-1}\mu_1 - \mu_2'\Sigma_2^{-1}\mu_2 \leqslant \ln|\Sigma_2\Sigma_1^{-1}| - 2\ln[C(1|2)\pi_2/C(2|1)\pi_1]$$

and to group 2 otherwise.

Since the classification rule is quadratic in X_n, we refer to this as "*quadratic classification.*"

Alternatively, if the group covariance matrices are equal, Rule 1 reduces to a linear function.

Rule 3. Assign an observation with characteristics X_n to group 1 if

$$X_n'\gamma - \alpha \geqslant \ln[C(1|2)\pi_2/C(2|1)\pi_1]$$

where γ are weights of the discriminant function described earlier

$$\gamma = \Sigma^{-1}(\mu_1 - \mu_2)$$

$$\alpha = (\mu_1 + \mu_2)'\gamma/2$$

and to group 2 otherwise. This is commonly termed "*linear classification.*"

Notice that Rule 3 implies a very simple classification heuristic. $X_n'\gamma$, which is often termed an observation's *discriminant score*, is computed as a simple linear weighting of X_n. The discriminant score is compared to a preset "cutoff," $\alpha + \ln[C(1|2)\pi_2/C(2|1)\pi_1]$. If the score is above the cutoff, the observation is assigned to group 1, otherwise to group 2.

This procedure is very similar to the linear probability model. In fact, if we use sample means and covariances and relative sample sizes as estimates of *a priori* probabilities, the linear classification rule will be identical to the linear probability model using .5 probability as a cutoff. Thus classification predictions will be identical.

Another noticeable aspect of the classification rules is the fact that they are invariant with respect to scale. For example, both sides of Rule 3 could be multiplied by any positive number, or an arbitrary constant could be added to each side, without effecting classification.

The difference between quadratic and linear classification is illustrated by Figures I.8 and I.9. In each case we assume a single X variable measured along the horizontal axis, with group densities measured along the vertical axis. The line X_c denotes the optimal cutoff assuming equal *a priori* probabilities and costs of misclassification. In the linear case, the cutoff is half way between μ_1 and μ_2, with observations simply assigned to the group whose mean is closest. Classification is more complex for the quadratic model and requires computing "weighted" distances to each mean.

As in the case of computing group probabilities, when population parameters are unknown, Anderson (1958) proposes substituting sam-

Figure I.8. Quadratic Classification

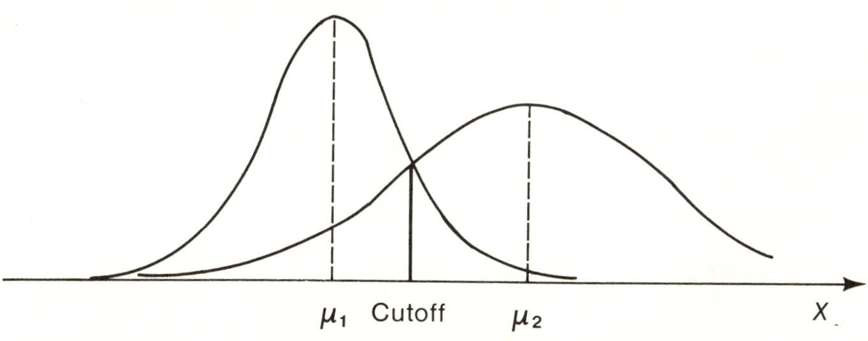

Figure I.9. Linear Classification

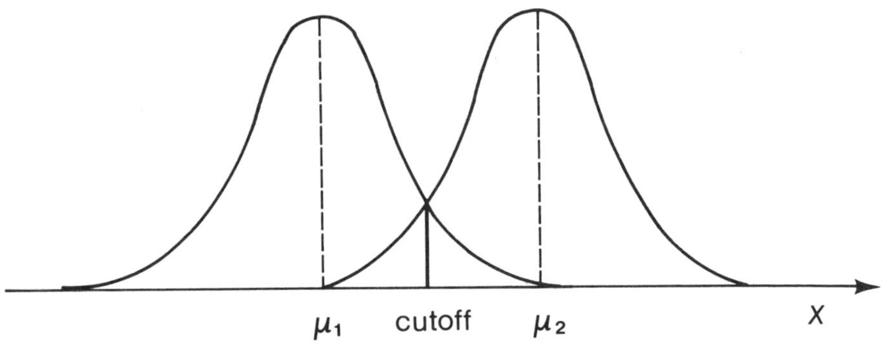

ple estimates $\{\bar{X}_1,\bar{X}_2,S_1,S_2,S\}$ for $\{\mu_1,\mu_2,\Sigma_1,\Sigma_2,\Sigma\}$ in the classification rules. Assuming random sampling with known groups, rules constructed from sample parameters will be consistent estimators of the true population rules. The use of sample parameters, however, may create problems if researchers want to estimate "expected" error rates associated with different rules. Since the rule parameters are themselves subject to sample errors, classification errors will result both from random unavoidable misclassifications and errors in estimating the correct classification rule. These problems are discussed in Chapter III.

Significance Tests and Examinations of Group Overlaps

In the introduction to this section, we suggested that discriminant analysis lacked a formal model. Thus, estimation issues could be discussed only in the context of a specific research objective. In the previous subsection, we discussed the construction of probabilities and classification rules for predictive purposes. Often, however, researchers are interested in more than predictive questions. In particular we may be interested in inferential questions such as testing hypotheses concerning group means and variance–covariance structures. In this subsection, we consider the general problem of inference in discriminant analysis.

Again using the example of bankruptcy, assume that an m length vector of firm characteristics X is distributed multivariate normally within both the bankrupt and nonbankrupt groups, with means μ_1, μ_2, and variance–covariance (dispersion) matrices Σ_1,Σ_2, respectively. Suppose that the researcher wishes to test the null hypothesis

$$H_0\colon \mu_1 = \mu_2$$

If we further assume equal covariance matrices, $\Sigma_1 = \Sigma_2 = \Sigma$, as a maintained hypothesis, H_0 is equivalent to testing whether the bankrupt and nonbankrupt groups are in fact drawn from the same population.

(Later in this section we discuss how to test equality of covariance matrices as well.)

Anderson (1958) demonstrates that for a random sample of size N_1 and N_2 for groups 1 and 2, respectively, H_0 can be tested under the assumption of equal, but unknown, covariance matrices by the following statistic

$$\frac{N_1 + N_2 - m - 1}{N_1 + N_2 - 2} \cdot \frac{1}{m} \cdot \frac{N_1 N_2}{N_1 + N_2}$$

$$(\bar{X}_1 - \bar{X}_2)' S^{-1} (\bar{X}_1 - \bar{X}_2) \sim F^{m}_{N_1 + N_2 - m - 1} \qquad (1.39)$$

where S is the sample within-groups variance–covariance matrix and $\bar{X}_1$ and $\bar{X}_2$ are the sample group mean vectors. When H_0 is true, the test statistic has an F distribution with m and $N_1 + N_2 - m - 1$ degrees of freedom. The null hypothesis can be rejected when the value of the test statistic is greater than the tabled value of F for the desired level of significance.

The expression given in Eq. (1.39) may look unfamiliar to those with previous exposure to discriminant analysis. There are a number of related multivariate statistics that have been developed over the years and that are more commonly seen. For example,

$$D^2 = (\bar{X}_1 - \bar{X}_2)' S^{-1} (\bar{X}_1 - \bar{X}_2)$$

is the commonly used Mahalanobis' D^2 statistic;

$$T^2 = \frac{N_1 N_2}{N_1 + N_2} (\bar{X}_1 - \bar{X}_2)' S^{-1} (\bar{X}_1 - \bar{X}_2)$$

is referred to as Hotelling's T^2;

$$\Lambda = \frac{N_1 + N_2 - 2}{T^2 + N_1 + N_2 - 2}$$

is called Wilks' Lambda; and

$$V = T^2/(N_1 + N_2 - 2)$$

is Hsu's V. Notice that the test statistic given in Eq. (1.39) can be expressed as a function of each of the above statistics, i.e.,

$$\begin{aligned} F^{m}_{N_1 + N_2 - m - 1} &= \frac{N_1 + N_2 - m - 1}{N_1 + N_2 - 2} \cdot \frac{1}{m} \cdot \frac{N_1 N_2}{N_1 + N_2} D^2 \\ &= \frac{N_1 + N_2 - m - 1}{N_1 + N_2 - 2} \cdot \frac{1}{m} T^2 \end{aligned}$$

$$= \frac{N_1 + N_2 - m - 1}{m} \cdot \frac{1 - \Lambda}{\Lambda}$$

$$= \frac{N_1 + N_2 - m - 1}{m} \cdot V$$

Thus each of these statistics could be used to construct the same test. [See Porebski (1966) for a more comprehensive discussion of the interrelationships.] Indeed, if you were to construct a dependent variable y_n, which had a value 1 for bankrupt group observations and 0 for nonbankrupt firms, and to regress y_n against X_n and a constant, the regression F-statistic (tests the null hypothesis that all coefficients but the constant are zero) would be identical to Eq. (1.39). Thus a regression program could be used to test the null hypothesis of group mean equality. Note that the regression model would be identical to the linear probability model discussed earlier.

There are a number of other hypothesis tests that may be of interest. Researchers may wish to test the equality of group mean vectors without imposing the assumption of equality of group covariance matrices. This is a classical statistical problem known as the "Behrens–Fisher problem." If sample sizes are equal, i.e., $N_1 = N_2 = N$, and observations are randomly ordered, Anderson (1958) shows that

$$\frac{N - m - 1}{m(N - 1)} \cdot T_N^2 \sim F_{N-m-1}^m \tag{1.40a}$$

where

$$T_N^2 = N(\bar{X}_1 - \bar{X}_2)' S_N^{-1} (\bar{X}_1 - \bar{X}_2)$$

$$S_N = \frac{1}{N - 1} \sum_{n=1}^{N} [(X_{1n} - \bar{X}_1) - (X_{2n} - \bar{X}_2)][(X_{1n} - \bar{X}_1) - (X_{2n} - \bar{X}_2)]'$$

is distributed as a F-statistic with m and $N - m - 1$ degrees of freedom under the null hypothesis $\mu_1 = \mu_2$. If $N_1 < N_2$, Anderson proposes the test statistic

$$\frac{N_1 - m - 1}{m(N_1 - 1)} T_{N_1}^2 \sim F_{N_1-m-1}^m \tag{1.40b}$$

where

$$T_{N_1}^2 = N_1(\bar{X}_1 - \bar{X}_2)' S_{N_1}^{-1} (\bar{X}_1 - \bar{X}_2)$$

$$S_{N_1} = \frac{1}{N_1 - 1} \sum_{n=1}^{N_1} \left[(X_{1n} - \bar{X}_1) - \left(\frac{N_1}{N_2}\right)^{1/2} \left(X_{2n} - \frac{1}{N_1} \sum_{p=1}^{N_1} X_{2p} \right) \right]$$

$$\left[(X_{1n} - \bar{X}_1) - \left(\frac{N_1}{N_2}\right)^{1/2}\left(X_{2n} - \frac{1}{N_1}\sum_{p=1}^{N_1} X_{2p}\right)\right]$$

Notice that only N_1 observations of group 2 are used.

Another test of interest is for equality of group covariance matrices, i.e.,

$$H_0: \Sigma_1 = \Sigma_2 = \Sigma$$

This test is particularly useful in choosing whether to use a linear or quadratic classification rule. Box (1949) shows that given a sample of size $N_1 + N_2 = N$, an approximate F-statistic may be developed from group sample covariance matrices S_1 and S_2, and the within-group covariance matrix S

$$A = \ln[|S|^{N-2}/(|S_1|^{N_1-1}|S_2|^{N_2-1})]$$

$$B = \left[\frac{1}{N_1+1} + \frac{1}{N_2+1} - \frac{1}{N-2}\right][2m^2 + 3m - 1]/6(m+1)$$

$$C = \left[\frac{1}{(N_1+1)^2} + \frac{1}{(N_2+1)^2} - \frac{1}{(N-2)^2}\right](m-1)(m+2)/6$$

$$D = m \cdot (m+1)/2$$

$$E = (D+2)/|B^2 - C|$$

If $B^2 > C$, the test statistic is

$$\left(\frac{E}{D}\right)\left[\frac{A(1 - B + 2/E)}{E - A(1 - B + 2/E)}\right] \sim F_E^D \qquad (1.41a)$$

If $C > B^2$, the test statistic is

$$\left(\frac{A}{D}\right)(1 - B - D/E) \sim F_E^D \qquad (1.41b)$$

Each is distributed as a F-statistic with D and E degrees of freedom when the null hypothesis is true.

Each of the above tests concerns comparisons between groups. Often, however, researchers may be interested in hypotheses concerning one particular group. A common hypothesis, for example, would be to compare the mean vector of a group to a preset, fixed vector, μ^0. Taking group 1 as an example, we want to test

$$H_0: \mu_1 = \mu_1^0$$

Assuming an unknown group covariance matrix, this hypothesis can be tested using a variation of Hotellings T^2

$$T^2 = N_1(\bar{X}_1 - \mu_1^{0})' S_1^{-1} (\bar{X}_1 - \mu_1^{0})$$

where S_1 is the sample group covariance matrix. Hotelling (1931) shows that

$$\frac{N_1 - m}{(N_1 - 1)m} T^2 \sim F^{m}_{N_1 - m} \tag{1.42}$$

is distributed as an F-statistic with m and $N_1 - m$ degrees of freedom when the hypothesis is true. Practical considerations in using these tests are discussed in Chapter III.

Finally, throughout this section we have spoken of the vector X_n as though it were of fixed given size m. In reality, researchers often consider a set of possible variables. Questions are often raised as to which variables are "important" discriminators between groups. Unlike regression, probit, or logit analysis however, there are no explicit causal relationships or coefficients. Thus it is more difficult to define what we mean by "significant" variables. This subject will be discussed in more detail in the chapter on discriminant analysis applications; however, it is worth a brief mention of the possible tests one might employ. A possible representation of an "insignificant" variable is that there is an "insignificant" difference between the two groups in the mean of that variable. Taking variable j as an example, this univariate hypothesis can be tested similarly to Eq. (1.39)

$$\frac{N_1 N_2}{N_1 + N_2} \frac{(\bar{X}_1^{(j)} - \bar{X}_2^{(j)})^2}{S^{(j)}} \sim F^{1}_{N_1 + N_2 - 2} \tag{1.43}$$

where $\bar{X}_1^{(j)}$ and $\bar{X}_2^{(j)}$ are the means of variable j in groups 1 and 2, respectively and $S^{(j)}$ is the jth diagonal element of the within-groups covariance matrix. This test statistic is identical to the square of the coefficient t-statistic if the 0–1 bankruptcy variable y_n were regressed against variable j and a constant.

As in the regression framework, univariate tests may not adequately reflect the "importance" of variables. For example, a variable might have a large significant univariate difference in the means yet not "contribute" to classification when other variables are used as well. A test that is often employed and that takes into account the multivariate nature of the discriminant analysis model is one proposed by Rao (1952). Defining Λ as the Wilks' Lambda statistic using all m sample variables and $\Lambda^{(j)}$ as Wilks' Lambda computed from all $m - 1$ variables except the jth variable, Rao proposes the test statistic,

$$\left(\frac{\Lambda^{(j)} - \Lambda}{\Lambda}\right)(N_1 + N_2 - m - 1) \sim F^1_{N_1+N_2-m-1} \quad (1.44)$$

which is distributed as a F-statistic with 1 and $N_1 + N_2 - m - 1$ degrees of freedom when the null hypothesis is true. This statistic tests the null hypothesis that the *conditional mean* of variable j *given* the other $m - 1$ variables is the same for group 1 as for group 2. Rao's statistic is identical to the square of the t-statistic associated with the coefficient of the jth variable when the 0–1 bankruptcy variable y_n is regressed against the entire m variable set and a constant (the linear probability model).

In a manner similar to regression restriction tests, we may also test the null hypothesis that the conditional means of a set of J variables, given the remaining $m - J$ variables, are the same for both groups. Defining $\Lambda^{(J)}$ as Wilks' Lambda computed from the remaining $m - J$ variables, the test statistic is

$$\left(\frac{\Lambda^{(J)} - \Lambda}{\Lambda}\right)\left(\frac{N_1 + N_2 - m - 1}{J}\right) \sim F^J_{N_1+N_2-m-1} \quad (1.45)$$

which is distributed as a F-statistic with J and $N_1 + N_2 - m - 1$ degrees of freedom under the null hypothesis. One should be careful in drawing too strong an inference from the conditional means tests. As indicated above, the null hypothesis cannot be directly interpreted in terms of a coefficient or causal relationship. Under the assumption of equal group covariances, equal conditional group means for a variable will indeed imply that the variable will not contribute in classification or in the calculation of group probabilities. However, the linkage between the significance tests and classification should not be overplayed. The conditional mean tests are dependent upon the assumption of equal group covariance matrices. If this assumption is violated, the tests are biased, and variables may contribute in classification even if their conditional means are equal.

Discriminant Functions

In the earlier subsection on classification, we described the discriminant function, showing that it was the linear weighting of an observation that extracted all information used in linear classification. It can also be shown that the same function is a component of the significance tests of the difference of group means. It is the discriminant function that provides the common linkage between a collection of somewhat unrelated data analysis procedures that we call discriminant analysis.

For this reason, it is worth a brief discussion of the function and a demonstration of its uses.

We previously defined the population discriminant function as the vector weighting

$$\gamma = \Sigma^{-1} (\mu_1 - \mu_2)$$

where Σ^{-1} is the within-groups covariance matrix and μ_1 and μ_2 are group mean vectors. We showed that for a given observation X_n, the discriminant score $X_n' \gamma$ contained all observation-specific information used in linear classification. If population parameters are unknown but random group samples are available, we could construct

$$b = S^{-1}(\bar{X}_1 - \bar{X}_2) \tag{1.46}$$

as a sample estimate of the discriminant function vector. R.A. Fisher (1936) demonstrated that an interesting thing happens if we compute the discriminant score of each observation for the sample used to compute the sample discriminant function, i.e.,

$$X_n^* = X_n'b$$

Fisher points out that the difference of the group mean discriminant scores

$$\sum_{n=1}^{N_1} \frac{X_{1n}^*}{N_1} - \sum_{n=1}^{N_2} \frac{X_{2n}^*}{N_2} = (\bar{X}_1 - \bar{X}_2)b$$

$$= (\bar{X}_1 - \bar{X}_2)'S^{-1}(\bar{X}_1 - \bar{X}_2)$$

is the Mahalanobis' D^2-statistic used in the test of group mean equality. Fisher also shows that the sample within-groups variance of X_n^* is

$$\begin{aligned} S^* &= b'\left[\sum_{n=1}^{N_1} (X_{1n} - \bar{X}_1)(X_{1n} - \bar{X}_1)' \right. \\ &\quad \left. + \sum_{n=1}^{N_2} (X_{2n} - \bar{X}_2)(X_{2n} - \bar{X}_2)'\right] b/(N_1 + N_2 - 2) \\ &= b'Sb \\ &= (\bar{X}_1 - \bar{X}_2)'S^{-1} \cdot S \cdot S^{-1}(\bar{X}_1 - \bar{X}_2) \\ &= (\bar{X}_1 - \bar{X}_2)'S^{-1}(\bar{X}_1 - \bar{X}_2) \end{aligned}$$

or Mahalanobis D^2 again. Suppose that we constructed a test of equality of group means using the transformed data X_n^* instead of the full observation vectors X_n. The test statistic corresponding to Eq. (1.39) would be

$$\frac{N_1 + N_2 - m - 1}{N_1 + N_2 - 2} \cdot \frac{1}{m} \cdot \frac{N_1N_2}{N_1 + N_2} (\bar{X}_1{}^* - \bar{X}_2{}^*)'(S^*)^{-1}(\bar{X}_1{}^* - \bar{X}_2{}^*)$$

$$= \frac{N_1 + N_2 - m - 1}{N_1 + N_2 - 2} \cdot \frac{1}{m} \cdot \frac{N_1N_2}{N_1 + N_2} [(\bar{X}_1 - \bar{X}_2)'S^{-1}(\bar{X}_1 - \bar{X}_2)] \cdot$$

$$[(\bar{X}_1 - \bar{X}_2)'S^{-1}(\bar{X}_1 - \bar{X}_2)]^{-1} \cdot$$

$$[(\bar{X}_1 - \bar{X}_2)'S^{-1}(\bar{X}_1 - \bar{X}_2)]$$

$$= \frac{N_1 + N_2 - m - 1}{N_1 + N_2 - 2} \cdot \frac{1}{m} \cdot \frac{N_1N_2}{N_1 + N_2} (\bar{X}_1 - \bar{X}_2)'S^{-1}(\bar{X}_1 - \bar{X}_2)$$

which is identical to the test statistic constructed from the entire observation vector. Thus, the discriminant function summarizes all relevant sample information, not only for classification but also for testing group mean differences. This is not unlike predicted y values in a regression, which summarize all information in the independent variables relevant for predicting y. We stress, however, that in discriminant analysis, either for classification or testing, the discriminant function is useful *only* under the assumption of equal group covariances.

The classification and significance test results will hold for any vector proportional to b, i.e., $b^* = \delta b$. However, the "cutoff" value $\alpha + \ln[C(1/2)\ \pi_2/C(2/1)\pi_1]$ of the linear classification Rule 3 must also be multiplied by δ. This has given rise to a number of different discriminant function vectors, each proportional to b. Several of these are derived from the familiar decomposition of sample variance. The *total deviation sums of squares* matrix,

$$T = \sum_{n=1}^{N_1} (X_{1n} - \bar{X})(X_{1n} - \bar{X})' + \sum_{n=1}^{N_2} (X_{2n} - \bar{X})(X_{2n} - \bar{X})'$$

where $\bar{X}$ is the sample grand mean vector, is always equal to the *sum* of the *within-groups deviation sums of squares matrix*

$$W = \sum_{n=1}^{N_1} (X_{1n} - \bar{X}_1)(X_{1n} - \bar{X}_1)' + \sum_{n=1}^{N_2} (X_{2n} - \bar{X}_2)(X_{2n} - \bar{X}_2)'$$

and the *between-groups deviation sums of squares* matrix

$$B = \sum_{n=1}^{N_1} (\bar{X}_1 - \bar{X})'(\bar{X}_1 - \bar{X}) + \sum_{n=1}^{N_2} (\bar{X}_2 - \bar{X})(\bar{X}_2 - \bar{X})'$$

$$= \frac{N_1N_2}{N_1 + N_2} (\bar{X}_1 - \bar{X}_2)(\bar{X}_1 - \bar{X}_2)'$$

Ladd (1966) shows that b (or a vector proportional to b) can always be derived from any two of these matrices. These include

(a) $b_1^* = W^{-1}(\bar{X}_1 - \bar{X}_2) = b/(N_1 + N_2 - 2)$

(b) $b_2^* = T^{-1}(\bar{X}_1 - \bar{X}_2) = b\left[1 - \dfrac{N_1N_2}{N_1 + N_2}(\bar{X}_1 - \bar{X}_2)'b_2^*\right]$

$$/(N_1 + N_2 - 2)$$

(c) $b_3^* = \dfrac{N_1N_2}{N_1 + N_2} T^{-1}(\bar{X}_1 - \bar{X}_2) = b\dfrac{N_1N_2}{N_1 + N_2}\left[1 - (\bar{X}_1 - \bar{X}_2)'b_3^*\right]$

$$/(N_1 + N_2 - 2)$$

b_2^* and b_3^* are particularly interesting in that they are the regression coefficients calculated from regressing a dependent variable that has values

$$y_n = \begin{cases} 1/N_2 & \text{if in group 1} \\ -1/N_1 & \text{if in group 2} \end{cases}$$

for b_2^* and

$$y_n = \begin{cases} 1 & \text{if in group 1} \\ 0 & \text{if in group 2} \end{cases}$$

for b_3^*, against X_n and a constant. Thus, a regression program could be used to calculate the sample discriminant function vector b (b is easily derived from the regression coefficients using the factors of proportionality shown above.) This also illustrates the computational commonality between the discriminant analysis model and the linear probability model, which would be identical to the 0–1 regression. However, since the models are based on different assumptions, interpretation of the coefficients may be quite different.

The discriminant function transformation is particularly important in that it reduces the dimension of the data from m to a single variable, yet retains all information relevant for group mean testing and linear classification. Using the population discriminant function, we could think of transforming all sample observations

$$x_n^* = X_n'\gamma$$

to a single variable or discriminant score. The space of the transformed variables is often called *reduced space.* Transformed space group means are commonly referred to as *centroids*

$$\mu_1^* = \mu_1'\gamma$$

$$\mu_2^* = \mu_2'\gamma$$

and reduced space within-groups variance as

$$\Sigma^* = \gamma'\Sigma\gamma$$

If population parameters are unknown, each could be estimated by their sample equivalent.

The discriminant function transformation is illustrated by Figure I.10, using a transformation of a two-variable, $X_n = \{x_n^{(1)}, x_n^{(2)}\}$ problem as an example. The discriminant function maps data from the two-dimensional space given by the axes $x^{(1)}$ and $x^{(2)}$ to reduced space shown along the line x^*. The ellipses indicate the locus of points of equal likelihood within each group in $[x^{(1)}, x^{(2)}]$ space, and the normal "humps" indicate density in reduced space. Note that all observations along any

Figure I.10. Reduced Space Transformation

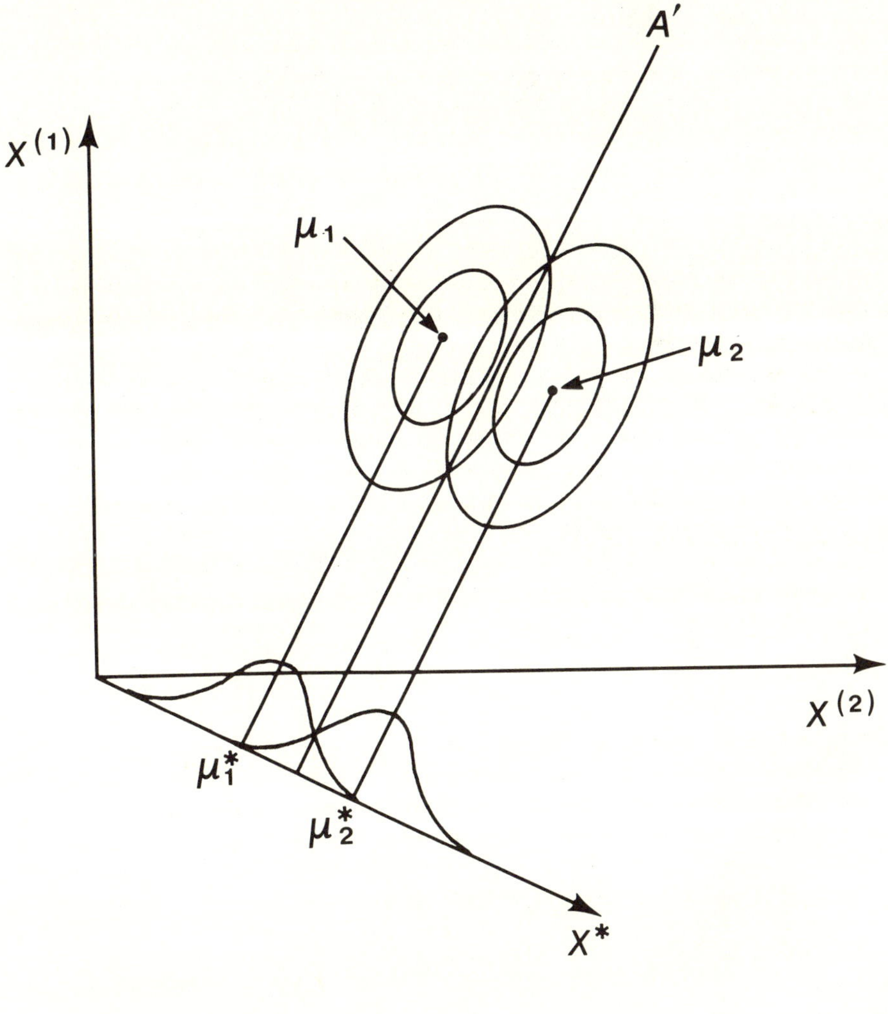

ray that is perpendicular to x^* (such as A') will have the same reduced space value. The transformation preserves the relative position of all observations as defined by the likelihood ratio $f_1(X_n)/f_2(X_n)$. Thus as shown before, classification would yield results in reduced space that are equivalent to results in the space of the original m variables.

Before leaving our discussion of reduced space, let us note another characteristic of the discriminant function transformation that will prove useful in the multigroup problem discussed in Chapter II. The linear transformation given by the discriminant function (or any proportional vector) has the following property. If we consider the class of linear transforms $\tilde{b}$ and transformed data,

$$\tilde{X}_n = X_n'\tilde{b}$$

where we restrict the sample deviation sums of squares of $\tilde{X}_n$ to a preset constant ϕ, i.e.,

$$\phi = \sum_{i=1}^{2} \sum_{n=1}^{N_i} \tilde{b}'(X_{in} - \bar{X})'(X_{in} - \bar{X})\tilde{b}$$

the sample discriminant function vector b, maximizes the ratio of the between-groups sample variance of $\tilde{X}_n$ to the within-groups variance. Because of the interrelationship between the variance measures, b also minimizes the ratio of within-groups variance to total variance and maximizes the ratio of between-groups variance to total variance. This is analogous to the fact that the least squares coefficient vector maximizes the ratio of predicted deviation sums of squares to residual sums of squares holding the deviation sums of squares of the dependent variable constant. As we shall see later, this fact is important in constructing discriminant functions with more than two groups.

Example—Director Interlocks III

We illustrate the discriminant analysis model using the same example used for the linear probability, probit, and logit models. Briefly, we examine whether the affiliation status

$$A = \begin{cases} 1 & \text{if commercial bank affiliated with a mutual} \\ 0 & \text{if not} \end{cases}$$

of 38 New Hampshire commercial banks is related to values of two variables

$$\text{TSD} = \frac{\text{Total Savings and IPC Time Deposits}}{\text{Total Savings and IPC Time and IPC Demand Deposits}}$$

$$\text{RL} = \frac{\text{Total Conventional Residential Real Estate Loans}}{\text{Total Loans and Gross Discounts}}$$

Modeled as a discriminant analysis problem, the example has a slightly different interpretation than when modeled as a probit or linear probability model. The affiliation variable defines two discrete groups: 24 affiliated banks (AFF) and 14 unaffiliated banks (UAFF). We are interested in two related questions: (1) Does the distribution of RL and TSD differ significantly between the two groups; and (2) how accurately can we predict group membership from values of RL and TSD? We address the distributional questions first.

The basic data used for almost all discriminant analysis estimates are the sample group means, variance–covariance matrices, and the "within-groups" variance–covariance matrix. For the Interlock problem these are

Group means

$$\overline{\mathrm{TSD}}_{\mathrm{AFF}} = .291 \qquad \overline{\mathrm{TSD}}_{\mathrm{UAFF}} = .674$$

$$\overline{\mathrm{RL}}_{\mathrm{AFF}} = .113 \qquad \overline{\mathrm{RL}}_{\mathrm{UAFF}} = .312$$

Group variance-covariance matrices

$$S_{\mathrm{AFF}} = \begin{bmatrix} .0162 & .0226 \\ .0226 & .0757 \end{bmatrix} \quad S_{\mathrm{UAFF}} = \begin{bmatrix} .0356 & -.0006 \\ -.0006 & .0089 \end{bmatrix}$$

Within-groups variance-covariance

$$S = \begin{bmatrix} .0232 & .0142 \\ .0142 & .0515 \end{bmatrix}$$

The hypothesis of equal group mean vectors can be tested by computing Mahalanobis D^2

$$D^2 = 3.290$$

and the test statistic

$$F^2_{35} = 14.14$$

which can be rejected at the 1 percent level.

Similarly the null hypothesis of group covariance matrix equality can be tested by the test statistic

$$F^3_{23181} = 7.014$$

which can also be rejected at the 1 percent level.

Classification schemes can be constructed under the assumption of equal or unequal group covariance matrices. If covariances are assumed to be unequal (quadratic classification, Rule 2) and *a priori* probabilities are given by the ratio of sample sizes (24/14), the classification rule is

Assign to AFF if
$78.0\ RL^2 - 68.6\ RL \cdot TSD - 90.3\ TSD^2 + 14.8\ RL + 147.6\ TSD - 53.7 \leqslant .26$

If covariance matrices are assumed to be equal (linear classification, Rule 3), the classification rule is

Assign to AFF if
$- 6.09\ TSD - 4.83\ RL + 3.96 \geqslant -.539$

Using these rules, 19 of the 24 sample affiliated banks were classified correctly by both rules, and 10 by the linear rule and 12 by the quadratic rule of the 14 unaffiliated banks classified correctly. Since we use the relative sample sizes as *a priori* probabilities, the linear rule classification results are identical to the linear probability model reported earlier.

The weights of the sample discriminant function can be obtained from the linear classification rule. They are

$$b_{TSD} = -6.09$$

$$b_{RE} = -4.83$$

Note that these are proportional to the OLS linear probability model coefficients estimated earlier. Observation discriminant scores can be formed using the discriminant function weights. Group centroids in the transformed (reduced) space would be

$$\text{AFF} = -2.32$$

$$\text{UAFF} = -5.61$$

Classification can also be performed using the discriminant scores and a calculated cutoff of -4.50. A rule that assigns scores larger than -4.50 to the affiliated group yields identical classification to the linear rule.

APPENDIX

MAXIMUM LIKELIHOOD ESTIMATION

For a number of the models presented in this chapter and Chapter II, we have proposed maximum likelihood estimators of the coefficient vectors. Because some readers may not have been exposed to the intricacies of maximum likelihood, we give a brief overview of the method in this appendix. This is by no means a complete discussion, for which we refer readers to a text such as Rao (1965), Theil (1971) or Maddala (1977).

Assume a random sample of N independent observations $y_1, y_2, \ldots, y_n$, each drawn from a density function $f(y;\theta)$, where θ is a K-length vector of unknown parameters. The joint density of the observations is then

$$\prod_{n=1}^{N} f(y_n;\theta) \tag{A1.1}$$

which we call the *likelihood function* of θ, $L(\theta)$. We could think of this as the likelihood of the sample. Maximum likelihood (ML) estimation is based on the intuitive principle of choosing estimates of the parameter vector $\hat{\theta}$ that maximize the observed sample likelihood. This is equivalent to maximizing the sample *log-likelihood*

$$\ln L(\theta) = \sum_{n=1}^{N} \ln f(y_n;\theta) \tag{A1.2}$$

which is often more convenient to deal with. For continuous densities with continuous first and second derivatives, the first order conditions necessary for $\ln L(\theta)$ to be at a maximum at $\hat{\theta}$ are that the first derivatives of $\ln L(\theta)$ evaluated for each element of $\hat{\theta}$ be zero, i.e.,

$$\sum_{n=1}^{N} \frac{\partial \ln f(y_n;\hat{\theta})}{\partial \theta} = 0 \tag{A1.3}$$

which are called the *likelihood equations.* We also require second order conditions, i.e., that the matrix of second derivatives evaluated at $\hat{\theta}$

$$\sum_{n=1}^{N} \frac{\partial^2 \ln f(y_n;\hat{\theta})}{\partial \theta \partial \theta'}$$

be negative semidefinite. For a unique maximum this must be a negative definite matrix.

For complex likelihood functions, satisfaction of first and second order conditions may not be sufficient to insure a global maximum. However all of the normal-derivative and logit likelihood functions discussed in this book will be single peaked if set up properly. Thus, satisfaction of first order conditions will be sufficient to insure a maximum.

Unfortunately the likelihood equations of many problems (including probit and logit) are highly nonlinear and thus require iterative solutions. These may be expensive, although there are many excellent methods and programs available (see Goldfeld and Quant, 1972). We have had good success, for example, in solving probit and logit likelihood equations using the Davidon–Fletcher–Powell method (see Fletcher and Powell, 1963).

The attraction of ML estimators is that under very general regularity conditions (see Theil, 1971: 392–393) they will have the following desirable properties:

1. *Consistency:* that they converge to the true parameters with probability one as the sample size goes to infinity.
2. *Asymptotic normality:* that as the sample size goes to infinity the distribution of the ML estimators converges to a multivariate normal distribution with mean θ and variance–covariance matrix equal to the inverse of the *information matrix,* $I(\theta)^{-1}$, where

$$I(\theta) = -E\left[\sum_{n=1}^{N} \frac{\partial^2 \ln f(y_n;\theta)}{\partial\theta\partial\theta'}\right]$$

   $I(\theta)$ is also known as the Cramer–Rao lower bound.
3. *Asymptotic efficiency:* that as the sample size goes to infinity, the limiting distribution of the ML estimators will have a smaller variance than any other estimator.

For the class of likelihood problems we deal with, the regularity conditions have been shown to hold; thus, these properties will follow. Of particular note is the asymptotic distribution of the ML estimators. Technically, the covariance matrix of the estimators is the inverse of the negative of the expectation of the second derivative matrix of the log-likelihood evaluated at the true parameters. However, we can consistently estimate this matrix by the second derivative matrix evaluated at the estimated parameters

$$I(\theta)^{-1} = \left[\sum_{n=1}^{N} \frac{-\partial^2 \ln f(y_n;\hat{\theta})}{\partial\theta\partial\theta'}\right]^{-1} \tag{A1.4}$$

Alternatively, $I(\theta)^{-1}$ can also be consistently estimated by a function of the cross-products of the first derivatives

$$I(\theta)^{-1} = \left[\sum_{n=1}^{N} \frac{\partial \ln f(y_n;\hat{\theta})}{\partial\theta} \frac{\partial \ln f(y_n;\hat{\theta})'}{\partial\theta}\right]^{-1} \tag{A1.5}$$

Coefficient standard error estimates can be computed as the square roots of the diagonal elements of the covariance matrix. Since the estimators are asymptotically normal, the elements of $[\hat{\theta} - \theta]$, divided by their standard errors, will be asymptotically distributed as t-statistics. This allows hypothesis testing similar to the regression framework. We can also compute what are called *likelihood ratio tests.* These are calculated as follows: Suppose we impose q restrictions on the K-elements of the parameter vector θ (e.g., set some elements to zero). Let $\ln L(\hat{\theta})$ be the sample log-likelihood [Eq. (A1.2)] computed from the unrestricted ML parameter vector. Let $\ln L(\theta^*)$ be the sample log-likelihood computed when the q restrictions are imposed in estimating ML estimators. Then the statistic

$$-2\ln[L(\theta^*)/L(\hat{\theta})] = 2[\ln L(\hat{\theta}) - \ln L(\theta^*)] \sim \chi^2(q) \qquad \text{(A1.6)}$$

is asymptotically distributed as a chi-square with q degrees of freedom when the restrictions are true.

Chapter II

Multigroup Classification Techniques: Conceptual Issues

INTRODUCTION

In Chapter I we focused on problems where the dependent variable is dichotomous and can take on only two variables. We presented a number of model specifications that can be used to characterize these problems. In this chapter we consider problems where the dependent variable can take on more than two values. We will show that many of the dichotomous models can be readily extended to the polytomous case. However, as we will also show, the complexity of many of the models increases dramatically.

Multivalued dependent variables problems have been characterized by a number of names—polytomous, multigroup, or multiple-choice. In each case, the dependent variable is assumed to take on a number of different values, such as membership in a particular group, choice of a decision maker, or preference rankings. Technically this definition would include continuous dependent variables. However, we restrict ourselves to cases where the number of possible groups, choices, or values is finite and small in number. Problems are generally classified according to whether the possible dependent variable values can be ranked or not. Within the ranked category we can also subdivide by whether the ranking is ordinal or cardinal, i.e., can we just tell that one value is "better" than another or can we quantify how much better. Each of these characterizations gives rise to a different set of potential model forms. We will consider a subset of these models that are polytomous extensions of the linear regression, probit, logit, and discriminant analysis models presented in Chapter I.

In the first section of this chapter, we focus on multichoice extensions of the regression, probit, and logit models. We divide our discussion into ranked and unranked models. We include discussion on issues of model assumptions and structure and parameter estimation. In the second section, we present a discussion of the multigroup discriminant analysis model. We restrict ourselves primarily to technical concerns, leaving application issues to Chapter III. Finally, the last section considers problems in model and sample selection. We include a discussion of model selection and a comparison of the virtues of the models presented in the chapter.

REGRESSION, PROBIT, AND LOGIT—MULTIPLE CHOICE

Introduction

The dichotomous regression, probit, and logit models can each be generalized to the polytomous case where the dependent variable can take on many values. However, expanding the number of choices available also increases the potential complexity of the models. If the dependent variable can take on only two values, the structure of the model need only predict when one choice will be chosen over the other. However, with many possible choices, the model must specify when choice one is chosen over two, and two over three, etc. The great variety in the way these choices can be structured has led to a number of different model specifications, each with their own statistical assumptions.

The multiple-choice models can be broadly classified into two general categories. For one type, we assume that the dependent variable can take on many values; however, there is a natural ranking that can be associated with each of the choices. For example, a restaurant critic might award one to five stars depending on quality of services. Thus there would be five possible dependent variable values. Yet clearly they are ordered as five stars is "better" than four, which is "better" than three, etc.

For the second type of model, alternative dependent variable values are assumed to be unordered. For example, a model to predict career choice by college seniors might include a number of possible careers. Yet it would be difficult to rank these choices, i.e., say that doctors were "better" than lawyers. Although, as we shall see, this taxonomy is quite useful, there are many problems that cannot easily be assigned to one of these categories. For example, voters might vote yes, no, or abstain. One view might be that abstain lies between yes and no, thus choices are ordered. However, it could just as easily be argued that abstainers are inherently different than voters, and thus their preferences cannot necessarily be placed in the middle.

Because there are more differences between the ranked and unranked choice models than between the probit/logit or regression specifications, we shall focus on the former distinction. We first discuss ranked choice models, then turn to unranked alternatives.

Ordered Multiple Choice

Suppose that the dependent variable of a problem can take on only k possible values. Furthermore, suppose that the values can be *ex-ante* ranked in an ordinal sense but not necessarily with a cardinal scale. Thus, for the nth observation we assume that

$$y_n = 1 < y_n = 2 < \ldots < y_n = k$$

according to some ordinal ranking. Thus, for example, if $y_n = 2$ (i.e., falls in the second category) this is "better" than $y_n = 1$, but "worse" than $y_n = 3$. We make no statement about how much better or worse it is. We also assume that no observations are *a priori* precluded from any of the k choices. We want to model the conditional probability that choice i occurs for the nth observation (i.e., the probability $y_n = i$), as a function of an m-length vector of independent variables X_n,

$$P_{in} = P(\text{choice } i|X_n) = F_i(X_n) \qquad i = 1, \ldots, k \tag{2.1}$$

We refer to this class of problems as ordered multiple choice. An example of where this arises in finance is the rating of bonds (see Chapter V). Bond ratings clearly represent an ordinal ranking from "best" (Aaa) to "worst" (C), which a number of studies have tried to predict from firm financial data.

There are a number of different ways that this problem can be modeled, each of which implies a different functional form $F_i(\ )$ in Eq. (2.1). One obvious approach is to assume that the k choices of y_n can be ordered not only ordinally, but also cardinally. This means, for example, that not only do we know that choice 2 is "better" than choice 1, but we know how much better. Defining $Y_n = g_i(y_n)$ as the value of the dependent variable as measured on a cardinal scale and $g(\ )$ as the function that maps y_n into Y_n, the researcher's problem might be restated as computing $E(Y_n|X_n)$ rather than calculating probabilities for each choice. If we further assume that $E(Y_n|X_n)$ is linear in the X's, i.e.,

$$E(Y_n|X_n) = X_n'\beta$$

then

$$Y_n = X_n'\beta + \varepsilon_n \tag{2.2}$$

where ε_n is a zero mean stochastic error. Thus, the problem can be expressed as a linear regression model. Consistent coefficient estimates of β could therefore be calculated by OLS applied to a random sample of Y's given X. If distributional assumptions about ε are made and the inverse function $g_i^{-1}(\ )$ is single-valued, estimates of the expectation of Y_n could be used to construct estimates of the probabilities of y_n. We note that this model suffers from many of the problems of the linear probability model. Observations with predicted values above the largest value of Y_n or below the lowest value of Y_n cannot have an expectation of zero for ε_n. Furthermore, the variance of ε_n is unlikely to be constant and will depend on X.

In order to appropriately apply the regression model, we must know the function $g(\ )$ that assigns cardinal values to each of the ordinally ranked choices. It is this transformation that allows us to alter the problem from one of predicting the probability of a choice to predicting the value of a dependent variable. Furthermore, if the researcher is not certain what the transformation function is, arbitrary choices can significantly alter the results. To give an example, Horrigan (1966) approached the bond rating problem by arbitrarily assigning the dependent variable Y_n the cardinal values 9 = Aaa, 8 = Aa, ..., 1 = C. Horrigan then regressed Y_n against a set of independent variables X_n proporting to estimate Eq. (2.2). Implicit in this model is the assumption that the bond ratings represent equal intervals on a cardinal scale, i.e., Aaa is to Aa what Ba is to B. If researchers do not want to make what may be an arbitrary assumption of this type, then the regression model cannot be used.

The Ordered Logistic Model

A number of authors (e.g., Aitchison and Silvey, 1957; Gurland, Lee, and Dahm, 1960) have proposed alternative models that retain the ordinal ranking of choices, but unlike the regression, do not impose a cardinal scale. These models are basically multiple-choice extensions of the dichotomous probit and logit models. Perhaps the most commonly seen is the ordered logistic model.

Suppose that y_n can take on k ordinally ranked values, with $y_n = 1$ the "lowest" and $y_n = k$ the "highest." Furthermore, suppose that

$$\begin{aligned} P_{1n} &= F(X_n'\beta) \\ P_{1n} + P_{2n} &= F(\alpha_2 + X_n'\beta) \\ &\ \ \vdots \\ P_{1n} + P_{2n} + \dots + P_{k-1,n} &= F(\alpha_{k-1} + X_n'\beta) \qquad (2.3) \\ P_{kn} &= 1 - F(\alpha_{k-1} + X_n'\beta) \end{aligned}$$

where

$$\alpha_{k-1} > \alpha_{k-2} > \ldots > \alpha_2 > 0$$

and

$$F(\alpha_i + X_n'\beta) = \frac{1}{1 + \exp[-\alpha_i - X_n'\beta]}$$

is the cumulative logistic function. This is called the *ordered logistic model.* Notice that Eq. (2.3) can also be expressed as

$$\begin{aligned} P_{1n} &= F(X_n'\beta) \\ P_{2n} &= F(\alpha_2 + X_n'\beta) - F(X_n'\beta) \\ &\vdots \\ P_{k-1,n} &= F(\alpha_{k-1} + X_n'\beta) - F(\alpha_{k-2} + X_n'\beta) \\ P_{kn} &= 1 - F(\alpha_{k-1} + X_n'\beta) \end{aligned} \tag{2.4}$$

Thus the probability of each choice is given by the difference of two cumulative logistics. Note that if $k = 2$, the model reduces to the binary logit problem, with $y_n = 1$ denoting the occurrence of the event (bankruptcy, etc.) and $y_n = 2$ denoting nonoccurrence.

To motivate the kind of model given in Eqs. (2.3) and (2.4), consider the following scenerio (see McKelvey and Zavoina, 1975). Suppose that there is a continuous but unobserved variable Y_n. Furthermore, assume that Y_n is a linear function of the X's and a stochastic, mean zero, standard logistic variable ε_n (alternatively, ε_n could be a standard normal that would give rise to an ordered probit model). Thus

$$Y_n = -X_n'\beta + \varepsilon_n \tag{2.5}$$

Furthermore, assume that the observed choice y_n is determined by the value of Y_n

$$\begin{aligned} y_n &= 1 && \text{if } Y_n \leq 0 && \Rightarrow \varepsilon_n \leq X_n'\beta \\ y_n &= 2 && \text{if } 0 < Y_n \leq \alpha_2 && \Rightarrow X_n'\beta < \varepsilon_n \leq \alpha_2 + X_n'\beta \\ & && \vdots && \vdots \\ y_n &= k - 1 && \text{if } \alpha_{k-2} < Y_n \leq \alpha_{k-1} && \Rightarrow \alpha_{k-2} + X_n'\beta < \varepsilon_n \leq \alpha_{k-1} + X_n'\beta \\ y_n &= k && \text{if } \alpha_{k-1} < Y_n && \Rightarrow \alpha_{k-1} + X_n'\beta < \varepsilon_n \end{aligned} \tag{2.6}$$

The width of each range is fixed across observations. However, the probability of Y_n falling in each range will vary by observations as $X_n'\beta$

changes. Note that this formulation implies probabilities of each choice that are identical to Eq. (2.4).

Though we have implied that there is a cardinal scaled variable underlying the ordinally ranked choices, since Y_n is unobserved its scale will be unknown. In the above formulation we have arbitrarily normalized Y_n by scaling ε_n to a standard logistic and normalized the location (mean) of Y_n by setting the upper bound of the range of $y_n = 1$ to zero (the X vector should also include a constant). Although similar to the regression model in that we have implied a cardinal scaling to the choices, the ordered logistic model differs fundamentally in that with the exception of the above arbitrary normalizations, the researcher does not have to impose the scaling. The scaling variables $\{\alpha_2, \ldots, \alpha_{k-1}\}$ are estimated by the data rather than externally imposed.

An example of an application of this type of model in finance is given by Kaplan and Urwitz (1979), who modeled Moody's bond ratings as an ordered choice problem. They assumed the existence of an underlying continuous "bond risk" variable, which Moody's breaks into categories. Each bond is assigned the ordinal rating (Aaa, Aa, etc.) of the category that its risk falls into. An inherent assumption of this model is that Moody's observes the ε_n's (hence Y_n) even though the econometrician does not.

Like the binary logit model, feasible estimation procedures for the ordered logistic model will depend upon whether multiple repetitions are observed for each value of X_n. If there are repeated trials on y given X_n, Theil (1970) shows that the model parameters can be consistently estimated by a regression method similar to the Berkson–Theil procedure (see Chapter I, Probit and Logit Analysis section). This can be shown as follows.

Suppose we have data on R_n repeated trials on y given X_n, and let r_{in} be the number of times choice i occurs, i.e., $y_n = i$, with $\tilde{P}_{in} = r_{in}/R_n$. Proceeding as in the dichotomous dependent variable case, a Taylor series expansion of the relationships given in Eq. (2.3) yields the following $k - 1$ approximate equations:

$$
\begin{aligned}
\ln[\tilde{P}_{1n}/(1 - \tilde{P}_{1n})] &= X_n'\beta + \tilde{\varepsilon}_{1n} \\
\ln[(\tilde{P}_{1n} + \tilde{P}_{2n})/(1 - \tilde{P}_{1n} - \tilde{P}_{2n})] &= X_n'\beta + \alpha_2 + \tilde{\varepsilon}_{2n} \qquad (2.7) \\
&\vdots \\
\ln\left[\sum_{i=1}^{k-1} \tilde{P}_{in}\Big/\left(1 - \sum_{i=1}^{k-1} \tilde{P}_{in}\right)\right] &= X_n'\beta + \alpha_{k-1} + \tilde{\varepsilon}_{k-1,n}
\end{aligned}
$$

where each $\tilde{\varepsilon}_{in}$ is a zero mean, normally distributed, random variable. The dependent variable in each equation is similar to the sample "logit" or log-odds of the binary logit model. Given a sample with sufficient variation in the X's, each of the equations could be estimated separately by OLS. However, since the β vector appears in each equation, it will be more efficient to "stack" the $k - 1$ equations and impose the cross-equation restrictions. Thus the $k - 1$ log-odds equations for each X_n would be treated as $k - 1$ observations (for a total of $Nk - N$) with the same X variables, but dummy variables for the second through $(k - 1)^{\text{th}}$ equations to estimate α_2 through α_{k-1}.

As in the dichotomous case, the large sample properties of the OLS estimators can be improved by adding $1/(2R_n)$ to the numerator and denominator of the probability ratio in each dependent variable. We could similarly improve our estimates by fitting a weighted least squares regression. However, unlike the binary case, we also have to worry about the covariance of the errors of the $k - 1$ observations for each X_n. The $k - 1$ observations will have a $(k - 1) \times (k - 1)$ covariance matrix Σ, with a typical element given as approximately

$$\Sigma_{jj'} = \frac{1}{N\left(1 - \sum_{i=1}^{j} \mathrm{P}_{in}\right)\left(\sum_{i=1}^{j'} \mathrm{P}_{in}\right)} \qquad j \leq j' \tag{2.8}$$

The actual observed probabilities $\tilde{\mathrm{P}}_{in}$, or estimates calculated by fitting Eq. (2.7) without the error covariance adjustment can be used to estimate this matrix. The computed $(k - 1) \times (k - 1)$ covariance matrix for each X_n is then inverted and used to calculate modified generalized least squares estimates in the usual fashion.

In many problems, researchers will not have the multiple repetitions on y for each X_n required for regression estimation. Like the binary logit model, an alternative in this case is to use *maximum likelihood* methods. Assuming a random sample of N observations, with N_i observations observed for each choice i, $\sum_{i=1}^{k} N_i = N$, and defining X_{in} as observations where choice i is chosen, the sample log-likelihood can be written as

$$\begin{aligned}
\ln L &= \sum_{i=1}^{k} \sum_{n=1}^{N_i} \ln(P_{in}) \\
&= \sum_{n=1}^{N_1} -\ln[1 + \exp(-X_{1n}'\beta)] \\
&+ \sum_{n=1}^{N_2} \ln\left[\frac{1}{1 + \exp(-\alpha_2 - X_{2n}'\beta)} - \frac{1}{1 + \exp(-X_{2n}'\beta)}\right] \qquad (2.9) \\
&\;\;\vdots \\
&+ \sum_{n=1}^{N_k} \ln\left[1 - \frac{1}{1 + \exp(-\alpha_{k-1} - X_{kn}'\beta)}\right]
\end{aligned}$$

Differentiating with respect to β and α, first order conditions for β are

$$\sum_{n=1}^{N_1} (1 - \hat{P}_{1n})X_{1n} + \sum_{n=1}^{N_2} (1 - 2\hat{P}_{1n} - \hat{P}_{2n})X_{2n}$$
$$+ \sum_{n=1}^{N_3} (1 - 2\hat{P}_{1n} - 2\hat{P}_{2n} - \hat{P}_{3n})X_{3n} \qquad (2.10a)$$
$$+ \ldots + \sum_{n=1}^{N_k} -(1 - \hat{P}_{kn})X_{kn} = 0$$

and for the α's

$$\sum_{i=2}^{3} (-1)^i \sum_{n=1}^{N_i} (\hat{P}_{1n} + \hat{P}_{2n})(1 - \hat{P}_{1n} - \hat{P}_{2n})/\hat{P}_{in} = 0$$
$$\vdots \qquad \vdots \qquad (2.10b)$$
$$\sum_{i=k-1}^{k} (-1)^i \sum_{n=1}^{N_i} (\hat{P}_{1n} + \ldots + \hat{P}_{k-1,n})(1 - \hat{P}_{1n}$$
$$- \ldots - \hat{P}_{k-1,n})/\hat{P}_{in} = 0$$

Unlike the binary logit model, the second order condition (which we do not show) will not hold for all coefficient vectors, although it should hold at the maximum. Since the first order conditions are nonlinear, maximum likelihood estimates of β and the α's will have to be solved for by iterative methods.

The Ordered Probit Model

Much of the above analysis also can be applied to what is called the *ordered probit model.* The only difference is that instead of the cumulative logistic in Eq. (2.3), we use the cumulative standard normal

$$F(\alpha_i + X_n'\beta) = \int_{-\infty}^{\alpha_i + X_n'\beta} f(z)dz \qquad (2.11)$$

where $f(\,)$ is the standard normal density function

$$f(z) = [1/(2\pi)^{1/2}] \exp(-z^2/2)$$

If the ε_n's of the model given in Eqs. (2.5) and (2.6) are standard normal instead of logistic, then choice probabilities will be given by the probit equivalent to Eq. (2.4)

$$P_{1n} = \int_{-\infty}^{X_n'\beta} f(z)dz$$

$$P_{2n} = \int_{X_n'\beta}^{X_n'\beta+\alpha_2} f(z)dz \tag{2.12}$$

$$\vdots$$

$$P_{kn} = \int_{X_n'\beta+\alpha_{k-1}}^{\infty} f(z)dz$$

Estimation of the parameters of the ordered probit model can proceed in a similar manner to the ordered logit. If there are multiple repetitions on y for each X_n, regressions similar to the Berkson–Theil procedure can be run. However, instead of log-odds dependent variables in the $k - 1$ equations of (2.7), sample "probits" should be used as shown in Eq. (1.23) of Chapter I. The ordered probit regression estimates can also be improved by a weighted least squares procedure similar to Eq. (2.8). However, the covariance terms (which we do not show) will differ from those shown in Eq. (2.8).

Maximum likelihood estimation of the ordered probit model is almost identical to the logit case. Again assuming a random sample with $\Sigma_{i=1}^{k} N_i = N$ observations and denoting X_{in} as observations where choice i is chosen, the sample log-likelihood is

$$\begin{aligned} \ln L &= \sum_{i=1}^{k} \sum_{i=1}^{N_i} \ln(P_{in}) \\ &= \sum_{n=1}^{N_1} \ln[F(X_{1n}'\beta)] \\ &+ \sum_{n=1}^{N_2} \ln[F(\alpha_2 + X_{2n}'\beta) - F(X_{2n}'\beta)] \\ &\vdots \\ &\sum_{n=1}^{N_k} \ln[1 - F(\alpha_{k-1} + X_{kn}'\beta)] \end{aligned} \tag{2.13}$$

Differentiating with respect to β and α, first order conditions for β are

$$\begin{aligned} &\sum_{n=1}^{N_1} \frac{f(X_{1n}'\hat{\beta})}{F(X_{1n}'\hat{\beta})} X_{1n} + \sum_{n=1}^{N_2} \frac{f(\hat{\alpha}_2 + X_{2n}'\hat{\beta}) - f(X_{2n}'\hat{\beta})}{F(\hat{\alpha}_2 + X_{2n}'\hat{\beta}) - F(X_{2n}'\hat{\beta})} X_{2n} \\ &\qquad + \dots + \sum_{n=1}^{N_k} \frac{-f(\hat{\alpha}_{k-1} + X_{kn}'\hat{\beta})}{1 - F(\hat{\alpha}_{k-1} + X_{kn}'\hat{\beta})} X_{kn} = 0 \end{aligned} \tag{2.14a}$$

and for the α's

$$\sum_{n=1}^{N_2} \frac{f(\hat{\alpha}_2 + X_{2n}'\hat{\beta})}{F(\hat{\alpha}_2 + X_{2n}'\hat{\beta}) - F(X_{2n}'\hat{\beta})}$$

$$- \sum_{n=1}^{N_3} \frac{f(\hat{\alpha}_2 + X_{3n}'\hat{\beta})}{F(\hat{\alpha}_3 + X_{3n}'\hat{\beta}) - F(\hat{\alpha}_2 + X_{3n}'\hat{\beta})} = 0 \qquad (2.14b)$$

$$\vdots \qquad \vdots$$

$$\sum_{n=1}^{N_{k-1}} \frac{f(\hat{\alpha}_{k-1} + X_{k-1,n}'\hat{\beta})}{F(\hat{\alpha}_{k-1} + X_{k-1,n}'\hat{\beta}) - F(\hat{\alpha}_{k-2} + X_{k-1,n}'\hat{\beta})}$$

$$- \sum_{n=1}^{N_k} \frac{f(\hat{\alpha}_{k-1} + X_{kn}'\hat{\beta})}{1 - F(\hat{\alpha}_{k-1} + X_{kn}'\hat{\beta})} = 0$$

Since first order conditions are nonlinear, computation of the maximum likelihood estimates will again require iterative solution methods. At the maximum, the second order condition (which we do not show) should also hold.

Before concluding our discussion of the ordered response models, let us make a few brief comments on their practical application. We have had reasonable success in estimating ordered response models, although maximum likelihood estimation is generally more expensive than binary logit/probit problems of the same size. The model however is quite sensitive to violations of the implied ordering of observations. If, in fact, choices are not ordered in the manner assumed by the researcher, parameter estimation will probably fail to achieve convergence. Signals of this will be values of α that get very close to one another or are made arbitrarily large. Another interesting aspect of the ordered choice models is that because the choice categories can be different sizes, it is possible that observations will not have the highest predicted probability for the choice in whose range $X\hat{\beta}$ lies. This same phenomena can occur in discriminant analysis with unequal group *a priori* probabilities.

Unordered Multiple Choice

In the ordered choice models, we assume a natural *a priori* ranking of the choices available for the dependent variable. In many applications, however, there will be no natural ranking of alternatives. For example, a model to predict choice of transportation mode will have no natural "best" or "worst" choice. Similarly models of the selection of automobiles will entail choices among basically unranked alternatives. College or career choices will also feature unranked or unordered alternatives. We emphasize the distinction of *a priori* unranked choices. Clearly each individual will have a ranking of automobiles or colleges;

however there will be no natural correspondence of these rankings across individuals. There will be no reason to believe that the "first" choice of one individual would be the same as that of another.

Because the unordered multiple choice problems are the least structured of any of the problems in this book, it is not surprising that a variety of ways have been proposed to analyze and model them. We shall focus on four different models: an extension of the linear probability model, two variations of what is called the "multinomial logit model," and the multinomial probit model. We begin with the linear probability model.

Consider the extension of the linear probability model to the case where instead of only two values, the dependent variable can take on k values. Furthermore, assume that the probability of *each* choice for the nth observation given a vector of exogenous variables X_n', is

$$
\begin{aligned}
P_{1n} &= P(\text{choice } 1|X_n) = X_n'\beta_1 \\
P_{2n} &= P(\text{choice } 2|X_n) = X_n'\beta_2 \\
&\vdots \\
P_{kn} &= P(\text{choice } k|X_n) = X_n'\beta_k
\end{aligned}
\tag{2.15}
$$

Thus, the probability of each choice is linear in the X's. A reasonable estimation procedure would be to estimate each equation as a separate linear probability model by OLS, where the dependent variable of the ith equation equals 1 if choice i is chosen and 0 otherwise. Any of the modifications suggested for the linear probability model (such as the heteroskedastic adjustment) could also be employed. However, this approach ignores the restrictions across the equations; particularly the fact that the dependent variables sum to one for each observation and that the predicted probabilities in theory should as well. Pindyck and Rubenfeld (1976), however, show that if X_n contains a constant, predicted probabilities from the OLS regressions will always sum to 1, i.e.,

$$\sum_{i=1}^{k} X_n'\hat{\beta}_i = 1$$

They also show that the intercept terms will sum to 1 and each of the other β's sum to 0. This implies that only $k - 1$ regressions will actually have to be run because the parameters of the remaining equation can be derived easily.

If the X's differ for each choice, the problem becomes more complex. Predicted probabilities will no longer necessarily sum to zero, although this restriction could be imposed. Zellner and Lee (1965) also suggest a generalized least squares procedure to take into account correlations across the equations. Domencich and McFadden (1975), however, voice reservations over the applicability of the linear probability model in the multiple choice setting. They argue that constraining probabilities to the zero–one interval and to sum to one imposes much more cumbersome burdens than in the binary model. Coupled with concerns over the sensitivity of the linear probability model to specification error, they conclude that alternative models may be preferable.

Multinomial Logit Model

One alternative to regression is the *multiple-choice unordered logit model.* This model, also known as the *multinomial logit model,* has been examined by many authors (e.g., Luce, 1959; Theil, 1969, 1970; Nerlove and Press, 1973; and McFadden, 1974). Each of these authors considers a model of the following basic form: For each observation, assume that the dependent variable y_n can take on k discrete values and that the conditional probability of each choice i, given X_n (i.e., the probability $y_n = i$) is

$$P_{in} = P(\text{choice } i | X_n) = \frac{\exp(X_{in}'\beta_i)}{\sum_{j=1}^{k} \exp(X_{jn}'\beta_j)} \tag{2.16}$$

This formulation differs from previous models we've looked at in several respects. First, we have subscripted both the β vectors and the X variables by choices. This implies that both the "relevant" X variables and their weightings may differ by choice. If each β is an m-length vector, it implies that the total variable set X_n could be of size $k \cdot m$ with $k \cdot m$ unknown coefficient weights. Although we shall later relax this assumption, we continue to assume that all k choices are *a priori* available for each observation.

Algebraic manipulation of Eq. (2.16) yields an interesting result. Computing the ratio of the probabilities of choice i to the sum of i and ℓ yields

$$\begin{aligned}\frac{P_{in}}{P_{\ell n} + P_{in}} &= \frac{\exp(X_{in}'\beta_i)/\sum_{j=1}^{k} \exp(X_{jn}'\beta_j)}{\exp(X_{\ell n}'\beta_\ell)/\sum_{j=1}^{k} \exp(X_{jn}'\beta_j) + \exp(X_{in}'\beta_i)/\sum_{j=1}^{k} \exp(X_{jn}'\beta_j)} \\ &= \frac{\exp(X_{in}'\beta_i)}{\exp(X_{\ell n}'\beta_\ell) + \exp(X_{in}'\beta_i)} \qquad (2.17) \\ &= \frac{1}{1 + \exp(X_{\ell n}'\beta_\ell - X_{in}'\beta_i)}\end{aligned}$$

or the cumulative logistic function. Since

$$\frac{P_{in}}{P_{\ell n}} = \frac{P(\text{choice } i|\text{choice } i \text{ or } \ell;X_n)}{P(\text{choice } \ell|\text{choice } i \text{ or } \ell;X_n)} \frac{P(\text{choice } i \text{ or } \ell|X_n)}{P(\text{choice } i \text{ or } \ell|X_n)}$$
$$= \frac{P(\text{choice } i|\text{choice } i \text{ or } \ell;X_n)}{P(\text{choice } \ell|\text{choice } i \text{ or } \ell;X_n)} \qquad (2.18)$$

it also follows that the conditional probability of choice i given that either choice i or ℓ is chosen is also a cumulative logistic function.

We have subscripted both the coefficients and X variables by choice. Although some normalizations are generally necessary, it is possible to both specify and estimate parameters of this general model. In practice, however, almost all applications have taken the form of one of two different restricted versions. In one version, which we refer to as the *multiple-data model,* the X variables are still subscripted by choices; however there is assumed to be only one coefficient vector. In the other commonly used version of the model, which we term the *multiple-weighting model,* the coefficient vectors are subscripted by choices; however, there is assumed to be only one vector of data. Because these models cover almost all applications of the multinomial logit model, they are worth discussing in more detail. We consider first the multiple-data model.

Suppose that the X's in Eq. (2.16) are subscripted by choice, but the β's are not. Choice probabilities are then

$$P_{in} = \frac{\exp(X_{in}'\beta)}{\sum_{j=1}^{k} \exp(X_{jn}'\beta)} \qquad (2.19)$$

Although we term this a *multiple-data model,* it has also been referred to as the *conditional logit model* (see McFadden, 1974). This type of specification arises quite naturally in problems where the X variables represent characteristics (including intercept shifts) of the choices not the choice maker. For example, Ben-Akiva and Watanatada (1980) examine the choice of transportation mode using such variables as travel time and expense. These variables will differ for each transportation mode; however, there is no reason to believe that bus and auto expenses should be weighted differently, hence the β vector is constant for all choices. Another example would be the choices by individuals in a multiple brand market. We would expect that X variables representing brand characteristics would vary by products. However, a given individual would not weigh values of these characteristics differently across products.

Since the choice probability in Eq. (2.19) is a ratio, we can divide both the numerator and denominator by any constant without changing the probabilities. Thus, if we divide by $\exp(X_{1n}'\beta)$ (choosing choice 1 arbitrarily)

$$P_{in} = \frac{\exp[(X_{in}' - X_{1n}')\beta]}{\sum_{j=1}^{k} \exp[(X_{jn}' - X_{1n}')\beta]} \tag{2.20}$$

the probabilities are unaffected. This implies that only relative X values, $(X_{in}' - X_{1n}')$, are needed. Note that it also implies that any variable that is constant for all choices cannot be used (since $X_{jn}' - X_{1n}'$ will be 0 for all j). This means that we cannot use X variables that represent characteristics of the decision maker, such as income and home location in the transportation mode problem, unless they are interacted with choice variables.

Instead of the above specification, suppose that the β's in Eq. (2.16) are subscripted by choices; however the X's are not. Choice probabilities are then

$$P_{in} = \frac{\exp(X_n'\beta_i)}{\sum_{j=1}^{k} \exp(X_n'\beta_j)} \tag{2.21}$$

We refer to this as a *multiple-weighting* model. This model, examined by Nerlove and Press (1973) among others, applies most naturally in cases where the X variables represent characteristics of the decision maker and not the choices. This is similar to the ordered-choice problems discussed in the previous section, where the model is designed to predict the choices, given information only on the decision maker. An example of this type of problem would be the selection of a college major given test scores of an individual. Since the data represent variables of the individual, they would not vary by choice. Coefficients, however, would be expected to vary by choice and to reflect different weightings of skills across disciplines. If X contains a constant, the corresponding elements of the β_i's would represent shifts across the choices.

Like the multiple-data model, the multiple-weighting model is identified only up to scale. In particular, we can add an arbitrary vector γ to each β_i and not affect the choice probabilities, i.e.,

$$P_{in} = \frac{\exp(X_n'\beta_i + X_n'\gamma)}{\sum_{j=1}^{k} \exp(X_n'\beta_j + X_n'\gamma)}$$

$$= \frac{\exp(X_n'\beta_i) \;\; \exp(X_n'\gamma)}{\sum_{j=1}^{k} \exp(X_n'\beta_j) \exp(X_n'\gamma)} \tag{2.22}$$

$$= \frac{\exp(X_n'\beta_i)}{\sum_{j=1}^{k} \exp(X_n'\beta_j)}$$

Thus, to uniquely identify coefficients it is necessary to impose a normalization. Nerlove and Press (1973) propose requiring the β's to sum to zero, i.e.,

$$\sum_{j=1}^{k} \beta_j = 0$$

Alternatively, Theil (1970) proposes picking a "base choice" i and setting $\beta_i = 0$. In either case, the β's will represent relative rather than absolute weightings. The choice of normalization will not affect the model "fit" in estimation or choice probabilities.

Probabilistic Choice

When we discussed binary models in Chapter I, we tried to motivate the logit and probit probability models as reduced forms arising from individual utility-maximizing choice models. Before proceeding further in our discussion of the multiple-choice model, it will be useful to examine whether these results will carry over into the multiple-choice setting. We will show, following the argument of McFadden (1974), that under certain conditions the binary choice results will also apply to multiple choices. This argument can be summarized as follows.

Suppose the nth decision maker is faced with a choice among k alternatives, say choosing which of the Big Ten colleges to attend or whether to buy a McDonald's, Burger King, or Wendy's hamburger. Furthermore, assume that they observe a vector of m characteristics on each choice—$X_1, X_2, \ldots, X_k$—and that the *utility* of each choice is given by the functions

$$\begin{aligned} U_{1n} &= X_{1n}'\beta_1 + \varepsilon_{1n} \\ U_{2n} &= X_{2n}'\beta_2 + \varepsilon_{2n} \\ &\vdots \\ U_{kn} &= X_{kn}'\beta_k + \varepsilon_{kn} \end{aligned} \tag{2.23}$$

where $\beta_1, \beta_2, \ldots, \beta_k$ are coefficient vectors and $\varepsilon_{1n}, \ldots, \varepsilon_{kn}$ are zero mean stochastic errors independent of the X's and unobserved by the econometrician but known to the decision maker when choices are made. We have subscripted both the β's and X's, although our discussion is equally applicable to both the multiple-data and multiple-weighting models.

This formulation is identical to that of the two-choice problem discussed in Chapter I. As in the two-choice problem, the decision maker is assumed to always choose the alternative with the highest utility. Thus, for example, choice 1 will be chosen if and only if

$$\begin{aligned} X_{1n}'\beta_1 + \varepsilon_{1n} &> X_{2n}'\beta_2 + \varepsilon_{2n} \\ &\vdots \\ X_{1n}'\beta_1 + \varepsilon_{1n} &> X_{kn}'\beta_k + \varepsilon_{kn} \end{aligned} \tag{2.24}$$

Therefore, the probability of choice 1 being chosen given the X's is

$$P(\text{choice } 1|X) = \int_{-\infty}^{-\infty} \int_{-\infty}^{D_{12}} \cdots \int_{-\infty}^{D_{1k}} f(\varepsilon_{2n}, \varepsilon_{3n}, \ldots, \varepsilon_{kn}|\varepsilon_{1n}) f(\varepsilon_{1n}) d\varepsilon_{kn} \ldots d\varepsilon_{1n} \tag{2.25}$$

where

$$\begin{aligned} D_{12} &= X_{1n}'\beta_1 - X_{2n}'\beta_2 + \varepsilon_{1n} \\ &\vdots \\ D_{1k} &= X_{1n}'\beta_1 - X_{kn}'\beta_k + \varepsilon_{1n} \end{aligned}$$

We showed in the two-choice case that the assumption that the ε's were bivariate normally distributed implied that Eq. (2.25) would be of the form of a probit model. Similarly we argued that if the ε's were extreme value distributed, Eq. (2.25) would have the cumulative logistic form. Both of these results will carry over to the multiple choice model; however, the generalization bears some comment.

If the ε's are multivariate normal, then choice probabilities will be given by what is termed the *multinomial probit model.* We shall develop this model in greater detail later in this section; however, it will turn out that the multinomial probit presents significant computational problems. Because of these computational problems, most practical attention has been focused on the multiple-choice logit model. Similar to the two-choice case, McFadden (1974) proves that if the errors $\varepsilon_{1n}, \ldots, \varepsilon_{kn}$ are *independently* and identically distributed extreme value random variables, then choice probabilities will be given by the multinomial logit model Eq. (2.16), i.e.,

$$P(\text{choice } i|X) = \frac{\exp(X_{in}'\beta_i)}{\sum_{j=1}^{k} \exp(X_{jn}'\beta_j)} \tag{2.26}$$

This is an extremely important result in justifying the use of the multinomial logit model. It allows us to argue that the specification of multinomial choice probabilities is consistent with an underlying model of choices made by utility-maximizing individuals. Care, however, must be taken before the multinomial logit model is blindly applied. In deriving the choice probabilities [Eq. (2.26)] from the utility functions, [Eq. (2.23)], McFadden needed to impose what Luce (1959) termed the "axiom of independence of irrelevant alternatives." This axiom states that for all possible pairs of choices, the probability that one choice will be chosen over the other, given that one of the two must be chosen, must equal the relative probability that one choice will be chosen over the other when the entire choice set is available. In other words, the relative odds of one alternative being chosen over another does not depend on what other choices are available. For the logit model, this assumption is operationally equivalent to the assumption that the utility function error terms are independent. If this assumption does not hold, the multinomial logit model should not be used.

As a number of authors (e.g., Tversky, 1972; McFadden, 1974) have pointed out, the "axiom of independence of irrelevant alternatives" may be inappropriate for many problems. The assumption that utility function errors representing "left out variables" are uncorrelated between close substitutes, for example, may be very implausible. McFadden (1980) cites a classic example where the axiom is violated: Suppose commuters choose between three alternative modes of travel—red buses, blue buses, and autos. Furthermore, suppose they treat the two buses as equivalent and are indifferent between autos and buses. Thus, given the paired choice of either bus and the auto, the probability of choosing the bus would be 1/2 and the auto 1/2. Yet if all three choices were available, we would expect each bus to be chosen 1/4 of the time and the auto 1/2 of the time. Thus the relative odds of choosing the auto over either of the buses would be 2 to 1, violating the independence of irrelevant alternatives assumption. As this example suggests, the application of the multinomial logit model should be restricted to situations where, given the X variables, the alternatives are distinct and any remaining information (or randomness in the utility function) is not patterned among the alternatives.

If the assumption of independence from irrelevant alternatives is met, the introduction of a utility-maximizing choice model has several important implications for the interpretation and estimation of the multinomial logit model. It provides us with an interpretation of the coefficients and predicted values $X_{in}'\beta_i$ in terms of the relative utilities of alternative choices. We can, for example, compute the expected value of utility

$$E[\max(U_{1n}, \dots, U_{kn})] = \ln\left[\sum_{j=1}^{k} \exp(X_{jn}'\beta_j)\right] + .577 \qquad (2.27)$$

This allows comparisons of consumer utility when choices are restricted. The independence from irrelevant alternatives assumption also allows us to mix observations with different choice set sizes. Thus we can drop the assumption that k is fixed across observations, an important consideration in many individual selection problems.

Multinomial Logit—Parameter Estimation

Like the binary and ordered response logit models, estimation procedures for the multinomial logit will depend upon whether repeated trials on y are observed for each X_n. If multiple trials are observed, parameters can be estimated by a regression procedure similar to the binary Berkson–Theil method. Differentiating between the multiple-weighting and multiple-data models, this can be seen as follows.

Assume we have data on R_n repeated trials on y given X_n, and let r_{in} be the number of times choice i occurs, i.e., $y_n = i$, with $\tilde{P}_{in} = r_{in}/R_n$. Theil (1970) demonstrates that the sample log-odds of any *pair* of choices, i and ℓ, can be approximated by the equation

$$\ln(\tilde{P}_{in}/\tilde{P}_{\ell n}) = X_{in}'\beta_i - X_{\ell n}'\beta_\ell + \tilde{\varepsilon}_{i\ell n} \qquad (2.28)$$

where $\varepsilon_{i\ell n}$ is a zero mean, normally distributed random variable. Theil termed the dependent variables in these equations "conditional logits." He shows that although there are $k(k - 1)/2$ possible choice pairs, there are only $k - 1$ independent equations. Therefore, he suggests selecting a "base response" and defining $k - 1$ equations as determinants of the conditional logits of each of the other $k - 1$ choices relative to the "base response." Arbitrarily defining choice 1 as the base response, this leads to the following $k - 1$ equations for the multiple-data model

$$\begin{aligned} \ln(\tilde{P}_{2n}/\tilde{P}_{1n}) &= (X_{2n}' - X_{1n}')\beta + \tilde{\varepsilon}_{2n} \\ &\vdots \\ \ln(\tilde{P}_{kn}/\tilde{P}_{1n}) &= (X_{kn}' - X_{1n}')\beta + \tilde{\varepsilon}_{kn} \end{aligned} \qquad (2.29)$$

and, normalizing by setting $\beta_1 = 0$, to the following $k - 1$ equations for the multiple-weighting model

$$\ln(\tilde{P}_{2n}/\tilde{P}_{1n}) = X_n'\beta_2 + \tilde{\varepsilon}_{2n}$$

$$\vdots \qquad \vdots \tag{2.30}$$

$$\ln(\tilde{P}_{kn}/\tilde{P}_{1n}) = X_n'\beta_k + \tilde{\varepsilon}_{kn}$$

Each of these equations could be estimated separately by OLS. However, because the coefficient vector is the same for each equation of the multiple-data model, it will generally pay to "stack" these equations and run them as one regression [i.e., run one regression with $N \cdot (k - 1)$ observations].

Although we have assumed that the choice set size is the same k for all observations, as we indicated in our discussion of probabilistic choice, this assumption is not necessary. If some observations have choice set sizes of fewer than k, say k', they should be used in only $k' - 1$ equations. Note though that for the multiple-weighting model, each observation must have choice 1 available or a more complicated specification than Eq. (2.30) will have to be used. Because it doesn't involve the coefficients, the selection of a "base response" is much more arbitrary for the multiple-data model. Thus choice 1 could be a "different" choice for each observation.

Many of the modifications suggested in the dichotomous case to improve the large sample properties of the OLS estimators will also apply to the polytomous model. One such improvement is to slightly alter the conditional logits to $\ln[(\tilde{P}_{in} + 1/(2R_n)/(\tilde{P}_{1n} + 1/(2R_n)]$. Another is to take account of the variances and covariances of the errors of either Eq. (2.29) or Eq. (2.30). The variance of $\tilde{\varepsilon}_{in}$ is approximately

$$V(\tilde{\varepsilon}_{in}) = \frac{1}{R_n}\left(\frac{1}{P_{in}} + \frac{1}{P_{1n}}\right) \tag{2.31a}$$

Similarly the covariance of any two errors is approximately

$$C(\tilde{\varepsilon}_{in}, \tilde{\varepsilon}_{\ell n}) = \frac{1}{R_n} \cdot \frac{1}{P_{\ell n}} \tag{2.31b}$$

Using either actual observed probabilities $\tilde{P}_{in}$ or probabilities predicted from a "first pass" OLS regression, an estimate of the $(k - 1) \times (k - 1)$ error covariance matrix for each observation could be inverted and used to compute modified generalized least squares estimates. We note, however, that since the X variables are the same for each of the $k - 1$ equations of the multiple-weighting model, there will be no gain from considering the covariances of the errors (as in seemingly unrelated regression). Thus each of the $k - 1$ equations can be estimated separately as a heteroskedastic weighted regression, taking into account only the variances of the errors. The weight used for each observation would thus be $w_{in} = [R_n P_{in} P_{1n}/(P_{in} + P_{1n})]^{1/2}$.

Finally, we can also formally test the multinomial specification by means of a χ^2 test. Theil (1970) proposes the test statistic

$$\sum_{n=1}^{N} R_n \sum_{i=1}^{k} [(\tilde{P}_{in} - \hat{P}_{in})^2/\hat{P}_{in}] \sim \acute{\chi}^2$$

where $\hat{P}_{in}$ is the predicted probability of each choice. When the model is true, this is asymptotically distributed as a chi-square with $N(k - 1) - D$ degrees of freedom, where D is the number of estimated parameters.

In many problems there will be insufficient repetitions on y for each X_n to use the Berkson–Theil procedure. McFadden (1974), for example, suggests as a rule-of-thumb that each choice be chosen at least five times as a minimum criteria. One alternative procedure suggested by Walker and Duncan (1967) and Amemiya (1976) is a nonlinear weighted least squares solution. This procedure, which requires iterative solution, is asymptotically equivalent to *maximum-likelihood* methods, which we outline as follows.

Assume a random sample of N observations, with N_i observations observed for each choice i, $\sum_{i=1}^{k} N_i = N$. Defining $X_n^{(i)}$ as observations where choice i was chosen, the sample log-likelihood is

$$\begin{aligned} \ln L &= \sum_{i=1}^{k} \sum_{n=1}^{N_i} \ln(P_{in}) \\ &= \sum_{i=1}^{k} \sum_{n=1}^{N_i} \left\{ X_{in}^{(i)\prime}\beta_i - \ln\left[\sum_{j=1}^{k} \exp(X_{jn}^{(i)\prime}\beta_j)\right]\right\} \end{aligned} \qquad (2.32)$$

Since maximization of the log-likelihood function of the multiple-data and multiple-weighting models will differ somewhat, let us discuss them separately. For the multiple-data model, the log-likelihood can be simplified to

$$\ln L = \sum_{i=1}^{k} \sum_{n=1}^{N_i} \ln\left\{\sum_{j=1}^{k} \exp\left[(X_{jn}^{(i)\prime} - X_{in}^{(i)\prime})\beta\right]\right\} \qquad (2.33)$$

Note that this requires data only on the difference in X between the selected choice i and the other (inferior) choices. Differentiating with respect to β, we obtain first order conditions

$$\frac{\partial \ln L}{\partial \beta} = \sum_{i=1}^{k} \sum_{n=1}^{N_i} \left(X_{in}^{(i)} - \sum_{j=1}^{k} \hat{P}_{jn} X_{jn}^{(i)}\right) = 0 \qquad (2.34)$$

where

$$\hat{P}_{jn} = \exp(X_{jn}^{(i)\prime}\hat{\beta}) / \sum_{\ell=1}^{k} \exp(X_{\ell n}^{(i)\prime}\hat{\beta})$$

with $\hat{\beta}$ the estimated parameters.

Note that if the X's contain dummy variables for each choice, satisfaction of the first order conditions implies that the observed fraction of the sample choosing each choice will be identical to the mean predicted probability of each choice. The second order condition requires that the matrix

$$\frac{\partial^2 \ln L}{\partial\beta\partial\beta'} = -\sum_{i=1}^{k}\sum_{n=1}^{N_i}\sum_{j=1}^{k}\left[\left(X_{jn}^{(i)} - \sum_{\ell=1}^{k} X_{\ell n}^{(i)}\hat{P}_{\ell n}\right)\hat{P}_{jn}\left(X_{jn}^{(i)} - \sum_{\ell=1}^{k} X_{\ell n}^{(i)}\hat{P}_{\ell n}\right)\right] \qquad (2.35)$$

must be negative definite.

For the multiple-weighting model, normalizing by setting $\beta_1 = 0$, the log-likelihood simplifies to

$$\ln L = N_1 + \sum_{i=2}^{k}\sum_{n=1}^{N_i} X_n^{(i)\prime}\beta_i - \sum_{i=1}^{k}\sum_{n=1}^{N_i} \ln\left[1 + \sum_{j=2}^{k}\exp(X_n^{(i)\prime}\beta_j)\right] \qquad (2.36)$$

Differentiating with respect to β_j, $j = 2, \ldots, k$, we obtain first order conditions

$$\frac{\partial \ln L}{\partial\beta_j} = \sum_{n=1}^{N_j} X_n^{(j)} - \sum_{i=1}^{k}\sum_{n=1}^{N_i} \hat{P}_{jn}X_n^{(i)} \qquad (2.37)$$

where

$$\hat{P}_{jn} = \exp(X_n^{(i)\prime}\hat{\beta}_j) / \left[1 + \sum_{\ell=2}^{k}\exp(X_n^{(i)\prime}\hat{\beta}_\ell)\right]$$

If X contains a constant, satisfaction of the first order conditions implies that the actual fraction of the sample choosing each alternative will be identical to their mean predicted probabilities. The second order condition is that the matrix of second derivatives be negative definite with submatrices

$$\frac{\partial^2 \ln L}{\partial\beta_j\partial\beta_j'} = -\sum_{i=1}^{k}\sum_{n=1}^{N_i} \hat{P}_{jn}(1 - \hat{P}_{jn})\, X_n^{(i)}X_n^{(i)\prime}$$

$$\frac{\partial^2 \ln L}{\partial\beta_j\partial\beta_\ell'} = \sum_{i=1}^{k}\sum_{n=1}^{N_i} \hat{P}_{jn}\hat{P}_{\ell n}X_n^{(i)}X_n^{(i)\prime} \qquad j \neq \ell \qquad (2.38)$$

Because the first order conditions of both the multiple-data and multiple-weighting models are nonlinear, computation of the maximum likelihood estimates will require iterative solution methods. It is straightforward to show that if the X's are not collinear, second order conditions will always hold for both models; hence $\ln L$ will be globally concave and have a unique maximum when first order conditions hold.

Although both the multiple-data and multiple-weighting models may be theoretically defined, in practice there are times when maximum likelihood estimates cannot be computed. Signals of this will be failure to converge and/or coefficients driven to $\pm\infty$. The most common occurrence of this is when the logit model is a perfect "predictor" or "classifier." This will occur in the multiple-weighting model, for example, whenever there exists a linear combination of the X's, say $X_n'b$, such that whenever $X_n'b$ is greater than some constant α, choice i is chosen, and choice i is never chosen when $X_n'b$ is less than α. This implies that the range of each X variable for the subsample selecting each choice must overlap the range of the same X for another choice. It also implies that if β_i has dimension m, there must be at least m observations selecting each choice. For the multiple-data model, perfect prediction will occur whenever there exists a linear weighting b such that $X_{in}'b$ is larger for the chosen choice of every sample observation than any other choice. X's that are constant across all choices will also cause failure to converge.

Multinomial Probit Model

When we discussed the dichotomous dependent variable problem in Chapter I, we presented the logit and probit models in tandem, arguing that they were essentially the same model. Our discussion of unordered multiple choice models, however, has focused entirely on the multinomial logit model. The reason for our apparent neglect of the probit model is that in the multiple-choice setting, the probit and logit models diverge both in their underlying assumptions and their computational ease. Severe computational problems of the multiple-choice probit model make it a much less attractive alternative than in the two-choice case. However, unlike the logit model, the underlying behavioral model that gives rise to the probit model need not require the axiom of independence of irrelevant alternatives. For this reason, despite its computational problems, let us briefly outline the model.

It is easiest to develop the multiple-choice probit model by starting with an underlying model of probabilistic choice. Assume that the nth decision maker always chooses the choice with the highest utility where the utility of choice i is given by $U_{in} = X_{in}'\beta_i + \varepsilon_{in}$, with ε_{in} a stochastic error. As we demonstrated earlier, the probability of each choice (using choice 1 arbitrarily) is given by Eq. (2.25), which we recall is

$$P(\text{choice } 1|X) = \int_{-\infty}^{\infty} \int_{-\infty}^{D_{12}} \cdots \int_{-\infty}^{D_{1k}} f(\varepsilon_{2n} \ldots \varepsilon_{kn}|\varepsilon_{1n}) f(\varepsilon_1) d\varepsilon_{kn} \ldots d\varepsilon_{1n} \quad (2.39)$$

where

$$D_{12} = X_{1n}'\beta_1 - X_{2n}'\beta_2 + \varepsilon_{1n}$$

$$\vdots$$

$$D_{1k} = X_{1n}'\beta_1 - X_{kn}'\beta_k + \varepsilon_{1n}$$

If the ε's are multivariate normal, then this formulation describes the *multinomial probit model.*

Since the above specification is somewhat unwieldy, let us illustrate the choice probabilities for a simpler three-choice model. Assuming that the three utility function errors are multivariate normally distributed with zero mean and covariance matrix

$$\Sigma = \begin{bmatrix} \sigma_1^2 & \sigma_{12} & \sigma_{13} \\ \sigma_{12} & \sigma_2^2 & \sigma_{23} \\ \sigma_{13} & \sigma_{23} & \sigma_3^2 \end{bmatrix}$$

the choice probabilities are

$$\begin{aligned} P_{1n} &= \int_{-\infty}^{D_{12}} \int_{-\infty}^{D_{13}} f(\delta_{12}, \delta_{13}; \rho_1) d\delta_{13} d\delta_{12} \\ P_{2n} &= \int_{D_{12}}^{\infty} \int_{-\infty}^{D_{23}} f(\delta_{12}, \delta_{23}; -\rho_2) d\delta_{23} d\delta_{12} \qquad (2.40) \\ P_{3n} &= \int_{D_{13}}^{\infty} \int_{D_{23}}^{\infty} f(\delta_{13}, \delta_{23}; \rho_3) d\delta_{23} d\delta_{13}, \end{aligned}$$

where $f(\,)$ is a standardized bivariate normal density function with correlations

$$\rho_1 = (\sigma_1^2 - \sigma_{13} - \sigma_{12} + \sigma_{23})/[(\sigma_1^2 + \sigma_2^2 - 2\sigma_{12})(\sigma_1^2 + \sigma_3^2 - 2\sigma_{13})]^{1/2}$$

$$\rho_2 = (\sigma_2^2 - \sigma_{12} - \sigma_{23} + \sigma_{13})/[(\sigma_1^2 + \sigma_2^2 - 2\sigma_{12})(\sigma_2^2 + \sigma_3^2 - 2\sigma_{23})]^{1/2}$$

$$\rho_3 = (\sigma_3^2 - \sigma_{13} - \sigma_{23} + \sigma_{12})/[(\sigma_2^2 + \sigma_3^2 - 2\sigma_{23})(\sigma_1^2 + \sigma_3^2 - 2\sigma_{13})]^{1/2}$$

and bounds

$$D_{12} = (X_{1n}'\beta_1 - X_{2n}'\beta_2)/[\sigma_1^2 + \sigma_2^2 - 2\sigma_{12}]^{1/2}$$

$$D_{13} = (X_{1n}'\beta_1 - X_{3n}'\beta_3)/[\sigma_1^2 + \sigma_3^2 - 2\sigma_{13}]^{1/2}$$

$$D_{23} = (X_{2n}'\beta_2 - X_{3n}'\beta_3)/[\sigma_2^2 + \sigma_3^2 - 2\sigma_{23}]^{1/2}$$

This model was originally proposed by Thurstone (1927) and has been applied by Hausman and Wise (1978). As in the logit model, restrictions across either the data or coefficients can be imposed to yield the multiple-weighting or multiple-data model, with similar normalizations of the β vectors required. In addition, for identification it will also generally be necessary to impose at least one normalization, such as $\sigma_1^2 = 1$, on the error covariance matrix. In the multiple-data model, where choice numbers have no special meaning, researchers might want to normalize each variance to one (i.e., $\sigma_1^2 = \sigma_2^2 = \sigma_3^2 = 1$).

One extremely attractive feature of the multinomial probit model is that unlike the logit model, we do not have to assume that the ε's are independent. This permits us to model problems where the axiom of independence of irrelevant alternatives does not have to hold. Thus, problems such as McFadden's "red bus–blue bus" problem could be represented as multinomial probits without violating the model's assumptions. If the ε's are not required to be independent, estimates of their correlations would allow us to identify patterns among choices. Choices with high error correlations, for example, could be inferred to be close substitutes.

Unfortunately, the greater generality of the multinomial probit model comes at a high computational cost. Estimation of the parameters of the three-choice model just presented is expensive but feasible, either by maximum likelihood methods with individual data or by Berkson–Theil regression techniques with repetition data. Although we don't present them here, Hausman and Wise (1978) have worked out the first order conditions of maximum likelihood estimation of the three-choice model. The computations involve the evaluation of bivariate normal integrals of the type shown in Eq. (2.40), which can be calculated by standard formulas. However, with more than three choices, computational costs become prohibitively expensive, requiring numerical integrations for exact solutions. Albright, Lerman, and Manski (1977) have proposed an approximate method of evaluating probit choice probabilities with larger sets of choices, which offers some promise of inexpensive calculation. However, the properties of this approximation have not been fully verified, leaving questions regarding its use. Until better computational methods are developed, the multinomial probit model will remain as an attractive conceptual model, yet one that is computationally intractable with more than three choices.

Sequential Models

In our discussion of the multinomial probit and logit models, we did not touch on the issue of how choice comparisons are made. There is the inference that decision makers evaluate the utility of each choice using all information available, then choose the alternative with the highest utility. However, particularly where information is costly, it is easy to think of choice selection processes where comparisons are made sequentially with different information sets. Tversky (1972) and Tversky and Sattath (1979), for example, have proposed a model that we do not discuss in detail and that they term "elimination-by-aspects." Decision makers are assumed to evaluate alternatives on the basis of a sequential list of aspects. For each aspect any alternative failing to have that aspect is eliminated from future consideration. This process continues until only one alternative is left. If each alternative represents a unique aspect, this model reduces to the unordered multiple-choice model. Otherwise, it implies a different structure.

Instead of sequential comparisons by aspects, it is also possible to think of sequential comparisons by choices. Decision makers could be thought of as confronting a sequential queue of alternatives without replacement. For each alternative, the decision maker must decide either to choose that alternative or continue searching and forego the opportunity to choose the discarded alternative. Many models of job search, for example, assume this kind of process. Many consumer purchase decisions might also be similarly modeled.

Although many other specifications are possible, Amemiya (1975) has proposed a formal representation of the sequential comparison by choice models based on the probit and logistic functions. He assumes that decision makers must choose from k alternatives, which they confront sequentially in order 1, 2, 3, ..., k. If the decision maker chooses an alternative, the process stops. Otherwise, they continue on to the next choice. Amemiya models the choice probabilities for the nth decision maker as

$$\begin{aligned} P_{1n} &= F(X_{1n}'\beta_1) \\ P_{2n} &= [1 - F(X_{1n}'\beta_1)]\, F(X_{2n}'\beta_2) \qquad (2.41) \\ &\vdots \\ P_{kn} &= \prod_{j=1}^{k-1} [1 - F(X_{jn}'\beta_j)] \end{aligned}$$

where

$$F(X_{in}'\beta_i) = \frac{1}{1 + \exp(-X_{in}'\beta_i)}$$

for the *sequential unordered logistic model,* and

$$F(X_{in}'\beta_i) = \int_{-\infty}^{X_{in}'\beta_i} \frac{1}{(2\pi)^{1/2}} \exp(-z^2/2)dz$$

for the *sequential unordered probit model.* The choice probabilities are formed under the implicit assumption that each decision is made independently. This assumption makes parameter estimation quite simple by reducing the model to a sequence of independent dichotomous choices. The coefficient vector β_1 can be estimated by fitting a binary logit or probit to the entire sample with $y_n = 1$ if choice 1 is chosen and 0 otherwise. β_2 could be similarly estimated by fitting a binary logit or probit model to the subsample of observations where choice 1 was not chosen and coding $y_n = 1$ if choice 2 was chosen and 0 otherwise. Repeating this process $k - 1$ times allows all parameter vectors to be estimated.

MULTIPLE DISCRIMINANT ANALYSIS

Introduction

Like the probit and logit models, discriminant analysis can be generalized quite readily to multiple groups. (In our discussion of probit and logit, we refer to "choices." Because it is more consistent with terminology used in other textbooks, we will use the term "group" when referring to the discriminant analysis model. Both terms refer to different values of a polytomous dependent variable.) Instead of two groups, we are concerned with comparisons of the distribution of one or more variables across a set of k discrete groups or populations. These could be automobiles, career choices, bond ratings, political parties, or any discrete, mutually exclusive, and identifiable taxonomy.

Other than the fact that it deals with k groups instead of two, descriptive and inferential multiple-group procedures are very similar to two-group discriminant analysis. It can be broadly described as a collection of techniques dealing with (1) predicting group membership for observations given only information on their values for certain independent variables and (2) testing for differences in the distribution of variables among groups. Analysis is based on the following set of assumptions.

We assume k discrete, mutually exclusive, identifiable populations or groups. Each group is assumed to contain observations that are each characterized by measurements on m independent variables, X. Within each group we assume observations are distributed with a multivariate normal distribution. Thus, denoting X_{in} as a typical observation of the ith group,

$$X_{1n} \sim N(\mu_1, \Sigma_1) \text{ (group 1)}$$

$$X_{2n} \sim N(\mu_2, \Sigma_2) \text{ (group 2)}$$

$$\vdots$$

$$X_{kn} \sim N(\mu_k, \Sigma_k) \text{ (group } k\text{)}$$

where $\mu_1, \ldots, \mu_k$ are m-length mean vectors and $\Sigma_1, \ldots, \Sigma_k$ are $m \times m$ variance–covariance (dispersion) matrices. These assumptions characterize what is termed the *multiple discriminant analysis* model. In the remainder of this section, we shall briefly outline the theory of discriminant analysis, following a similar outline to that used for the two-group model. Our focus will be primarily on theory, leaving issues of application to Chapter III.

Classification Probabilities

The multigroup discriminant analysis classification problem is based on the same principles as the two-group case. Given a set of k well-defined groups or populations and a sample of observations with measurements on m characteristics drawn from the groups, we wish to construct a scheme to "classify" unknown future observations into one of the groups based only on their values of the m characteristics. This can take two different forms. We may want to compute specific probabilities of group membership or merely derive an assignment rule that assigns observations to the "most likely" group.

Let us consider first the construction of group membership probabilities. As in the two-group case, this basically amounts to deriving a posterior on group membership using standard Bayesian logic. Probabilities are calculated from group likelihoods weighted by group *priors* (*a priori* probabilities) as follows.

Assume we observe characteristics of the nth observation (firm, individual, etc.) X_n, but do not know its group membership. The likelihood that an observation with these characteristics would be generated for each group is

$$\begin{aligned} f_1(X_n) &= \frac{1}{(2\pi|\Sigma_1|)^{1/2}} \exp \frac{-(X_n - \mu_1)'\Sigma_1^{-1}(X_n - \mu_1)}{2} \\ &\;\;\vdots \qquad\qquad\qquad \vdots \\ f_k(X_n) &= \frac{1}{(2\pi|\Sigma_k|)^{1/2}} \exp \frac{-(X_n - \mu_k)'\Sigma_k^{-1}(X_n - \mu_k)}{2} \end{aligned} \tag{2.42}$$

To compute "proper" probabilities we have to weight the likelihoods by *a priori* probabilities. As before, these can be interpreted as classical Bayesian *priors* or alternatively as population weights that take into account different group sizes. Defining $\pi_1, \ldots, \pi_k$ as the group *a priori* probabilities, group probabilities can be solved for as ratios of weighted likelihoods

$$
\begin{aligned}
P(\text{group } 1|X_n) &= \frac{\pi_1 f_1(X_n)}{\sum_{j=1}^{k} \pi_j f_j(X_n)} \\
&\vdots \\
P(\text{group } k|X_n) &= \frac{\pi_k f_k(X_n)}{\sum_{j=1}^{k} \pi_j f_j(X_n)}
\end{aligned}
\tag{2.43}
$$

Since we have assumed groups have different covariance matrices, the probabilities in Eq. (2.43) will correspond to *quadratic classification.*

The group probabilities are often expressed as

$$
P(\text{group } i|X_n) = \frac{(\pi_i/|\Sigma_i|^{1/2}) \exp(-1/2\chi_i^2)}{\sum_{j=1}^{k} (\pi_j/|\Sigma_j|^{1/2}) \exp(-1/2\chi_j^2)} \tag{2.44}
$$

where

$$
\chi_i^2 = (X_n - \mu_i)'\Sigma_i^{-1}(X_n - \mu_i) \tag{2.45}
$$

is called the *chi-square of group i.* It follows as a characteristic of the normal distribution that if you were to collect all observations of group i, and compute the variable χ_i^2, that it would be distributed as a chi-square with m degrees of freedom. This statistic can be used as a descriptive measure of the "closeness" of a particular observation to the center of a group. The significance level (p-value) of the χ^2 of an observation can be evaluated for each group. This number, like a type-I error, gives the percentage of the observations of that group that could be expected to lie further from the center of this group than the observation being evaluated. Observations with equi-probabilities for a group are sometimes said to be on the same *group contour line* (see Cooley and Lohnes, 1971).

To illustrate, suppose for a 4-variable problem, we computed a value of 8.0 for χ_1^2 (using the means and covariance matrix of group 1) for an observation. Looking up in a book of chi-square tables, we find a p-value .09158 for a chi-square of 8.0 with 4 degrees of freedom. Thus 9.1 percent of the observations of group 1 would be expected to lie further from the center (means) of the group than the observation of interest.

It follows from Eq. (2.44) that the probabilities of group membership will be weighted functions of the χ^2's. If weights $(\pi_i/|\Sigma_i|^{1/2})$ are equal, the group with the highest contour line (or lowest χ^2) will have the highest probability of group membership. Thus, the distance function

(2.45) "captures" all observation information relevant for evaluating group probabilities.

The expression for group probabilities simplifies significantly if we impose the assumption of equal group covariance matrices, i.e.,

$$\Sigma = \Sigma_1 = \Sigma_2 = \ldots = \Sigma_k$$

Group probabilities corresponding to *linear classification* are for the representative ith group

$$P(\text{group } i|X_n) = \frac{\pi_i \exp(-1/2\tilde{\chi}_i^2)}{\sum_{j=1}^{k} \pi_j \exp(-1/2\tilde{\chi}_j^2)} \qquad (2.46)$$

where

$$\tilde{\chi}_i^2 = (X_n - \mu_i)'\Sigma^{-1}(X_n - \mu_i) \qquad (2.47)$$

$\tilde{\chi}_i^2$ is similar in interpretation to χ_i^2. Both are distributed as chi-squares with m degrees of freedom; however, the linear classification chi-square $\tilde{\chi}_i^2$ requires the assumption of equal covariances. It appears at first glance that Eq. (2.46) is almost as complex as Eq. (2.44); however, we will show later in this section that the dimensionality of the linear classification scheme can be reduced significantly.

The question of sample versus population parameters is treated identically in the multiple as in the two-group model. Assuming random samples of sizes $N_1, \ldots, N_k$ drawn from each group, authors dating from Fisher (1936) have advocated using the sample mean estimates

$$\hat{\mu}_1 = \bar{X}_1 = \sum_{n=1}^{N_1} X_{1n}/N_1$$

$$\vdots \qquad \vdots \qquad \vdots$$

$$\hat{\mu}_k = \bar{X}_k = \sum_{n=1}^{N_k} X_{kn}/N_k$$

group covariance matrix estimates

$$\hat{\Sigma}_1 = S_1 = \sum_{n=1}^{N_1} (X_{1n} - \bar{X}_1)(X_{1n} - \bar{X}_1)'/(N_1 - 1)$$

$$\vdots \qquad \vdots \qquad \vdots$$

$$\hat{\Sigma}_k = S_k = \sum_{n=1}^{N_k} (X_{kn} - \bar{X}_k)(X_{kn} - \bar{X}_k)'/(N_k - 1)$$

and within-groups covariance matrix

$$\hat{\Sigma} = S = \left[\sum_{j=1}^{k} \sum_{n=1}^{N_j} (X_{jn} - \bar{X}_j)(X_{jn} - \bar{X}_j)' \right] / (N - k)$$

where

$$N = \sum_{j=1}^{k} N_j$$

When population parameters are unknown (as they usually are), these estimates will generally be consistent and provide consistent estimates of group probabilities. The selection of group *a priori* probabilities should also be subject to the same concerns as raised in the two-group model (see Chapter III also).

Before leaving our discussion of group probabilities, let us just briefly comment on the relationship of the discriminant analysis and logit models. The form of the probabilities in Eqs. (2.44) and (2.46) is remarkably similar to that of the multinomial logit model (particularly the multiple-data model) discussed earlier in this chapter. In both cases, the numerators of the group probabilities is given by e raised to a function of the X vector and weights particular to that group. The denominator is simply the sum of the numerator over all groups. We also note that like the logit model, the discriminant analysis conditional probability of group i over group ℓ, given that one of the two groups is chosen, reduces to a simple two-group discriminant analysis probability. This property implies the existence of an underlying assumption similar to the axiom of irrelevant alternatives.

Classification—Group Assignments

Let us now consider the problem of classifying observations into one of k populations. Often this problem reduces to assigning an observation to the group with the highest predicted probability by Eq. (2.44) or (2.46). However, we can consider more general assignment rules, particularly those with costs of misclassification. The general classification problem can be stated as follows (see Anderson, 1958).

Suppose the researcher perceives costs of misclassification $C(i|j)$ for assigning an observation to group i when it truly comes from group j, with *a priori* probabilities, $\pi_1, ..., \pi_k$. The researcher's objective is to divide the "space" of the X variables into k exhaustible regions denoted $G_1, ..., G_k$, where if an observation falls in region G_i, it is assigned to group i. The expected loss for a given assignment rule is

$$L = \sum_{i=1}^{k} \int_{X_n \varepsilon G_i} \left[\sum_{\substack{j=1 \\ j \neq i}}^{k} C(i|j) \pi_j f_j(X_n) \right] dX_n \qquad (2.48)$$

Anderson (1958) shows that the loss function (2.48) is minimized for k multivariate normal populations by the assignment rule:

Rule 1. Assign an observation with characteristics X_n to group i if for all other groups j

$$\sum_{\substack{\ell=1 \\ \ell \neq i}}^{k} C(i|\ell)\pi_\ell f_\ell(X_n) \geq \sum_{\substack{\ell=1 \\ \ell \neq j}}^{k} C(j|\ell)\pi_\ell f_\ell(X_n)$$

Notice that the expression in Rule 1 represents the total expected costs of misclassification if an observation is assigned to group i or group j.

Knowledge of (or estimates of) the *priors*, costs, means, and covariances of each group [to calculate $f_\ell(X_n)$] is sufficient to construct and use Assignment Rule 1. Usage, however, could be rather cumbersome, requiring comparison of k sums over $k - 1$ groups for each observation. If we assume that the costs of misclassifying an observation are the same regardless of which group it is assigned to, i.e.,

$$C(-|i) = C(1|i) = C(2|i) = \ldots = C(k|i)$$

then Rule 1 can be simplified significantly.

Rule 2. Assign an observation to group i if for all other groups j

$$C(-|i)\pi_i f_i(X_n) \leq C(-|j)\pi_j f_j(X_n)$$

If group covariances are not equal, i.e., $\Sigma_i \neq \Sigma_j$, Rule 2 can be expressed as a quadratic function.

Rule 3. Assign an observation to group i if for all other groups j

$$X_n'(\Sigma_i^{-1} - \Sigma_j^{-1})X_n - 2(\mu_i'\Sigma_i^{-1} - \mu_j'\Sigma_j^{-1})X_n + \mu_i'\Sigma_i^{-1}\mu_i - \mu_j'\Sigma_j^{-1}\mu_j$$
$$\geq \ln|\Sigma_j \cdot \Sigma_i^{-1}| - 2\ln\frac{C(-|j)\pi_j}{C(-|i)\pi_i}$$

Because Rule 3 is quadratic in X_n, we refer to it as a *quadratic classification rule.* It is identical to a series of pairwise group comparisons using the two-group quadratic classification rules.

The linkage to the two-group rules is even more apparent if we assume group covariances are equal, i.e., $\Sigma = \Sigma_1 = \ldots = \Sigma_k$. Rule 2 becomes

Rule 4. Assign an observation to group i if for all other groups j

$$X_n'\gamma_{ij} - \alpha_{ij} \geq \ln\frac{C(-|j)\pi_j}{C(-|i)\pi_i}$$

where γ_{ij} are weights of the two-group discriminant function defined for groups i and j

$$\gamma_{ij} = \Sigma^{-1}(\mu_i - \mu_j)$$

$$\alpha_{ij} = (\mu_i + \mu_j)'\gamma_{ij}/2$$

Rule 4 thus amounts to a series of pairwise two-group *linear classification* comparisons requiring only linear functions of X_n. Like the logit model "axiom of independence alternatives," it tells us that the choice between any two groups i or j does not depend upon the characteristics of any other group (the same holds for the quadratic rules). Notice, however, that instead of one linear function, it is necessary to calculate a different set of weights for each pair of groups. It appears that we would have to calculate $k \cdot (k - 1)$ sets of weights. However, since the functions differ only by the mean vectors, there are at most $(k - 1)$ independent functions. For example, note that

$$\gamma_{ij} = -\gamma_{ji}$$

and

$$\begin{aligned}\gamma_{\ell j} - \gamma_{\ell i} &= \Sigma^{-1}(\mu_\ell - \mu_j) - \Sigma^{-1}(\mu_\ell - \mu_i)\\ &= \Sigma^{-1}(\mu_i - \mu_j)\\ &= \gamma_{ij}\end{aligned}$$

Thus it is possible to construct Rule 4 from only $k - 1$ linear functions.

Sample versions of Rules 1–4 are easily derived by substituting $\bar{X}_i$, S_i, and S for their population counterparts. Again they will yield consistent estimates of the population assignment rules.

For Rules 2–4, the costs of misclassification, $C(—|i)$ always appear together with the *a priori* probabilities. In fact, if we set $\pi_i^* = C(—|i)\pi_i$, we could substitute π_i^* in all the rules and drop the costs entirely; although note that only if costs of misclassification are equal across groups will $\pi_i^* = \pi_i$. It also follows that if π_i^* is substituted for π_i, the assignment rules implied by Rules 2–4 are identical to assigning observations to groups with the highest predicted probability from Eqs. (2.44) or (2.46). For this reason, it is common to see *a priori* probabilities treated as a mixture of *priors* and misclassification costs. We caution however, that our ability to simplify Rule 1 to Rules 2–4, hence use π_i^*, rested on the assumption that misclassification costs depend only on true group membership, not on group assignment. In many applications in finance where groups are structured, such as bond ratings, this assumption may be unrealistic.

Significance Tests

Researchers are often interested in inferential rather than predictive questions regarding the relationship of the groups and the independent X variables. In Chapter I we introduced several statistics that could be used to test various hypotheses concerning group means and variance–covariance matrices. Many of these statistics (although not all) can be readily generalized to the multiple-group case; a topic we pursue in this subsection.

The significance tests most commonly seen are tests of the null hypothesis that all group mean vectors are equal, i.e.,

$$H_0: \mu_1 = \mu_2 = \ldots = \mu_k$$

where μ_i is the m-length population mean for group i. The principle underlying this test is that acceptance of H_0 suggests that the distribution of the X variables does not differ significantly across the groups. Researchers may also infer (though not necessarily correctly) that acceptance of H_0 suggests that the values of the X variables are not useful in "explaining" or "predicting" groups. Note though that the alternative hypothesis is that at least one mean vector is not equal to the others. Thus H_0 could be rejected because one group differed, although other groups did not have significantly different means. We briefly mention these issues before presenting the tests (they are discussed more fully in Chapter III), because blind use of the significance tests should be approached with caution.

In the simpler two-group case, we suggested a number of statistics, such as Hotellings T^2, Mahalanobis' D^2, which could be used to test H_0 under the maintained assumption of equal group covariance matrices, i.e.,

$$\Sigma = \Sigma_1 = \ldots = \Sigma_k$$

Although we will suggest other test criteria later, almost all test statistics in the multiple-group case are based on Wilks' Lambda (Λ) which is computed as follows.

Assume we have a random sample of sizes $N_1, \ldots, N_k$ for each of k groups, and let $\bar{X}_1, \ldots, \bar{X}_k$ be sample mean vectors for each group. Consider the following decomposition of the sample variance. Define the *total deviation sums of squares* matrix

$$T = \sum_{i=1}^{k} \sum_{n=1}^{N_i} (X_{in} - \bar{X})(X_{in} - \bar{X})'$$

where $\bar{X}$ is sample mean vector; the *within-groups deviation sums of squares* matrix

$$W = \sum_{i=1}^{k} \sum_{n=1}^{N_i} (X_{in} - \bar{X}_i)(X_{in} - \bar{X}_i)'$$

and the *between-groups deviation sums of squares* matrix

$$B = \sum_{i=1}^{k} N_i(\bar{X}_i - \bar{X})(\bar{X}_i - \bar{X})'$$

By construction it will *always* be the case that $T = B + W$. The Wilks' Lambda Statistic can be formed in several equivalent ways. The most commonly seen is from the determinant ratio

$$\Lambda = \left|\frac{W}{T}\right| \tag{2.49}$$

Because $T = B + W$, we will show later that Λ can also easily be computed from W and B or B and T.

Wilks' Lambda can be used to test H_0 under the assumption of equal group covariances; however, its usage is more complicated than in the two-group case. Unfortunately, the exact distribution of Λ under H_0 has been derived for only a subset of cases [when the number of variables m is even or the number of groups k is odd]. For this reason, researchers have tended to work with approximations of various distributions of Λ. The most commonly seen approximations are two proposed by Bartlett (1947) and Rao (1952).

Bartlett (1947) proposes the statistic

$$V = \left(\frac{m + k}{2} + 1 - N\right) \ln \Lambda \sim \chi^2(mk - m) \tag{2.50}$$

where $N = \Sigma_{i=1}^{k} N_i$ is the total sample size. Bartlett shows that V is asymptotically distributed as a chi-square with $m(k - 1)$ degrees of freedom when H_0 is true. A value of V greater than the tabular value at the desired significance level would lead to a rejection of H_0.

Rao (1952) has proposed an alternative approximation

$$F_\Lambda = \frac{1 - \Lambda^{1/c}}{\Lambda^{1/c}} \cdot \frac{dc - m(k - 1)/2 + 1}{m(k - 1)}$$

$$\sim F^{m(k-1)}_{dc - m(k-1)/2 + 1} \tag{2.51}$$

where

$$c^2 = \frac{m^2(k - 1)^2 - 4}{m^2 + (k - 1)^2 - 5} \qquad d = N - 1 - (m + k)/2$$

with

$$c = 1 \qquad \text{if } m^2 + (k - 1)^2 = 5$$

F_Λ is approximately distributed as an F-distribution with $m(k - 1)$ and $dc - m(k - 1)/2 + 1$ degrees of freedom when H_0 is true. If $m \leqslant 2$ and/or $k \leqslant 3$, F_Λ is exactly distributed as an F. In these instances, F_Λ simplifies to

$$\begin{aligned} F^{m}_{N-m-1} &= \frac{1 - \Lambda}{\Lambda}\frac{N - m - 1}{m} && \text{when } k = 2 \\ F^{2m}_{2(N-m-2)} &= \frac{1 - \Lambda^{1/2}}{\Lambda^{1/2}}\frac{N - m - 2}{m} && \text{when } k = 3 \\ F^{k-1}_{N-k} &= \frac{1 - \Lambda}{\Lambda}\frac{N - k}{k - 1} && \text{when } m = 1 \\ F^{2(k-1)}_{2(N-k-1)} &= \frac{1 - \Lambda^{1/2}}{\Lambda^{1/2}}\frac{N - k - 1}{k - 1} && \text{when } m = 2 \end{aligned} \tag{2.52}$$

Each statistic is distributed as a F with the indicated degrees of freedom when H_0 is true.

Although not as widely used, Hotelling (1951) has proposed a multigroup generalization of his T^2 that can also be used to construct an approximate test of H_0. Defining

$$T_0^2 = \text{Trace}[W^{-1}B] \cdot (N - k) \sim \chi^2(mk - m) \tag{2.53}$$

Hotelling shows that T_0^2 is asymptotically distributed as a chi-square with $m(k - 1)$ degrees of freedom when H_0 is true. Schatzoff (1966) conducted Monte Carlo tests comparing Wilks' Lambda and Hotelling's statistics with a number of different population characteristics, concluding that there is no clear advantage of one over the other.

There are several other hypotheses that may be of interest in the multigroup setting. The hypothesis of group mean equality can be tested without assuming equal covariances (the Behrens–Fisher problem). Unfortunately, most proposed procedures involve sample randomized pairings of observations similar to Anderson's (1958) procedure shown in Chapter I. We shall not present any of these proposals, referring readers to Timm (1975) for a comprehensive discussion.

Another commonly desired test is a test of the hypothesis of the equality of group covariance matrices, i.e.,

$$H_0\colon \Sigma_1 = \Sigma_2 = \ldots = \Sigma_k$$

Anderson (1958) and Box (1949) develop an approximate test of H_0 as follows. Defining S_i as the sample covariance matrix of group i

$$S_i = \sum_{i=1}^{N_i} (X_{in} - \bar{X}_i)(X_{in} - \bar{X}_i)'/(N_i - 1)$$

and letting

$$A = \ln[|W|] - \sum_{i=1}^{k} (N_i - 1)\ln[|S_i|]$$

$$B = \left(\sum_{i=1}^{k} \frac{1}{N_i - 1} - \frac{1}{N - k}\right) \frac{2m^2 + 3m - 1}{6(k - 1)(m + 1)}$$

Timm (1975) suggests the approximate test statistic

$$T = (1 - B)A \sim \chi^2(m(m+1)(k-1)/2) \tag{2.54}$$

which approximates a chi-square with $m(m + 1)(k - 1)/2$ degrees of freedom when H_0 is true. Anderson (1958) and Box (1949) propose a more precise approximation, particularly when m and/or k is greater than 6. Further defining

$$C = \left[\sum_{i=1}^{k} \frac{1}{(1 + N_i)^2} - \frac{1}{(N - k)^2}\right] \cdot \frac{(m - 1)(m + 2)}{6(k - 1)}$$

$$D = \frac{(k - 1)m \cdot (m + 1)}{2}$$

$$E = \frac{D + 2}{\text{abs}|B^2 - C|}$$

If $B^2 > C$, the test statistic is

$$\left(\frac{E}{D}\right)\left[\frac{A(1 - B + 2/E)}{E - A(1 - B + 2/E)}\right] \sim F_E^D \tag{2.55a}$$

If $C > B^2$, the test statistic is

$$\left(\frac{A}{D}\right)(1 - B - D/E) \sim F_E^D \tag{2.55b}$$

Each is approximately distributed as an F-statistic with D and E degrees of freedom when H_0 is true.

In Chapter I we presented an extensive discussion of hypothesis tests of the importance of individual variables—tests similar to tests in regression. We also deal with this subject at great length in Chapter III. Much of this discussion carries over into the multiple-group setting. There are three general types of tests that have been used to "rank" variables or to assist in making decisions on what variables to include in a model.

One test widely employed is to rank variables by their univariate Wilks' Lambdas. For the jth variable define

$$\Lambda_j = \frac{W^{jj}}{T^{jj}}$$

as the ratio of the jth diagonal elements of W and T. The test statistic

$$F^j = \frac{1 - \Lambda_j}{\Lambda_j} \frac{N - k}{k - 1} \sim F^{k-1}_{N-k} \tag{2.56}$$

can be used to test the unconditional hypothesis of the equality of group means just for variable j. It is distributed as an F-statistic with $k - 1$ and $N - k$ degrees of freedom when the hypothesis is true. Variables are sometimes ranked by the size of their respective univariate F-statistics (inverse of Λ_j)—the larger F, the "more important" the variable. This test, however, does not take into account the multivariate nature of the model.

A variable ranking test analogous to a multivariate t-test in a regression is one proposed by Rao (1952). This test, sometimes referred to as the conditional deletion method, amounts to dropping each variable in turn from the model and testing the effect on Wilks' Lambda. It formally tests the null hypothesis that the conditional mean of a variable given the other $m - 1$ variables is the same for all groups. Defining $\Lambda^{(j)}$ as the Wilks' Lambda of the remaining $m - 1$ variables when variable j is removed, the statistic

$$F_j = \frac{1 - \Lambda/\Lambda^{(j)}}{\Lambda/\Lambda^{(j)}} \cdot \frac{N - m + 1 - k}{k - 1} \sim F^{k-1}_{N-m+1-k} \tag{2.57}$$

is distributed as an F-statistic with $k - 1$ and $N - m + 1 - k$ degrees of freedom when the conditional mean of variable j is equal across groups. Variables can be ranked according to the size of this statistic. The larger the statistic, the more "important" the variable.

It is also possible to test hypotheses concerning the conditional means of a set of J variables. Defining $\Lambda^{(J)}$ as Wilks' Lambda computed from the remaining $m - J$ variables, the test statistic

$$F_J = \frac{1 - (\Lambda/\Lambda^{(J)})^{1/c}}{(\Lambda/\Lambda^{(J)})^{1/c}} \cdot \frac{dc - J(k - 1)/2 + 1}{J(k - 1)}$$

$$\sim F^{J(k-1)}_{dc-J(k-1)/2+1} \tag{2.58}$$

where

$$c^2 = \frac{J^2(k - 1)^2 - 4}{J^2 + (k - 1)^2 - 5} \qquad d = N - (m - J) - \frac{J + k + 2}{2}$$

is approximately distributed as an F with $J(k - 1)$ and $dc - J(k - 1)/2 + 1$ degrees of freedom when the J conditional means are equal across groups. If $J = 2$ or $k = 3$ (the case $J = 1$ is shown above and $k = 2$ in Chapter I), the statistic is distributed with an exact F

$$F_J = \frac{1 - (\Lambda/\Lambda^{(J)})^{1/2}}{(\Lambda/\Lambda^{(J)})^{1/2}} \cdot \frac{N - m - k + 1}{k - 1} \sim F^{2(k-1)}_{2(N-m-k+1)} \qquad \text{when } J = 2$$

$$F_J = \frac{1 - (\Lambda/\Lambda^{(J)})^{1/2}}{(\Lambda/\Lambda^{(J)})^{1/2}} \cdot \frac{N - m - 2}{J} \sim F^{2J}_{2(N-m-2)} \qquad \text{when } k = 3 \qquad (2.59)$$

with the indicated degrees of freedom.

Discriminant Functions

In our discussion of the two-group model, we described the discriminant function as a linear transformation that extracted all information relevant for linear classification or testing group mean equalities. This transformation had the highly desirable feature of reducing an m-length observation vector to a single variable. We also showed that the weights of the discriminant function would be proportional to the coefficients of the linear probability regression model. Most of these findings can be extended to the multiple-group case. However, instead of a single discriminant function, we will generally have two or more. The tie-in to the regression model will also no longer hold; however, discriminant function weights will be directly related to canonical correlation coefficients. These can be shown as follows. Before proceeding, we note that in the two-group case we referred to both "population" and "sample" discriminant functions. In the multiple-group extension, however, we will focus only on the sample version.

Consider a random sample of k groups numbering $N_1, ..., N_k$ and recall the within-groups deviation sums of squares matrix W, the between-groups deviation sums of squares matrix B, and the total deviation sums of squares matrix T. Furthermore, consider the determinantal equation

$$|B - \lambda W| = 0 \qquad (2.60)$$

where W is assumed to be of full rank m, and therefore, positive definite. The number of nontrivial solutions to this equation will be determined by the rank of B, which is

$$r = \min(m,k - 1)$$

The solutions $\lambda_1, ..., \lambda_r$ will be given by the r nonzero roots (eigenvalues) of the matrix $W^{-1}B$. Let us consider the m-length eigenvectors associated with the r roots, which we denote as $V_1, ..., V_r$. It is these vectors that constitute the discriminant functions in the multiple-group discriminant analysis model. Like the two-group function they have a number of interesting characteristics. Note that if $k = 2$, then V_1 (there is only one nonzero root since $r = 1$) will equal the two-group discriminant function.

As eigenvectors, the discriminant functions will be unique only up to scale. Thus, they are generally normalized, such that they have a length of 1 (the coefficients squared sum to 1). *Each* discriminant function will consist of m weights that could be used to transform an observation vector to a single variable. Thus, the r discriminant functions could be used to transform an m length observation vector X_n to r variables, i.e.,

$$x_n{}^{*(1)} = X_n{}' V_1$$

$$\vdots \qquad \vdots$$

$$x_n{}^{*(r)} = X_n{}' V_r$$

or compactly

$$X_n{}^* = V'X_n$$

where

$$X_n{}^* = (x_n{}^{*(1)}, \ldots , x_n{}^{*(r)})'$$

$$V = (V_1, \ldots , V_r)$$

We refer to the space of $X_n{}^*$ as the *reduced space.* For the two-group problem, it has only one dimension, although in general it will have r dimensions.

Consider what happens when we transform the observations used to compute the original sample statistics. The sample mean vector of the observations of each group will be

$$\bar{X}_i{}^* = V'\bar{X}_i$$

which we refer to as *centroids.* Similarly the group covariance matrix will be

$$S_i{}^* = V'S_iV$$

The reduced-space total, within-groups, and between-groups deviations sums of squares matrices would be

$$T^* = V'TV$$

$$W^* = V'WV$$

$$B^* = V'BV$$

Fisher (1936) and numerous others show that if we form the reduced-space Wilks' Lambda

$$\Lambda^* = |W^*|/|T^*|$$

it is identical to the original-space Wilks' Lambda $|W|/|T|$. Because Wilks' Lambda is the basis of the significance tests of group mean equality, all relevant observation information for these tests will be retained in reduced space.

Equally important, if we form linear (and only linear) classification rules in reduced space, using centroids $\bar{X}_i^*$ and the transformed within-groups dispersion matrix

$$S^* = V'SV$$

classification will be *identical* to that assigned when we use $\bar{X}_i$ and S. For example, the comparable rule in reduced space corresponding to the sample version of Rule 4 is

Rule 5. Assign an observation with transformed characteristics X_n^* to group i if for all other groups j

$$X_n^{*\prime}\gamma_{ij}^* - \alpha_{ij}^* \geq \ln \frac{C(-|j)\pi_j}{C(-|i)\pi_i}$$

where

$$\gamma_{ij}^* = S^{*-1}(\bar{X}_i^* - \bar{X}_j^*)$$

$$\alpha_{ij}^* = (\bar{X}_i^* + \bar{X}_j^*)'\gamma_{ij}^*/2$$

Rules 5 and 4 will yield identical classification results. Note that since the linear rules are based on $k - 1$ pairwise discriminant functions, these two-group functions will also be retained in the reduced space. It will not be the case, however, that quadratic classification will be identical in reduced space to the original space. Moreover, because the derivation of the discriminant functions is dependent on the assumption of equal group covariances, quadratic classification should not even be performed in reduced space [except when covariance matrices are proportional, see Lohnes (1961)].

We have assumed so far that all r variables of the transformed space are retained for testing and/or classification. It may be the case, however, that fewer than r of the variables will perform almost as well as the entire set. For example, if we graphed observations in reduced space and found very little variance in $x_n^{*(2)}$, then the second reduced-space dimension could be dropped without serious harm. The idea of further reducing the dimension of the reduced space can be formally tested. The test is derived as follows.

Since the determinant of a matrix is equal to the product of its roots, and Wilks' Lambda $\Lambda = |W|/|T|$, it follows that Λ will also be equal to the product of the r nonzero roots of the determinantal equation, $|W - \Psi T| = 0$. Because $T = W + B$, the solutions to this equation will be directly related to the roots of the determinantal equation $|B - \lambda W| = 0$, which is associated with the discriminant functions. That is, if the roots Ψ_i and λ_i are ordered so that

$$\Psi_1 > \Psi_2 > \dots > \Psi_r \text{ and } \lambda_1 > \lambda_2 > \dots > \lambda_r$$

then the *i*th root

$$\Psi_i = \frac{1}{1 + \lambda_{r+1-i}}$$

Therefore, the smallest root Ψ_r equals $1/(1 + \lambda_1)$ where λ_1 is the largest root of $|B - \lambda W| = 0$. Furthermore

$$\Lambda = |W|/|T| = \prod_{i=1}^{r} \cdot \Psi_i = \prod_{i=1}^{r} \frac{1}{1 + \lambda_i}$$

Thus, Wilks' Lambda can be expressed as the product of the roots associated with the discriminant functions. Since Wilks' Lambda is inversely related to the separation of group means, the larger λ_i, the greater its contribution to group mean separation. Moreover, since the roots are directly linked to reduced space variables (the largest root λ_1 is associated with V_1, etc.), we can use the contribution of each root to Wilks' Lambda as a measure of the contribution of the associated reduced-space dimension to classification and group separation. To formally test this, Rao (1952) shows that if the roots are ordered as above, the test statistic associated with the *i*th root

$$T = [N - (m - k)/2]\ln(1 + \lambda_i) \sim \chi^2(m + k - 2i) \qquad (2.61)$$

is approximately distributed as a chi-square with $m + k - 2i$ degrees of freedom. It can be used to test the significance of the contribution of the *i*th function, conditional on the previous $i - 1$ functions being used.

In the two-group model, the discriminant weights were proportional to the coefficients that would be obtained if a 0–1 dependent variable representing group membership were regressed against the vectors X_n and a constant. A similar analogy can be developed for the multigroup case as follows.

The discriminant functions can also be derived as solutions to what is known as the *discriminant criterion.* It can be shown that the discriminant function V_1 associated with the largest root λ_1 is the vector (up to a factor of proportionality) that maximizes the ratio

$$E = \frac{|V_1' \, BV_1|}{|V_1' \, WV_1|} \qquad (2.62)$$

Thus, V_1 is the transformation that maximizes the between-groups variance relative to the within-groups variance in the space implied by the transformation. V_2, or the function associated with λ_2, is the transformation that maximizes E subject to the restriction that projections on it be uncorrelated with projections on V_1. (Normally eigenvectors will be orthogonal; however, because $W^{-1}B$ is not symmetric, this will not necessarily follow unless $r = m$. By "uncorrelated" we mean that the transformed variables $x_n{}^{*(1)}$ and $x_n{}^{*(2)}$ will be uncorrelated.) Furthermore, V_3 will be the vector that maximizes E subject to the restriction that projections on it be uncorrelated with projections on both V_1 and V_2, etc.

This process of deriving the discriminant functions is equivalent to a form of *canonical correlation.* If we code $k - 1$ dummy variables (assume $r = k - 1$) such that

$$D_1 = \begin{cases} 1 & \text{group 1 observations} \\ 0 & \text{otherwise} \end{cases}$$

$$\vdots$$

$$D_{k-1} = \begin{cases} 1 & \text{group } k - 1 \text{ observations} \\ 0 & \text{otherwise} \end{cases}$$

and arrange the nth observation such that it consists of its values for the $k - 1$ D variables and the m X variables, canonical correlation consists of finding the set of weights

$$U = [u_1, \ldots, u_m]'$$

for the X variables and another set of weights

$$Z = [z_1, \ldots, z_{k-1}]'$$

for the D variables such that the correlation between

$$P_X = U'X = u_1 x_n{}^{(1)} + \ldots + u_m x_n{}^{(m)}$$

and

$$P_D = Z'D = z_1 D_1 + \ldots + z_{k-1} D_{k-1}$$

is largest for our particular sample. This is the first canonical correlation. The weights can be estimated with a well-established procedure that we do not show (see Tatsuoka, 1971). The second canonical correlation consists of finding the sets of weights that maximize the correlation of P_X and P_D subject to the restriction that they be respectively uncorrelated with P_X and P_D derived for the first canonical correlation. Weights for higher canonical correlations are defined similarly.

Set up as above, the canonical weights associated with the first canonical correlation U will be identical (up to proportionality) to the first discriminant function V_1. Weights associated with the second canonical correlation will be identical to V_2, etc. Thus, a canonical correlation program could be used to generate the discriminant functions.

SPECIAL TOPICS

Nonrandom Sampling

Throughout our discussion in this chapter and the previous one, we have assumed random data samples. For example, for the probit and logit models, we assumed that given the independent variables, samples were randomly drawn with respect to choice or group. Similarly, for discriminant analysis, we assumed random data selection from the entire population. There are countless situations, however, where samples will almost certainly not be random. A natural question therefore, is to ask to what extent the properties of the statistical procedures we have discussed will be affected by stratified sampling. This is particularly a relevant issue for researchers who may face different costs in collecting random versus nonrandom data.

We will not attempt to provide a comprehensive discussion of nonrandom sampling—an old and much discussed problem in statistics. However, we want to touch briefly on two important types of stratification likely to occur in categorical dependent variable models—stratification according to independent variables and stratification by dependent variable (group or choice). Since these have different implications for estimation and inference, we shall look at each problem separately.

In each of the models we have discussed, we assumed that observations were characterized by measurements on a vector of "independent" variables X_n and a "dependent" variable (or group) y_n. In estimating parameters of each model, we assumed that the X's were a random sample from the population. Suppose, however that they are not randomly drawn. For example, suppose that one of the firm characteristics used in a model to predict bankruptcy is the ratio of gross profits to sales and that all firms with negative gross profits are excluded from the sample. Interestingly, the effect of such stratification is dramatically different for the discriminant analysis model than for the linear probability, logit, and probit models. The estimation procedures we have proposed for the latter three model forms are conditioned only on the assumption that the distribution of the y's given the X's be random. The X's themselves, however, need not be random. Thus, standard estimation procedures will still yield consistent parameter estimates even when the sample is stratified by the independent variables. This does not mean to say that X variable stratification will have no effect on the value of empirical estimates. Sample stratification can limit the generalizability of results and makes them more susceptible to problems of robustness.

Stratification of the sample by the independent variables can cause much more severe problems for the discriminant analysis model. The estimation procedures we've proposed require that within each group, the distribution of the *X* variables be random. If there is stratification by the *X*'s, then sample estimates of the group means and covariances will be biased. For example, excluding negative profit firms would give misleadingly high mean profit estimates for firms. As shown in Avery (1977), such stratification will also bias estimates of the discriminant functions, measures of importance of variables, and classification results. Moreover, it is difficult to predict the direction of the bias because it depends upon how the stratification effects each group.

If the stratification scheme is known, then Avery (1977) presents a procedure that can be used to calculate unbiased estimates of the discriminant analysis model parameters. The adjustment, however, is computationally complex and does not appear to be distributionally robust. In practice, researchers have often just ignored the problem of stratification. Even though such practices are invalid on purely statistical grounds, they are often defended on the grounds of empirical practicality. We caution, however, that such estimates are severely limited in their generalizability. A discriminant analysis model, for example, based on samples including only positive profit firms, can only be applied to like populations. Results and predictions from this model should not be applied to the population at large.

Avery(1977) also presents a procedure which can be used to calculate consistent estimates of the discriminant analysis parameters when the stratification scheme is random. This procedure requires that the probability of an observation appearing in the sample be a known (or estimable) function of the X's. Interestingly, Avery shows that parameter estimates can be obtained much easier than in the case where stratification is exact. Consistent estimates of group means and covariances can be obtained by weighting observed observations by the inverse of their probability of occuring in the sample.

Exactly the opposite results occur if samples are stratified by the dependent variable. This has been sometimes referred to as group- or choice-based sampling. The selection procedure normally followed consists of sampling the groups or choices at different rates, but within each group observation, selection is random. For example, in the bankruptcy problem, researchers might sample virtually all failed firms, yet only a fraction of the nonfailed firms. A symptom of stratified sampling by the dependent variable is that the ratio of failed to nonfailed firms in the sample will not be the same as in the population.

Unlike stratified sampling by the independent variables, stratification by group will not cause severe problems for the discriminant analysis model. As long as observations are randomly drawn within groups, sample means and covariances will be unbiased and consistent estimates of group distribution parameters. Discriminant functions and classification rules can therefore be consistently estimated and hypothesis tests conducted with the stratified sample. In constructing classification rules, however, remember that *a priori* probabilities should reflect the "true" population ratios, not the sample proportions.

Stratification by groups or choices, however, poses a much more serious problem for the linear probability, logit, and probit models. Such stratification violates the inherent assumption required for standard estimators of these models, that given the X's, the y's be randomly drawn. Manski and Lerman (1977) prove that if observations are differentially sampled by choice, normal maximum likelihood estimates of logit, probit, or regression model parameters will generally not be consistent. However, they propose a relatively simple fix-up procedure, which they show will yield consistent estimates. For the nth observation they define a weight

$$w_n = Q_n/H_n \tag{2.63}$$

where Q_n is the true fraction of the population choosing the choice chosen by the nth observation and H_n is the fraction of the sample choosing that choice. Note that if sampling is completely random, the expectation of w_n is one. Manski and Lerman (1977) then show that the parameters that maximize the weighted sample log-likelihood

$$\sum_{n=1}^{N} w_n \ln f(y_n;\theta) \tag{2.64}$$

will be consistent. Note that this adjustment is similar to the *a priori* probabilities in discriminant analysis. Manski and Lerman (1977) also show that estimates of the standard errors of the coefficients can be derived from the second derivative matrix of the weighted log-likelihood function.

The Manski–Lerman adjustment makes it relatively easy to handle stratification by group or choice even for the probit and logit models, as long as the stratification scheme is known. This is a particularly important consideration when observations may have different collection costs and information content. For example, in transportation mode studies it may be easier to collect information at the train and bus station on known riders (thus sample by choice) than to sample the population at large and have to discard noncommuters. Stratification by choice may also severely reduce the number of required data points in studies of low probability events, such as firm bankruptcy, where random sampling might require a large number of observations to have an adequate number of failures. These topics are discussed more fully in Manski and McFadden (1980) and Cosslett (1980) and are important considerations in sample design. A key point that must be emphasized when samples are stratified by choice is that the true population proportions must be known (or estimated) for either discriminant analysis (for *a priori* probabilities) or probit/logit.

We have discussed problems where sample stratification is by either the independent or the dependent variable and where the stratification scheme is known. If stratification is by both independent and dependent variables or the stratification form is unknown, fix-up techniques become much more complex. In the case of unknown stratification, there are no obvious adjustments that could be used to obtain consistent estimates of model parameters. The case of stratification by both independent and dependent variables, though not necessarily intractable, is likely to cause headaches, since it implies that both the standard logit/probit and discriminant analysis model estimates will be biased. Fix-up techniques will have to be constructed on a problem-by-problem basis, although several general cases should be noted.

One general class of problems is considered by Heckman (1979), who discusses estimation of probit and regression models when sample stratification is by another variable that is correlated, although not perfectly, with the dependent variable. Another relatively common form of stratification by both independent and dependent variables is the paired sample. This occurs when a sample of one value of the dependent variable (such as failed firms) is matched observation by observation with a sample drawn from the other value of the dependent variable (nonfailed firms) according to characteristics of independent variables (such as firm size, location, product line). This is clearly a case of stratified sampling by group (failed firms are sampled at a much higher rate than nonfailed firms) and if the matching variables are correlated with the variables used in the analysis, with the independent variables as well. This is likely to cause particularly severe problems for the discriminant analysis model, suggesting that results from such a sample would almost certainly not be generalizable. Moreover, the particular matching scheme will also invalidate the simple Manski–Lerman (1977) probit/logit weighting adjustment, requiring a much more complex adjustment. Given these complications it makes much more sense in modeling low probability events to stratify by choice, but then to choose randomly within each group.

Model Selection—Goodness of Fit

The similarity of the regression, logit, probit, and discriminant analysis models we have presented in this book raises the question as to how the choice of model should be made. Although some authors have argued otherwise [e.g., Gunderson (1974), who says that the linear probability model is "inherently a wrong functional form,"], there is nothing that should categorically exclude any of the models from consideration. Either on the grounds of computational ease, theoretical structure, or functional flexibility, a case could be made for each of the models we have presented. Indeed, as we have pointed out, there are conditions where data can be consistently described by more than one model. Unfortunately, a number of authors [such as Gunderson (1974) and Moore (1973)] have tried to argue the general superiority of one model form over another on the basis of specific empirical studies or Monte Carlo data. It is our contention that it is dangerous to generalize. We believe that model selection is an imperfect science and must be problem-specific, depending upon theoretical grounds, fit of the data, and indeed even upon computer programs at the user's disposal.

Although the choice of model will often not greatly affect the implications of a study (because different model forms will lead to similar empirical conclusions), there are a number of considerations that can be used in making the choice. These range from the researcher's beliefs as to the theoretical causal structure of the process being modeled to the "fit" of each potential model with actual data. In this subsection and the one that follows, we discuss these considerations, starting with methods of measuring data fit. We conclude with the application of these ideas to the director-interlock problem presented in Chapter I. Although much of our discussion could apply equally as well to other aspects of model selection (such as the choice of variables), we will concentrate our discussion on the choice of model form, i.e., probit, logit, linear probability model, or discriminant analysis. We will assume individual level data, although most arguments will carry over to data with multiple repetitions per cell. We begin with a discussion of how empirical evidence can be used to choose among models.

There are a number of ways that researchers can evaluate the "quality" of an empirical model. Coefficient signs, magnitudes, and significance levels, for example, can be compared with *a priori* expectations or findings from other models. The most common way, however, is to examine how well the model "fits" or "predicts" the observed dependent variable(s). On the basis of such judgments, choices can be made on model form and composition, as well as evaluations of specific hypotheses. Unfortunately, there is no one "correct" way to measure a model's fit. Particularly for the discrete dependent variables we are considering, there are several different ways to measure fit. These can be broadly classified into two classes. Model fit can be judged by how well the model correctly classifies observations. The criteria of fit is measured by how often the predicted "most likely" group or choice actually occurs. Alternatively, model fit can be measured by how accurately predicted probabilities reflect observed group or choice frequencies.

Judgments of the first type are perhaps those most commonly seen in the literature. A sample with known values of the dependent variable is used to construct predictions based only on the values of the independent variables. The group or choice with the highest predicted probability (thus the most likely) is taken as the prediction of the model for each observation. These are compared with the actual values of the dependent variable to determine which of the observations the model correctly classifies. Results can be displayed as illustrated in Table II.1 for a model to predict horse race results. Observations on the diagonal are correctly classified and those off-diagonal misclassified. The misclassification rates of models can be compared and used to select the best model. Thus, for example, if a discriminant analysis model predicted better than a logit model, then the discriminant analysis model would be chosen. Although this is an attractive mechanism for model selection, several words of caution should accompany its use.

First, there is a question of which sample to use. If the original sample used to estimate parameters is used, as Lachenbruch and Mickey (1968) show, misclassification rates will be biased in small samples. Alternatively, another or "holdout" sample could be used. This yields unbiased estimates of misclassification rates, however it has the disadvantage of requiring large samples and not using all the data to estimate the model. In Chapter III, in a more comprehensive discussion of this topic for the discriminant analysis model, we present a method attributable to Lachenbruch (1967), which combines the original sample and holdout methods. However, particularly when comparing different models, none of these methods is unambiguously superior.

A second concern is that it is difficult to compare misclassification rates across samples of different compositions and probabilities. This is because "naive" or "base rate" predictions (predictions with no model) vary significantly across problems. For example, in the horse race prob-

Table II.1. Horse Race Model

Actual Placement		*Prediction*				
	Total	*Win*	*Place*	*Show*	*Other*	*Misclassification (rate %)*
Win	30	6	5	5	14	80
Place	30	3	6	6	15	80
Show	30	3	6	5	16	83
Other	110	3	5	7	95	14

lem, a naive model would predict that all horses would finish out of the money and thus be correct 55 percent of the time. However, since industrial firm failure rates are only about 1/250 per year, a naive model of firm failure would be correct 99.6 percent of the time. To crudely correct for this, Simon (1971) proposes an index that he terms the "Index of Predictive Efficiency" (P.E.), where

$$\text{P.E.} = \frac{\#\text{ misclassifications using naive model} - \#\text{ misclassifications with model}}{\#\text{ misclassifications using naive model}} \tag{2.65}$$

The P.E. index can be used to measure the improvement that a model offers over the naive version.

Even using the P.E. adjustment, particular concern should be exercised in using misclassification rates from stratified samples. This is particularly true when samples are stratified by group. For example, the higher the percentage of out-of-the-money horses in the sample, the better the horse race model would appear to predict. If the evaluating sample is stratified, true population ratios (*a priori* probabilities) should be used to adjust misclassification rates to reflect a random sample of the population.

A fourth concern with using misclassification rates is that it weights all misclassifications equally. Clearly, however, as the horse race example illustrates, this may not always be desirable. It may be significantly more costly to misclassify an out-of-the-money horse as a win than as a show.

Finally, perhaps the most serious flaw with using misclassification rates to choose among models is that it is sensitive only to observations with probabilities near thresholds (such as .5 in a two-group problem) and cannot detect differences among models with extreme observations. This is particularly true in problems involving low probability events such as firm failure where it is likely that all models will predict nonfailure for virtually all observations. Since bankruptcy is such a rare event, the evidence of a good model will not be that it predicts failed firms with probabilities of .5 or more (since no model can do that); rather that it predicts failure with higher probabilities for failed firms than for nonfailed firms. This would be obscured in focusing on the misclassification rate, because all models will do as well as the naive model.

Several proposals have been made to adjust the misclassification rate criteria for low probability problems. One is to alter the classification cutoff, such as lower the prediction of firm failure from a failure probability of .5 to .2. To be sure, this will increase the number of failed firms correctly classified. However, this will be more than offset by an increase in the number of nonfailed firms incorrectly classified, and thus is not recommended. As we showed in Chapter I, the optimal cutoff point for two-group discriminant analysis models with equal costs of misclassification, and generally for other models as well, is a probability of .5. Deviations will only increase the number of total sample misclassifications.

The inadequacies of the misclassification rate criteria have led to alternative measures of model fit that take into account the predicted group or choice probabilities, not just "most likely" predictions. One suggested approach is to compare the average predicted probabilities for each group. For example, the mean predicted failure probability for known failed firms could be compared to the mean probability for nonfailed firms. The wider the difference, the better the model. Another similar approach is to rank observations by predicted probabilities and compare the actual failure rates of, say, the lowest decile to the next lowest, etc. Both of these approaches are primarily descriptive. Other, more objective criteria have been proposed that are variations of the regression multiple correlation coefficient R^2.

Using the two-group problem, where $y_n = 1$ or $y_n = 0$ as an example (although the discussion can be easily generalized to multigroup problems), let $\hat{P}_n$ be the estimated probability that $y_n = 1$ for a given model given values of the independent variables X_n. In a manner similar to that for a standard regression problem, we could define the sum of sample squared residuals as

$$\text{RSS} = \sum_{n=1}^{N} (y_n - \hat{P}_n)^2 \tag{2.66}$$

Since, as we have noted before, these residuals will have different variances, $P_n(1 - P_n)$ Eq. (2.66) can be corrected for heteroskedasticity

$$\widetilde{\text{RSS}} = \sum_{n=1}^{N} (y_n - \hat{P}_n)^2/(\hat{P}_n(1 - \hat{P}_n)) \tag{2.67}$$

By itself, this statistic is not particularly meaningful. Domencich and McFadden (1975), however, suggest constructing a similar residual for a naive model where all observations are assumed to have the same probability (or equivalently where the X vector consists only of a constant.) In all the models we have considered, the naive model probability $\hat{P}$, would just be the fraction of the actual sample where $y_n = 1$. The adjusted naive model residual sums of squares are

$$\overline{\text{RSS}} = \sum_{n=1}^{N} (y_n - \hat{P})^2/(\hat{P}_n(1 - \hat{P}_n)) \tag{2.68}$$

Domencich and McFadden (1975) then propose the statistic

$$R^2 = 1 - \widetilde{\text{RSS}}/\overline{\text{RSS}} \tag{2.69}$$

which they argue can be used analogously to the regression R^2 as a measure of fit and can be used to compare models. They caution, however, against the use of this statistic in small samples, proposing a more robust alternative based on the log-likelihood function.

Defining a model's sample log-likelihood function as

$$\ln L = \sum_{n=1}^{N_1} \ln(\hat{P}_n) + \sum_{n=1}^{N_0} \ln(1 - \hat{P}_n) \tag{2.70}$$

where N_1 consists of observations where $y_n = 1$ and N_0 consists of observations where $y_n = 0$, Domencich and McFadden (1975) suggest constructing a similar statistic for the corresponding naive model

$$\overline{\ln L} = N_1 \ln(\hat{P}) + N_0 \ln(1 - \hat{P}) \tag{2.71}$$

These two statistics can be used to test the null hypothesis that all model coefficients except the constant are 0 (thus that the naive model is true) by the likelihood ratio statistic

$$-2[\ln L - \overline{\ln L}] \sim \chi^2 (m - 1) \tag{2.72}$$

which is distributed asymptotically as a chi-square with $m - 1$ (m is the dimension of X_n) degrees of freedom when the hypothesis is true. Domencich and McFadden (1975) also propose the pseudo R^2 statistic

$$p^2 = 1 - \ln L / \overline{\ln L} \tag{2.73}$$

which they argue provides a practical and theoretically sound index of goodness of fit.

An attractive feature of these R^2 measures of goodness of fit is that they can be used to compare the performance of different model forms on the same data. If, for example, the logit model appeared to have a significantly better data fit than the discriminant analysis model, it would offer a persuasive argument to adopt the logit model form. Morrison (1972) shows that indeed the "true" model of the probability P_n (given a set X_n vector) will have a higher expected R^2 (or p^2) for a randomly drawn data sample than alternative model forms. However, these statistics should not be blindly used. Goldberger (1973) and Westin (1974) argue that Morrison's results will hold only in expected value terms, and thus it is quite possible for "wrong" models to perform better in some samples. These results are also quite sensitive to the distribution of the independent variables and may lead to different recommendations for different ranges of the X's.

Model Selection—Theoretical Considerations

In our discussion on model selection, we have focused on measures of how different model forms fit actual data. Often, however, researchers may have to make model decisions before examining data. It may also be desirable to have the model decision guided by theoretical rather than empirical considerations and to choose the model form most consistent with the structure of the problem being modeled. In this subsection, we focus on the problem of model selection on theoretical grounds. We will consider arguments for and against the linear probability, probit, logit, and discriminant analysis models. Most of our discussion will involve comparisons of the first three models and discriminant analysis.

To begin with, there is nothing inherently wrong with any of the models we have presented. Each rests on sound statistical grounds and under appropriate assumptions can be properly used to model any categorical dependent variable problem. Statements such as "it is improper to use a linear regression model with a 0–1 dependent variable" or "discriminant analysis cannot be used if groups are ranked" are dangerous and inaccurate generalizations. However, each of the models rests on different distributional and, to some extent, structural assumptions. Thus, for a given problem, it may be that the assumptions required for one model are more appropriate than those of other models and therefore argue for that model's use. The researcher's goal is to match the assumptions to the problem. Running the risk of violating our own caveat about generalizations, several general guides can be used in matching problems and models.

Most empirical problems can be classified as one of two types: those involving *causal relationships* and those involving *conjoint relationships*. By causal we mean that the values of certain variables determine the values of certain other variables. Thus, if values of the first variables are changed, those of the second will change in a predictable and determined way. The researcher normally relies on theory to suggest causal models and structures, which they then wish to test or estimate. In conjoint models, the researcher does not specify any causal linkages. Model variables, for example, may be assumed to be jointly determined by other unspecified variables. The researcher is normally interested in describing or estimating the relationship between variables in their model for forecasting, monitoring, or other purposes. There is no pretense, however, of measuring a causal structure. A critical difference between causal and conjoint models is that there is no inference in a conjoint model that changing the value of one variable will necessarily change the values of any others; or if it does, it is not clear how those values will change.

If the researcher's problem involves measuring the conjoint relationship between a discrete variable y and a vector of variables X, where the goal is to estimate parameters of the forecasting function $E(y|X)$, then theoretical considerations should not preclude any model. The regression, probit, logit, and discriminant analysis models merely represent different expectation functions. Model selection in these circumstances should be much more an issue of empirical fit and statistical considerations. Robustness, computing costs, and sampling concerns may also be important. This does not mean, however, that theoretical considerations are totally irrelevant. If, for example, in a multichoice problem, data is available on the choices but not the decision makers, such as in the transportation mode problem, it would be virtually impossible to use a discriminant analysis model. Similarly, if groups are ranked, then ordered logit or probit may be desirable. We caution, however, that if the problem is basically conjoint, then causal inferences should not be drawn from estimated coefficients and parameters. It would be a mistake to choose a model because it "fit well" and then interpret its parameters as supportive of a particular causal hypothesis.

If the researcher, however, is interested in estimating and/or testing a causal model, then there may be strong theoretical reasons for choosing one model over another. In the discrete dependent variable models there are two potential lines of causality: The y variable or group could determine the value of the X variables or the X variables determine y. If the relationship is the former, then a very strong argument can be made for discriminant analysis, which inherently embodies a causal link running from the groups to the X variables. Of course, even if y is believed to cause X, we could always estimate the conjoint function $E(y|X)$ and could do this with any of the model forms. However, we should not interpret these as causal models.

The vast majority of discrete dependent variable problems are likely to be based on the assumption that the X's cause the y's. It appears that a strong argument can be made for probit and logit in this case. In Chapter I and the multinomial probit and logit section of this chapter, we showed how logit and probit reduced forms could be derived from utility-maximizing models, where values of the X variables did indeed determine the value of y. We also suggested that the validity of the axiom of independence of irrelevant alternatives could be used to help decide between the probit and logit models. These arguments are indeed attractive and provide a direct causal interpretation for the probit and logit model coefficients. However, McFadden (1976b), shows that a case can be made for the discriminant analysis model, even if the X's are assumed to cause the y's. He shows that if appropriate distributional and *a priori* probability assumptions are made, then discriminant analysis statistics will provide consistent estimates of the parameters of an underlying causal process running from the X's to y. We gave an explicit example of this in Chapter I, where we showed a case where the two-group linear discriminant function coefficients would be proportional to the logit function parameters and the discriminant analysis group probabilities would have exactly the same form as the logit model. This suggests that the use of a discriminant analysis model could be defended. McFadden (1976b), however, also voices concern that this justification of the discriminant analysis is not very robust with respect to assumptions, particularly on the *a priori* probabilities. He argues that unless there is strong confidence that these assumptions are met, then logit, regression, or probit causal models should be used.

Example—Director Interlocks IV

Many of the arguments that we have presented in this section on theoretical and empirical model selection are best illustrated by use of an example. To do this we return to the running example we used in Chapter I on director interlocks (Eisenbeis and McCall, 1971). If you recall, this example investigates whether the affiliation status

$$A = \begin{cases} 1 & \text{if commercial bank affiliated with a mutual} \\ 0 & \text{if not} \end{cases}$$

of 38 New Hampshire commercial banks is related to values of two variables

$$\text{TSD} = \frac{\text{Total Savings and IPC Time Deposits}}{\text{Total Savings and IPC Time and IPC Demand Deposits}}$$

$$\text{RL} = \frac{\text{Total Conventional Residential Real Estate Loans}}{\text{Total Loans and Gross Discounts}}$$

The objective of the Eisenbeis–McCall study was primarily conjoint rather than causal in nature. They were interested in whether the affiliated status of banks was related to the two independent variables. There is an inference that affiliation affects the banks' behavior but no suggestion of a strong causal structure. There is particularly no inference that the *X*'s cause affiliation. Viewed in this way, as a conjoint relationship, there is no particular theoretical reason to favor one model form over another. However, it means that the estimated parameters of any model should not be given a causal interpretation.

Since there is no strong theoretical argument, it seems reasonable to rely on measures of model fit in selecting a model form. In Chapter I we presented estimated parameters for the affiliation problem when modeled as a regression, logit, and discriminant analysis model. Each of these models was used to construct a predicted probability of affiliation for the original sample. These predictions for each of six models are given along with the values of the TSD and RL for each sample observation in Table II.2. To further illustrate the differences among the six models, the classification cutoff lines are presented in Figure II.1. Note, that as they should be, the linear probability and linear discriminant analysis cutoffs are identical.

It is difficult to judge the relative quality of the model fits even with a table of every predicted probability. To provide a more concrete measure of model fit, we prepared Table II.3 which presents the misclassification rates, mean probabilities, Domencich and McFadden's

Figure II.1. Classification Cutoffs

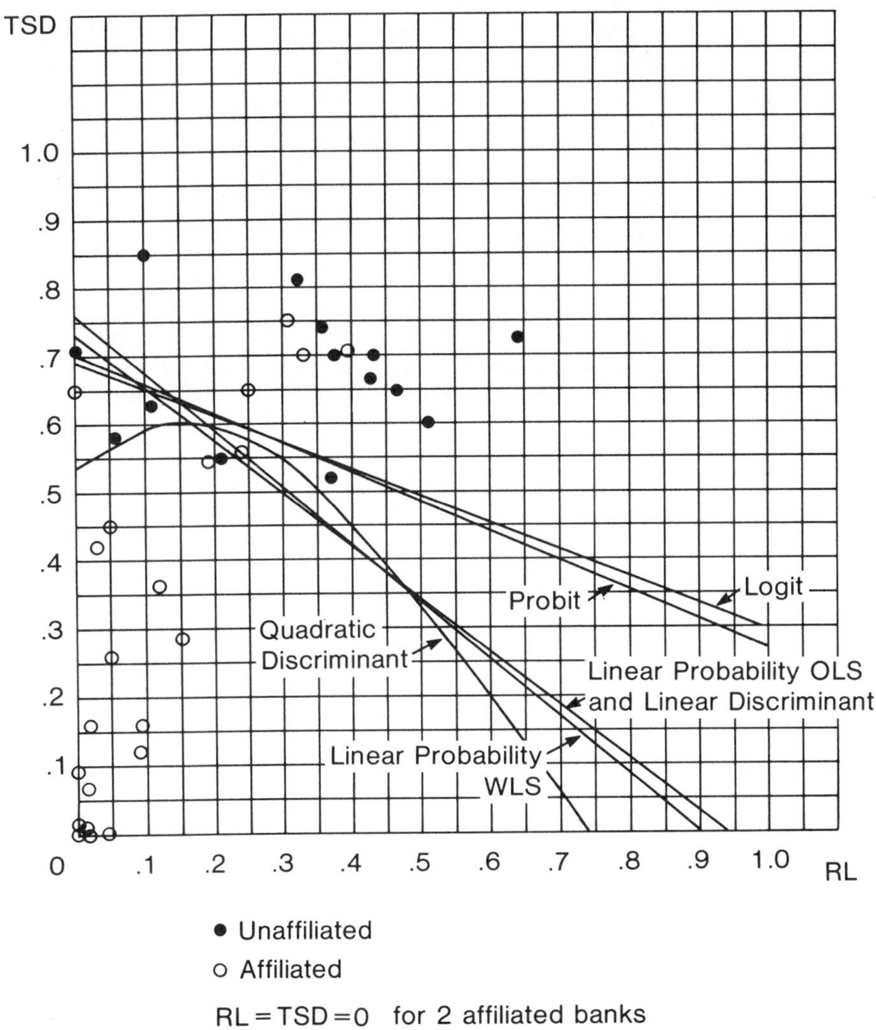

Table II.2. Predicted Probabilities Director Interlocks

TSD	*RL*	*Linear Probability OLS*	*Linear Probability WLS*	*Logit Model*	*Probit Model*	*Linear Discriminant*	*Quadratic Discriminant*
				Unaffiliated (14 banks)			
.740	.358	.26	.26	.19	.19	.15	.17
.849	.101	.34	.35	.18	.19	.24	.21
.665	.421	.28	.28	.25	.26	.17	.07
.705	.375	.28	.27	.22	.23	.17	.13
.698	.434	.25	.24	.20	.20	.14	.06
.721	.639	.10	.07	.10	.09	.05	.01
.518	.365	.44	.44	.57	.56	.40	.36
.810	.320	.23	.22	.13	.13	.12	.32
.600	.512	.28	.27	.30	.30	.16	.01
.715	0	.52	.54	.47	.48	.54	.06
.578	.060	.59	.61	.68	.68	.67	.51
.635	.111	.51	.53	.54	.54	.53	.36
.552	.207	.52	.53	.62	.62	.54	.67
.647	.465	.27	.26	.25	.26	.16	.03

Affiliated (24 banks)

0	0	1.11	1.15	.99	1.00	.99	1.00
.717	.399	.26	.25	.19	.20	.14	.10
.753	.306	.29	.28	.20	.20	.17	.25
.069	.022	1.04	1.08	.99	1.00	.98	1.00
.016	0	1.10	1.14	.99	1.00	.99	1.00
.008	.017	1.10	1.13	.99	1.00	.99	1.00
.265	.049	.86	.89	.96	.97	.93	1.00
.422	.034	.74	.76	.89	.89	.85	.98
.362	.120	.73	.75	.91	.91	.85	1.00
.121	.089	.95	.98	.99	.99	.97	1.00
.654	.249	.41	.41	.39	.40	.34	.33
.158	.090	.92	.95	.98	.99	.96	1.00
.449	.050	.71	.73	.86	.86	.82	.96
0	0	1.11	1.15	.99	1.00	.99	1.00
.650	0	.57	.59	.59	.60	.63	.13
.161	.018	.97	1.00	.98	.99	.97	1.00
.699	.329	.32	.31	.26	.27	.21	.20
.288	.154	.77	.79	.94	.95	.88	1.00
0	.320	.90	.90	.99	1.00	.95	1.00
0	.001	1.11	1.15	.99	1.00	.99	1.00
.542	.185	.54	.55	.65	.65	.58	.72
.090	0	1.03	1.08	.99	1.00	.98	1.00
0	.044	1.08	1.12	.99	1.00	.99	1.00
.565	.238	.49	.49	.57	.57	.48	.57

Table II.3. Model Fits

	Linear Probability OLS	*Linear Probability WLS*	*Logit Model*	*Probit Model*	*Linear Discriminant*	*Quadratic Discriminant*
Percentage Unaffiliated Banks Misclassified	28.6	28.6	28.6	28.6	28.6	28.6
Percentage Affiliated Banks Misclassified	20.8	20.8	16.7	16.7	20.8	20.8
Mean Probability Unaffiliated Banks	.35	.35	.34	.34	.29	.21
Mean Probability Affiliated Banks	.80	.82	.80	.80	.78	.80
R^2 (adjusted)	.43	.44	.42	.41	.40	.49
p^2 (likelihood ratio)	.56	.54	.55	.53	.51	.52

(1975) R^2, and likelihood ratio measures. These results illustrate the ambiguity likely to characterize many problems. The logit and probit models have marginally better rates of misclassification. However, the quadratic discriminant analysis model scores best on the other measures of model fit, albeit only marginally. These results are too similar to argue strongly for one model form, suggesting that all of the six models would perform approximately the same. Thus, it would be very hard to say which model form is "best."

Chapter III

Discriminant Analysis Application Problems

INTRODUCTION

Of the multivariate classification techniques discussed in the previous chapters, discriminant analysis has been most widely used. However, despite the existence of a fairly extensive body of literature on various theoretical aspects of the technique, most of the applications to date appear to have suffered from statistical or methodological problems that have limited the practical usefulness of their results.

The methodological difficulties have centered around what has often been the application of an inappropriate statistical technique to the problem at hand. Usually not enough thought is given to matching the statistics to the underlying theoretical problem. Instead the researcher proceeds to apply what appears to be a new or "hot" technique to data that is readily available. One of the objectives of this book is to make clearer the types of problems that the various techniques discussed are designed to accommodate and how one would determine which statistical procedure is appropriate for the problem being investigated.

Of nearly equal concern are the host of statistical problems that have repeatedly plagued the applied literature. While these problems are not unique to economics, business, or finance, it does seem that the topics and data are such that statistical difficulties are encountered more frequently in these areas than in many others.

This chapter focuses on the statistical problems associated with discriminant analysis. This technique has been so widely used and abused that we felt that a separate chapter should be devoted especially to it. The statistical problems that have been most common are of several different types, among which are those associated with

1. Violation of the underlying assumptions of the classical linear discriminant analysis model. These include
   a. Deviation of the distribution of the variables within each group from multivariate normality.
   b. Unequal group covariance matrices.
   c. The lack of distinct definitions of the groups.
2. Interpretation of the relative importance of individual variables in the model.
3. Reduction of dimensionality and elimination of insignificant variables.
4. Specification of the appropriate classification scheme, including
   a. Selection of *a priori* probabilities and/or costs of misclassification.
   b. Estimation of classification error rates.
5. Application of the techniques in time-series prediction.

Each of these problem areas is discussed in detail in the following sections.

VIOLATION OF THE ASSUMPTIONS OF THE DISCRIMINANT ANALYSIS MODEL

The key assumptions of the classical linear discriminant analysis model are that (1) the variables describing the members of the group observations are multivariate normally distributed within each group, (2) the group covariances are equal across all groups, and (3) the groups are discrete, mutually exclusive, and identifiable. The following subsections consider these three general problem areas.

Multivariate Normality

The classical linear discriminant analysis procedures presented first by Fisher (1936) assume that the variables used to describe or characterize the members of each of the groups being investigated are multivariate normally distributed. In practice, deviations from this normality assumption, at least in economics and finance, tend to be the rule rather than the exception. The tests of significance and estimated classification error rates may be biased when the normality assumption is violated. Hence, it is of interest to determine whether the assumption holds and what effects its relaxation may have on the statistical tests and on the ensuing classification. In the applied literature, the problem of testing for the appropriateness of the distributional assumption has been largely ignored, probably due to lack of familiarity with the available test procedures and their properties.[1]

Equally important, however, is the fact that if the normality hypothesis is rejected, then one is still faced with the practically impossible task of deriving the appropriate joint probability density functions and constructing alternative classification schemes. In practice, the tactic adopted by most researchers is to simply ignore the problem. They seem to be content to assume that the standard discriminant analysis procedures yield reasonable approximations and proceed as if the normality assumption holds. There are circumstances, however, under which the results may not be robust and are biased.

The theoretical and statistical work dealing with normality has been of three major types. First, some have simply abandoned discriminant analysis procedures entirely. The examples of logit, probit, and related quantile choice models presented earlier and reviewed and discussed by McFadden (1976) or Nerlove and Press (1973, 1976) are illustrative of this approach. It should be noted that the choice of these models depends upon more than simply a response to or to avoid a statistical problem. Rather the choice goes to the very heart of the research problem and involves identifying and specifying the underlying structure of the model to be estimated. Second, some have utilized discriminant analysis schemes that have been developed for specified types of nonnormality, especially for cases involving binary and other discrete variables. Finally, some have used standard discriminant analysis procedures but have attempted to evaluate the bias in the significance tests and classification results introduced when the normality assumptions are violated in known ways. The robustness of the significance tests and classification results to nonnormality are discussed in the next two subsections.

The Effects of Nonnormality on Tests of Significance. The multivariate tests for the equality of group mean vectors in discriminant analysis typically assume multivariate normality. Most of these tests are based upon Hotelling's T^2 or related statistics.[2] The robustness of Hotelling's T^2 to nonnormality has received considerable attention in the statistics literature. Mardia (1975b), for example, has recently reviewed the empirical work that consists of Monte Carlo studies of the effects of different types of nonnormality. These studies are mainly bivariate studies for numerous alternative distributions, populations, and sample sizes.[3] The results suggest that Hotelling's T^2 is robust for even small samples. Mardia concludes that T^2 seems to be more sensitive to the presence of multivariate skewness than kurtosis, and the sensitivity to skewness (in the two-samples case) seems greater when the sample sizes are unequal than when they are equal. No results are readily available for cases involving more than two groups or more than two variables.

The Effects of Nonnormality on Classification Performance. Hills (1967) develops optimal (nonclassical discriminant analysis) rules for the case where all of the variables are discrete. He also discusses alternative nonparametric methods of estimating log-likelihood ratios that can be used to construct classification schemes.[4] When the number of variables are small, he argues that the log-likelihood ratio can be estimated by enumeration of the relative frequencies. However, when the number of variables is large, he proposes use of a nearest neighbor procedure to estimate the likelihood ratio.[5]

Although Hills (1967) states that this nearest neighbor procedure is not consistent, it does have the advantage of being less subject to sampling variability than the direct enumeration procedure for estimating the likelihood ratio.[6] Linhart (1959) also considers the case where all the variables are discrete and solves the classification problem, essentially by enumeration, as did Hills (1967).

Often in financial applications, and in particular in credit scoring and bond rating schemes, many of the important attributes tend to be categorical in nature. Hence, the resultant models contain mixtures of both discrete and continuous variables. Hills (1967) and Linhart (1959) both consider the case of mixed discrete and continuous variables. The usefulness of the rules they propose hinge on the extent to which one is willing to assume that the discrete variables are independent of the continuous variables. In cases where they are independent, the samples can be split on the discrete variables and separate discriminant functions estimated for the subsamples using the remaining continuous variables. Chang and Afifi (1974) have investigated Bayes' rules for the simple two-group case with one dichotomous variable and with both one and several continuous variables. Similar to Linhart (1959), their results indicate that it is appropriate to split the samples and then to construct separate discriminant functions and classification rules for the pairs of samples. This procedure was recently used in an industrial bond rating study by Pinches (1975) and in a discussion of that application by Eisenbeis (1978). Krzanowski (1975) extends the approach of Chang and Afifi (1974) to more than one dichotomous variable. The optimal rules he derives require a different set of functions to be estimated for each combination of cells, with different cutoff points to be applied for each cell. Others, including Cochran and Hopkins (1961), Glick (1973), and Linhart (1959) have suggested that the continuous variables should be transformed into discrete variables and then the methods designed for multinomial classification applied.[7]

The studies discussed above focus on nonstandard procedures for nonnormal data. A number of studies have examined the performance and robustness of the standard discriminant analysis techniques when nonnormality exists. Gilbert (1968) compared the classification performance of the linear discriminant function, when all the variables were discrete, with the performance of two logit models, a full multinomial model and a model assuming that the variables are mutually independent. The experiments show that, for the limited range of covariance structures considered, the loss from using the linear discriminant function is small and not of great importance. Furthermore, it is argued that as the number of variables is increased, the results should be quite stable. If one applies the standard linear discriminant techniques with dichotomous variables, as Gilbert (1968) did, it is quite easy to show that the assumption of equal group covariances is also violated. Hence, a better comparison might have been with the performance of the quadratic model. Thus, Gilbert's Monte Carlo experiments really were comparing deviations from both multivariate normality and equal group covariances.

Moore (1973) expands upon Gilbert's (1968) results in several respects. He notes that the sampling results were derived from a first order interactive model that has limited applicability in the class of populations it can generate. He also argues that the populations sampled were not readily described in terms of means and variances, which makes comparisons with other populations more difficult. To correct this, Moore examines a broader range of populations than Gilbert.[8] Furthermore, in addition to three of the five methods considered by Gilbert (1968), he considers two other classification methods—a quadratic discriminant function and one utilizing second order approximations to the full multinomial probabilities.[9] Moore's evidence suggests that the application of the linear discriminant function to problems with binary variables gives mixed results. The linear discriminant function yields very small errors and outperforms the quadratic function for those cases where the binary variables are uncorrelated. Performance decreases significantly, however, in those cases where the log-likelihood ratio undergoes "reversals." That is, when the log-likelihood is graphed against the number of variables in the vector having values equal to one and the function does not increase monotonically, the likelihood ratio is termed to have undergone a "reversal." In such instances, the quadratic model outperforms the linear model, although it is inferior to the other second order method investigated.

More recently, Dillon and Goldstein (1978) discuss a classification rule based upon a distance metric proposed by Matusita (1954). They compare the performance of this new rule with four of the five methods used by Moore (1973) (the quadratic rule is not included). The results suggest again that the performance of the linear discriminant function is quite acceptable as long as the correlations among the discrete 0–1 variables are moderate (e.g., less in absolute value than .2 to .3) and the difference between the group means is relatively large (e.g., greater than .10).[10] Furthermore, like those of Moore (1973), the results also suggest that the linear function performs substantially worse in cases of population "reversals" where the binary variables are all moderately correlated with each other. This result was also observed in the Monte Carlo simulations of Krzanowski (1977).

Krzanowski (1975, 1977) also considers the performance of the linear discriminant function in the case where there are both discrete and continuous variables. He shows that the linear discriminant function may yield substantially biased error estimates (as high as 50 percent error) whenever there is interaction between the binary and continuous variables. The bias of the linear discriminant function also increases whenever there are moderately positive correlations between the binary variables.[11] A high correlation between binary and continuous variables in one population and a low correlation in another, or a change in sign, represent cases, according to Krzanowski (1977), in which the linear discriminant function would be expected to yield biased error estimates. Thus, inspection of the group correlation matrices should provide useful clues as to when the linear discriminant function, as opposed to the other alternatives described above, could be applied and be expected to give satisfactory error estimates. In the absence of correlation, the linear function performed quite well. He also notes that dichotomizing the continuous variables according to the method of Cochran and Hopkins (1961) and application of the multinomial method of Hills (1967) yields consistently biased and worse performance than do the methods that treat those variables as continuous.

The robustness of both the linear and quadratic discriminant functions to other types of nonnormality, other than discrete multinomial distributions, has been studied by Lachenbruch, Sneeringer, and Revo (1973). They investigate the robustness of both linear and quadratic procedures for three specific nonmultivariate normal distributions. These distributions are transformations of normally distributed variables, so the true classification errors are known. The three distributions are the log normal, the logistic, and the inverse hyperbolic sine normal. The authors conclude that the standard linear procedures may be quite sensitive to nonmultivariate normality and yield badly misleading estimates of the error rates. However, they also suggest that the problems may not be as great when the distributions are bounded, such as in the case with the logit normal distribution, rather than unbounded. They found that the estimated overall classification error rates were not affected as much as the individual group error rates. They also observed that even attempts to adjust for inequalities of the group covariances by using quadratic classification rules did not significantly improve the results, and in many cases, they were worse. Subrahmaniam and Chinganda (1978) examined the linear function when the variables follow an Edgeworth series distribution. Subrahmaniam and Chinganda found that the errors introduced are small when the skewness factor is small; this finding is similar to the results of Lachenbruch et al. (1973) for bounded distributions. As the skewness factor increases, the estimated group error rates deviate from the true rates, but the overall error rate is largely unaffected.

Lachenbruch et al. (1973) suggest that, if possible, data should first be transformed to approximate normality. Then standard tests for the equality of the group covariances should be employed to determine whether linear or quadratic techniques should be used.

The use of certain transformations to transform data prior to estimating discriminant function has been a common procedure. The natural log and standard log are the most frequently used transformations. Pinches and Mingo (1973), Bates (1973), Carleton and Lerner (1969), Horton (1970), and Altman et al. (1977) all used such transformations in their studies. This is because many of the variables employed, such as firm size, loan size, and population, tend to be highly skewed with a few large values and a number of small values. Hence, a much greater proportion of the values lie to the left of the variable mean than to the right. If a distribution is skewed to the right, the effect of the natural log transformation is to make the marginal distribution of the variable more symmetric and probably more normal. But the cautions noted previously from the work of Lachenbruch et al. (1973) still apply.

As a final point, it should also be recognized that the application of a transformation may change the interrelationships among the variables and may also affect the relative positions of the observations in the groups. In the case of the log transformation, there is also an implicit assumption being accepted. When such a transformation is employed, the transformed variables give less weight to equal percentage changes in a variable when the values are larger than when they are smaller. If, for example, the variable being transformed was firm size, the implication would be that one does not believe that there is as much difference between a \$1 billion- and a \$2 billion-size firm as there is between a \$1 million- and a \$2 million-size firm. The percentage difference in the log will be greater in the latter case than in the former case. Use of such transformations changes the implicit structure of the underlying model being estimated. Considerable attention is usually given in regression models to the implications that transformations of the variables have for the model being estimated. Little attention has been given in discriminant analysis to this problem, but the same types of considerations would seem to apply.

Unequal Group Covariance Matrices

A second critical assumption of classical linear discriminant analysis is that the group covariance (dispersion) matrices are equal across all groups. Relaxation of this assumption affects not only the significance tests for the differences in group means but also affects both the usefulness of the so-called "reduced-space transformations" and the appropriate form of the classification rules.

Some attention has been given to the effects of unequal covariances on the hypothesis test of the equality of group means and to the development of exact tests when the covariances are unequal.[12] Anderson (1958) presents an exact test for the equality of the means for the limited case when the sample sizes are equal. He provides an approximate test for the case when there are unequal sample sizes (see Chapter I).[13] To date, however, such tests do not appear to have been programmed, or at least they have not been made readily available to researchers.

As was the case with departures from normality, it is of interest to investigate the bias that might be introduced if the standard significant test based upon Hotelling's T^2 for equality of group means is applied when the group covariances are in fact unequal. Holloway and Dunn (1967) investigated the robustness of Hotelling's T^2 for the two-group case with populations distributed in the form N_1 (0, I) and N_2 (M, $\sigma \cdot$ I) with equal eigenvalues. Drawing upon the work of Scheffé (1959), Hopkins and Clay (1963), and Ito and Schull (1964), they conclude that robustness of the test depends upon both the number of variables and relative sample sizes in the groups.[14] For the univariate case, the test seems to be affected very little as long as the samples are equal or nearly equal in size, especially for larger samples. With widely disparate sample sizes, the actual significance level is greater than the hypothesized level. Thus, the null hypothesis would be rejected more frequently than it should when the means are in fact equal. When the number of variables increases, both the significance level and the sensitivity to unequal sample sizes increases. According to Holloway and Dunn (1967), "Equal sample sizes help in keeping the level of significance close to the supposed level, but do not help in maintaining the power of the test."

Cooley and Lohnes (1962, 1971), Rulon, Tiedeman, Tatsuoka, and Langmuir (1967), and Tatsuoka (1971), among others, have discussed the advantages of the reduced-space transformations that can be used to reduce the original m-dimensional variable test space to an r-dimensional space.[15,16] The transformation is selected as the matrix of eigenvectors associated with the roots of the determinantal equation $|T - \lambda W| = 0$, which has (r) nonzero roots.[17] The reduction in dimensionality is possible because the linear transformation from test to reduced space preserves relative euclidian distances among observations and leaves the significance tests and classification results unaffected. But this property holds, if and only if, the group covariance matrices are equal. If the covariances are not equal, the transformation to reduced space is no longer distance preserving. The result is a warping of the relative positions of the observations in reduced space, and this affects the reduced space significance tests and changes the resulting classifications. Lohnes (1961) has examined a portion of this problem by comparing linear test and linear reduced-space classifications when the group covariances are unequal. However, his results are difficult to assess and are not particularly useful since he does not compare the linear results with the appropriate quadratic test-space results. Since the assumption of equal covariances is used in transforming the data from test to reduced space, the differences he observes are due solely to the warping of the reduced-space transformations in response to the unequal covariances in his data.

Considerably more attention has been given to the effects of unequal covariances on the classification procedures and results. Gilbert (1969) has investigated and compared the effects on classification error rates and conditional probabilities of the use of a linear rule (assuming equal covariances) when, in fact, the covariances are unequal (implying a quadratic rule should have been used). Only the two-group case with known parameters is examined. The results indicate that significant differences can occur and that these are directly related to the differences in the covariances, the number of variables, and the separation among the groups. Classification disagreement between the two rules increases as the differences between the covariances and the number of variables increase. However, the further apart the groups are for given covariances, the less significant are the differences between the linear and quadratic results.[18] Gilbert (1969) also provides tables that can serve as a useful guide in judging how the linear and quadratic rules may deviate for problems involving groups with particular parameter characteristics.

In a more recent Monte Carlo study, Marks and Dunn (1974) investigated the performance in the two-group case of Fisher's linear discriminant function, the "best" linear function proposed by Clumies-Ross and Riffenburgh (1960) and Anderson and Bahadur (1962), and the quadratic classification rule. Sample estimates of population parameters were used, and the overall probability of misclassification was used as the performance criterion. For large samples, the authors conclude that the relative performance of the quadratic procedures improves as the groups converge and as the number of variables increases. For small samples, they indicate that the linear procedures perform better for small numbers of variables and reasonably similar covariance matrices, and this performance improves further as the number of variables increases. However, as the covariances become more dissimilar, the quadratic rules dominate. These results seem quite reasonable when one considers what is involved in constructing the sample functions and classification rules. For the two-group *m*-variable linear case, 2m variable means and 1/2 m(m + 1) different elements of the pooled within-groups covariance matrix must be estimated. This represents a total of 1/2 m(m + 5) parameters. In the quadratic case, m(m + 3) different parameters are estimated; this is nearly twice the number estimated in the linear case. For fixed but small samples, the resulting degrees of freedom of the pooled within-groups covariance matrix used in the linear rules are substantially larger than for the individual group covariances used in the quadratic rules. When the covariances are similar, relatively more efficient linear classification results are obtained that are not swamped by the effects of averaging the group covariances. However, as the differences in the covariances increase, the efficiency of the linear parameter estimates begins to be dominated by the effects of the unequal covariances. Marks and Dunn (1974) provide tables indicating the points where tradeoffs between sample size and inequality of the covariances occur. However, their tables are of limited practical usefulness because they investigated only a few specific types of covariance inequality. It is not clear how general their conclusions are.

Wahl and Kronmal (1977) expand upon Marks and Dunn's (1974) Monte Carlo results to consider greater sample sizes and more varied covariance structures using essentially the same methodology. Their conclusions are essentially the same as that of Marks and Dunn (1974).[19] When the mean and covariance matrices are quite similar, it makes little difference which method is used. However, as the covariances become greatly dissimilar, quadratic rules dominate, provided the sample sizes are large enough. In fact they argue that sample sizes are an important consideration in deciding between the two procedures, and they provide some rules of thumb (for the two-group case) to aid the user. Marks and Dunn (1974) suggest that for more than six variables and less than 25 observations per group, the linear model is preferred. Wahl and Kronmal's (1977) work indicates that for four variables, 25 observations per group is sufficient to use the quadratic model, and they suggest that for every two additional variables, another 25 observations per group should be available to employ a quadratic model. With more than 100 observations, they indicate that the quadratic model is favored because the asymptotic properties are reached fairly quickly.

A number of the applied studies using quadratic classification techniques that have recently appeared in the literature tend to support the tentative observations of Gilbert (1969), Marks and Dunn (1974), and Wahl and Kronmal (1977).[20] For example, in his classic three-group Iris problem, Fisher (1936) used linear procedures. Recently, Eisenbeis and Avery (1972) have shown, using Fisher's data, that although the hypothesis of the equality of the covariance matrices was rejected beyond any measurable level of significance, the use of quadratic classification rules, as shown in Table III.1, yield identical results to those using the linear rules. The reason for this becomes quite clear when the estimates of the group overlaps are examined in Table III.2.[21] The group means are so far apart that there is almost no significant overlap among the groups.[22]

Related to the work of Gilbert (1968), who investigated the performance of the linear function when all the variables were discrete, it can be shown that if a dichotomous variable is included in the variable set, the assumption of equal covariances will almost assuredly be violated. This again implies that quadratic and not linear classification procedures should be used.[23,24]

A priori there is little reason to believe that any one application area is likely to be more susceptible to this problem than any other, except to the extent that categorical variables may arise more frequently in certain types of problems than in others. The available evidence does indicate, however, that rejection of the hypothesis of equal group covariances may have a significant and undesirable impact on the test for the equality of group means. More importantly, depending upon the sample sizes, number of variables, and differences in the dispersions, use of linear classification rules when quadratic rules are indicated may have drastic effects on the classification results and in particular on individual assignments and on the respective group error rates. Logically then, the test for the equality of the covariances matrices should precede both the test for the equality of group means and the estimation of classification errors.

The Definitions of the Groups

A third, and implicit assumption of discriminant analysis, is that the groups being investigated are distinct and discrete. That is, it is assumed that an observation is a member of one and only one group. Furthermore, in the parameter estimation process, it is assumed that it is known

Table III.1. Classification Results—Iris Data[a]

		Linear Classification Results Predicted Groups			*Quadratic Classification Results Predicted Groups*		
Actual Groups	*Total*	*Iris Setosa*	*Iris Versicolor*	*Iris Virginica*	*Iris Setosa*	*Iris Versicolor*	*Iris Virginica*
Iris Setosa	50	50	0	0	50	0	0
	(100.0)	(100.00)	(0.00)	(0.00)	(100.00)	(0.00)	(0.00)
Iris Versicolor	50	0	48	2	0	48	2
	(100.00)	(0.00)	(96.00)	(4.00)	(0.00)	(96.00)	(4.00)
Iris Virginica	50	0	1	49	0	1	49
	(100.00)	(0.00)	(2.00)	(98.00)	(0.00)	(2.00)	(98.00)

[a]Percentages are shown in parentheses.

Table III.2. Expected Group Overlap-Iris Data[a]

	Percentage Overlap Assuming Unequal Covariances			*Percentage Overlap Assuming Equal Covariances*		
Groups	*Iris Setosa*	*Iris Versicolor*	*Iris Virginica*	*Iris Setosa*	*Iris Versicolor*	*Iris Virginica*
Iris Setosa	100.0000	$.2058 \times 10^{-18}$	$.1927 \times 10^{-32}$	100.0000	$.1401 \times 10^{-15}$	$.1013 \times 10^{-34}$
Iris Versicolor	$.1150 \times 10^{-65}$	100.0000	.7830	$.1401 \times 10^{-15}$	100.0000	.1767
Iris Virginica	0.0[b]	.1311	100.0000	$.1013 \times 10^{-34}$	.1767	100.0000

[a]The table is read as follows: The means of the row group lie closer to the means of the column group than X% of the column group's observations.
[b]Less than 10^{-76}.

in which group each sample observation belongs. However, in the applied literature, numerous examples occur that violate these assumptions or that exhibit related problems with the groups that limit the practical usefulness of the classification results.

Perhaps the most extreme case of a problem with the definition of the groups occurs when an inherently continuous variable is arbitrarily segmented and used as a basis to form groups. Several examples of this method of forming groups can be found in the applied literature. Walter (1959), for example, attempts to discriminate between large industrial corporations with high and low earnings–price ratios. He arbitrarily divides firms into quartiles based upon the distribution of their earnings–price ratios and then uses discriminant analysis to distinguish between those firms in only the first and fourth quartiles ("low" and "high" earnings–price ratios). Shick and Verbrugge (1975) use a similar approach to segment banks with high and low P/E ratios. Banks with a ratio .5 standard deviation above the mean are assigned to the "high" P/E group and those with a ratio .5 standard deviation below the mean are assigned to the "low" P/E group.[25]

There are four basic problems with the use of this type of criterion to form groups. First, the groups are arbitrary and are not truly distinct. There is no theory to suggest that quartiles or standard deviations (or functions thereof) delineate relevant groups or that the independent variables are related to groups formed using such criteria. There is certainly nothing magical about the use of quartiles as distinct from, for example, deciles as a grouping criterion, and hence, it is not clear how many groups should be formed. In fact, there are an infinite number of different grouping critera that could be specified to form groups on the basis of segmenting a continuous variable. Furthermore, an infinite number of different sets of groups could be specified using a given criterion, and a particular observation could be a member of each of several groups. Hence, neither the groups nor group membership are really distinct. Second, in forming the classification scheme, both Walter (1959) and Shick and Verbrugge (1975) do not include all of the groups. Walter (1959) leaves out firms in the second and third quartiles and Shick and Verbrugge (1975) drop banks whose P/E's were within .5 standard deviation of the mean. As a result, the estimated classification rules in Walter's study, for example, can only make comparisons of whether a given observation appears more like a first or fourth quartile firm and must classify firms accordingly. The possibility of a firm actually belonging to, or having a higher probability of being a member of, the second or third quartile groups is not considered by the model. Firms drawn from that portion of the population would be forced into the first or fourth quartiles. Third, any attempt to assess expected error rates for the two-group model using either samples drawn from only the first and fourth quartiles, or alternatively, drawing samples from the entire population (i.e., firms whose E/P ratios are distributed across all four quartiles) will result in classification errors, since firms from the second and third quartiles will be assigned to the first and fourth quartiles. It thus gives biased estimates of the expected true error rates. At the very least, a four-group model should be estimated with each quartile representing a separate group; this would not, however, eliminate the other problems discussed earlier. Finally, such problems do not really lend themselves to predictive discriminant analysis. They involve forming groups on the basis of a variable or factor that is, in fact, observable at the same time the "independent" or "explanatory" variables are. For example, if one observes a firm's level of profits, it can be assigned to the proper quartile without reference to the other variables. Hence, there is no need to use other variables to predict in which quartile the criterion variable should be expected to lie.

As a practical matter, the only time it really makes sense to form groups based upon the distribution of a continuous-type variable is if natural breaks or discontinuities appear. Otherwise, segmenting an inherently continuous variable effectively discards information about the relationships between the independent (or explanatory) variables and the grouping criterion variable that might more appropriately be captured in a regression, logit or other causal model. In most instances there are good alternative model specifications for such problems.[26]

This problem of omitting groups or portions of populations has occurred to a greater or lesser degree in other studies, such as Altman (1968) and Edmister (1972), who only look at relatively small firms. Joy and Tollefson (1975) have given particular attention to this problem. They emphasize that in order to obtain useful and interpretable results, particularly with respect to classification, it is important that the populations sampled to estimate discriminant functions and classification error rates correspond to the populations generating the new observation to which the model is to be applied. Divergence between the two population sets has been a common failing with certain types of applications. For example, in the development of credit scoring systems, the objective is usually to develop models to discriminate between those *new* loan applicants who are, and are not, likely to default on their loans. Characteristically, however, loan performance data with which to estimate the discriminant function are not available on the population of *all* applicants, but rather on only the subset of applicants who were previously granted loans. Omitted are data on that portion of the population that applied for loans but did not receive them. Some of these loans may or may not have defaulted. Technically, a model constructed in such a fashion should not be applied to new loans that are drawn from a broader population. Rather, a more appropriate use is as an internal loan review device since it was developed from and the estimates of error rates are applicable to the population of loans that were granted. The practitioner should keep in mind that the estimates of the error rates do not apply to new loan applicants. It has been argued by Eisenbeis (1977) that if one is willing to assume (1) that the initial loan review process screened out the "bad" loan tail of the distribution of potential default loans and (2) relatively few of the good loans have been eliminated, it is likely that the resultant or screened populations of good and bad loans would have (1) closer centroids and (2) probably greater overlap than the true population. Hence, the estimated error rates from the "screened" populations are likely to represent conservative estimates of the true error rates. This conclusion, however, may not be correct. Avery (1977) has investigated the effects of using truncated samples from normal populations to estimate population parameters and classification error rates. As might be expected, he found that use of truncated samples resulted in biased estimates of the group means and covariances. One might even reject the hypothesis of the equality of the group covariance matrices and employ quadratic classification procedures when the true group covariances were in fact equal. Use of truncated samples also leads to biased estimates of the true error rates and the true cutoff point in the model. Avery (1977) shows that the size and direction of the bias depend upon the original truncation points of the samples, which he argues are usually not known. Thus, without knowledge of the method by which samples may have been truncated, it is not possible to make inferences about the bias that may be associated with a given system.

Closely related to the problem of omitting groups or portions of populations in constructing classification schemes are situations where the researcher has a new observation to classify and may be unsure whether it arose from any of the groups used in constructing the model. The problem occurs frequently in anthropology when a fossil is discovered and one wants to decide whether it belongs to one of a number of known groups of fossils or whether it is representative of an as yet unknown group. In Walter's study, the problem would be to decide whether a new sample firm belonged to either the first or fourth quartile groups used to construct the model or whether it may have been drawn from the second or third quartile group, which had been omitted.

No general procedures for this problem have been developed as yet. However, Rao (1965) proposes a chi-square test for the case when the observation is assumed to have arisen from a population collinear with known groups having known parameters and equal covariances.[27] McDonald, Lowe, Smidt, and Meister (1976) extend Rao's test for the case with unknown parameters and small samples.[28]

Another type of group identification problen can be found in the paper by Adelman and Morris (1968). They arbitrarily grouped countries into three groups according to their prospects for economic development. Eight criteria were used to construct the groups and then discriminant functions were estimated using some of these same grouping variables as independent variables. The original samples were reclassified and group assignments were made based upon that classification. Then a second discriminant analysis was performed. Not surprisingly, the final results appeared quite impressive. Of course, the authors were not really performing a discriminant analysis, but rather were employing a crude form of cluster analysis to group the countries based upon their similarities. Again, the original groups were formed essentially arbitrarily, and group membership was not unique. Observations were reassigned, and the final groups were redefined based upon the initial discriminant analysis and classification.

A final grouping problem that is common in business and finance relates to the use of arbitrarily defined groups where the original group definitions were made by someone other than the researcher. This is a feature of studies by Pogue and Soldofsky (1969), Pinches and Mingo (1973), Carleton and Lerner (1969), and Altman and Katz (1975), who all looked at bond ratings. Bank examiner capital adequacy ratings were investigated by Dince and Fortson (1972), and problem bank groups were studied by Stuhr and Van Wicklen (1974) and Sinkey (1975). In all these studies, the group definitions appeared discrete as far as the researcher was concerned. But because the groups were taken as given only masks the fact that someone else had already made what may have been an arbitrary grouping decision. The possibility still exists that the original assignments may have been in error. In such cases, the best that the researcher could hope to do is to replicate or simulate the original grouping decision. Use of such grouping schemes introduces an additional source of error into the assessment of classification error rates. That is, one can never be sure whether observations have been misclassified because of overlaps among the groups or because of errors in the original assignment by an examiner, bond rater, etc. Moreover, if one is interested in the "true" model, such assignment errors can bias the sample discriminant functions and estimated probabilities of misclassification.

Lachenbruch (1966) and McLachlan (1972, 1977) have investigated the effects that certain assignment errors have on classification errors. They conclude that for the equal covariance, two-group case, when each of the group assignment errors are random and equal, there is little or no effect on the estimated classification errors. Furthermore, as long as the assignment errors are (1) small or (2) symmetric and not too different from each other, there will not be a significant effect on the estimated error rates for both large and small samples. More recently, Lachenbruch (1979) has investigated the effects of random assignment errors when a quadratic function is used. Unlike the linear case, initial misclassifications have important and serious impacts and can bias the individual expected group error rates. The degree of bias introduced depends upon both the differences in the group covariances and the initial assignment errors.

Because the assumption of random assignment errors is not particularly realistic, Lachenbruch (1974) has also investigated two models with nonrandom assignment errors. As might be expected, the estimated error rates using the more common methods are biased and unreliable.

THE RELATIVE SIGNIFICANCE OF INDIVIDUAL VARIABLES

In the applied literature, one of the most widely misunderstood aspects of discriminant analysis relates to the problem of determining the relative importance or contribution of individual variables to the analysis. Unlike the case with the classical linear regression model, where the normal equations define a unique set of coefficients as a solution, discriminant function coefficients are not uniquely defined; only their ratios are.[29] Therefore, it makes little sense to attempt to test whether a particular coefficient is equal to some nonzero value in a manner analogous to the tests for the significance of coefficients in regression analysis. That is, there are no tests for the absolute value of a particular discriminant coefficient. Moreover, once the analysis is extended beyond two groups to the case of k groups, there is an added problem because there is more than one coefficient for a given variable. There are the coefficients associated with the classification rules and there are the coefficients of the $(k - 1)$ eigenvectors defining the $k - 1$ dimension of difference between the groups.

It is this aspect of discriminant analysis—the difficulty of isolating and testing behavioral hypotheses about the role of individual variables in a model—that is probably more upsetting to economists than to those more interested in data analysis. It seems to be the nature of the hypotheses in economics and finance that they require the influence of specific variables to be isolated and quantified in a cardinal sense.

Regression models, as well as some of the others discussed in Chapters I and II, are better suited for such problems, since they allow tests of hypotheses about whether certain variables are, *ceteris paribus*, significantly different from specific values. On the other hand, very few problems give rise to hypotheses about the ratios of coefficients that are unique in discriminant analysis.[30]

As is discussed in Chapter IV, the passage of the Equal Credit Opportunity Act and the promulgation of the Federal Reserve's Regulation B makes it increasingly important for legal reasons to be able to isolate the role and importance of individual variables in credit scoring models, especially since many of these models employ discriminant analysis. In the absence of tests for individual discriminant function coefficients, the problem becomes one of defining a metric or specifying a criterion against which to assess the "importance" of a variable. Various conditioning methods have been developed to measure the contribution of variables to the various F-statistics that are used to test for the significance of the difference between group means. Other researchers have focused on the role of specific variables in classification. Each method appears to use a slightly different criterion to measure and assess a variable's "importance," and thus the selection of one method over the other should be gauged against the requirements of the specific problem under investigation.

A number of different criteria for evaluating the contribution of individual variables have been proposed.[31] Among these are ranking of variables on the basis of (1) their univariate F-statistics, (2) their discriminant function coefficients weighted by the square roots of the diagonal elements in the pooled within-groups covariance (or deviation sums of squares) matrix, (3) stepwise forward selection methods giving conditional contribution to the multivariate F-statistics, (4) stepwise backward methods as in (3), (5) a conditional deletion method that removes each variable in turn from the m-variable set, with replacement, (6) a method of Mosteller and Wallace (1963) that weights the two-group discriminant function coefficients by the difference in the group means divided by the difference in the mean discriminant scores,[32] and (7) the expected probabilities of misclassification. (See Table III.3 for a description of these methods.[33])

Several relevant points should be made about these ranking methods. First, the ranking method (6) proposed by Mosteller and Wallace (1963), which measures the gross contribution of a variable to the overall Mahalanobis D^2 as a percentage of D^2, has little to recommend it. The weights are difficult to interpret because they (a) are signed (e.g., plus or minus), (b) can be greater than one, and (c) do not sum to one.[34] Moreover, the method is not readily generalizable to more than two groups.

Table III.3. Criteria for Determining the Importance of Variables

Method	*Metric*	*Description of Conditioning Procedure*	*References*
1. Univariate *F*-statistic	$F_j = (1 - \Lambda_j)\left(\sum_g N_g - k\right)/\Lambda_j(k - 1)$ $\Lambda_j = (W_{jj})/(T_{jj})$	Variables ranked on the basis of F_j. The lower its significance level, the greater is the univariate power of the variable. Method assumes that variables are independent	Eisenbeis and Avery (1972); Eisenbeis, Gilbert, and Avery (1973); Weiner and Dunn (1966)
2. Scaled discriminant function coefficients	$b_j\,(W_{jj})^{1/2}$	For the two-group case, the *j*th coefficient is weighted by the square root of the pooled within-groups covariance matrix or the deviation sums-of-squares matrix. The larger the absolute value of the coefficient, the greater is the power of the variable. Method assumes independence, or nearly so; and can not be readily generalized to more than two groups. See Eisenbeis and Avery (1972) for an heuristic generalization	Weiner and Dunn (1966); Eisenbeis, Gilbert, and Avery (1973)

Table III.3. (Continued)

Method	*Metric*	*Description of Conditioning Procedure*	*References*
3. Stepwise forward method	For the ith variable in the jth size subset $F_{\Lambda_i(j\|j-1)} = \frac{1-\Lambda_i(j\|j-1)}{\Lambda_i(j\|j-1)} \cdot \frac{\sum_g N_g - j + 1 + k}{k-1}$ where $\Lambda_i(j\|j-1)$ is the conditional Wilks' lambda for the jth size subset consisting of variable i and those variables in the previously selected $j-1$ subset. $\Lambda_i(j\|j-1) = \frac{\Lambda_i(j)}{\Lambda_i(j-1)}$ where $\Lambda_i(j-1)$ is the Wilks' lambda for the $j-1$ subset and $\Lambda_i(j)$ is the Wilks' lambda for the jth subset consisting of variable i and those variables in the previously selected $j -$ subset.	Variables are added sequentially. The first variable selected is the variable with the highest univariate F-statistic. The best two-variable set is chosen such that it contains the best univariate variable as one of the two variables included. The process is continuous with the relative importance of variables determined by their order of entry	Weiner and Dunn (1966); Eisenbeis, Gilbert, and Avery (1973) See Chapter II eq. 2.57 p. 95
4. Stepwise backward method	For the ith variable at the jth level $F_{\Lambda_i(j-1\|j)} = \frac{1-\Lambda_i(j-1\|j)}{\Lambda_i(j-1\|j)} \cdot \frac{\sum_g N_g - j + 2 - k}{k-1}$ where $\Lambda_i(j-1\|j)$ is the conditional Wilks' lambda for the $j-1$ subset with the ith variable deleted from the jth subset. $\Lambda_i(j-1\|j) = \frac{\Lambda(j-1)}{\Lambda(j)}$ where $\Lambda(j)$ is the Wilks' lambda for the jth subset and $\Lambda(j-1)$ is the Wilks' lambda with the ith variable deleted from the jth subset.	Variables are deleted sequentially from the m-variable set beginning with the variable that reduces the F-statistic the least; this is the least important variable. Given that the least important variable is deleted, the second least important variable	Eisenbeis, Gilbert, and Avery (1973) See Chapter II eq. 2.57 p. 95

		is deleted from the remaining $(m - 1)$ variables. Variables are ranked in reverse order of their removal	
5. Conditional deletion method	For the ith variable $$F_{\Lambda_i(m-1\|m)} = \frac{1 - \Lambda_i(m - 1\|m)}{\Lambda_i(m - 1\|m)} \cdot \frac{\sum_g N_g - m + 2 - k}{k - 1}$$ where $\Lambda_i(m - 1\|m)$ is the Wilks' lambda for the $m - 1$ subset formed after deleting the ith variable from the m variable set. $$\Lambda_i(m - 1\|m) = \frac{\Lambda(m - 1)}{\Lambda(m)} \text{ where } \Lambda(m) \text{ is}$$ the total Wilks' lambda and $\Lambda(m - 1)$ is the Wilks' lambda for the $m - 1$ level subset excluding variable i.	Variables are deleted in turn from the m-variable set and the reduction in the resulting $(m - 1)$ F-statistic is examined. The variable reducing the F-statistic the most is the most significant variable; the variable reducing the F-statistic the least is the least significant variable	Eisenbeis and Avery (1972); Eisenbeis, Gilbert, and Avery (1973); Bartlett (1939); Kshirsager (1972) See Chapter II eq. 2.57 p. 95
6. Mosteller and Wallace weighted coefficients for two groups	$$\frac{b_i(\bar{X}_1 - \bar{X}_2)}{(\bar{X}_1 - \bar{X}_2)'B}$$	Weighted coefficients represents the relative contribution of a variable to the Mahalanobis distance between group means	Mosteller and Wallace (1963); Joy and Tollefson (1975)
7a. Error rates	For two groups $P = Q(-1/2\sqrt{D^2})$ where D^2 is Mahalanobis D^2 and Q is cumulative normal density function	For two groups, the metric is equivalent to simply working with the metric D^2. Thus, conditioning methods described in 3, 4, or 5 above can be used	Urbakh (1971); Habbema and Hermans (1977)

Table III.3. (Continued)

Method	*Metric*	*Description of Conditioning Procedure*	*References*
7b. Error rates	$G^{-1}(\alpha) = \frac{Q(D,p) - Q(D_j,p_j)}{(D,D_j)}$ $G^{-1}(\alpha)$ = value of inverse normal distribution $Q(D)$ = estimated conditional risk (ecr) for full variable set $Q(Dj)$ = ecr for variable subset j $\sigma(D,D_j) = \{v(D) + v(D_j) - 2\}. \frac{D_j g(-1/2\ D) v(D_j)}{D g(-1/2 \cdot D_j)}$ $v(D) = \{g(-1/2 \cdot D)\}^2(1/4n_1 + 1/4n_2 + D^2/8N)$ $N = n_1 + n_2 - 2$ g = normal density function D = Mahalanobis D^2 for full variable set D_j = Mahalanobis D^2 for variable set; n_i = sample size of group i	Any of the conditioning methods in 3–5 above can be used	McLachlan (1976)

Second, methods (2), (3), and (4) all employ essentially the same metric—the conditional F-statistic based upon the conditional Wilks' Λ. All take into account the correlations among the variables, but they differ in their conditioning procedure or criterion. In the case of the stepwise forward and backward methods [methods (2) and (3)], the relative contribution of a given variable is measured against an increasing (decreasing) number of variables. For example, in the stepwise forward method, the second variable to enter is the second most important variable, given that the best univariate variable is already included. Similarly, the third variable to enter is the most important variable, given that the first two have already been included. Once a variable is included in a set, it always remains in all subsequent sets. The selection of additional variables is conditional on others having been included, and the method does not consider that a variable might enter and subsequently be dropped as other variables are added.

On the other hand, the backward selection method is designed to sequentially delete variables from the original set, beginning with the variable that reduces the significance of the remaining $m - 1$ variable F-statistics the least. The second variable is chosen so as to reduce the significance of the remaining $m - 2$ variables the least, given that the first variable has already been omitted, and so on. The last variable to remain is thus the most important.[35]

The conditional deletion method (4) focuses on the contribution of a specific variable to the multivariate F-statistic, given that all the other $m - 1$ variables have already been included. Because no other variables are dropped, the conditional deletion method assesses the relative importance of each variable in terms of its net contribution to the criterion statistic, assuming all of the other variables have been included, and not just its contribution (as is the case with the forward and backward methods) to selected subsets of variables.

Interestingly, Bartlett (1939) and more recently Kshirsagar (1972) show that this conditional deletion method has more than intuitive appeal. It was stated previously that whereas discriminant function coefficients are not unique, their ratios are.[36] Hence, while it is not appropriate to test whether a given coefficient is significantly different from some nonzero number, it does make sense to test whether the ratio of two coefficients is equal to α, i.e.,

$$H_0: \frac{b_i}{b_j} = \alpha$$

When $\alpha = 0$, Kshirsagar (1972) demonstrates that this is equivalent to testing whether the addition of a given variable to an $m - 1$ set significantly increases the overall discriminatory power of the set. This is also the essence of the conditional deletion method, which tests for the equality of conditional group means and ranks the *m* variables according to the discriminatory power that each variable adds to the overall set, given that the other $m - 1$ variables have already been included. Kshirsagar (1972) shows that in the two-group case, when a dichotomous independent variable is being regressed on the independent variables to take into account the computational equivalence between regression and discriminant analysis, regression coefficient *t*-tests can also be used to test this hypothesis.[37] Hence, they may be interpreted identically to the conditional deletion tests for the significance of the contribution of the variable, given that the others have been included.[38]

Third, methods (1) and (2), and to some extent (6), employ metrics that assume that the individual variables are independent. Cochran (1964) has shown, however, that seemingly insignificant or unimportant variables on a univariate basis may be very important when combined with other variables.[39] Some authors, such as Edmister (1972), Pinches and Mingo (1973), and Zumwalt (1975), in applying discriminant analysis, exclude highly correlated variables because of their belief that "multicollinearity" was harmful. Cochran's analysis, however, should not be interpreted as indicating that correlations are "harmful" or that multicollinearity biases specific significance tests.[40] Cochran focused on a variable's net (or joint) contribution to the overall discriminatory power of a set of variables by comparing its contribution to the Mahalanobis D^2 with what that contribution would be under the assumption that the variable was independent of the others in the set. He relied on the well-known result that when variables are independent, the multivariate Mahalanobis D^2 is the sum of the univariate D^2's. In cases where the population parameters are known, the "worst" situation would be that a variable would add nothing to the Mahalanobis D^2 and the "best" situation would be that the multivariate D^2 would be increased by more than the univariate D^2 of the variable under consideration.

Against this background, Cochran's results for the two-variable case indicate that any negative correlations and all extremely high positive correlations between the variables will increase the combined discriminatory power of the other variables. Moderate or low positive correlations mean that the combined power of the set will be somewhat less than the sum of the univariate D^2's, and may not be much greater in some instances than one of the univariate D^2's taken alone.[41] Thus, assessing a variable's contribution to the overall discriminatory power of a set of variables by use of its univariate Mahalanobis D^2 (or *F*-statistic) will tend to overstate the variable's contribution when its correlations with the other variables are moderately positive and will tend to understate its contribution whenever the correlations are either negative or highly positive.[42,43] In this sense, use of the univariate *F*-tests in discriminant analysis raises problems similar to those when the *t*-tests from bivariate regressions (one dependent and one independent variable) are used to make inferences about the role of variables in a multivariate regression. The results may be misleading. However, use of the conditional deletion method to measure a variable's contribution to the multivariate D^2 is not subject to these same problems, provided there is not perfect collinearity among the variable set. As is the case with multivariate regression, the basic properties of the coefficients and the overall estimates of the error rates are unaffected by the existence of, or the lack of, correlation among the variables. In this sense, Kmenta's (1971) conclusions about the importance of multicollinearity as a property of samples is directly applicable. High multicollinearity is a characteristic of samples. It implies that the estimated coefficients may be relatively unreliable in that they may have high variances. But this is irrelevant to the inferences one may draw about the importance of a variable.

Fourth, method (7) differs from the others in the sense that it employs a different metric—the estimated error rate—but not a different conditioning scheme. Urbakh (1971) expresses the probability of misclassification for the two group case as

$$P = Q(-1/2\sqrt{D^2})$$

where D^2 is the familiar Mahalanobis D^2 and Q is the cumulative normal density function. It becomes immediately plain that because the density function is monotonic and increasing in D^2, it is sufficient to focus solely on a variable's contribution to D^2.[44] Thus, in the two-group case, a ranking based on such error rates is identical to the ranking that would be found using the conditional *F*-statistic as a metric. For the two-group case, McFadden (1976) proposes a confidence coefficient criterion for measuring the significance of the change in expected error rates resulting from a change in the size of a variable set. Again, however, the criterion should yield the same ranking as methods employing the *F*-statistic.

However, Habbema and Hermans (1977) point out that for more than two groups, there is no clear relationship between the value of the *F*-statistics and estimated error rates. In general, the *F*-statistic "tends to separate well-separated populations further, instead of trying to separate badly separated populations." They propose a kernel method for direct estimation of density functions and error rates.[45] They apply the criterion for selection of subsets of variables but do not use it in connection with various algorithms to rank variables. For the reasons stated earlier, the conditional deletion method would seem to be suggested for use with this criterion.

Finally, all the metrics employed in (1)–(7) assume that the group covariance matrices are equal. In cases where the covariance matrices are unequal, Karson and Martell (1977) provide a discussion of the use of James' (1954) statistic which can be used with samples in place of the univariate and multivariate D^2.

In summary, in the absence of what appear to be well-defined tests for the significance of individual discriminant function coefficients, a number of different metrics—including conditional F-statistics and error rates—and conditioning methods have been employed to evaluate the contribution of individual variables to the overall performance of the function. For the two-group case, use of either the F-statistics based upon Mahalanobis D^2 (or equivalent statistics) or the overall error rate as a metric will yield the same results. For more than two groups, the contribution of variables to the D^2 will not necessarily indicate their relative importance in classification. Thus choice of the metric depends on whether the primary interest is in the importance of variables in separating group centroids or in classification. In terms of the conditioning methods, the conditional deletion method, which assesses the net contribution of a variable, given that the effects of all the other variables have already been taken into account, seems likely to be most consistent with the objectives most researchers will have in examining the relative importance of variables. For this reason, it would seem to be the preferred method. Finally, despite the concerns of many, multicollinearity poses no special problems for discriminant analysis. The basic properties of the coefficients (in terms of being unbiased) and of the overall function are unaffected. The precision of the estimates of the coefficients may be reduced, but since the coefficients are not unique, this would seem to pose even less of a problem than in regression analysis.

REDUCTION OF DIMENSIONALITY AND ELIMINATION OF INSIGNIFICANT VARIABLES

Closely related to the problem of evaluating the role of individual variables in discriminant analysis is that of dimension reduction. The two principal ways for reducing dimensionality are to eliminate (1) those variables or (2) those discriminant functions (in the reduced space k-group case) that do not contribute significantly to the overall ability to discriminate among groups.

Assessment of the appropriateness of alternative dimension-reducing procedures rests upon a knowledge of the metrics and conditioning methods involved and an understanding of how the reducing procedures chosen relate to the overall research objective. This can be particularly important for problems in business, economics, and finance, where there has been a tendency for some researchers to skip the process of developing a theoretical model to generate the variables for analysis and the hypotheses about their relative importance. Instead, they sometimes employ an embarrassingly large number of variables and data from which purely statistical variable reduction procedures are permitted to suggest which variables should be in the final model.

This would clearly seem to be an inappropriate research methodology. Indeed, Roy (1958), in one of the first papers on the use of stepwise conditioning procedures, makes the point that the conditional tests are based upon the formulation of nested sets of linear hypotheses. He argues that the procedures should only be employed "when the variates can be arranged on *a priori* grounds." Stevens (1973) also indicates that there should be some theoretical rationale to dictate such an ordering.

Pure search techniques for reducing the size of a variable set may be justified in certain problem areas. For example, in medical diagnostic problems, the objective may be to identify a disease from its symptoms. Or in taxonomy or anthropology, individuals are to be classified by their characteristics. In such cases, the statistical problems are basically in data description and there is no intent to infer causality. In fact, in diagnostic problems, the direction of causality is reversed. The predictor symptoms (or independent variables) are the result of, or are caused by, the disease, which is the event to be predicted. As Weiner and Dunn (1966) note, the high cost of obtaining patients relative to the cost of obtaining measurements, the extent of known interrelationships among factors, and often the lack of hypotheses at the outset of the research in medicine can lead to the generation of a large number of variables, many of which can later be ignored. Pure data description problems are not as common in economics and finance. Thus it can be concluded that variable reduction techniques are not to be used as a substitute for theory or to derive underlying causal relationships or models. With these caveats, we now turn to discussion of the specific dimension-reducing techniques that are often employed.

Variable Selection Methods

Most of the methods for reducing the number of variables relevant for discrimination have focused on determining whether a given variable or subset of variables contributed significantly to Wilks' lambda—

or related statistics—used in testing for differences in group means.[46,47] The methods all have three characteristics in common: (1) a metric—usually an *F*-statistic or conditional *F*-statistic,[48] (2) a conditioning method or searching algorithm, and (3) a stopping criterion for determining how large a subset is required.

Use of the statistics employed to test for the equality of group means as metrics is appropriate if the research goal is to maximize the separation among group means using the minimum number of variables. If, however, the aim is to construct a classification scheme, then use of the aforementioned metrics may not leave the classification results unaffected, even if seemingly insignificant variables are omitted. As Habbema and Hermans (1977) point out, except for the two-group case a more significant *F*-statistic may not indicate better classification performance. Eisenbeis and Avery (1973) have examined in a heuristic manner the relationship between the significance tests for the equality of group means and the problem of investigating group overlap, which is relevant for classification purposes.[49] They argue that the existence of statistically significant differences among group means, especially when the sample sizes are large, does not convey much, if any, useful information about the ability to construct a successful classification scheme. Following Cooley and Lohnes (1962), they suggest that chi-square methods of describing group overlaps (which can be adjusted for unequal covariances) could be used as metrics to make inferences about probable classification performance.[50] Thus, it would seem that choice of a metric for variable selection should be rooted in the research objective—either classification or distinguishing among group means.

Having selected a metric, the problem then becomes one of searching among the variables to find the subset that yields the best value of the metric, e.g., maximizes the *F*-statistic or minimizes the error rates. Clearly, as McCabe (1975) indicates, the optimal search procedure would be to evaluate all possible subsets of a given size. Even for variable sets as small as 15–20 variates, however, the computational time required can be prohibitively expensive. Thus, it has become common to search for other algorithms that may not necessarily yield the optimal or the best set but that economize on computation and provide at least acceptable results.[51] Hence, the stepwise forward, backward, and other conditioning methods used to determine the relative importance of variables have also been employed to select variable subsets.

Eisenbeis, Gilbert, and Avery (1973) have described and compared six such methods employing the algorithms 1–5 in Table III.3, plus a completely exhaustive technique as well. The methods were illustrated using data from a 15-variable, two-group study by Gilbert (1974) of potential competition in banking. The example clearly shows how the different conditioning methods and metrics could yield different subsets and different classification performance. Moreover, it also illustrates how statistically insignificant variables on a univariate basis could both improve the separation between the group centroids and improve the classification results.

Once a metric and a conditioning method have been selected, the final problem is to decide what size subset should be chosen. When employing the F-statistics based on the conditional Wilk's lambda described in Chapter II, Eqs. 2.57–2.59, it is possible to test for the significance of the remaining variables, given that the first j variables have been taken into account. Assuming that there are m variables in the set and following Rao (1952) and Anderson (1958), the conditional Wilks' lambda may be expressed as

$$\Lambda^{(j)} = |W^{(j)} \div T^{(j)}|$$
$$= \frac{|W_{mm}| \div |T_{mm}|}{|W_{jj}| \div |T_{jj}|}$$

where W and T are the pooled within-groups deviation sums of squares matrix and total deviation sums of squares matrix. It can be seen that in the latter expression, the numerator is the Wilk's lambda for the total m-variable set, whereas the denominator is the Wilk's lambda for the first j variables alone. The advantage of this formulation is that it can be used to compare any subsets.

The percentage significance levels of the associated F-statistics for different size subsets $j = 1, \ldots, m$ indicate the reduction in discriminating power for each subset j.[52] Relatively little work has been done to indicate what percentage significance level of the conditional F-statistic could be used in order to be sure that little information will be lost by leaving variables out. However, Eisenbeis, Gilbert, and Avery (1973) state that the choice depends upon the conditioning method being used and the costs associated with the number of subsets to be evaluated. In this respect, the completely exhaustive method is the most expensive, whereas the univariate F-test and weighted coefficient methods are cheap. Eisenbeis et al. (1973) suggest that significance levels in the high 90s can serve as "targets at which little information is likely to be lost."

When expected error rates are used as the metric for variable selection, McLachlan (1976) provides a method for calculating a confidence level at which the error rate is not increased upon deletion of a variable or set of variables.[53] Unfortunately, the method is only applicable to the two-group case as yet. But for that case, it can be shown that there is a one-to-one correspondence between a variable's contribution to Wilk's lambda and its effect on expected error rates.

Elimination of Discriminant Functions

In the k-group linear case, it is possible to transform the original m-variable problem to, at most, a $(k - 1)$-variable problem. Each of the new $k - 1$ variables is a linear transformation of the original m variables. The transformations are the eigenvectors associated with the eigenvalues found as the solution to the determinantal equation

$$|B - \lambda W| = 0$$

Where B is the between-groups deviation sums of squares matrix and W is the pooled within-groups deviation sums of squares matrix. The relative sizes of the eigenvalues indicate the relative proportion of the total sample variance accounted for by each dimension. Furthermore, since Wilks' lambda can be expressed as a direct function of these $(k - 1)$ eigenvalues (e.g., $\Lambda = \Pi_{k-1}\ 1/(1 + \lambda_i)$), it is reasonable to ask if all of the $(k - 1)$ dimensions contribute significantly to the differences between the group centroids. Rao (1952) discusses an approximate conditional chi-square test for the importance of an eigenvalue (and hence eigenvector or discriminant function), but such tests should be used with caution. It can be shown that excluding even an insignificant dimension can affect the classification results.

Eisenbeis and Avery (1972) compare the classification results using one of two discriminant functions based upon a three-group, 12-variable, security analysis problem originally studied by Smith (1965). The analysis of the significance of the roots is shown in Table III.4 and the one and two linear discriminant function classification results are shown in Table III.5. The data clearly indicate that although the second root is statistically insignificant according to the usual standards, the omission of the second dimension significantly affects the classification results in two ways.

Table III.4. Significance of the Roots in the Security Analysis Problem

Root Number	*Value of Root*	*Percentage of Total Variance Accounted for by Root*	*Value of Chi-Square Statistic*	*Degrees of Freedom*	*Significance Level (%)*
1	3.945974	83.462	40.76363	13	0.010407
2	0.7818336	16.537	14.72933	11	19.520000

Table III.5. Comparison of One- and Two-Dimensional Linear Classification Results—Security Analysis Problem

Actual Groups		*Predicted Groups*[a,b]					
		One Eigenvector Used			*Two Eigenvectors Used*		
Group	*Total*	*Investment Group*	*Trading Group*	*Speculative Group*	*Investment Group*	*Trading Group*	*Speculative Group*
Investment	11 (100.000)	7 (63.636)	4 (36.364)	0 (0.000)	11 (100.000)	0 (0.000)	0 (0.000)
Trading	11 (100.000)	1 (9.091)	10 (90.909)	0 (0.000)	0 (0.000)	9 (81.818)	2 (18.162)
Speculative	11 (100.000)	0 (0.000)	0 (0.000)	11 (100.000)	0 (0.000)	2 (18.182)	9 (81.818)

[a]Percentages are shown in parentheses.
[b]Equal *a priori* probabilities were assumed.

First, the overall accuracy fell off from 87.9 to 84.8 percent. Even more importantly, there were significant changes in the individual group error rates. Thus, if classification is a primary goal, dropping even an insignificant dimension or variable may be undesirable. Habbema and Hermans (1977) have made the point that a variable's contribution to the multivariate F-statistic may not, in the k group case, be a good indicator of its role in classification. The same conclusion must necessarily hold for individual discriminant functions for the linear reduced-space case.

SPECIFICATION OF CLASSIFICATION SCHEMES

Usually one of the main reasons for performing a discriminant analysis is to construct a classification scheme. When the population means, covariances, and *a priori* probabilities (and perhaps costs of misclassification) are known, it is a straightforward process to construct rules that will minimize expected error rates. However, when these parameters are unknown and estimated from samples, one is interested in how well the rules formed with sample parameter estimates might be expected to perform on random samples from the group populations. Performance depends critically on the choice of *a priori* probabilities and costs of errors. In addition, assessment of that performance may be influenced by the methods used to estimate the expected errors. These problems are explored in the remainder of this section.

The Selection of the Appropriate A Priori Probabilities and Costs

The standard discriminant analysis classification rules incorporate *a priori* probabilities to account for the relative occurrence of observations in different populations and misclassification costs to adjust for the fact that some classification errors may be more serious (e.g., costly) than others. The importance of the *a priori* probabilities and/or costs of misclassification have been grossly overlooked, partly due to the lack of computer programs that easily incorporate them into the rules. Lest too much be made of this point, we want to state that any program that accommodates *a priori* probabilities can easily accommodate error costs as well.

It is not uncommon for many applied studies to employ the techniques without using random samples from the populations or without making any mention of what *a priori* probabilities are used. Many others simply assert that equal *a priori* probability and costs were assumed, with no apparent thought as to how this might affect classification performance.

It can be easily shown by example that unless the groups are truly equally likely, the estimated error rates assuming equal *priors* might bear little relationship to what the true error rates are in the population. Consider the example in Table III.6 which is taken from a recent business loan study and which shows six-group quadratic classification results using both equal *a priori* probabilities and sample proportions as the estimated population *a priori* probabilities.[54] The overall expected probability of misclassification was 51.1 percent for the equal *a priori* probability case as compared with 45.5 percent for the unequal *a priori* probability case. More important, however, than the overall improvement between the unequal and equal *a priori* cases was the fact that some of the individual group error rates shifted radically. For example, 88 percent of group 2 were correctly assigned assuming equal *priors* whereas 100 percent were misclassified in the unequal *priors* case. This illustrates that one can be drastically misled about the effectiveness of a classification scheme if the correct *priors* are not employed.

In the absence of knowledge of the population *priors*, it has become common practice to use sample proportions as estimates. This is appropriate, provided the pooled data would represent a random sample from the combined group populations. Otherwise, of course, the resulting classifications would only minimize the classification errors in the sample rather than provide estimates of the population error rates. It is for this reason, for example, that Meyer and Pifer (1970), in their study of bank failures (which had equal sample sizes), found that an equal *a priori* rule minimized their classification errors. They simply discovered that they had equal numbers of observations in each sample.

Using independent estimates of the population *priors* relieves the researcher of the burden of worrying that the pooled sample over all the groups represents a random sample from the combined population. It does not, however, relieve the researcher of the problem of assuming that the samples are representative of the groups being investigated. Alternative sampling methods such as the paired methods of Meyer and Pifer (1970) or Sinkey (1975) are representative of nonrandom schemes that have been used. Nonrandom methods, which attempt to control for certain factors [such as bank size, regulatory status, number of branches, and location in the study by Sinkey (1975)], may be appropriate for investigating the importance of certain variables but not for estimating classification error rates. To the extent that the control variables are not independent of the other included variables, one would expect the covariances and group means in the control sample to be different from a random sample drawn from the population. If this is true, then the resulting classification rules would be biased, and even

Table III.6. Equal and Unequal *A Priori* Quadratic Classification Results—Business Loan Study

Actual Group Number	Total	Equal *A Priori* Probability Results: Predicted Groups[a] 1	2	3	4	5	6	Unequal *A Priori* Probability Results: Predicted Groups[a] 1	2	3	4	5	6	Estimated *A Priori* Probabilities
1	73 (100.00)	72 (98.63)					1 (1.37)	70 (95.89)					3 (4.11)	.04
2	125 (100.00)		110 (88.00)		5 (4.00)		10 (8.00)				125 (100.00)			.07
3	81 (100.00)	17 (20.99)		46 (56.79)			18 (22.22)	14 (17.28)		46 (56.79)			21 (25.93)	.05
4	676 (100.00)		213 (31.51)		73 (10.80)	390 (57.69)					263 (38.91)	413 (61.09)		.38
5	699 (100.00)		111 (15.88)		59 (8.44)	529 (75.63)			2 (.29)		138 (19.74)	559 (79.97)		.39
6	115 (100.00)	33 (28.70)	12 (10.43)	25 (21.74)	9 (7.83)		36 (31.30)	32 (27.83)		21 (18.26)	29 (25.21)		33 (28.70)	.07

[a]Percentages are shown in parentheses.

use of appropriate *priors* would not yield valid estimates of the population error rates. An alternative method for such a study would have been to draw random samples from both groups, include the control variables as the *j* variables in the conditional Wilk's lambda statistics shown previously, and then examine the conditional significance of the other variables.

Little or no attempt has been made to date explicitly to incorporate costs into the applied models. Dince and Fortson (1972) attempted to rationalize *ex post* their use of a zero cutoff point based upon a poll of bank supervisors from whom they obtained subjective cost estimates that approximately balanced their *a priori* probability estimates.[55] Both Sinkey (1975) in his study of problem banks and Meyer and Pifer (1970) in developing their model of bank failure discuss the development of rules that would maximize the returns from applying their screening models. However, these discussions are only general in nature. Moreover, in neither study did they attempt explicitly to specify or estimate the model they proposed, nor did they apply it in the empirical portion of this paper. More recently, Altman and Eisenbeis (1978) and Joy and Tollefson (1975) discuss the effect of both the estimation of *a priori* probabilities and the costs of errors on the assessment of the performance of the bankruptcy model of Altman (1968). Both proposed crude estimates of the *a priori* probabilities but neither directly attempted to estimate population parameters or costs. Harter (1973), in his scoring model for mortgage loans, considers both the opportunity cost (in terms of an average markup), the demand for mortgage money, collection costs, and charge-off costs per dollar of loan in determining the appropriate cutoff. He does not provide estimates of error rates, however.

The most complete discussion of error costs in the context of an applied problem has been provided by Altman (1977). He focuses on commercial bank costs in a credit scoring model, and in particular uses several techniques to estimate expected bank loss and loss-recovery experiences. Altman did not, however, consider explicitly all relevant costs he identifies nor does he apply his estimates in an actual credit scoring model. Altman, Haldeman, and Narayanan (1977), however, do incorporate estimates of both *a priori* probabilities and costs of errors in their Zeta model for bankruptcy classification.

In general, we must conclude that although the general procedures for incorporating costs of misclassification into the classification procedures have been developed, they need to be explored further in the applied literature.

Assessment of Classification Error Rates

The major purpose of employing discriminant analysis is usually to construct a classification scheme. Most often the parameters of the populations being studied are unknown and hence must be estimated from samples. A central problem then is to assess the performance of those sample rules.

It has been well publicized in the economics and finance literature, due in part to a paper by Frank, Massy, and Morrison (1965), that reclassification of the original sample used to estimate the sample rules as a means to estimate expected error rates leads to biased and overly optimistic prediction of how well the rules would perform in the population. A number of alternative methods have been suggested and evaluated for estimating classification errors.[56] These methods are basically of three types: those using samples, those using the assumption of normality, and those using jackknife procedures. These methods are described in Table III.7 and their limitations or strengths are noted. In general, most of the methods have relied upon the assumption of normality; of these, the majority have attempted to adjust for the bias in alternative estimates of the sample Mahalanobis D^2, which enters into each of the error rate estimators.

The comparative performance of these estimators has received considerable attention. Specifically, Lachenbruch and Mickey (1968), Cochran (1968), McLachlan (1974a,b,c), and Sorum (1973) have conducted fairly exhaustive Monte Carlo studies comparing the various methods.[57] Lachenbruch and Mickey (1968) review several of the methods listed in Table III.7,[58] looking at 2-, 4-, 8-, and 20-variable cases. They concluded that for large numbers of variables, the OS, and $\bar{U}$ methods perform better than the rest; for small numbers of variables, all methods perform equally well. Overall, the OS method seems the best, except for small samples, in which case the U or $\bar{U}$ methods appear to be the best. However, it should also be noted that the U, original sample, and H methods are most easily generalizable to more than two groups as well as to cases with unequal covariances.[59] In this respect, then, as well as based upon Lachenbruch and Mickey's (1968) evidence, the U method would appear to be superior, especially when coupled with its applicability to both small and large dimensional problems.[60]

Sorum (1972) also performed Monte Carlo experiments for the 2-, 4-, 8-, and 20-variable cases. He compares the performance of nine estimators of the conditional probability of misclassification (P^*), the average probability of misclassification (P^{**}), and the optimum probability of misclassification (P^{***}).[61] For both P^{**} and P^{***}, when the number of variables is small, *DS*, *B*, and O are superior to R and U. For P^{***}, when the number of variables increases to 20, *DS*, *B*, and O remain superior, whereas U and OS are better than R, *D*, Q_3, and Q_5. For P^{**} on the other hand, OS, O, *B*, and *DS* outperform the rest, with U being intermediate. For P^*, the ordering is almost the same as

Table III.7. Error Estimation Methods for Two-Group, Equal Covariances Case

Method	*Estimator*	*Properties and Other Comments*	*Reference–Source*
1. Resubstitution method-R	P_1 and P_2 are sample proportions of misclassified observations	Estimates are consistent but may be badly biased and overly optimistic for small samples in particular	Lachenbruch and Mickey (1968)
2. Holdout method-H	Samples are split with one used to estimate functions that are then employed to classify the other (or holdout) sample and estimate P_1 and P_2	Estimates are consistent and unbiased but require large samples. Intuitively, the estimates may be less efficient than other methods	Lachenbruch and Mickey (1968); Frank, Massy, and Morrison (1965)
3. Population method	When population parameters are known, i.e., $N_1(\mu_1,\Sigma)$, $N_2(\mu_2,\Sigma)$ and Δ^2 is the population Mahalanobis distance [$\Delta^2 = (\mu_1 - \mu_2)'\Sigma^{-1}(\mu_1 - \mu_2)$] used to calculate error rates	Errors are true errors in population	Lachenbruch and Mickey (1968); McLachlan (1974a,b,c)
4. D method	Estimator of Δ^2 = sample D^2 where $D^2 = (\bar{X}_1 - \bar{X}_2)' S_W^{-1} (\bar{X}_1 - \bar{X}_2)$	Estimates of D^2 are consistent but upward biased, hence error rate estimates are consistent but may also be badly biased downward, particularly for small samples	Lachenbruch and Mickey (1968); McLachlan (1974a,c)
5. D^{*2} method	Estimators of $\Delta^2 = D^{*2} = \left(\dfrac{N_1 + N_2 - 3 - p}{N_1 + N_2 - 2}\right) D^2 - \dfrac{p(N_1 + N_2)}{N_1 N_2}$	Estimates of Δ^2 are unbiased and consistent as are estimated error rates, but if N_1 and N_2 are small relative to p and D^2 is small, then D^{*2} may be negative, which precludes it use	Lachenbruch and Mickey (1968)
6. DS method	Estimator of $\Delta^2 = DS^2 = \left(\dfrac{N_1 + N_2 - p - 3}{N_1 + N_2 - 2}\right) D^2$	Estimator is consistent but slightly biased, such that error rates are slightly underestimated	Lachenbruch and Mickey (1968)

Table III.7. (Continued)

Method	*Estimator*	*Properties and Other Comments*	*References–Source*
7. O method	Estimator of conditional probabilities of misclassification $P_1 = G(-\frac{1}{2}D) + g(-\frac{1}{2}D)\{-\frac{1}{4}(p-1)/D + \frac{1}{16}D\}/N_1 + g(-\frac{1}{2}D)\{\frac{3}{4}\cdot(p-1)/D + \frac{1}{16}D\}/N_2$ Reverse notation on N_1 and N_2 for P_2	Allows separate estimates of P_1 and P_2. Where groups are close together and sample sizes are small, the method performs poorly. When D^2 is large, the O method performs similarly to D method because factors are proportional to $1/D^2$	Lachenbruch and Mickey (1968); Moran (1975)
8. OS method	Substitute DS^2 for D^2 in (7)	Allows separate estimates of P_1 and P_2. Performs better than O method	Lachenbruch and Mickey (1968)
9. *B* method	Estimator of $\Delta^2 = B^2$ $= D^2\left(\frac{4N_1(N_1-1)(N_1+N_2-p-4)}{(2N_1-1)^2(N_1+N_2-2)}\right)$ for use as estimator in P_1, reverse notation for estimator of P_2		Broffit (1969); McLachlan (1974c)
10. U method[a]	The method holds out one observation at a time, estimates the discriminant functions based upon $N_1 + N_2 - 1$ observations and classifies the holdout observation. Process is repeated until all observations are classified. The proportions of observations P_1^{**} and P_2^{**} are used as estimates of average conditional error rates. Confidence intervals around P_1^{**} and P_2^{**} are given by $\frac{2N_iP_i^{**} + Z^2 \pm [(2N_iP_i^{**} + Z^2)^2 - 4N_iP_i^{**}(N_i + Z^2)]^{1/2}}{2(N_i + Z^2)}$	Method gives almost unbiased estimates of the confidence intervals. Moreover, it may be used to get around sample size limitation of the H method. Intuitively, one would expect the method to be more efficient than the H method. Kshirsagar (1972) feels the method may not be sensitive to normality assumption	Lachenbruch (1967) McLachlin (1975)

11. Ū method	Estimator of $\Delta^2 = \frac{D^2_i}{S_i^2}$ where $D^2_i = \frac{1}{N_i}$ times sum of N_i scores from group i in (10). S_i = sample standard deviation of scores in (10)	Lachenbruch and Mickey (1968) argue that the method performs well when compared to others using normal distribution	Lachenbruch and Mickey (1968)
12. D_3 method	Estimator of $\Delta^2_i = D^2_i = D^2\left(\frac{N_1}{N_1 + 1}\right)$ reverse notation for group 2		Sorum (1972)
15. M_1 method	As in (7) $G(-D/2) - g(-D/2)[\{D/16 - (p - 1)(1/4D)\}(1/N_1 + 1/N_2) + (D/32)\{D^2 - 4(2p + 1)\}/(N_1 + N_2 - 2) + \{g(-D/2)/1024\}[D\{D^2 - 4(2p + 1)\} + (p - 1)(16/D)\{(p - 1) + (p - 3) \cdot (4/D^2)\}](1/N_1 + 1/N_2)^2 + [D^5 - 12(p + 1)D^3 + 16(2p^2 + 1)D + (p - 1)(2p - 1)(64/D)][1/N_1(N_1 + N_2 - 2) + 1/N_2(N_1 + N_2 - 2)] + (D/12)[3D^6 - 4(12p + 19)D^4 + 16(12p^2 + 24p + 7)D^2 + 192(4p^2 + 4p - 1)] + (N_1 + N_2 - 2)^2$		McLachlan (1974c)
16. M_2 method	As (7) and (15) above $G(-D/2) + g(-D/2)[\{(p - 1)/D\}/N_1 + (D/32)\{4(4p - 1) - D^2\}(N_1 + N_2 - 2)^{-2} + O_2(\text{bias})$		McLachlan (1974c)

[a]P_i^{**} = conditional probability of group membership; it is assumed that *a priori* probabilities are equal.
[b]G = normal distribution function; N_1 and N_2 are group sample sizes; g = standard normal density function; p is number of variables.

that found by Lachenbruch and Mickey (1968), with OS dominating and U in an intermediate position. In all cases, R and D perform very poorly.

Most recently McLachlan (1974b,c) proposed two other estimators, M_1 and M_2. Their performance in estimating the same three error rates, P^*, P^{**}, and P^{***} are compared with the estimators OS, U, D, DS, O, B, Q_3, and Q_5. The Asymptotic Mean Square Error (AMSE), as well as Monte Carlo experiments, are compared as performance criteria. With respect to the conditional error estimators for P^* (the probability of misclassification for an individual observation) and P^{**}, McLachlan (1974a) finds that no estimator was uniformly superior. Generally speaking, the OS and M_1 method was superior to the O, DS, and D methods. For P^{***}, McLachlan (1974c) indicates that B and DS are preferred except for small values of Mahalanobis D^2 (e.g., less than 2) where M_1, M_2, and O perform better; OS is inferior overall.

In summary, of the methods proposed to estimate error rates, those relying on the assumption of normality tended to outperform the R or U methods. On the other hand, most were not readily generalizable to more than two groups, nor were there any studies to indicate the appropriate form of these estimators when the *a priori* probabilities were unequal. The U method on the other hand does not rely on the assumption of normality, hence it is a less restrictive method. Moreover, it can be easily extended to more than two groups and can take into account unequal *a priori* probabilities. These features, plus what was generally an intermediate, but acceptable, performance based on the Monte Carlo and AMSE criteria, would seem to make it a desirable method. If one had to pick an estimator relying on the normality assumption, then the OS, DS, or B methods would be preferred; however, it should also be recognized that no one method was superior overall.

TIME-SERIES APPLICATIONS

In business, economies, and finance, many of the classification problems to which discriminant analysis has been applied involve time-series prediction. This includes such problems as failure prediction, rating bonds, and credit scoring. Here the aim is to predict an event one, two, or more periods into the future based upon data taken from a single time period or previous periods as opposed to simply predicting the likelihood of an event occurring. Since time-series prediction is not explicitly incorporated into discriminant analysis, its application to such problems raises a host of issues, almost none of which have been dealt with in the theoretical literature. Some of these problems have been briefly discussed by Joy and Tollefson (1975), Eisenbeis (1977), and Altman and Eisenbeis (1978).

The first problem relates to the form and structure of the models specified. The process by which an observation moves from one group to another over time might reasonably be expected to be a continuously evolving one. This suggests that the relationships among the relevant variables (e.g., means, variances, and covariances) change over time. Hence, the appropriate model might be different, both in terms of parameters and variable composition, for each separate time period into the future for which prediction is to be made.

A second difficulty concerns the selection and estimation of the appropriate *a priori* probabilities in time-series problems. To the extent that the relative expected occurrences of the groups in the population may vary from period to period, it is not at all obvious what the population *priors* should be or how they should be estimated. For example, in the problem bank study of Sinkey (1975), the number of problem banks has varied quite significantly from year to year-from a low of around 150 in some years to more than 349 in early 1976. Under such circumstances, it is not clear whether it is more appropriate to use the relative group frequencies from a given year as estimates of the *a priori* probabilities or to attempt to use some average of past frequencies. In the absence of theoretical guidance, it would seem that the research design and goals should determine the method to be used. Clearly, in the problem bank study, the expected frequencies of problem and nonproblem banks are not independent of the state of the economy. During unstable times, then, a simple average of past years' frequencies might tend to understate the expected frequencies of the problem group. A second aspect of this same problem arises when data from several time periods are pooled to make predictions over the same span of time periods (e.g., Altman, 1968) or over future time periods (e.g., Pinches and Mingo, 1973 or Gilbert, 1974). This is usually done when observations for one of the groups occur relatively infrequently and pooling is necessary to get a large enough sample with which to work. Again, it is not clear what the appropriate *a priori* probabilities are or how they should be estimated. In such instances, gross sample proportions are probably inappropriate. Selection and estimation of the *priors* should be geared to the type of classification statements that the researcher wishes to make. For example, if a one-period classification is to be made, then it would seem reasonable to use an average of the relative frequencies over several time periods to estimate the *priors*. On the other hand, if predictions are to be made over several time periods, such as Gilbert (1974) did, then it may be more appropriate to pool data over the same time period to estimate frequencies.

Another problem explicitly considered by Joy and Tollefson (1975) and Altman and Eisenbeis (1978) centers on the methods of validation and estimation of expected error rates. Specifically, Joy and Tollefson

(1975) argue that if data from time t are used to predict an event in time $t + 1$, then it is not sufficient to select another sample from time period t and predict and validate the model based upon the results from time period $t + 1$. Rather, they suggest that data from a future time period such as $t + 2$ should be used to predict an event in time period $t + 3$. Altman and Eisenbeis (1978) point out that "The essence of J&T's argument is that in time series type applications, a discriminant analysis model is only useful for prediction purposes if the basic underlying relationships and parameters are stable over time".[62] Otherwise, the model and estimated error rates will only be valid for the specific periods investigated. The results cannot be extrapolated beyond the original sample period with the same expected performance. Thus, unless a known process is involved, a function derived from data in one time period will be different and will yield different error rates from a function estimated over another period.[63] Moreover, the former model may not perform well on the latter period's data. Hence, even following Joy and Tollefson's suggestion and validating a model using a sample from a time period outside the original sample period will yield error estimates of questionable or only limited value unless the underlying model is stable (or stationary) over time. This discussion of the role of *ex post* classification suggests that comparison of classification results from within the sample period with those outside the same period may itself serve as a crude test for stationarity. Agreement would serve to justify making inferences about expected error rates, the predictive content of the model, and the role of individual variables.

Finally, there is another aspect of the problem of stationarity that arises in cases where pooled data are employed, such as in the Altman (1968) study.[64] In that study, data one period before failure for the failed firms were used to estimate the discriminant function. However, the failures were selected over the years 1946–1965. Hence, the sample of failed firms involved pooling of data across several time periods. However, if the basic cross-sectional relations among the means and variances are not stable over time, then pooling of data in such a manner is also inappropriate. Again, comparison of the cross-temporal and intertemporal classification results may serve as useful guides to the validity of the pooling approach and to the stationarity of the parameters of the models.[65,66]

SUMMARY AND CONCLUSIONS

In this chapter we have explored several of the more common problem areas appearing in the applied discriminant analysis literature. If we had to rank the problems according to the importance of their effects on the usefulness of the techniques, the problems related to classification would be most critical. Violation of the normality assumptions, particularly when the underlying distributions are unbounded can significantly bias the estimated error rates, or more importantly, lead to an inferior classification scheme. Perhaps even more important, however, are the issues surrounding the selection of *a priori* probabilities. In particular, the failure to relate the estimates of the *a priori* probabilities to the appropriate population *priors* limits the ability to make any meaningful inferences about the overall performance or accuracy of the classification scheme. The selection of the appropriate form of the classification rules (linear versus quadratic) depends critically upon sample characteristics.

The problems of nonnormality, the selection of a criterion for variable selection and interpreting the significance of individual variables are less easy to resolve. Until further research is done, one must simply temper the conclusions reached by recognizing that the empirical results represent approximations that may be significantly biased.

NOTES

This chapter is an expanded version of Eisenbeis (1977).

1. Most available normality tests are for univariate and not multivariate normality. For discussions and review of this literature see Shapiro, Wilk, and Chen (1968) and more recent papers by D'Agostino (1973), Shapiro and Francia (1972), and Andrews, Gnanadesikan, and Warner (1973). Mardia and Zemrock (1975) present a Fortran subroutine to calculate measures of multivariate skewness and kurtosis relevant for some of the proposed tests for multivariate normality. See Mardia (1975b) for a discussion of these tests. Pinches and Trieschmann (1974) provide an application of the tests for multivariate normality.

2. See Porebski (1966) for a discussion of the relationships among the various statistics used in multivariate analysis.

3. Mardia (1975a) reviews the one-sample studies of Arnold (1964), Chase and Bulgren (1971), and Mardia (1970), which cover the following bivariate distributions: uniform-independent, uniform-Morgenstern, double exponential-independent, negative exponential-independent, negative exponential-Marshall and Olkin. The two-sample studies of Hopkins and Clay (1963) and Mardia (1971) cover the following cases: mixed normals, negative exponential-independent, Pareto, and uniform-Plackett.

4. The likelihood ratios are of the form: $\ln[P_1(X) \div P_2(X)]$, where $P_1(X)$ and $P_2(X)$ are (in the two-group case) the multinomial densities of the variable vector X in the two populations.

5. For cases where the variables each have only two states, the log-likelihood ratio is estimated as:

$$\ln\left[\frac{n_2}{n_1} \cdot \frac{r_1 + \sum_m r_{1i}}{r_2 + \sum_m r_{2i}}\right]$$

where n_1 and n_2 are the number of observations in groups 1 and 2, respectively, r_j is the number of observations in group j that have $X = X_0$, and r_{ji} is the number of observations in group j that differ from $X = X_0$ on i number of variables.

6. Hills (1967) does generalize his results to cases where the variables in the vector X have more than two states and to more than two groups.

7. As will be discussed later, this method is not preferred.

8. All the means and correlations were restricted to be identical within most of the populations sampled in Gilbert's study.

9. The three methods evaluated by both Moore and Gilbert are the full multinomial, independent variables, and the linear discriminant function.

10. Negative correlations were less harmful than positive correlations. Note that because 0–1 binary variables are used, the variables means are all between zero and one; hence, the differences between the means must be at least 10 percentage points in this binary case.

11. This result parallels the simulations with all binary variables.

12. Logically, one should test for the equality of group covariances and for multivariate normality before testing for the equality of group means. Box (1949) presents a test for the equality of the group covariances, which is described in Chapters I and II. Neyman and Pearson (1931), Bartlett (1939), Plackett (1947), Hartley (1940), and Lehmann (1959) have also proposed tests. In general, these tests seem to be sensitive to departures from normality based upon the Monte Carlo work of Ghosh (1972), Hopkins and Clay (1963), and Mardia (1971, 1975). This has also been discussed in Pinches (1978). Samruiddin and Atiqullah (1975) present new statistics for testing the equality of variances for both normal and nonnormal populations.

13. Other tests have been proposed by Bennett (1951), Yao (1965), James (1951, 1954), and Welch (1947); the first three have been evaluated in Subrahmaniam and Subrahmaniam (1973). The method of James (1954) has been programmed and Martell and Fitts (1978) have recently applied it to problems in determining trust department usage. Lee and Gurland (1975) review the size and power of tests proposed by Fisher (1935), Banerjee (1960, 1961), Welch (1947), Pagurova (1968), Wald (1955), Welch (1949), and Aspin (1948) and their own proposed test. These results suggest that their test and that of Welsh–Aspin behave quite well.

14. Because most of their examples had equal eigenvalues, this tends to limit somewhat the generality of their conclusions.

15. r equals the minimum of m and one minus the number of groups (i.e., $k - 1$).

16. Moreover, as m increases, the reduced-space variables are more likely to be multivariate normal because of the Central Limit Theorem (Lohnes, 1961).

17. T is the total deviation sums of squares matrix and W is the pooled within-groups deviation of squares matrix. See Eisenbeis and Avery (1972).

18. Altman's (1968) study of corporate failures provides an example of the kind of data where nearly identical results can be achieved using either a linear or quadratic model (see also Altman and Eisenbeis, 1978).

19. Similar results were achieved by Michaelis (1973), Van Ness and Simpson (1976), and Van Ness (1979).

20. See Gilbert (1974, 1975), Eisenbeis and Avery (1972), Eisenbeis and McCall (1971), Bates (1973), Lane (1972), Eisenbeis and Murphy (1974), Sinkey (1975), for recent examples of the use of quadratic procedures.

21. See Cooley and Lohnes (1962) or Eisenbeis and Avery (1972) for an explanation of the derivation of these tables.

22. A similar result was found by Altman, who reestimated his original bankruptcy model using quadratic procedures, and the results were virtually identical (see Altman and Eisenbeis, 1978).

23. Note that Gilbert (1968) used only linear instead of quadratic procedures. Hence, her results reflect a mixture of problems associated with violation of both the normality assumption and the equality of covariances assumption as well.

24. For example, consider a Bernoulli variable X that takes only two values [0, 1] with the probability $P(X = 1) = p$ and $P(X = 0) = 1 - p = q$. The mean of X in group 1 is $\mu_{x1} = p_1$ and the variance is $\sigma^2_{x,1} = p_1(1 - p_1) = p_1 \cdot q_1$. For linear discriminant analysis to be appropriate in any problem including the variable X, the variance elements in the group covariance matrices for X must be equal. That is, $\sigma^2_{x,1} = \sigma^2_{x,2}$. But this will hold only if (1) the mean in group 1 equals the mean in group 2 (i.e., $p_1 = p_2$) in which case X is not an important discriminator in itself, or (2) if $q_2 = p_1$, which represents a very limiting case. See Kshirsagar (1972) for a discussion of discrimination when there are zero mean differences of which this is a special case. Conversely, if $p_1 \neq p_2$ or $p_1 \neq q_2$, then $\sigma^2_{x,1} \neq \sigma^2_{x,2}$. Therefore, if these two variance elements of the covariance matrix are unequal, then the covariance matrices $\Sigma_1 \neq \Sigma_2$, and quadratic rather than linear classification should be employed.

25. Other studies using similar procedures to arbitrarily specify groups are Klemkowsky and Petty (1970), Norgaard and Norgaard (1974), and Haslem and Longbrake (1971).

26. In fairness to Walter (1959), he does state that his discriminant analysis methodology is not meant to be a substitute for a regression analysis approach.

27. The test is of the form

$$(X - \mu_1)' \Sigma^{-1} (X - \mu_1) - \frac{[(X - \mu_1)' \Sigma^{-1} (\mu_2 - \mu_1)]^2}{(\mu_2 - \mu_1)' \Sigma^{-1} (\mu_2 - \mu_1)} \sim \chi^2_{(m-1)}$$

A value of χ^2 that is significant indicates that observation did not arise from the two known populations.

28. The test is H_0: X belongs to population 1,2

$$(X - \bar{X}_i)'S^{-1} (X - \bar{X}_i) > \frac{N_i - 1}{N_i} \cdot \frac{p(n - 2)}{n - p - 1} F^p_{n-p-1}$$

29. One way discriminant function coefficients may be derived is by maximizing the ratio of the between-groups variance to pooled within-groups variance. But because it's not possible to uniquely maximize such a ratio, the usual procedure is to maximize the between-groups variance subject to the constraint that the within-groups variance is equal to a constant, which is usually selected to be 1. That is, the variance ratio is homogeneous of degree zero; hence, the resulting coefficients are only unique up to a factor of proportionality. See Kshirsagar (1972), Rao (1965), Eisenbeis and Avery (1972), Ladd (1966), Anderson (1958), or Lachenbruch (1975) for further discussions of this point.

30. There is some confusion in the applied literature about the interpretation of the t-statistics when a dummy independent variable regression model is used, because of computational equivalence, to estimate a discriminant function. It will be shown later that the regression t-statistics can be used, but the resulting tests are of a slightly different hypothesis than in a straight regression problem. See Carleton and Lerner (1969) or Meyer and Pifer (1970) for example of the use of the dummy regression approach to calculate discriminant function coefficients and of the incorrect use of the resulting t-statistics.

31. See Cooley and Lohnes (1962, 1971), Eisenbeis and Avery (1972), Rao (1965), Joy and Tollefson (1975), Mosteller and Wallace (1963), Urbakh (1971), and McLachlan (1976) for discussions. Five of these criteria were reviewed by Eisenbeis, Gilbert, and Avery (1973); Weiner and Dunn (1966) examine four methods including (1), (2), and (3), above.

32. It represents the gross contribution of the ith variable to the Mahalanobis distance between the group means divided by that Mahalanobis distance.

33. Other metrics have been proposed. For example, Urbakh (1971) examines the conditional contribution to Mahalanobis D^2 statistic and McKay (1976) employs Hotelling's T^2 statistic. It can easily be shown that these methods are equivalent to the ones using

F-statistics, discussed above and in Table III.3, based upon Wilk's Λ. See Porebski (1966) for a discussion of the relationship among these statistics.

34. The weighted coefficient represents the contribution of the ith variable to the Mahalanobis distance between the group means. In the two-group case, where b_i is the coefficient of the ith variable, the measure of relative percentage contribution is

$$\frac{b_i(\bar{X}_{i1} - \bar{X}_{i2})}{(\bar{X}_1 - \bar{X}_2)'B}, B' = (b_1, b_2, ..., b_j).$$

35. Note that there is no reason to believe that the stepwise forward and backward methods will agree or will even result in the same variable being found to be the most important.

36. See Eisenbeis and Avery (1972) or Kshirsagar (1972) for proofs.

37. See Eisenbeis and Avery (1972), Anderson (1958), and Ladd (1966).

38. In the k-group case, the regression analog becomes the canonical correlation between $k - 1$ dummy variables corresponding to the k groups. See Bartlett (1939) and Porebski (1966).

39. Eisenbeis, Gilbert, and Avery (1973); Altman (1968) and Katz (1974) also provide further empirical evidence that seemingly unimportant variables on a univariate basis may be important discriminators in a multivariate context.

40. This is provided the correlations are not so high as to cause ill-conditioned or singular covariance matrices.

41. Elashoff, Elashoff, and Goldman (1967) show that for the case where all the variables are dichotomous, exactly the opposite conclusions hold. Small positive correlations increase discrimination, whereas negative correlations may not be helpful.

42. Cochran expands his results to several variables, but no one has studied mixtures of positively and negatively correlated variables.

43. Depending upon how one corrects for the bias in the sample estimate of D^2, it is possible for addition of a variable to actually reduce the overall power of the set, see Lachenbruch and Mickey (1968) or McLachlen (1974b).

44. He shows that the contribution of the ith variable to D^2 is β_i^2/ρ_{ii} where β_i is the coefficient of the ith variable and ρ_{ii} is the ith diagonal element in the inverse of the correlation matrix.

45. In practice, their method is very expensive because of the large number of computations required.

46. See Eisenbeis and Avery (1972), Eisenbeis, Gilbert, and Avery (1973), or Weiner and Dunn (1966) for examples of these methods.

47. These methods have all assumed equal covariances. For this reason, use of the standard F-statistics and related metrics when the group covariance matrices are unequal are subject to the same limitations and problems that apply to their use in testing for the equality of group means.

48. McHenry (1978), Roy (1958), Weiner and Dunn (1966), Stevens (1973), McCabe (1975) and McKay (1976, 1978) all employ Wilk's lambda as a metric. Murray (1977), Van Ness and Simpson (1976), and Goldstein and Robinowitz (1975) all use probabilities of correct classification or expected overall error rates as metrics. Graphical methods are discussed in McKay (1978). Goldstein and Dillion (1977) discuss a variable selection procedure for discrete variables.

49. Joy and Tollefson (1975), Frank, Massy, and Morrison (1965), and Morrison (1976), also touch on this point.

50. Using the following chi-square measure

$$\chi^2_{m,gh} = (\bar{X}_g - \bar{X}_h)' S_w^{-1} (\bar{X}_g - \bar{X}_h)$$

which is distributed with m degrees of freedom; the resultant significance level α indicates that the means of group g lie closer to the means of group h than $\alpha \cdot 100\%$ of the members of group h. If the group dispersions are equal, then the pooled within-groups dispersion matrix S_w is used in the χ^2, otherwise the individual dispersion matrix S_h is used.

51. See also McCabe (1975), Stevens (1973), McKay (1976), Van Ness and Simpson (1976), Goldstein and Robinowitz (1975), Roy (1958), McHenry (1978), and Weiner and Dunn (1966).

52. In this case, the higher the significance level, the lower is the loss in power by omitting the $m - j$ variables given the first j variables have been included.

53. The confidence level is given by

$$G^{-1}(\alpha) = \frac{Q(D_1p) - Q(D_1,P_1)}{\sigma(D, D_1)}$$

where terms are defined in Table III.3 under method 7b.

54. For illustration purposes, it is assumed that the sample proportions were the population *a priori* probabilities (see Eisenbeis and Avery, 1972).

55. The cutoff point in the linear case is equal to

$$\ln \frac{C(g|h)\pi_h}{C(h|g)\pi_g} = \ln(1) = 0$$

if the ratio of the costs $[C(g|h)/C(h|g]$ and the ratio of the *a priori* probabilities π_h/π_g are approximately offsetting.

56. See Lachenbruch (1967, 1968, 1975), Lachenbruch and Mickey (1968), Frank, Massy, and Morrison (1965), Dunn (1971), Dunn and Varady (1966), Moran (1975), Sorum (1971, 1973), Sedransk and Okamoto (1971), Hills (1966), Smith (1947), Okamoto (1963), McLachlan (1974a,b,c, 1976), and Broffit (1969).

57. Sorum (1973) and Sedransk and Okamoto (1971) looked at the univariate case only.

58. These were the O, OS, D, DS, Ū, U, and R methods.

59. Eisenbeis and Avery (1972) have programmed the U method for all cases including quadratic classification. Pinches (1978) indicates the U method is also available in the Biomedical Computer Program (BMDP O7M).

60. For an example of how sample sensitive the R method is when compared to the U method, even when relatively large samples are employed, see Eisenbeis and Murphy (1974). Their estimates of expected group error rates between the U and R methods differed from 13 to 16 percentage points.

61. The estimators were R, U, DS, OS, O, D, B of Broffit (1969), and Q_3 and Q_5 described in Sorum (1971, 1973).

62. This is not a unique problem to discriminant analysis time-series applications; it also holds with regression and other statistical models attempting to project future events based upon past experience.

63. See Lachenbruch (1975) for an example of prediction over time where the predictor variables are parameters from a time-series regression.

64. See Chapter VII for a discussion of several failure prediction models. Virtually all of these models have this time-series problem.

65. It is not clear whether the time period for the intertemporal validations sample should span as many periods as the original sample.

66. Choice of the *a priori* probabilities is also a problem in such models.

Chapter IV

Credit Scoring Applications

INTRODUCTION

Since the mid and late 1960s, credit scoring and related loan review procedures have been applied with increasing frequency by financial institutions and other creditors.[1] Chandler and Coffman (1977), for example, report that use of such systems is known to be widespread today, and Hsia (1978) indicates that thousands are currently in place. However, given the proprietary nature of these systems, relatively little is known about their specific content and structure. There have been several credit scoring systems that have been constructed by university-based authors and have appeared in the journals. Of the 17 consumer loan models reviewed in this Chapter, 5 are represented by the authors as having been developed for actual use in some way by the lender and another 5 may have been placed in operation. To the extent, then, that these models are representative of the systems actually being employed in industry, careful review suggests that a number of them could be expected to suffer from methodological and statistical problems. This may have significant implications for the hundreds employing similar models. As Chandler and Coffman (1977) point out, these problems take on increasing importance with the passage of the Equal Credit Opportunity Act (ECOA) in 1974, its amendments in 1976, and the implementation of the act through the Federal Reserve's Regulation B. The 1974 Act prohibited discrimination in the granting of credit on the basis of sex or marital status, to which the March 1976 amendments added seven other prohibited factors. These included race, color, religion, national origin, age, receipt of public assistance benefits, and the good faith exercise of rights under the Consumer Credit Protection Act. Particularly relevant to the consumer credit area are the provisions under the act concerning the use of age in scoring models and the related interpretations under Regulation B. These describe the statistical criteria that the scoring systems must satisfy with respect to sampling and validation before they would legally qualify to employ the prohibited age variable. These laws and new regulations place an important burden on any institution employing numerical screening models to ensure that their systems are statistically and methodologically sound.[2]

This chapter reviews the issues concerning the development of credit scoring models. Particular emphasis in the next section is placed on the methodological approaches that have been taken in selecting and developing screening models. The third section discusses the various types of scoring models that have been developed and the fourth section explores the statistical problems associated with those models.

THE METHODOLOGY OF CREDIT SCORING MODELS

There have been a number of attempts to construct various credit scoring models. However, relatively few researchers have devoted specific attention to the underlying objectives one is trying to achieve in formulating or selecting among the alternative models that might be used. Notable exceptions have been Mehta (1968, 1970), Bierman and Hausman (1970), Dirickx and Wakeman (1976), Greer (1967a,b), Edmister and Schlarbaum (1974), and Long (1976).

One of the first to examine the problem of formulating an optimal credit granting policy was Greer (1967a); he proposed two models. One model was designed to determine the optimal number of credit applicants to accept by maximizing "credit-related profits." These returns were formulated to be a function of the present value of current period profits from credit sales, the present value of future profits from applicants granted credit in the current period and the present value of profits from current and future period cash sales. The second model was nearly identical to the first but included the additional consideration of granting loans to fewer than all applicants. Greer constructed the objective function for this second model to differ from the first by only a constant. Thus, it is not surprising that Greer finds that the optimal number of loans to grant is the same for either model. It is important to note that these models are multiperiod models; the decision on the optimal number of loans to grant this period depends not only upon the future value of the loans made but also upon the future value of the additional business that might be gained as a result of granting a given number of loans. As formulated, however, the models have several limitations. First, they are not credit scoring models *per se*. The models do not aid in actually making an individual credit decision. Second, they are based upon the firm's historical policies and portfolio experience. Both models rely on past experience for information on average default rates, costs of granting credit, costs of collections, and purchasing patterns of customers. As such, the proposed optimal policies only aid in deciding at what level to operate a given system. Moreover, they are not particularly useful for evaluating alternative systems that have not yet been placed in operation or for which there is no historical experience.

Following Greer's work, Mehta (1968, 1970) presented a series of sequential decision models that employed different and successively more costly bits of information to refine the credit granting process. Mehta's (1968) approach is quite straightforward and is based upon two simple observations. First, he assumes that an individual's past credit performance can serve as a useful guide to project future credit performance. Second, he argues that information is costly and that not all information may be needed to make a decision on every applicant. A creditor is thus faced with the problem of deciding how much information to collect before making the credit decision. Three costs become relevant, which Mehta (1968) defines to be:

1. Acceptance cost = bad debt cost + average investment cost + average collection cost[3]
2. Rejection cost = lost sales cost[4]
3. Cost of further information = cost of acquiring additional information + cost of additional decision

The process requires the creditor to go through a sequential process attempting, based upon past loan loss experience and historical costs experience, to select the alternative that minimizes costs. Each time the alternative to seek more information is selected, more costly information is assumed to be acquired.

In his second paper, Mehta (1970) extends his earlier static analysis to take into account optimal decisions for collection, which were previously assumed to be exogenous, and to recognize the value of future sales and credit requests that might result from granting a loan. A Markov process is used to estimate the values of the additional revenues and costs of collecting accounts i periods old. As was the case with Greer's models, Mehta's models are limited in that they rely on historical cost information and loan loss experience.

Bierman and Hausman (1970) focus on the class of models involving multiple requests for single period loans. In each case, it is assumed that a loan is granted and that it is either (1) repaid in full or (2) not collected and is written off during the period requested. At the end of each period a new loan may be requested, and so on for n periods. The essential features of the models are that they allow for consideration of estimates of prior probabilities of collection; consideration (or valuation) of the customer relationship over n periods; revision of the estimates of the probabilities of repayment based upon previous periods' payment performance; incorporation of discounting in valuing future period receipts and collection costs, consideration of the probability that a customer may terminate the customer relationship at some future date; and allow for the fact that the amount of credit granted may affect repayment performance. The models are formulated as dynamic programming models in which the revisions in the estimates of collection probabilities are assumed to follow a Beta distribution with parameters n and r, denoting n periods and r collections. Dirickx and Wakeman (1976) extended the Bierman–Hausman models to allow for collection after the end of the first period and to allow for partial repayments. The obvious weakness of the models is the limited representation of a loan as a single period instrument.

Edmister and Schlarbaum (1974) directly address the problem of selection and evaluation of alternative credit granting systems. Under the assumption that management's objective is to maximize the market value of shareholders' equity, they argue that the goal of any credit analysis system should be to maximize the "expected net present value of granting loans to applicants." They proceed to construct an objective (or criterion) function that is shown to be dependent upon (1) a credit system's acceptance rate, (2) the expected returns and losses on good and bad loans that have been accepted, and (3) the cost of credit analysis and processing. In addition, they recognize that certain dimensions of an institution's credit policies, such as interest rates and collection policies, will affect not only the number of applications received but also the net present values of good and bad loans. They do not deal with these endogenous components to evaluating credit systems and proceed to illustrate the selection among alternative systems with given net present values and number of applications. As such, their work is a partial equilibrium approach and is nonoptimal. Omission of consideration of the endogenous components eliminates the most interesting and relevant behavioral considerations in the loan granting problem. In addition, as Long (1976) points out, their approach ignores start-up and reestimation costs.

Long (1976) extends the Edminster and Schlarbaum approach to explicitly recognize (1) start-up and updating costs, (2) variation in system efficiency over time, and (3) changes in the number and quality of loan applicants. He then proceeds to investigate the effects of alternative assumptions about system decay on update policies. Long's (1976) work, however, is subject to the same limitations as that of Edmister and Schlarbaum with respect to the endogenous components of a credit system, namely, *given* net present values and numbers of applications.

From a review of the various approaches that have been taken to formulation of credit model selection objectives, it would appear that there are several key elements to the credit granting decision that have important implications for the construction of a credit scoring model.

First, the credit granting decision is in fact a multiperiod problem that may, depending upon the types of credits involved, have two dimensions. In the context of the Greer and Bierman–Hausman type models, the granting of credit in one period is but part of a customer relationship that extends over many periods. The decision to grant credit effects the value of that customer relationship both over the period of a particular loan and also over the life of the customer relationship. Clearly, such a view of the credit process is particularly applicable to the business loan activities of a financial institution and has in fact been modeled by Hester and Pierce (1975) and by Hester (1962). It is also relevant, however, to the consumer lending area, where it is quite clear that the provision of credit is tied or linked to the provision of other financial and nonfinancial services by creditors over periods greater than the life of a loan. In the case of merchants, as distinct from financial institutions, the decision to grant credit impacts future revenues from sale of merchandise as well as demands for further extensions of credit. It is also clear from the approaches of many of the authors, particularly Edmister and Schlarbaum (1974) and Long (1976), that a credit decision is really a multiperiod decision. The lender commits funds to a single borrower for many future periods over which the loan generates a flow of revenues until it is either (1) paid off in full or (2) defaults, after which a portion of the value of the principal may be recovered.[5] Thus, the value of a loan is determined not only by whether it is paid in full but also, in the case of default, by the length of time it is current, by collection costs, and by the realizable value of any collateral that may remain. In such a framework it could be that, even if the lender were 100 percent certain that a loan would not be paid in full, it may still be worthwhile to grant the loan if it remains current for a sufficient length of time. This is particularly true if collection costs are low and the collateral has sufficient recovery value. The possibility that a defaulted loan may still be profitable has been given little attention in the published work to date.

Second, Mehta (1968, 1970), Bierman and Hausman (1970), and Greer (1967a,b) make the point that there is a need to consider the cost of information in formulating a credit granting scheme. To the extent that information on a customer's past credit performance, while not costless, is relevant to assessing future credit performance, there is a need to weigh the value of collecting additional information against the costs before deciding when is the appropriate time to make the credit decision.[6]

Third, most of the credit policy models discussed explicitly or implicitly assume that the prospective lender makes a judgment of the riskiness of a borrower in terms of either default probabilities or opportunity costs in deciding whether or not to grant a loan. Greer (1967b) assumes such a ranking. Bierman and Hausman (1970) and Dirickx and Wakeman (1976) employ a Bayesian approach to estimating default probabilities. Edmister and Schlarbaum (1974), Long (1973, 1976), and Mehta (1968) rely on average historical loss experience for given categories of loans.

Finally, in multiperiod–multidecision-type models, such as the customer relationship approaches of Bierman and Hausman (1970) or Mehta (1970), there may be a need to readjust estimates of expected default probabilities over time based upon a customer's payment performance.

Having reviewed the general approaches that have been taken to the credit granting problem and having examined what appear to be the key features that a credit scoring model might be required to possess, we now turn to a brief review of the types of models that have been proposed in the literature to see how well they measure up.

REVIEW OF CREDIT SCORING MODELS

In general, the credit scoring models that have been developed have focused on two categories of loans: (1) loans to individuals[7] and (2) business loans.[8] Models of loans to individuals have focused on farm loans, mortgages, and consumer installment loans on automobiles, mobile homes, major appliances, and credit cards. Business loan review systems have been constructed for regular commercial and industrial loans, term loans, trade credit, and loans to minority and small businesses. Additionally, the models have been developed for application to two distinct phases of the lending function. Most have focused on the credit granting function and on providing a tool for the loan officer. But at least six studies have dealt with the loan servicing and review functions.[9] See Tables IV.1 and IV.2 for details of these studies.

Table IV.1. Consumer Loan Studies

Study, Purpose, and Sample Characteristics	*Statistical Methodology and Primary Variables*	*Unique and/or Interesting Aspects of Study and Some Critical Comments*
1. *Durand (1941).* Estimated separate linear discriminant functions for supplemental evaluation of consumer installment loans for five different types of financial institutions: commercial banks, industrial banks, automobile finance companies (separate functions were estimated for new and used cars), personal finance companies, and appliance finance companies. Samples were drawn from 21 banks, 10 industrial banks, 3 automobile finance companies, 2 personal finance companies, and 1 appliance finance company. Several samples were drawn for each class of institutions with approximately equal numbers of loans in each group of good and bad loans. About 7200 loans were collected in total; about 2700 from commercial banks, 1400 from personal finance companies, 1300 from industrial banks, 1400 from automobile finance companies, and 400 from appliance finance companies. Analysis sanples for commercial banks combined only about 190 observations in each group	*Linear discriminant models* were estimated, although not all are presented. Nine-variable model for commercial banks was built, including sex, occupation, years at present address, years at occupation, bank account, and life insurance. Four-variable model for the used car sample from automotive finance companies was constructed. Variables include price, down payment, income, and maturity. No classifications were performed	*Remains* the most comprehensive, best, and statistically correct application of discriminant analysis to appear in the credit-scoring literature. Properly recognizes the limitations of models derived from prescreened data. Value of study lies in presentation of appropriate statistical methodology and discussion of limitations of the models. Examples used scaled-weighted method to determine role of individual variables. No discussion of *a priori* probabilities. Good discussion of costs of errors. An arbitrary integer scale was assigned to represent occupations

Table IV.1. (Continued)

Study, Purpose, and Sample Characteristics	*Statistical Methodology and Primary Variables*	*Unique and/or Interesting Aspects of Study and Some Critical Comments*
2. *Myers and Forgy (1963).* To determine credit risk of conditional sales contracts on mobile homes. Used as original sample, 150 good accounts (no more than 2 or 3 late payments) opened between 1/1959 and 10/1960 and 150 bad accounts (made less than 18 payments and repossessed in 1960 or 1961) selected from central office of Universal Finance Co., Los Angeles, Cal. Same size holdout used for validation	*Compares classification results* from four models: discriminant analysis, stepwise regression, equal weights on all variables, and sequential discriminant analysis. Used 21 of 40 original variables selected on basis of univariate F-ratios. Variables are mixed discrete and continuous and included age, phone, bank account, credit reference, unpaid balance	*Discriminant and regression analysis.* Pooled data for 22 months. Did not consider *a priori* probabilities of membership. Used correlation between actual and predicted scores as index of predictive power of model. Methodology was inappropriate and gives biased estimates of error rates. Suffers from time-series problem and lack of theoretical justification for model
3. *Smith (1964).* Used pooled data for 5-1/2 years from one bank composed of 1516 good and 1234 bad direct personal loans. Covered period from mid-1952 to 1955	*Derived an additive scoring function* by summing univariate weights. The weights were determined as the conditional probability that a firm with a given factor would be bad. Used 13 of 20 continuous and categorical variables selected on basis of univariate chi-square tests. Variables include telephone, residence, bank account, purpose of loan, time in last residence, time on last job, sex, marital status, and age	*Univariate method* ignoring correlations and interactions among the variables. Used analysis sample to test predictive power. Method is essentially *ad hoc* and confuses conditional and cumulative probabilities. Suffers from time-series problem
4. *Reinsel and Brake (1966).* Construct linear dummy regression function to evaluate risks on loans to farmers provided through FHA and PCA.	*Linear discriminant model* estimated separate models for PCA and FHA borrowers. Six variables were selected (by an unknown method) for the PCA	*Biased classifications* due to reclassification of original sample. No discussion of *a priori* probabilities or of method selecting variables

Sample of 40 PCA borrowers for one analysis sample and 56 FHA borrowers. Data were from applications filed in 1950s and were collected on non-real estate dairy loans in two Michigan counties	model, including farm size, farming experience, borrow's rate of increase in net worth, ratio of non-real estate debt to total debt, number of credit sources used, and ownership of farm. Model correctly classified 38 of 40 borrowers in the analysis sample. FHA model used 7 variables, including insurance, borrower's rate of increase in net worth, family size, ratio of non-real estate debt to total debt, ratio of interest and principal payments to total income, running water. A total of 45 of 56 FHA borrowers in analysis sample were correctly identified	
5. *Pratt and McGhee (1967).* Developed a two-stage linear discriminant analysis model to simulate the accept–reject decisions of the credit analyst of a large independent oil company. Analysis sample consisted of 413 accepted loans and 506 rejected loans. Validation sample consisted of (1) a subset of 276 accepted loan and 453 rejected loans and (2) 184 good loans and 217 bad loans	*Linear discriminant model* estimated, using 8 categorical variables, which include location, home ownership, age, number of dependents, occupation (8 classes), and length of employment. Second stage was estimated adding four additional categorical variables from a more costly credit evaluation. This included references, employment of wife, banking accounts, and pay record	*Simulated* the loan evaluation process of the credit analysis. Included two-stage decision process that considered the cost of making a wrong decision and the cost of collecting additional data. Validated model on good and bad accounts, as such, really tested the accuracy of the credit analysis procedures rather than predicting good and bad credit risks. Model rejected 91.5 percent of the bad accounts that had been approved by the analyst and the only good accounts rejected were ones that in fact had not been activated. Used regression analysis and scaled-weighted method to select variables and determine their relative importance. Improperly used linear discriminant analysis techniques on categorical data. No discussion of *a priori* probabilities is provided

Table IV.1. (Continued)

Study, Purpose, and Sample Characteristics	*Statistical Methodology and Primary Variables*	*Unique and/or Interesting Aspects of Study and Some Critical Comments*
6. *Boggess (1967).* Discussed disguised application from one firm of a statistical scoring model to screen consumer credit in 1964–1967. No details on sample or actual statistical method used is presented	*Scaled weights* on 8 variables for 4 separate years are described. Actual method used to derive weights is unknown (probably discriminant analysis). Variables used are marital status, home ownership, auto, age, time at residence, bank reference, telephone, fewer than 3 children	Emphasis is on goals of model construction, including cost and revenue objectives, market segmentation, updating and revalidation of models to take into account dynamics, revising cutoff scores, and sample bias
7. *Chatterjee and Barcun (1970).* Employed a sample of 385 good and 389 bad personal loans from a New York City bank. All data consisted of categorical variables	*Nonparametric nearest neighbor techniques* of Hills (1966) were used for dealing with all categorical data. Variable selection procedures are discussed, comparing classification performance of the explanatory set with and without each variable. Variables used are incone, residence, debt owed, telephone, home ownership, length of time on job more than 3 years, type of job, marital status	*Method is distribution free.* Takes into account *a priori* probabilities, and does not scale the variables. Uses an almost unbiased jackknife procedure to obtain error estimates. Practical use of the technique requires a computer
8. *Evans (1971).* Constructed linear discriminant analysis loan review function to identify impending problems for 1965 sample of FHA and PCA farms with loans in 5 areas in South Dakota. A total of 200 loans	*Estimated linear discriminant analysis models* for the combined FHA and PCA samples, as well as for each separately. Fifteen variables were in each model, including age, number in household, production record, ratios of debt to net	*No classification* results are presented. Many of the variables in the model do not provide independent bits of information because some could be derived directly from the others. Improperly interpreted linear

were in the sample, 100 each for the FHA and PCA lenders with 50 good and 50 bad loans in each sample	worth and assets, composition of debt. Variables ranked in importance based on conditional deletion method. Most important features of unsuccessful borrowers were low production record, high cost of operation, high ratio of non-real estate debt to non-real estate assets and large family. A 23-variable model was tested as of the year of the last loan application and no significant differences were found between the successful and unsuccessful borrower at the time the loan was made	coefficients as indicating marginal increments to the probability of success or failure
9. *Hettenhouse and Wentworth (1971).* Discussed two-phase system to screen five different types of consumer loans for Indiana National Bank in Indianapolis, Indiana	*Two-phased model* consisted of a stepwise linear regression model (discriminant analysis) to drive scoring weights for five loan types: direct auto, personal, indirect auto, property improvement, and other indirect loans. No information is provided on variables in model, sample sizes, or other aspects of the estimation. It is indicated that a holdout sample was used for validation. A variant of the model is said to provide a continuous estimate of the potential yield or value of the loan. The second phase permits further subjective review by a loan officer	No details of the model or estimation is provided. Thus, the performance and structure cannot be evaluated

Table IV.1. (Continued)

Study, Purpose, and Sample Characteristics	*Statistical Methodology and Primary Variables*	*Unique and/or Interesting Aspects of Study and Some Critical Comments*
10. *Orgler (1971).* Developed models to evaluate and monitor the performance of existing consumer loans in a bank's portfolio as a tool for bank examiners and loan officers. Data were from two commercial banks. About 400 (200 good and 200 bad) loans were from one bank and 300 loans for a second bank. No details of the data are provided	*Stepwise dummy regression* analysis was used to derive three discriminant models, one for each of two banks consisting of 7 variables (different ones for each bank) and a combined model. Variables included: years at present employment, phone, checking account, auto, credit rating, type of account, and number of overdue notices	*Dummy regression model* used to estimate discriminant functions. Model is true loan servicing model in that loan payment history is included. Results also indicate different signs on some of same variables for two different banks. Classification results are biased because analysis sample was reclassified. Results indicate that about 80 percent of bad loans were correctly identified but from 49 to 36 percent of the good loans were assigned as bad loans or were placed in a third "no decision" group. Use of "no decision" group begs the classification question and is of questionable value. No discussion of *a priori* probabilities used
11. *Lane (1972).* Developed three-group discriminant analysis model to distinguish between personal bankrupts who will not repay from persons filing under Chapter XIII and debt counselors who enter programs and agree to repay. Data were 247 personal bankruptcy cases with assets under $40,000 and 250 Chapter XIII cases filed in U.S. District Court, L.A. between 1/1/1969 and 12/30/1966. Debt counselors were those filed in 1966 and early 1967 in southern California	*Quadratic classification rule* was employed assuming equal *a priori* probabilities. Seventeen continuous variables were used including income, months on job, months to acquire debt, household assets, and detailed breakdown of various components of debt	*First study* employing quadratic classification rules. Functions and rules are not reported. Wrong *a priori* probabilities were used. Also, data were pooled over slightly different time periods. Did not include a group of borrowers who did not default. Uses a cutoff and validation procedure that suggests results may be based upon pairwise comparisons rather than a true three-group conparison

12. *Harter (1973).* Derived a model for predicting the likelihood of default on single-family residential real estate loans. Data were selected from 7 New York City mutual savings banks and consisted of 109 forecloses and 77 loans that had been paid off or were current for at least 3 years; an analysis sample of 56 good and bad loans were used to develop the discriminant function	*An 11-variable linear model* was constructed from 23 original variables based on the standard errors of the coefficients. Variables include: monthly payment, down payment/purchase price, income, number in family, other income/total income, number of years married, employment, monthly debts payments/annual mortgage, monthly mortgage payment/annual income, monthly payment on mortgage/monthly housing expenses last 12 months	*One of the few* studies that attempted to take into account the costs of errors. Selected a cutoff score so as to maximize differences between return on good loans and foreclosure costs. Used suboptimal method for variable selection. Also no discussion of *a priori* probabilities or tests for linear versus quadratic model. Also had small analysis sample relative to the number of variables in the set
13. *Apilado, Warner, and Dauten (1974).* Constructed heuristic, univariate, and linear discriminant analysis models to predict good and bad credit risks in consumer installment loans. Analysis samples consisted of 431 good accounts and 404 bad accounts from files closed in 1970 and 1971 that were randomly selected from 307 banking offices and 18 finance companies from an industrialized southwestern state. A holdout sample of 47 good loans and 46 bad loans was also employed	*Used a univariate scaling method* to construct efficiency indexes as one method to rank the original 13 variables according to their discriminant power. Also used stepwise forward discriminant analysis procedures to reduce original 13-variable set to 8 variables. Does not mention what *a priori* probabilities were used in constructing several different classification models. Variables used in rough order of importance include home status, checking account, purpose of loan, number of dependents, number of monthly payments, age of borrower, amount of loan, and marital status. Some of the variables were categorical	*Classification results* emphasized comparison of alternative cutoff scores to eliminate bad accounts while eliminating a minimal number of good accounts. Linear model had 73.7 percent overall accuracy rate with 74 percent of the bad and 72 percent of the good loans correctly identified. Methods used paid little attention to *a priori* probabilities (probably used equal) or costs of classification errors. Incorrectly states that little improvement in discriminant analysis models results from use of more than four variables; claims to demonstrate this with heuristic model results. Pooled data from 2 years. Attempted to reduce number of variables before checking overall classification efficiency of the models. Found that age and martial status were important variables, but in case of the latter, it was impossible to tell from results presented in which direction

Table IV.1. (*Continued*)

Study, Purpose, and Sample Characteristics	*Statistical Methodology and Primary Variables*	*Unique and/or Interesting Aspects of Study and Some Critical Comments*
14. *Chandler and Ewert (1974a).* Describe two-stage procedure for a bank to use in issuing credit cards. Emphasis is on deciding when to approve or deny an applicant as opposed to seeking additional information. Data consist of 2000 applicants over 1-1/2 years (about 1973–1974) of which 1000 were good, 500 bad, and 500 rejected. Bad applications consisted of accounts written off and a sample of delinquent accounts. Analysis sample of about 700 observations and holdout sample of about 1300 observations were used	*Linear discriminant function* was constructed using 15 variables from application, including length of time on job, residency tenure, income. Classifications were compared with a second model using all variables from first model plus 5 variables, selected using stepwise procedures, from a purchased credit report, including credit rating and type of creditor	*No description* of the models or variables are provided. Two-step procedure is designed to balance expected payoff from seeking additional information against cost of additional data. But no details are provided of the example presented
15. *Ewert and Chandler (1974b).* Estimated dummy regression and quadratic discriminant functions to predict whether credit card accounts 1 month delinquent would become either current or 2 months delinquent. Data consist of an analysis sample of 165 good accounts and 49 delinquent accounts and a holdout of 84 good accounts and 25 delinquent accounts. The source or time span of the data is not indicated	*Both 16- and 18-variable linear and quadratic* discriminant analysis models were estimated. Variables selected according to predictive power, but method is unspecified. Only 8-variable model is described and all dummy variables are used. Variables include credit rating, previous payment record, year's purchase record, exceeded credit limit, prior month's purchase record, previous management review of account	*Quadratic classifications* worse than linear, indicating degrees of freedom problem for small samples. Only linear classifications are presented, using two arbitrary cutoffs. In 50–50 model only 54 percent of delinquent accounts and 78 percent of current accounts were correctly identified. Model is true account service function and represents more appropriate use of techniques than for credit granting decision since preselection sample bias is not a problem

16. *Sexton (1977).* Estimated separate linear function for low (less than $5000) and high income families for sample of consumer loans taken from Penneys', Wards, and Sears. Sample consisted of 3291 high income and 828 low income families. Purpose was to determine if the criteria that discriminated between high and low credit risks for high income families was the same as for low income families	*Linear discriminant functions* were estimated using a dummy dependent regression. Fourteen variables were employed, including a set of three dummy independent variables to represent marital status, a set of two dummy variables to represent home ownership, and a set of two dummies to denote two of the three retailers. Variables included were credit rating, marital status, number of dependents, age, income, supplemental income, home ownership, and telephone	*Statistical problems* limit generalizations that can be made. The two sets of exhaustive dummy variables suggest that the regression model should have been singular. In addition, inclusion of partial set dummy variables to denote the three retailers without a constant term also clouds ability to interpret specific coefficients. Many of the coefficients don't make economic sense, such as the marital status results and the negative coefficient on supplemental income for high income borrowers
17. *Gau (1978).* Developed a factor, discriminant, and cluster analysis taxonomic procedure to identify risk classes in conventional mortgages at time of origination. Data consist of 873 nondefaulted loans and 212 defaulted loans as of June 30, 1974 that were originated in 1967	*Factor analysis* of 64 variables were used to identify 17 independent dimensions. Factors were used in a discriminant analysis to identify which factors were important and to weigh the factors as input to a cluster analysis to identify 6 risk classes. A discriminant analysis was then developed to assign loans into one of 6 cluster groups. Three types of variables were used measuring financial characteristics of transactions, property, and borrower. Included several variables that would indicate potential EEO problems including age, sex, and marital status	*Methodology is devoid of theory* and basically employs statistical techniques to determine which variables (factors) are relevant. Implicit structure suggests that defaulted and nondefaulted loans arise from a population that is segmented into several risk classes. No mention of *a priori* probability costs of errors or whether tests indicated a linear structure was appropriate

Table IV.2. Commercial and Business Loan Studies

Study, Purpose, and Sample Characteristics	*Statistical Methodology and Primary Variables*	*Unique and/or Interesting Aspects of Study and Some Critical Comments*
1. *Cohen, Gilmore, and Singer (1966).* Describe a sequential process for commercial and industrial loan evaluation that incorporates the value of the loan to the bank. The actual credit rating section of the charted flow process incorporates an arbitrarily specified categorical scheme rather than a specific optimization rule. No empirical example is provided	*Process* is essentially a verbal disception of a computer flow chart. Heuristic model is not an optimization model nor does it provide estimatible parameters. Variables suggested as relevant to the loan evaluation process include purpose of loan, amount, maturity, payback schedule, security, financial condition and future prospects of the borrower, and exogenous factors, such as: industry characteristics, general economic climate, and state of monetary policy	Decision model was developed more as a teaching device and to describe the general loan granting process than to represent an optimal credit granting process. No multivariate statistical analysis of financial statement data is performed
2. *Ewert (1969).* Presents a model for evaluating risk associated with granting of trade credit. Data were supplied by a moderately large California manufacturing firm. Analysis sample consisted of 198 good and 109 bad accounts and a holdout sample of 100 good and 100 bad accounts from 1960–1964	*Used dummy linear regression* estimation technique to estimate linear probability function incorporating the adjustments for heteroskedasticity as described in Goldberger (1964: 248–250). Stepwise techniques were used to reduce the number of variables to 17. A 9-variable subset was also used. Variables included were credit rating, current ratio, net worth, growth in sales, sales relation to industry, paying and reporting experience of the suppliers receivables	*Model correctly classified* 82 percent of the accounts correctly. Recognized problems associated with costs of misclassification and sample bias due to previous screening. Had time problem due to pooling of 5 years of data

3. *Orgler (1970)*. Develops linear dummy regression model to review existing loans by duplicating bank examiner classifications. Data were taken from bank examination files in several eastern states. Analysis sample consisted of 75 classified loans and 225 good loans and a holdout sample of 40 classified loan and 80 good loans	*Stepwise regression routines* were used to reduce an unspecified (but large) number of variables to a 6-variable set of which 5 were dummy variables. These include secured status, past due status, audit status of borrower, profits of firm, working capital/current assets, past classification of the loan. In selecting variables, some were deleted due to problems of multicollinearity, whereas others were dropped if the signs were wrong or could not be explained. Used a third classification of "marginal" when generating predictions	*Employs double cutoff* or gray area into which most of the good loans were placed. Correctly identified over 75 percent of the bad loans. Considers problem of costs of misclassification, but costs are not incorporated in the model. Has problem with use of dummy variables in linear model. Also has an error in regression constant used for prediction due to unequal sample sizes. Ignores *a priori* probabilities
4. *Edmister (1971)*. Develops model of small business loan default under SBA guarantee and loan programs. Sample consisted of 21 good and 21 bad loans under SBA programs	*Discriminant function* was constructed from a set of 19 ratios, a total of 722 new variables (38 for each of the 19 ratios) were created. These ratios were then screened using unspecified stepwise procedures to derive a set of 7 dummy independent variables determined by whether or not each ratio differed from a critical value. The ratios included equity/sales, net working capital/sales relative to industry, current liabilities/equity relative to SBA average, funds flow/current liabilities, inventory/sales trend of industry, industry trend in quick ratio, trend in borrow's quick ratio relative to industry	Study had 17 times as many variables as observations. Incorrectly states that methodology requires equal numbers of sample observations in each group. Used linear techniques with all categorical variables. Validation results indicate 80 percent accuracy overall, but no consideration is given to *a priori* probabilities in estimating error rate

Table IV.2. (Continued)

Study, Purpose, and Sample Characteristics	*Statistical Methodology and Primary Variables*	*Unique and/or Interesting Aspects of Study and Some Critical Comments*
5. *Bates (1973).* Quadratic discriminant analysis between repaid and delinquent loans made under the SBA's project OWN to black businessmen and to white businessmen in the Boston, Chicago, and New York metropolitan areas. Samples consisted of 147 good loans and 125 bad loans (more than 60 days delinquent) to black businessmen and 132 good loans and 68 bad loans to white businessmen between 1967 and 1971	*Quadratic discriminant analysis* classification functions were separately calculated for loans to black and white businessmen. A total of 11 variables were used, 9 of which were in the model for black businessmen and 10 in the model for white businessmen. These included total assets of business, length of time loan outstanding, purpose of loan, credit rating, net worth, liquidity, repayment, owner's net worth, owner's outside income, years of managerial experience. Variables were selected by specifying all non-balance sheet variables and then using complete stepwise procedures to add the balance sheet variables	*Deletion of 30–60 day delinquents* implies a group specification problem exists. Used quadratic classification rules and used linear scaled-weighted coefficients to determine the importance of individual variables. Used qualitative variables and transformed skewed variables using log transformations. Use of a variable indicating number of months the loan was outstanding means the functions can be used only for loan review and not as a credit rating system. Does not use population *a priori* probabilities. Has time-series problems
6. *Chesser (1974).* Presents a logit model for forecasting commercial loan noncompliance. Data drawn from 4 commercial banks in 3 states for years 1962–1971. Sample consisted of paired sample of 37 satisfactory and unsatisfactory loans 1 year before	*A six-variable logit equation* was estimated from a larger set of 15 variables. The method of variable selection was based upon discriminatory power in a discriminant analysis. The six variables include cash and marketable securities/total assets, net sales/cash and marketable	Only application of logit analysis in the credit scoring area. Purpose of model was to estimate a "probability" of noncompliance. Incorrectly argued that discriminant analysis would not provide such an estimate. Model was about 76 percent accurate on both the analysis and

noncompliance and 21 pairs of loans 2 years before noncompliance	securities, gross earnings/total assets, total debt/total assets, fixed assets/net worth, working capital/net sales	holdout sample 1 year prior to noncompliance. Same model was used to predict noncompliance 2 years earlier with significant reduction in accuracy. A second model should have been estimated. Also a time-series problem exists due to pooling of data from a number of years. Model could be used either to grant loans or to review existing portfolios
7. *Altman, Margaine, Schlosser, and Vernimmen (1974)*. Constructs a linear discriminant function to evaluate the repayment performance of firms in the wool and cotton textile industry in France. Data consist of a sample of 35 problem firms and 99 good firms in the period 1968–1971	*Univariate analyses and principle components* were employed to identify potentially important discriminating variables from an initial set of 41. Two components were found to account for 40 percent of the variation and were interpreted as indicating the importance of margins and of cash flow. Also a 41-variable descriptive discriptive discriminant analysis was performed. A smaller 10-variable set was identified. Five variables were included that seemed to be the most efficient from the 41-variable set and 6 were included based upon correlations with the two main principal components. Variables included represented leverage, profitability, and value added	*Model performed poorly* in the sense that there were high errors of prediction. No mention is made of the *a priori* probabilities used and arbitrary cutoffs were employed. No holdout sample or equivalent method was employed to adjust for selection sample bias. A sample size problem exists since there were 41 original variables and only 35 observations in bad group. Pooling of data across 1968–1971 creates a time-series problem

Table IV.2. (Continued)

Study, Purpose and Sample Characteristics	*Statistical Methodology and Primary Variables*	*Unique and/or Interesting Aspects of Study and Some Critical Comments*
8. *Edelstein (1975)*. Evaluates the performance of the minority loan program sponsored by 8 Philadelphia banks and assesses banks' ability to select good and bad credit risks from the applicant pool of minority entrepreneurs. Population of 290 approved loans between April, 1968 and January, 1970 was analyzed. Consisted of 122 good loans (those whose payments were on time) and 168 delinquent or written-off loans. Analysis sample consisted of 145 of the 290 loans. Error rates for various cutoff points are presented. Also developed model to explain the accepted and rejected applicants from the pool, subperiod models of performance based upon changes in racial and other characteristics of neighborhood, and submarket models based upon differences in neighborhoods within the Philadelphia market	*Estimated linear probability* type model using two-stage least squares procedures to adjust for heteroskedasticity when a 0–1 dummy independent variable is employed. Estimates were interpreted as an index of performance. A total of 37 variables were evaluated but final model (whose method of selection is unspecified) included only 5 variables. These were size of loan, date issued, categorical variable indicating if employed more or less than 7 years, annual income and wealth, and categorical variable representing length of residence greater than 2 years	*Models estimated are* more descriptive of loan performance rather than credit scoring models *per se*. Time-series problem is present due to pooling of data. Use of the regression model requires the assumption that the probabilities of performance are linearly related to the independent variables

The typical approach in both the credit scoring and loan review models is to select a sample of loans that have been previously screened and approved by loan officers. These loans are then categorized into two (and possibly more) mutually exclusive groups. Loans defined as "good loans" are those that have been paid off or are current and those defined as "bad loans" are either slow paying, delinquent, or in default. For example, in their study of the default risk of conditional sales contracts on mobile homes, Myers and Forgy (1963) defined "good loans" as those accounts opened between January, 1959 and October, 1960 with no more than two or three late payments and "bad loans" as those for which less than 18 payments had been made and the collateral repossessed in either 1960 or 1961. Bates (1973), in his study of loans made to small businessmen under the SBA project OWN, called all current loans "good" and loans more than 60 days delinquent "bad." Edelstein (1975), in a similar study of a loan program for minority entrepreneurs sponsored by eight Philadelphia banks, defined "good loans" as those whose payments were on schedule; all other loans were considered to be "bad." Finally, in a study of personal bankruptcies, Lane (1972) employed three groups in an attempt to distinguish among those borrowers who would ultimately repay, those who would file under Chapter XIII of the bankruptcy laws, and those who would enter debt counselor programs and repay.

Once the samples have been selected, a discriminant analysis or some other type of classification procedure is usually proposed to distinguish between the groups. A classification function and/or rule is estimated from the pool of loans that have already been granted. The classification objective usually is to minimize the overall error rates or costs of misclassification. In the case of the loan review models, the objective is to construct a management tool to monitor and review the performance of an existing loan portfolio. In the consumer and commercial loan models developed by Orgler (1970, 1971), for example, the purpose was to develop for bank examiners a tool to assist in the assessment of asset quality. The models by Chesser (1974), Ewert and Chandler (1974b), and Evans (1971) were designed to determine whether loans in a portfolio that had missed payments or had otherwise indicated some difficulty, would require some type of collection or work-out effort or would return to current status.[10]

Of the consumer and commercial loan models cited in this chapter, none possess *all* of the key elements of a scoring model noted in the previous section. For example, none of the models are multiperiod. Moreover, none take into account the value of the customer relationship. Nor do they recognize that under certain circumstances a defaulted loan may still be profitable, albeit more risky.[11] In fact, the reported models deal only with the problem of assessing default probabilities. Even here, there are clear divisions among the models. Those of Lane (1972), Chatterjee and Barcun (1970),[12] and Durand (1941) specifically had as an objective to minimize the probabilities of misclassification. Harter (1973) took into account both the return on a correct decision and the cost of an error. Most of the remaining studies are silent on the objectives of their models, although it is probably fair to conclude that they are implicitly attempting to minimize the classification errors.

Although the models are limited in scope, it is worthwhile to note a few additional key features. Of the 17 consumer loan models described in Table IV.1, 11 included at least one of the variables that would now be prohibited under the Equal Credit Opportunity Act.[13] Interestingly, with respect to the three variables that occurred the most frequently—age, sex, and marital status—most of the models tended to favor women and older people as being less risky. However, several other studies found little predictive value to some of these factors. For example, the models of Smith (1964) and Durand (1941) favored women, whereas those of Myers and Forgy (1963), Pratt and McGhee (1967), and Apilado, Warner, and Dauten (1974) found sex not significantly related to credit worthiness. None of the models reported that women were *ceteris paribus* more risky than men. With respect to marital status, the models of Boggess (1967), Sexton (1977), Apilado, Warner, and Dauten (1974), and Smith (1964) tended to favor married versus single applicants; Smith's model suggested that divorced applicants were also risky.[14] On the other hand, Durand (1941) concluded that marital status was not important. The importance of the age variable varied the most among models. Smith (1964) found that the lowest risk borrowers were 65 and over; the model of Boggess (1967) gave preference to people in excess of 35; and Durand (1941) and Sexton (1977) found that older people were slightly better credit risks. Reinsel and Brake (1966), Pratt and McGhee (1967), and Apilado, Warner, and Dauten (1974) indicated that age was not significantly related to credit worthiness, whereas the model of Evans (1971) favored younger applicants. The results from examination of the models are not strictly comparable because of the discrete way that age was entered into the models.[15] Some used variables that only distinguished between young people (i.e., under 20 and over 20), whereas others employed continuous variables to capture age.

In addition to the specific variables included, a number of different statistical models have been used to construct credit rating schemes. Discriminant analysis models are by far the most prevalent; 13 of the 17 consumer loan studies listed in Table IV.1 and 4 of the 8 commercial loan models in Table IV.2 employed discriminant analysis techniques.

In addition, two studies, Edelstein (1975) and Ewert (1969) employed a linear probability function, one, Chatterjee and Barcun (1970) used a nonparametric nearest neighbor procedure, one, Chesser (1974) employed a logit model, and two others, Smith (1964) and Myers and Forgy (1963) used essentially *ad hoc* weighting schemes.

With few exceptions, then, the models discussed in this section are essentially directed toward only one dimension of the credit granting function, albeit a critical one, and that is the assessment of the likelihood that loans will default, go "bad," or experience difficulty over their life. Within the scope of this narrower objective, we now turn attention to how well it is carried out in terms of model specification and application of the relevant statistics.

METHODOLOGICAL AND STATISTICAL PROBLEMS IN CREDIT SCORING MODELS

Most of the models reviewed in the previous section suffer from methodological and statistical problems that may affect the reliability of the estimates of default probabilities. Particularly for the consumer credit granting models, it is important to understand the dimensions of these problems, since as Chandler and Coffman (1977) note, only if a credit scoring model is "demonstrably and statistically sound" can it satisfy the regulatory standards under the Federal Reserve's Regulation B. Moreover, to the extent that a model is subject to criticism on statistical grounds, vulnerability under the "effects test" is likely to be increased.[16]

Since all but a few of the models that have appeared in the literature have employed discriminant analysis procedures, this section mainly focuses on the problems that can be identified with the use of this technique.[17,18]

As has been noted in Chapter III, the statistical problems in the applied discriminant analysis literature may be categorized into about five different types.[19] These are

1. Violation of the underlying assumptions of the classical linear discriminant analysis model. These include
   a. Deviation of the distribution of the variables within each group from multivariate normality.
   b. Unequal group dispersions.
   c. The lack of distinct definitions of the groups.
2. Interpretation of the relative importance of individual variables in the model.
3. Reduction of dimensionality and elimination of insignificant variables.
4. Specification of the appropriate classification scheme, including

a. Selection of *a priori* probabilities and/or costs of misclassification.
b. Estimation of classification error rates.

5. Time-series analysis.

To these, a review of the credit scoring applications suggests that an additional problem is associated with

6. Selection of the analysis samples.

Each of these problem areas will be briefly discussed in turn. However, since the issues related to "reduction in dimensionality" pose no separate or special problems for credit scoring models, no discussion of that area is provided.

Distribution of the Variables

One of the critical assumptions in discriminant analysis is that the variables describing the members of the groups being evaluated are multivariate normally distributed. As noted in Chapter III, violation of the assumption of multivariate normality can result in biased tests for the equality of group means and biased classification results. None of the discriminant analysis or other models referred to in this chapter, except for Chatterjee and Barcun (1970), devote attention to this problem. Clearly, those discriminant analysis models employing categorical variables violate the distributional assumptions[20] and, hence, may be immediately open to challenge. A successful defense of a challenge to the statistical validity of the model would have to rest on a discussion of the robustness of the procedures employed to differing distributional assumptions.[21]

Alternatively, procedures described by Hills (1966, 1967), Linhart (1959), and Chang and Afifi (1974) and employing nearest neighbor techniques or methods of subdividing the populations might be used. Chatterjee and Barcun (1970) provide an application of the "nearest neighbor" rules described by Hills (1966) to the problem of screening personal loan applications for a New York bank. When the vector of loan characteristics is composed of binary variables, as was the case in Chatterjee and Barcun's application, the "nearest neighbor" rules are optimal. Moreover, they are nonparametric and distribution free.

It should also be noted that use of probit or normit or other similar techniques does not relieve one of the problems of worrying about underlying distributional assumptions. In the case of probit, logit, normit, and tobit analysis, it is assumed that the event probabilities follow particular distributions. Thus, theoretical rationalization of a particular technique employed rests to a significant degree upon how closely the distributional assumptions of the technique fit the problem at hand.

Equal versus Unequal Covariances

The decision to employ linear as opposed to quadratic sample discriminant analysis techniques theoretically rests upon tests for the equality of the group covariances. When the covariances are equal, then linear procedures should be employed, and when the covariances are unequal, then quadratic procedures are appropriate.[22] The one caveat is that Monte Carlo studies by Marks and Dunn (1974) suggest that there may be efficiency trade-offs between use of linear and quadratic rules and sample sizes. When samples are small and the number of variables relatively large, linear rules may give more efficient estimates of the expected error rates than quadratic rules, even when the population covariances are unequal. Of the credit scoring models reviewed, only Bates (1973), Lane (1972), Ewert and Chandler (1974b), and Durand (1941) devoted any attention to the appropriate functional form of the discriminant analysis model. All but Durand estimate quadratic rules after testing for the equality of the group dispersions.

The Role of Individual Variables

As Chandler and Coffman (1977) point out, there is a high probability that court tests of the validity of credit scoring models may place constraints on the variables included in a model and require the user to be able to demonstrate that each variable contributes significantly to the overall discriminatory power of the model. This possibility poses a serious potential problem for users of discriminant analysis procedures because there are no analogous statistical tests to those in regression analysis for the significance of individual coefficients. In the linear case, it is possible to test for the conditional significance of individual variables and presumably analogous tests could be formulated in the quadratic case. But as of yet these tests are not widely available in useable form.[23] The lack of exact tests and the need to rely on approximations would certainly complicate the defense of many discriminant analysis credit scoring models in court.[24] It is interesting that Chatterjee and Barcun (1970) illustrate how the "nearest neighbor" procedure can be used to test for the conditional contribution of individual variables to the classification results. They simply estimate overall classification accuracy, deleting the variable of interest, and compare the results to those with all the variables included. If the estimated error rates are not significantly different, then the variable of interest does not add to the power of the variable set. This is analogous to the discriminant analysis tests for the conditional contribution of variables to the multivariate *F*-statistic used to test for the differences in group means that was proposed by Eisenbeis, Gilbert, and Avery (1973). Presumably, the procedure proposed by Chatterjee and Barcun (1970) could be applied equally as well to determine the conditional contribution of individual variables to the discriminant analysis classification results.

Unlike the discriminant analysis models, probit, logit, and related techniques do not suffer from similar limitations with regard to testing for the significance of individual variables. Thus, had he chosen to, it would have been possible for Chesser (1974), in his model of commercial loan compliance, to test for the significance of individual variables in the model.

Problems in the Definitions of the Groups

Many of the available classification techniques discussed in Chapters I and II, and especially discriminant analysis, assume that the groups being investigated are discrete and identifiable. In most of the credit screening applications, this has been interpreted as categorizing loans into risk classes according to whether they were either "good" (in which case they were either current or had been paid) or "bad" (in which case they were in default or in some way delinquent). Since one of the prime purposes of a credit scoring model is to evaluate the credit worthiness of through-the-door applicants by assigning them to the appropriate risk classes, it is important that the groupings used exhaust those in the population from which the applicants are drawn. If the groups do not exhaust the population, then an applicant could be wrongly classified into one of a set of risk classes, none of which represented the class from which it arose. In this respect, some of the models reviewed in this chapter suffer from one or more deficiencies. The most common problem is omission of part of the population as a result of the group definitions used. Myers and Forgy (1963), for example, defined "good" loans to be those with no more than 2 or 3 late payments and "bad" loans as those for which fewer than 18 payments had been made and which had been repossessed. The study omits the possibility that a borrower could have made more than 18 payments and then defaulted. Similarly, it fails to consider that loans could miss more than 2 or 3 payments and yet not go into default. There is a second problem associated with their "good" group; that is, at the time the sample was constructed a loan might have passed the criterion to be a good loan, yet as time passed, the borrower could have defaulted before its payments were made. The problem of omitted portions of the population posed potential problems in the studies of Bates (1973), Smith (1964), and Sexton (1977), and examples of a potential time-dimension problem associated with the group definition can be found in the work of Edelstein (1975) and Chesser (1974).[25]

It should also be noted that the use of risk classes, or groups, as a basis for deriving a credit scoring model implies that one is using a discrete rather than continuous concept of risk. Such groupings appear to satisfy the required assumptions or discriminant analysis model, as long as one is willing to regard risk as being discrete and is willing to disregard recovery values or collateral as a means of reducing creditor risk exposure.

Use of Inappropriate A Priori Probabilities and Costs of Misclassification

The standard discriminant analysis classification rules—both linear and quadratic—incorporate *a priori* probabilities to account for the fact that the populations or groups being investigated occur with different relative frequencies in the poplulation. Furthermore, it is also possible to adjust for the fact that one type of misclassification may even be more costly than another. In this model, however, the costs of classification errors are fixed, in that the cost (for example) of making a "bad" loan is invariant with respect to the characteristics of the loan. That is, the classification rules assume that the expected losses or costs are the same for all errors of the same type. They do not allow for the fact that the expected loss or error cost may vary for each loan depending upon the value of collateral, recovery values, or other remedies that may be available.

Relatively little attention has been paid to the selection of the appropriate *a priori* probabilities in the development of the credit scoring models reviewed in this chapter, and most have simply assumed that both the *a priori* probabilities and costs of errors are equal. For example, of the studies listed in Tables IV.1 and IV.2 only Ewert (1969), Durand (1941), and Ewert and Chandler (1974b) give any indication of being aware of the importance of selecting or estimating proper *a priori* probabilities. Similarly only Pratt and McGhee (1967), Harter (1973), and Hettenhouse and Wentworth (1971) consider costs at all in those models employing discriminant analysis. Chatterjee and Barcun (1970) consider costs in their nearest neighbor scheme. In the logit model of Chesser (1974) and the probability models of Edelstein (1975) and Ewert (1969), the use of *a priori* probabilities are not an issue.

It can be demonstrated that proper choice of the *a priori* probabilities is critical to assessment of the performance of the model and estimates of the default rates. Use of *a priori* probabilities different from the population *priors* will result in estimates that may bear little relationship to what might be expected when the model is applied to the population or what the true error rates should be. Moreover, it will not result in minimization of the probabilities of misclassification. In the models reviewed in Tables IV.1 and IV.2, most simply assumed equal *a priori* probabilities or did not even mention what *priors* were employed.

Estimation of Classification Error Rates

Particularly critical under the ECOA will be the ability to accurately illustrate or estimate the overall performance of the credit scoring models in terms of the objective function employed. For those attempting to minimize classification error rates, the researchers will be forced to trade off the costs of sample size and expansion of the variance of error estimates. It has been well publicized that employing the samples used to construct the classification rules to estimate expected error rates leads to a biased and optimistic prediction of how well the model will perform. A number of alternative methods have been proposed, the most widely used and most expensive being the holdout method. It is also interesting to note, however, that tests indicate that the holdout method is not clearly superior to these alternate methods.[26] Of the applied work, Orgler (1970), Ewert (1969), Ewert and Chandler (1974b), Apilado, Warner, and Dauten (1974), and Myers and Forgy (1963) employ the holdout method. Hettenhouse and Wentworth (1971), Bates (1973), and Harter (1973) simply allow for user selection of desired error trade-offs, presumably based upon reclassification of the original samples. Lane (1972), Orgler (1971), and Altman, Margaine, Schlosser, and Vernimmen (1974) employ the original sample method, and Edmister (1971) uses a synthetic method. None of the studies have made use of either the Lachenbruch method, which provides almost unbiased estimates of the error rates, or the other methods listed in Table III.7, of Chapter III, which make use of the assumption of normality. The advantage of both the holdout and Lachenbruch methods is that they are more easily generalized to the cases when the group covariances are unequal and when there are more than two groups.

Selection of Analysis Samples

As Chandler (1977) notes, a special problem arises in credit scoring models because they are usually developed from samples of loans that have been granted; they are typically not based upon lending experience with the population of potential borrowers or through-the-door applicants. Short of granting loans to all comers, the potential user of a credit scoring model is usually forced to estimate a model with the truncated population of approved borrowers. Such a method is, however, subject to severe problems. Avery (1977) has investigated the effects on a scoring model (with known population parameters) of estimating the model with truncated-normal samples. His results are quite alarming. First, he notes that even when the underlying populations have equal covariances, use of truncated samples will lead one to reject the equal covariances hypothesis and employ quadratic rather than linear rules. Furthermore, one obtains biased estimates of the group means and dispersions, the true cutoff point, and true error rates. Lastly, the direction and extent of the bias is shown to depend upon the original truncation points and hence is not usually known *ex post.* In most instances then, without knowing the truncation system, it is not possible to estimate in which direction the bias lies. The results of Avery's work are of interest for two reasons. First, systems estimated from a sample of loans that have been previously screened are likely to be biased, and the direction and size of that bias is not known. Second, even if a lender decided to incur the costs of granting loans to all through-the-door applicants, there is still no assurance that such a sample would be representative of the population of potential borrowers. If borrowers are aware of an institution's credit policies, a self-prescreening may occur, which would make even the resulting through-the-door samples biased. On the other hand, since many institutions have such high acceptance rates, prescreening may not be a severe problem.

Chandler and Coffman (1977) discuss several alternatives to the problem of validation of the classification results when the model has been derived from prescreened samples, including an interesting heuristic method based upon sampling theory. Shinkel (1977) investigates two alternatives. One, employed by Long (1973), uses both "good" and "bad" accepted applicants together with the rejected applicants to estimate, based upon reclassification of the applicants, what proportion of the rejects are likely to be "good" and "bad." The second is a method called "augmentation," which weights the good and bad applicants in the accepted group by an estimate of the likelihood that each would be accepted. Shinkel (1977) concludes that both methods also yield biased estimates of the predictive ability of the scoring model. Avery (1977) has proposed a maximum likelihood method to correct for the bias in the estimates of the means and covariances to construct consistent estimates of these parameters that can be used to construct unbiased estimates of the error rates. This area is, however, as yet a new one for investigation and promises to be important in view of ECOA.

Few of the authors of particular scoring models, except perhaps Durand (1941), have recognized the limitations of models derived from prescreened data. Of course, the problems of prescreening are not relevant to the loan review models, since the focus is on the expected performance of loans that have been granted.

Time-Series Problems

The discussion of the underlying objective of a credit scoring model suggests that it is not only relevant to determine whether or not an applicant will default or otherwise experience financial difficulty over the life of the loan but also to determine when that difficulty is likely to occur. This is particularly the case if one wishes to enter profitability considerations into the loan granting process that might result in granting loans that are likely to default as long as they are current for a sufficient length of time for them to be profitable. This problem has not been considered in the applied credit scoring literature. There are some techniques, however, that have been proposed by Rulon et al. (1967) for use in personal classification that might be readily adapted to the problem of loan evaluation. Specifically, they involve the combined use of discriminant and time-series regression analysis. The attempt is to answer the question (given that a loan looks like it might be bad), "What's the likelihood that it will default in payment period 1, period 2, etc.?"

SUMMARY AND CONCLUSION

To place the applied literature in perspective, this chapter has reviewed the methodological foundations for the formulation and selection of credit scoring and loan review models. It was shown that existing scoring models have focused primarily on the minimization of default rates, which is, in fact, only one dimension of the more general credit granting problem. To the extent that profit maximization or cost minimization is, or should be, the objective of a scoring model, then most of the applied work seems incomplete. Even ignoring these problems, it is also shown that the applied work typically suffers from statistical deficiencies. Of equal concern is that some of the problems seem inherent in the discriminant analysis techniques employed or are not subject to easy remedy given the state of the art concerning estimation and sampling procedures.

NOTES

This chapter is a revised version of the paper by Eisenbeis (1978).

1. A large number of nontechnical pieces have appeared discussing the use of quantitative credit scoring models. See, for example, McGrath (1960); Biborosch (1965); Amstutze and Liebman (1966); Weingartner (1966); Cannellys (1967); Work (1967); Biborosch (1967); Abate (1969); Hammer and Orgler (1969); Coakley (1970); Roy and Lewis

(1970); Roy and Sanderson (1972); Gooch, Wagner, and Statham (1973); and Harter (1974).

2. For a model that contains several of the factors mentioned in the ECOA, see Gau (1978).

3. Bad debt cost = (probability of nonpayment) · (variable product cost).

4. Lost sales cost = (probability of payment) · (contribution margin).

5. Dirickx and Wakeman (1976) generalize the Bierman–Hausman (1970) model to include partial and/or full pay back over more than one period.

6. Both Greer (1967b) and Chandler and Ewert (1975) address this problem directly.

7. Work on consumer lending models and loans to individuals include Durand (1941); Myers and Forgy (1963); Smith (1964); Reinsel and Brake (1966); Pratt and McGhee (1967); Boggess (1967); Chatterjee and Barcun (1970); Hettenhouse and Wentworth (1971); Orgler (1971); Evans (1971); Lane (1972); Harter (1973); Apilado, Warner, and Dauten (1974); Ewert and Chandler (1974a); Chandler and Ewert (1975); Sexton (1977); and Gau (1978).

8. Business loan studies includes: Cohen, Gilmore and Singer (1966); Ewert (1969); Orgler (1970); Edmister (1971); Bates (1973); Chesser (1974); Altman, Margaine, Scholosser, and Vernimmen (1974); and Edelstein (1975).

9. These included: Orgler (1970, 1971); Evans (1971); Lane (1972); Chesser (1974) and Ewert and Chandler (1974b).

10. The critical analytical question is not simply to determine whether or not a loan will go into default. Rather, the problem centers on assessment of the probability of default in each period 1, 2, . . . , *i*, . . . , t over the life of the loan. In addition, the models of Mehta (1968, 1970) and Bierman and Hausman (1970) suggest that the probability of default in any period *i* may not be independent of previous payment performance in periods $(i - 1)$, $(i - 2)$, . . . , 1.

11. In this sense they are essentially single-period models with the period being the life of the loan. No attempt is made to determine at what specific intervals over the life of a loan it is more or less likely to default or become slow paying. An exception is the model of Ewert and Chandler (1974b) which focused on the likelihood that once a loan becomes slow paying in one period, it would continue to be slow paying in subsequent periods. This model is not, however, a credit granting model; it is a loan review and internal control model. In this respect, it is more closely linked to the work on optimal foreclosure policies of Pye and Tezel (1974) and Mitchner and Peterson (1957).

12. Chatterjee and Barcun (1970) did consider costs but only as a device to show how the cut-off points and error rates were shifted and not as an integral part of the model. Durand (1941) also considered costs but not as part of his empirical model.

13. These included Durand (1941); Myers and Forgy (1963); Smith (1964); Prat and McGhee (1967); Boggess (1967); Chatterjee and Barcun (1970); Evans (1971); Apilado, Warner, and Dauten (1974); Sexton (1977); and Gau (1978). No information was available on variables included in the study of Hettenhouse and Wentworth (1971).

14. Chatterjee and Barcun (1970) included martial status in their model but it was not possible to indicate what the direction of influence was. Sexton (1977) found that being married was a significant indication of credit worthiness, but being single, divorced or separated was not. Since these variables are perfectly collinear (with another set) the model is singular and, the results must be suspect. Harter (1973) found the number of years a person was married also indicative of credit worthiness.

15. It was not readily discernible what role age, marital status, and sex played in the study of Gau (1978).

16. See Chandler and Coffman (1977) for a discussion of the "effects test."

17. The models of Chatterjee and Barcun (1970); Chesser (1974); Cohen, Gilman, and

Singer (1966); Edelstein (1975); Smith (1964); and Myers and Forgy (1963) employ other statistical methods.

18. For a general discussion of the theory of discriminant analysis, see Eisenbeis and Avery (1972); Lachenbruch (1975); or Cooley and Lohnes (1962, 1971).

19. Each of these issues are explored in detail in Eisenbeis (1977) and Pinches (1978), with numerous references to the relevant theoretical and applied literature.

20. See Eisenbeis (1977) for a discussion and references.

21. All of the variables in Edmister (1971) are categorical and all but one in Orgler (1970) are dummy variables. Sexton (1977), as well as others, employed both continuous and binary variables.

22. In this connection, it is easy to show that use of dummy variables in a discriminant analysis model not only implies that the distributional assumptions are violated, but also that a quadratic model should be used.

23. Martell and Fitts (1977) employ a test proposed by James (1954) to test for the overall significance of the model when the group covariances are unequal.

24. At least six alternative methods have been proposed and employed; see Altman and Eisenbeis (1978). Several more are discussed in Chapter III.

25. It is not possible to determine whether group definition problems existed for the studies of Altman, Margaine, Schlosser, and Vernimmen (1974); Chatterjee and Barcun (1970); Orgler (1970); Ewert (1969); Pratt and McGhee (1967); Orgler (1971); Boggess (1967); Chandler and Ewert (1975); or Evans (1971).

26. For a discussion of the methods see Chapter III, Eisenbeis and Avery (1972) and also Eisenbeis (1977).

Chapter V

The Application of Statistical Classification Methods to Bond Quality Ratings

INTRODUCTION

Over the last decade, a relatively large number of research efforts and published materials have concentrated on the classification of fixed income securities of corporations and, to a lesser extent, of municipalities into formalized rating classes that supposedly represent gradients of default risk of the issuing entity. There are at least three private organizations in the United States that concentrate on the analysis of companies and municipalities and publish assessments of the investment quality of their publicly traded debt securities in the form of bond ratings. These ratings, supplied by Moody's, Standard & Poor's (S&P), and Fitch, receive wide publicity, are well-known and respected, and are thought to influence the market risk premium attached to securities. Studies by Harold (1938), Hickman (1958), and Atkinson and Simpson (1967) tend to confirm that there is indeed a high correlation between the bond ratings assigned and the eventual payoff of interest and principal.

Discussions with portfolio managers of insurance companies and bank trust departments verify that bond ratings are considered very seriously in the individual evaluation of securities. For example, West (1973) finds that ratings affect bond yields by influencing the "preferred list" of investment alternatives. In a study of recent new issues of industrial and public utility bonds, we observed that the percentage spread (underwriting commission) between the price paid by the public and the price received by the company on industrial bonds rated A or better was 0.875 percent of the issue, regardless of other aspects of the issue or the firm. All negotiated public utility bonds had a similar relationship. Bonds below A-rating did, however, show a wide differential in spread.

Because of the existence of bond ratings and their acceptance by investment analysts, market traders, and regulatory commissions, the subject has interested researchers enough to attempt to replicate, indeed predict, these ratings via published data and statistical techniques thought to be appropriate to the task—the general theory being that financial statement information and market related data, when analyzed in a sophisticated manner, can result in a precise evaluation of the issuing entity's risk characteristics, its market risk premium, and its bond rating. The review, discussion, and evaluation of these studies covering the period 1966–1979 is the subject of this chapter. It should be noted that rating agency executives consistently deny the possibility of replicating their ratings because the process is reflective, interpretive, and based on future as well as past factors and the ratings are not simply a "numbers game," e.g., Burke (1974) and Fraser (1976).

We will not attempt to explore each of the numerous bond rating studies in complete detail. This treatment is typically found in the initial part of each new research study, where the author reviews the past studies and explains why his approach is conceptually superior to past endeavors and then continues on to report his new empirical results. In addition to the basic research studies on bond ratings, the reader is referred to textbooks such as Lev (1974), where the "state of the art" is also reviewed quite well. Some detail, however, on the important studies is unavoidable because one of the main purposes of the book is to aid the researcher interested in financial analysis and statistical techniques applied in this area.

Each of the studies will be reviewed and categorized according to the statistical technique utilized to analyze bond risk premiums and bond quality ratings. Specifically, the techniques of multiple regression, linear and quadratic discriminant analyses, and logit analysis will form the categories. The latter two techniques are discussed in conceptual detail in prior chapters, and we assume that the reader is sufficiently familiar with regression techniques to follow the discussion. Related techniques such as factor and cluster analyses will be mentioned if they entered into the relevant studies. In our discussion of these studies, we will comment on the strengths and weaknesses of both the technique and how it was applied and also on the relative success it had on the analysis of the fixed income securities. We will then try to formulate a logical rationale for the success, or lack of success, of these studies with respect to their statistical explanatory power and predictive accuracies. Finally, we present a fairly complete review of the relevant studies in tabular form (Appendix A) with editorial commentary.

We concentrate on the *corporate* bond rating problem but also present a bibliography of municipal bond studies in Appendix B. We hasten to mention that the risk–return characteristics of municipal bonds are quite important in terms of the problems that analysts have had in the past and its potential future economic impact.

STATISTICAL BOND RATING ANALYSIS

It is important at the outset to define a bond rating and the rating process. Ratings are ordinal classifications that are typically expressed in letter(s) form—that is nonquantitative—but that are supposed to connote a certain hierarchy with respect to investment quality. Hence, the triple-A rated bonds are deemed less risky than double-A, and double-A less risky than single-A, etc., but there is no specific measurement attached with respect to the amount of risk differential. That is, the different values of the dependent variable (bond rating) represent an ordinal representation of risk but do not necessarily lie on a linear scale. In addition, within-group (rating) variability cannot be observed despite the opinion that differences in risk do exist. At least one of the rating agencies now assigns plus and minus designations as well as letters.

In this chapter studies that have analyzed the bond rating process are reviewed, and it is fair to say that the dominant objective, with few exceptions, was to *replicate* the bond rating process. Since the rating process itself is subjective and admittedly imperfect in many cases, it is not clear what we are observing when the various models manifest "errors." One possibility is that the model has misspecified risk characteristics and that stochastic random errors are observed. This type of error can be eliminated by more effective modeling. A second type of error might be the result of the *rater's* problem of faulty risk assessment on individual issues. This error cannot be corrected in the original model's construction even if the model is in fact capturing risk properly. Subsequent tracking of the fixed income security's bond rating might very well reveal that the *model's* result was more accurate than the *rater's* at the time of the model's construction. The model's classification accuracy would nonetheless be negatively affected.

The rating agencies oftentime do not agree with each other on the same security. "Split-ratings" for individual issues imply either that the various raters are looking at different indicators and/or their implicit weightings attached to the common indicators are not identical. Both reasons are likely to be the case, especially when one adds the subjective, expectation quality to the rater's analysis. Because most of the studies to be reviewed attempt to replicate either Moody's or Standard & Poor's ratings, one might argue that whichever rater is being examined, the model should reveal that agency's process. Alternatively, however, we would argue that the basic entity being rated—namely, the corporation—has fundamental risk characteristics and that split-ratings only confuse the issue. Modeling errors in classification of these firms' securities might be different from errors where the rating agencies agree. Even in the latter case, both or all raters could be "wrong." The split-rating problem is an interesting one, and we will return to it. In the final section of this chapter, more in-depth analysis of the rating and modeling process will be attempted in order to explain the results we have observed in the literature.

EVOLUTION OF STATISTICAL TECHNIQUES

One possible approach to the bond modeling process is to search for a type of dependent variable, other than the rating, that represents less ambiguous categorization. And this was exactly what occurred when Lawrence Fisher (1959) published his classic study on the explanation of market risk premiums on broad cross-sections of corporate data. This multiplicative-regression study was successful in explaining approximately three quarters of the variation in market risk premiums of bonds and is to this day a study that continues to be the basis for current analysis. Tambini (1969) updated Fisher's study with similar results. We shall see that Fisher's basic model has also been utilized for the bond rating problem (West, 1970).

Why then did the research emphasis shift to bond ratings rather than the more objective bond yields? The answer to this question is purely conjectural on our part, but perhaps several observations can help explain it. One can observe over time that the market yield on debt securities changes, in some cases dramatically (e.g., Lockheed's February, 1971 downrating), around the time bond ratings change. It is generally agreed that the primary yield movement in securities tends to change before the rating change, but evidence Katz (1974), Grier and Katz (1976) and Hettenhouse and Sartoris (1976), suggests that there remains some short-term reaction after the rating change. Weinstein (1977), however, showed that the "abnormal" return on bonds whose rating is changed is not significant in the period from 6 months prior to 6 months after the rating change. He did find some evidence of an "announcement effect," but the only real evidence of any prior adjustment is during the period from 1.5 to .5 years before the change is announced. He also finds, "contrary to Grier and Katz (1976), that there is no evidence of any adjustment after the rating change."

The rating change is an event; yield changes are continuous and timing is a less precise factor. Therefore, yield or return changes are difficult to explain and certainly more difficult to predict. Fundamental risk characteristics of firms do vary over time as well—probably changing less frequently than yields but certainly on a more continuous basis than rating changes. If prediction of bond rating changes could lead the actual change in rating by a sufficient amount of time, then the probability of trading profits and other benefits are clearly manifest. But how do we predict rating changes? The general feeling among researchers is that before you can predict an event, you must be able to understand the process—hence, the classification or replication stage. Therefore, one can observe that most bond rating studies have at least two integrated parts—the classification model and then some follow-up or prediction test sample. The latter test serves two purposes. First, it can help assess the model's reliability, and second, it provides some evidence on predictive accuracy.

The predictive curiosity and profit potential aspect of bond rating security analysis helped to stimulate research, and the number of related studies increased as well with the general emergence of modern, seemingly appropriate, statistical methodologies for the classification of qualitative dependent variable problems. In particular, discriminant analysis techniques applied to financial problems emerged in the late 1960s and early 1970s as a potentially interesting way to attack the bond rating phenomenon. As we will see, this change to discriminant analysis was partially the result of general skepticism toward the continued use of regression.

The number of bond rating studies has continued without abatement, partially due to the somewhat mediocre results accomplished to date. At a later point we will pursue this question of statistical accuracy and present a rationale for the fact that mediocre results are probably the best we can expect from this imperfect process known as bond ratings.

Multiple Regression Analysis Studies

After the initial regression study by Fisher (1959) on bond-market risk premiums, several studies attempted to pursue the bond rating problem with a similar statistical methodology. Horrigan (1966) utilized a two-step approach; first regressing a number of accounting data ratio profiles (from an initial group of 15 ratios) on the bond quality ratings of a sample of firms whose ratings were stable over a 6-year period (1959–1964). The dependent variable (ratings) was arbitrarily assigned values from 9 to 1 (Aaa to C), indicating a constant relationship between quality ratings. The "best" model (highest R^2) of many independent variable combinations was then used to predict the ratings of two other samples of bonds—new bond ratings and bonds that saw their ratings changed by the two major agencies. The prediction phase was indeed innovative but unfortunately created problems for attaining high predictive accuracy. The average value of five independent variables for each of the rating classes was calculated and multiplied by the estimated coefficients to arrive at a regression calculated rating (RCR) for *each rating*. This was done for the initial estimating sample. The second stage found each new bond being assigned an RCR based on its variable values compared with each rating's RCR. The closest rating class determined the prediction of bonds in the holdout samples.

West (1970) was critical of Horrigan's approach due to lack of a theory of the model and reliance on accounting data. He utilized the Fisher model's four independent variables (Appendix) and coded the dependent (rating class) measure in the same manner as Horrigan. West used log forms for all variables to allow for the interaction among the variables that were not assumed independent. Regression results from a single year's (1949) cross-section were used to predict the ratings of outstanding bonds 5 and 10 years hence. The actual prediction of a particular bond's rating was done in much the same manner as Horrigan's. Although West's results appear to be slightly superior to Horrigan's, West himself did not consider these results as particularly impressive or even significantly improved.

Several interesting issues arise when assessing the performance of the Horrigan and West studies. First, both utilized dependent variables as if they were on an interval scale; assigning the value 9 to the highest quality (Aaa) bonds and continuing down to a value of 1 for the lowest (C) quality ones. It is clear that ordinary least squares regression implies a nine-times risk differential between these two classes and at the same time a two-times risk differential between Aa (8) and B (4) rated bonds. While we can think of bond ratings as conveying ordinal imformation with respect to the relative investment quality of bonds, it is not correct to interpret these ratings as equal intervals of potential default. Since the rating process is by admission subjective in nature, such a precise interpretation is obviously without foundation. Horrigan (1966:45) admits that the interval coding of ratings may have been a problem.

With the assignment of "barrier" dependent variable values, it is clear that the error term of the regression equation will not equal zero and will probably not be normally distributed. McKelvey and Zavolina (1975) illustrate also that the variance of the error term will not be constant as a function of the independent variables. This would seem to be the case in both regression studies noted above and in the two group dichotomous (0–1) specifications used by Pogue and Soldofsky (1969) for bond rating analysis and by many others in failure prediction.

Pogue and Soldofsky (P&S) (1969) used a variant of ordinary least squares regression to classify bonds in the top four rating groups (Aaa–Baa) of industrial, public utility, and railroad bonds. In effect, the interval-scale problem referred to before was changed somewhat by only comparing two categories of bonds at a time, using the dummy (0–1) dependent variable technique. This sequential, pairwise comparison technique (essentially pairwise discriminant analysis) was used to *infer* multigroup relationships but still had many of the same problems as earlier studies, and a few new ones. The authors also implied an industry effect by segregating their analyses to the various sectors noted above.

The linear, two-group procedure utilized by P&S avoided multigroup interval comparison problems that were inherent in the Horrigan and West studies. By ignoring other groups, however, one has a built-in loss of information. Comparison of the Aaa and the Aa groups produces parameters that cannot account for the qualities of the lower rated bonds. If, as P&S also attempt, comparison is made between the extreme rating classes (Aaa and Baa) and nonadjacent classes (e.g., Aaa and A), then the qualities of the intermediate bonds are lost. In addition, since linear techniques pool covariance matrices in the determination of parameter estimates, intragroup differentials are not explicit and intergroup variances are assumed not equal. This latter problem is true of all linear techniques (regression, discriminant, logistic, etc.) and implies that more information is potentially gained by nonlinear structures that are not pooled. Even if P&S had tested for group variance equality between their two-group analyses and could not reject variance–covariance equality, simultaneous testing of groups may still reject it. Finally, their conclusion that differences in bond rating classification can be adequately explained by available financial data is suspect due to the statistical procedures that they utilized.

Before leaving the regression analysis section, we should mention that the most recent effort to accurately describe, via statistical analysis, the bond rating process is again a variant of the ordinary least squares regression technique—known as logit analysis (Kaplan and Urwitz, 1979). We will return to this framework after reviewing the discriminant analysis studies.

Discriminant Analysis Studies

The results of the several regression studies on replicating and predicting bond ratings left the issue of the statistical validity and accuracy unresolved (see discussion of results in a subsequent section). About the time that these regression studies were being completed, the application of discriminant analysis to finance problems was becoming popular and somewhat more sophisticated. Discriminant analysis, which assumes that the observations being evaluated come from different populations, seemed an appropriate extension of the work already completed and described above. The bond rating process is after all a qualitative one and the dependent variable clearly has no numerical value—*ex ante.* What's more, the quadratic variation of the classical linear discriminant approach has the potential to deal with differences between groups (bond-ratings) more effectively, but still does not consider the continuous nature of risk and default probability.

With discriminant analysis, a series of functions is computed to maximize the ratio of the squared distance between groups to the within-group squared deviations. Because the technique concentrates on selecting a set of variables that best separates groups, it obviates the need to impose an interval scale between the groups. Although the implicit interpretation of results that quantify (*ex post*) the "scores" of each bond is of an ordinal or scaled nature, the technique does not explicitly consider the ordinal nature of bond ratings in arriving at the "best" parameters. That is, separation is most important and not the theoretical spacing of the most credit-worthy category (Aaa) from the second most credit-worthy (Aa) category, and so on. In essence, it ignores the fact that the G (number of bond rating classes) groups can be viewed as categorized widths of unequal range with respect to the dimension that is implicit in any bond analysis—risk of default. While avoiding the interval scale assumption necessary in ordinary least squares regression studies, such as the ones by Horrigan and West, discriminant analysis cannot exploit all of the potential information in the ordinal bond rating structure.

The discriminant analysis technique does provide an important contrast to the regression studies and was pursued primarily by Pinches and Mingo (P&M) (1973, 1975) and Altman and Katz (1976). P&M evaluated newly issued industrial bonds, which were rated into five categories (Aa–B). They reasoned, incorrectly in our opinion, that independence of the discriminant explanatory variables was an important quality and therefore conducted their initial study in a two-step approach. First, factor analysis was employed on 35 accounting and financial variables to identify orthogonal components of the data. Then, supposedly the most important variable of each of the factors was selected for further analysis in the discriminant model. This type of sequential approach to discriminant analysis variable selection has intuitive appeal for some researchers because it takes the variable selection process a step removed from actual discriminant classification and attempts to reduce collinearity. Orthogonality will not be achieved, however, by selecting a single variable from the various factors because it is the latter that are independent of each other, not the variables (unless the factor loading is 1.0). In fact, a linear combination of *all* variables is found in *every* factor, and in the final analysis, the use of factor analytical techniques is not intuitively appealing at all.

Principal component analysis (Altman, Margaine, Schlosser, and Vernimmen, 1973) has been used for essentially the same purpose with only mediocre success at best. Cluster analysis (Morton and McLeavey, 1976) has been used to group firms by their credit worthiness characteristics, and the clusters were compared with Moody's bond ratings. Only one cluster (out of five) seemed to stand out as unambiguous, and comparison with ratings was insignificant.

Returning to P&M, seven factors were identified as containing different data dimensions among the firms that comprised the five bond rating classes. In fact, their final discriminant model contained data from only five of the factors (six different variables), but the reader is left unaware of why this was the case. A possible reason for this result is that orthogonality and factor loadings play little role in the construction of an accurate discriminant model. Collinearity is simply not a problem (except in extreme cases where matrix inversion is not possible) and, in fact, high negative correlations (Cochran, 1964; Altman, 1968) have been argued for and shown to be quite important in classification and predictive accuracy assessment. Clearly, little can be said about the individual variable significance tests when nonindependence among the discriminant variables exists, but (as was explained in detail in an earlier chapter) in discriminant analysis, the "name of the game" is group separation and accurate classification by the entire profile of variables and not by the individual components. The concern about multicollinearity in discriminant studies has been pervasive within the literature, and we want to make it clear that this should not be considered important. When prediction is the goal, it would seem inappropriate to begin discarding variables and dimensions without concern about what is being sacrificed in terms of overall accuracy.

In the final analysis, the original P&M bond rating discriminant model did not seem to consider the factor analysis information very much and the resulting linear discriminant model was accurate in certain bond ratings and unimpressive in others, primarily the Baa class. Because this class contains bonds of both subordinated and nonsubordinated status, and one of the P&M variables was a dichotomous dummy to designate presence or absence of subordination, the revised P&M study (1975) had as one of its objectives to assess the accuracy when the subordinated variable (which was also present in the Horrigan study) was eliminated. A second objective of the revised study was to consider a nonlinear form of the discriminant model—namely, quadratic—in order to capture group differences more effectively and to exploit the information content of nonhomogeneous covariance matrices from one bond rating group to another. The newer model (five variable quadratic) did improve upon the troublesome Baa class, but showed reduced accuracy in other classes.[1] Still, P&M claimed increased classification and predictive accuracies over the previous regression studies and continued the trend to try to "outdo the last bond rating study." This study also suffered from the lack of assessment of statistical significance of certain tests with and without the subordination variable, i.e., multivariate *F*, chi-square measure of group overlap, and overall classification accuracy tests.

Altman and Katz (1976) also applied quadratic discriminant analysis but limited their study to securities in the electric public utility industry. Unlike P&M, no prior testing or *a priori* screening of the variables was done, although the selection of potential variables was by no means arbitrary. Not being concerned with explanatory variable independence, i.e., multicollinearity, their model was composed of 14 variables—far more than in any other bond rating study. The *classification* results of this study were extremely high (over 90 percent) and the authors attributed this success to (1) concentration on a homogeneous business risk category, (2) quadratic as opposed to linear analysis, and (3) unambiguous bond ratings. The latter will be pursued in greater detail at a later point, but essentially only bonds that received the *same* rating by the two major rating agencies were considered and these bonds could not have been involved in a rating change (over the study period 1969–1971). In addition, they varied the *a priori* probabilities of group (rating) membership and observed its effect on classification results.

The Altman–Katz study can be criticized for not including all members of the bond population, i.e., mixed ratings by Moody's and S&P and changed rating bonds, and as such cannot be used with total confidence on new samples of bonds. In addition, the extensive fitting of the data with their model probably contributed to the high classification accuracy. This was partially shown to be the case when the Lachenbruch (1967) holdout sample technique revealed considerably lower overall accuracies (77 percent)—particularly apparent in the extreme (Aaa and Baa) classes. Still, the holdout accuracy was higher than in any previous or, for that matter, subsequent bond rating study. Whether restricting the study to unambiguously rated bonds was a virtue or not is a matter of methodological opinion that can be argued on both sides.[2] One might even postulate a "new" bond rating category that includes only those bonds that received mixed ratings between two adjacent categories. With the exception of Aa versus A bonds among electric utility securities, however, adjacent categories would not provide sufficient numbers of mixed ratings for statistical testing.

Rappaport, Murphy, and Parr (1979) also were concerned with the mixed rating problem, and like Altman–Katz, analyzed only those companies that were rated identically by Moody's and S&P. They did not find a significant difference in ratings between the two agencies but still restricted their analysis to equivalently rated securities. The authors analyzed 123 *commercial paper* ratings of industrial companies that were rated into the two highest categories in 1977. A factor analysis technique screened 37 original variables with the resulting stepwise quadratic discriminant function selecting six measures. Results were "modest but not overpowering" (Rappaport et al., 1979:10), with an overall classification accuracy level of 83 percent. The shift in emphasis to short-term financial instruments is an interesting extension of the bond rating subject.

Unfortunately, the authors of this commercial paper study do not test their model on holdout samples, do not attempt predictive evaluation and ignore a third rating category (lowest rating). We also find it suboptimal to first reduce the variable set via a factor analytical technique and then to utilize a stepwise discriminant methodology. Factor analysis, as we have seen earlier, is not particularly useful because it assumes all observations come from the same population, and in this case it reduced the variable set from 37 to 17 measures. The 20 "screened out" variables might have been helpful for classification purposes.

A slight variation on the bond rating replication procedure is to concentrate directly on the bond quality rating *change* event. Bhandari, Soldofsky, and Boe (BSB) (1979) utilized a two-group, linear discriminant function to classify bonds into either upgrades or downgrades and then attempted to examine the resulting discriminant score distribution to assign new observations into an additional category, i.e., no change in rating. Whereas many of the studies cited above have as their ultimate objective the prediction of rating changes, BSB attacked the problem directly. Utilizing traditional measures, with trends and stability estimates of these measures, their study examined rating changes of 49 industrial companies in 1974 and 1975 and had a "control" sample of 24 firms with no rating change in its bonds for comparison purposes.

The authors did not include the no-change category in their analysis for several reasons, including problems in (1) assigning *a priori* probabilities of group membership, (2) selection of a representative sample of firms belonging to the no-change group, and (3) the ability to specify that an arbitrarily defined zone that is between the actual two extreme groups "can accomplish the no-change predictions" (Bhandari et al., 1979:7). We remain unconvinced primarily because any function that ignores in its construction a substantial segment of the population will not have the ability to evaluate new observations representing the entire population. The parameters of the two-group model are unique to those samples and should only be utilized to classify and predict elements to these same *a priori* groups. In addition, it would appear to us that specification of realistic *priors* and selection of representative sample observations for a three-group analysis are easily specified.[3]

The results of the rating change model, like most others, are mediocre, with considerably more success in predicting upgrades than downgrades. A procedure for classifying new observations into one of the two original groupings or a third (no-change) group was suggested. This admittedly subjective approach is simulated for numerous alternative prediction strategies, with the choice of boundary scores left up to the analyst.

Logit Analysis

A recent attempt to statistically explain the somewhat illusive bond-rating issue utilized an approach that, it is argued, combines the best qualities of both ordinary least squares regression (OLS) and discriminant techniques. This study (Kaplan and Urwitz, 1979) uses logit analysis. This methodology is a variant of regression analysis but does not assume that the various assignments of dependent variable values represent equal intervals on a scale as do, for example, bond ratings of 1 to 9 found in the studies of Horrigan and West. Logit analysis also does not ignore the ordinal information content inherent in successively higher (or lower) bond ratings. Further, since it is a parametric technique using tests similar to OLS with respect to individual variable significance, it is argued that the results have greater economic meaning than if one used discriminant analysis. Actually, *individual* variable significance test ability is a mixed blessing. In order for the tests to have validity, assumptions about the normality of individual variable distributions are necessary, whereas in discriminant analysis only multivariate normality is assumed. Still, it would appear that the assumptions of discriminant analysis are more strict than logit analysis, and the latter technique is becoming increasingly popular in financial research.[4]

We have discussed in a previous chapter the theoretical nature of logit analysis. With respect to the specific application of this technique to bond ratings, the dependent variable can represent an ordinal but not necessarily a linear or equal scale. That is, A-rated bonds are less risky than Baa ones, but there is no theoretical *a priori* basis for determining how much less risky.

Kaplan and Urwitz (K&U) distinguish between the theoretical dependent variable of interest, Y = default risk, and the observed variable, Z = bond rating. Z is categorical, like discriminant analysis, and has M response categories, where M equals the number of bond ratings. By postulating $M + 1$ numbers for the dependent variable, with extreme values $\mu_0 = -\infty$ and $\mu_9 = +\infty$ and with K variables, the basis for postulating a nonlinear dependent variable is apparent. To identify the model, $\mu_1 = 0$ with $\sigma_1 = 1$. Maximum likelihood estimation techniques are applied to the problem with $M + K + 1$ parameters estimated; that is, $\mu_2, \ldots, \mu_{M-1}$ and the weights $\beta_0, \beta_1, \ldots, \beta_k$ are estimated.

K&U utilized the maximum likelihood, probit technique and compared their results directly with the prior regression studies of Horrigan and West. A model with a small number of independent variables was desirable to these authors but they inappropriately, in our opinion, cite the 14-variable Altman–Katz discriminant study as an example of too many variables. Actually, K&U also look at a relatively large number of potentially important explanatory variables themselves and settle on eight, including a dummy variable representing subordination status. Their original sample includes only unchanged rated bonds in the study period (1971–1972) and new issues for their holdout sample. The authors caution that their results are only preliminary, but despite the greater sophistication of their model *vis-à-vis* earlier OLS techniques, the results do not appear to be appreciably better; and they tentatively conclude that "OLS regression on bond ratings may not involve the pitfalls that we might have anticipated". K&U conclude that "Horrigan's model appears to have aged well" having *superior* explanatory power on K&U's sample than on his own and that "overall the OLS equation performs slightly better than the probit equation, which is contrary to our expectations" (Kaplan and Urwitz, 1979:43). They reason that perhaps the six rating (Aaa to B) classes give a close approximation to a continuous dependent variable.[5] A detailed discussion on empirical accuracy in bond rating studies follows.

HOW ACCURATE HAVE STATISTICAL BOND RATING STUDIES BEEN

We have reviewed most of the important corporate bond-rating studies and one thing is eminently clear. An enormous amount of time and effort have gone into their cumulative works. A fair question to pose therefore is just how effective have they been. The answer in strictly statistical terms seems to be that the results have been good but by no means significant enough to make true believers out of most market practitioners, and certainly not the raters themselves. When one reflects on the bond rating process itself, however, the overall conclusion is, in our opinion, that the results are just about as good as one could hope for. This section of the chapter will review the primary statistical results of the studies discussed in the preceding statistical methodology section. The following section will attempt to explain these results in view of the process and realities of bond ratings.

Table V.1 lists the statistical accuracy of results of the several studies noted above—starting with Horrigan (1966) and going through Kaplan and Urwitz (1979). These results are listed in terms of (1) original sample classification or explanation accuracy, and (2) results from various types of holdout (test) samples. The tests and samples are not identical from study to study and the techniques themselves are different; hence, exact comparisons are not possible. We feel, however, that the tests are similar enough to draw some comparative conclusions and the magnitude of the reported accuracies are indicative of some fairly clear absolute conclusions.

The two main standards utilized for evaluating the explanatory and predictive accuracy of the models are the regression studies' R^2 tests and the discriminant analyses percent-of-correct-observations assessment.[6] In the case of Pogue and Soldofsky's dummy dependent variable (0–1) specification, we can report both types of tests. As noted above, results are reported for the original sample (model construction) and for various types of holdout samples including (1) independent samples in the same time period as the original samples; (2) subsequent period samples; (3) Lachenbruch analysis; and (4) in the last column of Table V.1, a retrospective analysis of the explanatory accuracies of four of the studies (made by Ang and Patel, 1975). The latter presents holdout results based on several cross-sections in the years prior to the time the actual studies were carried out.

It is obvious that R^2 and percentage accuracy in classification are not identical, but less obvious is the fact that OLS regression R^2 results are not in fact the same as logit or probit analysis R^2's. The latter can be extremely biased upward because the dependent variable is essentially a range between two values and if the observation falls within this range (i.e., correct bond rating classification), there will be no contribution toward the residual sum of squares. For OLS, due to the estimation of a discrete dependent variable with a continuous model, any estimated value different from the discrete dependent variable (e.g., Aa = 8) will indeed contribute to the residual error, even if the observation is correctly classified. Hence, we observe that the Kaplan–Urwitz study shows extremely high R^2 values but the percentage accuracy tests are very similar to the Horrigan and West R^2s. In fact, K&U conclude that

Table V.1. Comparison of Empirical Results: Corporate Bond Rating Models

Study (Author and Date)	*Percentage of Success Model Building Sample (Original)*	*Percentage of Success Test Sample(s) (Holdout)*	*Ang and Patel (1975) Empirical Findings*
Horrigan (1966)	R^2 = 0.65 (Moody's) R^2 = 0.63 (S&P)	R^2 = 0.58,0.54 (Moody's) R^2 = 0.52,0.57 (S&P)	% Accuracy = 0.30
West (1970)	R^2 = 0.75 (Moody's)	R^2 = 0.62 (4 years) R^2 = 0.60 (12 years)	% Accuracy = 0.35
Pogue and Soldofsky (1969)	% Accuracy = 0.85 (Moody's Industrials) $\bar{R}^2$ = 0.60 (Industrials) $\bar{R}^2$ = 0.55 (Utilities, Aaa versus Baa) R^2 = 0.93 (Railroads)	% Accuracy = 0.80 (Moody's Industrials)	% Accuracy = 0.46
Pinches and Mingo (1973)	% Accuracy = 0.70	% Accuracy = 0.65 (Holdout)	% Accuracy = 0.39
Pinches and Mingo (1975)	% Accuracy = 0.65 (Test I) % Accuracy = 0.75 (Test II)	% Accuracy = 0.56 (New Issues)	
Altman and Katz (1976)	% Accuracy = 0.91 (Moody's and S&P combined)	% Accuracy = 0.77 (Moody's and S&P combined)	—
Kaplan and Urwitz (1979)	R^2 = 0.91 % Accuracy = 0.64 R^2 = 0.94 % Accuracy = 0.70	% Accuracy = 0.59 % Accuracy = 0.65	—

R^2 = Coefficient of determination; percentage of the variation in the dependent variable explained by the combined group of presumably independent explanatory variables.

% Accuracy = Overall percentage of observations in the sample categorized by the model correctly and placed in the actual bond rating.

despite the increased sophistication of their work *vis-à-vis* the other two models, the results indicate that there is little to be gained in terms of statistical accuracy.

All of the results listed in Table V.1 are for industrial bonds, with the exception of Altman–Katz and one sample of Pogue–Soldofsky. The latter's industrial results appear to demonstrate a slight edge in accuracy over the other industrial bond studies. This statistical edge could be explained by the bias inherent in a linear model that is used in sequential, paired-group analyses. The linear approach assumes equal covariance matrices of the *G* groups, and to the extent this is not the case, the results are biased. Despite this characteristic, Ang and Patel (1975) find that Pogue–Soldofsky consistently outperform the other industrial models. The relatively low R^2 results in these latter comparisons, however, cast considerable doubt on the effectiveness of any of the models. Further, Ang and Patel (1975) observe that the parameters of the various models are unstable and that the abilities of the models to predict eventual financial distress of corporations is limited to the short term and only in the short term (1 to 3 years) are these models able to outperform random selections methods. At the same time, in terms of predicting financial repayment problems, Ang and Patel (1975) conclude that in several instances the purely statistical models outperform the results implied by the ratings given by Moody's. What this all means is hard to say because the statistical model's primary objective was to *replicate* Moody's or S&P and not outperform them.

In the final analysis, one must conclude that the results of the various models are mediocre at best. The percentage accuracies range from just above 50 percent to close to 80 percent on holdout samples and this might be considered as evidence confirming what bond raters have always claimed—that statistical computerized models will never be able to duplicate the complex rating process. At the same time, we have seen evidence that the potentially low-cost (of operation), statistical models can do as well or better than bond raters in terms of default risk evaluation, which is far more important than the bond replication process itself. In terms of *replicating* the rating system, whether Moody's or S&P's, the results appear to leave a great deal of room for improvement. The next section will explore this observation and present arguments that future studies really *cannot* be expected to improve very much upon existing results, given the nature of the rating process.

RATING REPLICATION RESULTS—CAN THEY BE IMPROVED?

In our opinion, the ability of statistical models, which are based on reported financial data, to replicate the ratings given to fixed income securities by professional rating companies is not likely to improve. Theoretically, there is a great deal of room for improvement when studies yield 60–70 percent in observed explanatory power, i.e., adjusted R^2 or percentage of bonds accurately classified. We feel that existing studies have yielded these "mediocre" results for at least four reasons and only two of these imply any potential future improvement. The other two, however, concern the rating process itself, the nature of which seems to preclude the possibility of much improvement. The specific categorizations of our explanation of received results are statistical methodology; industry effects; bond ratings—a subjective process; and "mixed" bond ratings.

Statistical Methodology

Implicit in our prior discussion on bond rating studies is the search for an optimal methodology to utilize for this very special problem. Researchers have explored fairly sophisticated approaches including univariate and multivariate analyses; linear and nonlinear structures and various types of dependent variable specifications. If we knew the next *logical* step in the evolving statistical attack on bond ratings, we would be carrying out these tests ourselves at this very moment. The simple answer is that we do not know what will work to improve upon existing results. There are certainly many other potentially interesting approaches and we are confident that the exploration by researchers, both university-based and investment professionals, has not seen its final attempt. The next few paragraphs will discuss other rationales for limited success and, in so doing, hopefully explore changes in methodology to aid the researcher.

Industry Effects

Most of the studies discussed above concentrated on industrial bonds and quite naturally included firms in vastly different sectors of the economy. While the cross-sectional, diverse representation is not necessarily a problem, it may be if bond ratings themselves are not evenly distributed across industries—or better said—if industries are not evenly distributed across ratings. If the raters implictly are treating some industries as more risky than others (i.e., ascribing lower bond ratings on average), and the explanatory variables selected are not sensitive to this ordinal ranking, then lower accuracy will be observed *vis-à-vis* studies concentrating on a particular sector. This assumes, of course, that the variables are theoretically valid to measure one type of risk or another for a given type of firm, but not so for firms of different business characteristics. For instance, earnings instability might be measured by the standard error of estimate around a trend line of earnings/assets. But, if raters presume that one type of firm (e.g., food processing) can tolerate a certain degree of instability more effectively than another type (e.g., car manufacturing), then even if the measure is theoretically sound, it will create problems. Essentially we are saying that if there is an implicit industry effect, and the model does not provide for it, then results will suffer. This reason is tied up with the nature of the rating process and we will return to it in the next subsection.

The two studies mentioned earlier, which did attempt to isolate firms by industry, were Pogue and Soldofsky (industrials, railroads, and utilities) and Altman and Katz (electric public utilities only).[7] The former had the industry-effect problem in their industrial sample but not in the other samples. The latter did not have the problem. Both studies seem to demonstrate superior accuracies, but we cannot isolate the industry effect as a definite reason for these results. Still, it is logical to assume that, by restricting the analysis to a relatively homogeneous group, the likelihood of higher accuracy increases. Horrigan did attempt to handle the industry effect by directly adjusting the variables, but this does not seem to have been very successful. On the other hand, one might interpret his results as showing evidence of no industry effect. We leave the issue as potentially a factor but probably the least important of our reasons.

Bond Rating—A Subjective Process

Perhaps the primary restrictive factor is that statistical models based solely on reported data cannot effectively replicate a process that is subjective and likely to be irrational in some cases. The statistical model may very well register "errors" in classification but may indeed have captured a valid categorization of the bond. If the rating is itself, at the time of the model's construction, not effectively portraying potential risk of default of certain observations, then a "miss" will be recorded. Subsequent changes in the rating may vindicate the model, but still the error remains. One possible way to rectify this is to ignore errors of this type or else limit the sample to unchanged bond ratings in the near future as well as in the past (see Horrigan, 1967 and Altman and Katz, 1976). This will probably have a positive effect on results, but it will restrict the analysis to a subset of bonds.

Those who believe in efficient markets might claim that prices (or yields) do indeed reflect all available information and that the best model is one that is based on yields and not ratings. We have already seen that a model of this type (Fisher), when used to explain bond ratings (West), did not appreciably improve on other studies based on rating replication only. Of course, the Fisher model itself left a fair amount of market yield unexplained. To the extent that market yields are perfectly correlated with bond ratings, the subjective nature of the rating process should not bias expected results in the way we imply in the previous paragraph. If, however, the ratings themselves influence yield, then the subjective process could lead to errors in the objective statistical models.

Mixed Bond Ratings—An Observed Phenomenon

Our final rationale concerns the method by which the researcher sets up the problem and chooses his sample. In all but two of the studies noted earlier, the dependent variable is based on the ratings received from either Moody's or Standard & Poor's. To the extent that the two agencies do not agree on a particular bond's rating at a specific point in time, there will be ambiguity in the rating used and a source of potential error.

How serious is this problem of mixed rating? Table V.2 illustrates the timing of rating changes on bonds changed by both Moody's and Standard & Poor's in the electric public utility sectors from 1960 to 1976. This frequency distribution shows the number of months that one rater's change led or lagged behind the other rater's. Note that the rating changes by the two agencies took place in the same month in only 18 percent of the cases, with the average lead time when one agency changed first being 12 months (median of 6 months). Firms whose ratings were not changed by both agencies are not included. Therefore, there is an additional number of observations where one agency may have changed a rating to a grade different from the other,

Table V.2. Identical Rating Changes by Moody's and S&P on Public Utility Bonds, Summary Data on Comparative Timing (1960–1979)

Total number of observations	133
Number of instances when S&P changed rating earlier	58
Number of instances when Moody's changed rating earlier	53
Number of instances when both changed rating in same month	22
Average monthly timing difference for all changes	11.5
Median monthly timing difference for all changes	7

Source: Moody's and S&P Monthly Bond Guides and summary data provided by rating companies.

but because both did not change their ratings, those observations are not listed.

Comparison data of electric utility bonds rated as of July, 1979 showed that 17.6 percent of the bonds were rated differently by the two leading agencies. Mixed rating for individual issues imply that the various raters are looking at different indicators and/or that their implicit weightings attached to the common indicators are not identical. Both reasons are likely to be the case, especially when one adds the subjective, expectation quality to the rater's analysis.

In his analysis of municipal bonds, Morton (1975) presents some additional evidence on the mixed bond rating problem. He observed that of 137 city bonds rated by both Moody's and Standard & Poor's in 1972, identical ratings were found in only 70 percent of the cases. While ratings of the two agencies are probably not independent of each other, in the 30 percent (41 cases) where the ratings differed, Moody's ratings were higher in just two instances and Stardard & Poor's ratings were higher 39 times. Thus, for *cities* in Morton's sample, S & P tended to be more liberal in giving higher ratings. Public utility bond rating change data (Table V.3) indicate, however, that there has not been a significant difference over time in the propensity to change ratings earlier by either of the two agencies. Also, recent discussion with rating agency personnel revealed that criteria and procedures in rating corporate debt are constantly changing, especially for public utilities in the 1980s. Therefore, to generalize about the relative "liberalness" of one agency versus the other is not particularly meaningful.

Tables V.2 and V.3 illustrate that, over time, there are a considerable number of mixed or ambiguous ratings. Which rating should be used? One cannot say which rating service is "correct," and to the extent the two disagree, there will be an element in the methodology that adds to the number of "mistakes" in observed accuracy. One possible means of adjusting for this bias is to base the model only on those bonds that received the same rating by both agencies at the relevant cross-sectional point in time. If one further restricts the sample to those bonds whose rating remained unchanged over some relevant period, then the ingredients for a less ambiguous analysis are present. Of course, the danger is that information will be lost by omitting certain observations.

CONCLUSION

This chapter has reported on the evolution of statistical classification techniques applied to the corporate bond rating phenomena. In so doing, we have critiqued the various studies and presented our evaluation of the current state of the art. While the bond rating analysis

Table V.3. Number of Times and Duration That One Rating Agency's Change in Bond Rating Leads the Other (Public Utility Bonds, 1960–1979)

Lead Time in Months	*Instances When Standard & Poor Lead Moody's*	*Instances When Moody's Lead Standard & Poor*
0	—	—
1	10	5
2	0	5
3	4	4
4	3	4
5	1	3
6	2	4
7	2	1
8	3	0
9	2	0
10	3	2
11	0	2
12	6	2
13–24	11	11
25–36	5	4
>36	6	6
Total	58	53

subject has evolved with ever increasing sophistication, we feel that rating replication and prediction is presently at a plateau stage and the move to a higher level will not be an easy one.

Appendix A follows

APPENDIX A

Summary of Studies Using Statistical Classification Techniques for Corporate Bond Rating Purposes (In Chronological Order)

Study, Purpose, and Sample Characteristics	*Statistical Methodology and Primary Variables*	*Unique and/or Interesting Aspects of Study and Some Critical Comments*
1. *J. Horrigan (1966).* To explain industrial bond ratings of separate samples of nonchanged Moody's and S&P bonds (1959–1964). Used best model to predict changed rating bonds (1961–1964) and newly rated bonds (1961–1964). Over 150 bonds in each of the original models	*Multiple regression analysis;* two-step process of best regression model to determine a regression calculated rating (RCR) for each rating class. Firms in secondary samples then were compared to the RCR for rating assignment. Variables included (1) total assets, (2) working capital/sales, (3) sales/net worth, (4) operating profit/sales, (5) net worth/debt, and (6) subordination status	*First attempt to replicate/predict bond ratings.* Problem with equal-interval, linear dependent variable scaled from 9(AAA) to 1(C). Dummy subordination variable added significantly to explanatory power but introduces problems (see Pinches and Mingo, below). Best model from many attempts with different sets of variables; tries to adjust for industry effect
2. *T. Pogue and R. Soldofsky (1969).* To classify three samples of Moody's Industrials, Utilities, and Railroad bonds into four rating classes (Aaa–Baa). Sample size of 40 firms in each model covering the period 1961–1964	*Sequential dichotomous (0–1) dependent variable, multiple linear regression models;* adjacent bond ratings compared and also Aaa versus Baa. Explanatory variables included (1) debt/total capital; (2) net income/total assets, (3) coefficient of variation of (2); (4) interest coverage, and (5) total assets	*Small sample problems.* Sequential two-group models are not necessarily appropriate for multigroup conclusions due to nonhomogeneity of the group dispersion matrices. Recognized importance of separation by sectors although only holdout results given for industrials. Seems to have highest accuracy of industrial bond models
3. *R. West (1970).* To explain and predict ratings of Moody's Industrial bonds. Sample of 57 bonds in 1949 used to establish model for prediction of ratings on samples of existing bonds in 1953 and 1961	Utilized *Fisher's* (1959) *multiplicative, logarithmic regression model* in a similar two-step process to Horrigan (1966). Firms in secondary samples classified by their regression "score" compared with the various ratings' average scores. Explanatory measures include (1) coefficient of variation of net income/assets, (2) number of years of no solvency problems, (3) market value of equity/debt, (4) market value of outstanding debt	Used *market risk premium model* for bond ratings and problem of interval separation between dependent variable values; choice of "best" regression from many cross-sections is biased. Utilized market measures as well as accounting data. Results apppeared to be slightly superior to prior study (Horrigan) but author concedes his model is probably no better

4. *G. Pinches and K. Mingo (1973).* Classification of 180 newly issued industrial bonds into five Moody's rating classes (Aa–B) covering period 1967–1968. Holdout sample of 48 bonds in sample period and 48 new bonds issued in 1969	*Three-step process* of applying *factor analysis* to original sample to determine important factors and measures; then selected measures integrated into a 5-group linear discriminant model to establish classification criteria; finally, model tested on 2 holdout samples. Important discriminant variables include (1) subordination (0–1) status, (2) years of consecutive dividends (log), (3) issue size (log), (4) interest coverage (log), (5) debt/assets, and (6) income/assets	First to apply *factor-discriminant analysis statistical combination* but final model only partially reflects factor analysis results; established extreme importance of subordination feature but found its use a mixed blessing due to very low accuracy in group where bonds are both subordinated and not; utilized several trend (5-year means) variables; first to use discriminant model for interval scale problem of dependent variable but added ordinality problem
5. *E. Altman and S. Katz (1976)* Classification of Moody's and S&P electric public utility bonds into four rating classes (Aaa–Baa). Original and holdout samples consisted of 260 observations (1969–1971) of nonchanged and nonmixed rating bonds. Analysis done for Moody's and S&P combined and also separated. Observed accuracy in predicting rating changes in 1972–1975 period	*Quadratic, multigroup* discriminant analysis with Lachenbruch holdout test applied. Model contained 14 discriminant variables, the most important of which were (1) interest coverage, (2,3) variability of interest coverage and operating income, (4) return on assets, (5) total assets, (6) market value equity/book value equity, (7) retained earnings/assets, and (8) maintenance and depreciation/operating revenue	*First application of quadratic discriminant analysis* to bond rating problem; compared quadratic with linear results; extensive fitting of data to problem; problem with ordinality of dependemt variable concerned with the mixed (S&P differs from Moody's) bond rating problem; holdout results considerably lower than original although still the *highest percentage accuracy of all bond rating studies;* admitted and tested for nonindependence of observations. Modest predictive results on rating changes; tested for various *a priori* probability assumptions
6. *G. Pinches and K. Mingo (1975)* Same original sample as 1973 study, only divided the bonds into subordinated and nonsubordinated categories. Purpose to assess the bias in 1973 study of including subordinated bonds; similar problem that Horrigan (1967) and Kaplan-Urwitz (1979) had	Applied *quadratic discriminant structure* to two models; one contained the same variables as 1973 study except did not include subordination status (0–1) variable. The second separated subordinate from nonsubordinated bonds and had two samples; nonsubordinated (Aa, A, Baa) and subordinated (Baa, Ba, B)	Trade-off in results between higher accuracy in those ratings where *subordination* exists *vis-à-vis* lower accuracy where it does not exist. Did not completely compare old model with new one because old one was linear; also, did not use holdout samples in new model tests. Did not test for statistical significance with and without subordination variable; also, did not observe the actual classifications of individual bonds under different model assumptions

Study, Purpose and Sample Characteristics	*Statistical Methodology and Primary Variables*	*Unique and/or Interesting Aspects of Study and Critical Comments*
7. *J. Ang and K. Patel (1975).* Compared the accuracy of several (4) existing bond rating statistical models for *industrial* bonds in periods *prior to* the relevant studies' development. Also, compared prior studies' accuracy in predicting expost loss experience with that of Moody's. Sample of 414 bonds	Tested data from bonds in the periods 1928, 1932, 1934, 1936, and 1938 on existing rating models and compared their classifications of ratings with that of Moody's. Financial loss performance for each of five classes of bonds (uniformly distributed) created from each existing model compared with Moody's performance	Existing models built on data from 1949–1966 compared with actual ratings as much as 30 years *earlier* is a questionable but interesting test. *Common sample applied to all models* (good point). All models outperformed two naive models based on random assignments; arbitrary loss performance test
8. *T. Morton and D. McLeavey (1976).* Attempted to observe clusters of bonds that were statistically grouped according to their financial ratios and then clusters were analyzed based on their average values of variables. Industrial bonds (85) in period 1973–1975 used	Utilized a combination of *factor* and *cluster* analysis to group bonds. Factor analysis helped reduce number of ratios from 15 to 7 (highest correlated ratios with 7 factors). Variables include (1) total assets, (2) operating profit/sales, (3) long term debt/net worth, (4) operating expense/sales, (5) net income/total assets, (6) earnings per share, and (7) sales/total assets	Only one group of bonds showed significant and consistent differences from the other four groups; analysis restricted essentially to top three rating classes, but five clusters observed; another test had three clusters without much improvement. Clusters of bonds based on financial ratios were selected by an algorithm that could not consider credit worthiness as an implicit objective; *concluded* that Moody's *rating classes contain a rather heterogeneous group of firms*
9. *R. Kaplan and G. Urwitz (1979).* Attempted to improve upon existing regression and discriminant analysis models by using a variant of the OLS regression. Selected all (120) Moody's Industrial bonds with unchanged ratings in 1971–1972 period for original sample and all (53) new issues rated by	Applied logit-probit analysis, maximum-likelihood technique to bond rating problem; from at least 15 possible variables and 7 different models, the following variables were found to be most important; (1) subordination (0–1) status, (2) total assets, (3) net income/total assets; and (4) long-term debt/net worth; traditional measures like in-	*First* to *apply* the nonlinear *logit-probit approach;* appears to have eliminated the linear dependent variable-separation of rating class problem and the ordinality problem. *Results,* however, *not significantly better than past OLS models.* Biased R^2 results due to nature of dependent variable. Despite their criticism of search bias in other studies,

Moody's in same period as a holdout sample	terest and debt cash-flow coverage as well as the newer measures, earnings and price betas, were not very helpful	they too search for best model. Small holdout test; thoughtful, well-done study
10. *S. Bhandari, R. Soldofsky and J. Boe (1979).* Attempt to classify and predict rating changes of industrial bonds with 2-group discriminant functions. Samples of 49 original and 26 holdout firms from 1974–1975 period. Third "control" group of no-change rating bonds	Linear discriminant function comprises fixed charges earned, leverage, profitability, and earnings stability with some variables expressed in trend form as well	*First* to concentrate directly on *rating changes.* Small samples with holdout firms data partly coming from years prior to original sample. Use of 2-groups instead of 3-groups biases results. Conclusion and relevance to actual rating procedures is questionable
11. *A. Rappaport, J. Murphy, and A. Parr (1979).* Classified sample of 123 industrial commercial paper issues into higher and lower rated groups in 1977. Identically rated securities by Moody's and S&P	Two step methodology involved first *factor analysis* and *then stepwise, quadratic discriminant techniques.* Variables selected included three ratios (times interest earned, acid-test, and current ratio) and three market related measures (price-earnings, common stock beta, and number of investment companies holding common stock)	*First to apply discriminant analysis* to *commercial paper ratings.* Results were modest for classification but did not analyze model in a holdout or predictive setting. Ignored a third rating category with few observations and did not present actual model

APPENDIX B

Municipal Bond Study References

Bahl, R., "Measuring the Credit Worthiness of State and Local Governments: Municipal Bond Ratings," *Proceedings of the National Tax Journal*, September, 1971.

Bolten, S. and W. Kretlow, "Municipal Bond Ratings and the Cost of Capital: Suggestions For Municipal Financial Management", *Working Paper,* University of Houston, 1975.

Carleton, W. and E. Lerner, "Statistical Credit Scoring of Municipal Bonds", *Journal of Money, Credit and Banking,* November, 1969.

Edelman, R., "An Objective Technique to Numerically Score Publicly Issued Bonds," *Eastern Finance Association,* April, 1978.

Goodman, R., "Municipal Bond Rating Testimony", *Financial Analysts Journal,* May–June, 1968.

Hastie, K. L., "Determinants of Municipal Bond Yields", *Journal of Financial and Quantitative Analysis,* June, 1972.

Hempel, G., *Measures of Municipal Bond Quality,* (Ann Arbor: University of Michigan Press), 1967.

———, *The Postwar Quality of State and Local Debt,* (New York: National Bureau of Economic Research), 1971.

———, "Quantitative Borrower Characteristics Associated With Defaults on Municipal General Obligations", *Journal of Finance,* May, 1973.

Horton, J., "Statistical Classification of Municipal Bonds", *Journal of Bank Research,* Autumn, 1970.

———, "A Statistical Rating Index For Municipal Bonds", *Financial Analysts Journal,* March–April, 1969.

Jantscher, G., "The Effects of Changes in Credit Ratings on Municipal Borrowing Costs", *Brookings Reprint #177 1970,* Brookings Institution, Washington, D.C.

Morton, T. G., "A Comparative Analysis of Moody's and Standard & Poor's Municipal Bond Ratings", *Review of Business & Economic Research,* Winter, 1975–1976.

Parker, S., "Municipal Bond Ratings", *Financial Analysts Journal,* July–August, 1968.

Rubinfield, D., "Credit Ratings, Bond Deficits and Municipal Borrowing Costs: A New England Study", *Proceedings of National Tax Association,* October, 1972.

Rudolf, S., "The Effect of Credit Ratings on Municipal Bond Yields", *Municipal Finance Study Group,* State University of New York, Albany, 1971.

Sherwood, Hugh, *How Corporate and Municipal Debt is Rated: Inside Look at Standards & Poor's Corp.,* New York, N.Y., 1971.

Tyler, W., "How Are Those Municipal Bonds Rated", *The Institutional Investor,* May, 1968.

White, W., "Tax Exempt Bond Market Ratings", *Standard & Poor's Corp.,* New York, N.Y.

NOTES

1. Eisenbeis (1978) has devoted an entire paper to the Pinches and Mingo approach and commented on how they incorrectly attempted to test for the bias of the subordinated variable. He does, however, agree that the quadratic model was the appropriate one.

2. In fact, two of the authors of this book hold different opinions on this matter but it is clear what the trade-offs are—unambiguous ratings versus less than total population representation.

3. In fact, the paper does mention that a three-group analysis was attempted but not reported, probably due to poorer classification results. Inferior three-group classification

will always result compared to separate two-group tests. This is not sufficient rationale, however, for ignoring the more appropriate procedure.

4. Martin (1977) applied logit analysis to another financial problem—that of classification of problem and failed commercial banks. An in-depth discussion of this and other techniques applied to the commercial bank industry can be found in Sinkey (1979).

5. It is interesting to note that K&U find that their "objectively" assigned values for rating classes Aaa to B correspond quite closely to equal interval classes, i.e., values of 0, 1.57, 3.28, 5.19, and 6.76 (average intervals of 1.69 and a standard deviation of just 0.14).

6. It should be noted that R^2 is not measuring classification accuracy at all. It is equivalent to the multivariate F-test of discriminant analysis, which tests the significance of group mean differences.

7. Industry effects were explicitly considered by Edmister (1972) and Alves and Dambolena (1979) in faulure classification studies.

Chapter VI

Statistical Classification Models Applied to Common Stock Analysis

INTRODUCTION

The application of statistical classification techniques to various aspects of equity financing and returns performance has been an attractive and fairly prolific area of research in the last 10 to 15 years. Common stock markets exist in various forms of liquidity and allocational efficiency in numerous other domestic environments, including developing as well as industrial countries, whereas corporate debt markets are limited in number and importance. The various aspects of equity analysis relevant to classification techniques are more diverse than fixed income analysis and present more interesting empirical as well as theoretical challenges.

The purpose of this chapter is to review and comment upon numerous classification studies related to several aspects of common stock analysis and, in so doing, to provide a clear picture of the variety of equity application areas amenable to statistical classification techniques. These areas include (1) common stock investment categories; (2) price–earnings and risk–return equity classification; (3) information content and return performance; and (4) capital structure questions.

Our review of studies relevant to common stock statistical classification will focus on several recurring themes and problems. One important finding is that many studies are not comprehensive in that they do not examine representative firms from all groups comprising the entire population. Group selection, or rather omitted groups, is a critical concern; other concerns are variable selection and collinearity issues. The former is, in our opinion, an area where the analyst can significantly help determine the eventual success of the model. The latter remains a controversial point, although we feel it should not be given the same amount of prominence when discriminant analysis is the classification technique utilized compared to other multivariate techniques, such as regression analysis. We will also examine the accuracy of studies and the validity of the holdout test (if any) applied. We are especially interested in classification and predictive studies that have prescriptive as well as descriptive investment elements.

Where appropriate we will note the actual variables utilized by researchers, but in most cases we will defer this discussion and simply list the most prominent variables in a comprehensive Appendix. The order of presentation of studies in this Appendix parallels that of the text but can be referred to independently as well.

COMMON STOCK INVESTMENT CATEGORY CLASSIFICATION

Less widely known than bond quality ratings are ratings of investment quality of common stocks. In addition to Standard & Poor's and Moody's, several stock brokerage and investment banking firms categorize securities according to characteristics consistent with various types of investment strategies related to the risk–return trade-off. The central idea is that different investment objectives and investor utility functions require selection from among many classes or groups of securities, and one way to reduce the screening process is to rely on professional investment analysts to separate the population. This traditional procedure is an alternative to modern portfolio concepts, which stress only the statistical qualities of securities with respect to risk and return from a portfolio standpoint and all but dismiss the concept of individual security risk. The evidence remains, however, that security analysis and individual firm quantitative and qualitative estimates are still the dominant pragmatic process, and as such, the categorization of equities as, for example, growth versus return oriented or income versus speculative continues to be relevant. Statistical studies that add to our understanding of these qualities are potentially beneficial.

Although fixed income security quality ratings are better known and more sophisticated, the very first study that attempted to replicate the rating process of investment professionals via statistical procedures was, surprisingly, related to common equities (Smith, 1965). After Smith's work, numerous corporate analyses shifted to the fixed income area (Horrigan, 1966; Pogue and Soldofsky, 1969; West, 1970; Pinches and Mingo, 1973, 1975; Altman and Katz, 1976; and Kaplan and Urwitz, 1979. Only White (1975) has returned to the common equity market for further investigation of its rating characteristics. The purpose of this first section is to review and comment upon the Smith and White studies.

Smith's (1965) work is in many ways a seminal piece with respect to the application of discriminant analysis to a financial security analysis phenomenon, and although his work predates White's by over 10 years, limited evidence of the problem's evolution is demonstrated. Smith points out, correctly in our opinion, that equity classification is typically made on a univariate basis and because group definitions appear to be vague and several dimensions of a company's performance are involved, there is reason to expect that a multivariate parametric statistical technique can add to the understanding of raters and ratings.

Some interesting aspects of the two studies are that both are multigroup (more than two) analyses with Smith's (five groups) and White's (three groups) categories based on different raters. Smith's groupings concern investment, speculative, growth, and stability elements, whereas White uses three groupings (A, B+, B−) without discussing their meaning for investment analysis.

The variable selection process is quite different, with Smith relying on a melange of techniques, including (1) statistical significance of the various discriminant functions = [G (number of groups) −1]; (2) relative contribution of individual variables (scaled-vector approach); (3) intercorrelations between variables; and (4) the accuracy of reclassification. These procedures have formed the basis for several subsequent studies and statisticians are still arguing about the most appropriate measures to use for variable selection. For instance Smith, in discussing the benefits of multivariate discriminant analysis, notes its ability to exploit the information content of seemingly insignificant variables (on a univariate basis) which are, in fact, important contributors to overall discrimination. Cochran (1964) first showed this theoretically, and Altman (1968) and others have verified this aspect empirically. Both Smith and White measured individual contribution based on the scaled-vector method.

Both studies were concerned with high correlations between variables. White utilized factor analytical dimensions to screen an original list of 24 variables. In fact, factor analysis groups financial measures into distinct orthogonal elements and thereby eliminates "redundant" information with respect to the *population* (all groups) of observations. It does not necessarily aid in the separation of groups since within- and between-group differences must be assessed as well. [See Pinches and Mingo (1973) for an example of a two-step (factor analysis plus discriminant analysis) approach.] White's final discriminant model utilized variables from only six of the ten factors identified and he chose the most important variable from each of these six dimensions. Unfortunately, the author does not explain his statement, "while ten factors were important in describing the dimensionality of the data, variables from only six factors appear to be important for predicting common stock ratings" (White, 1975:5). We have often observed this failing in studies using factor–discriminant analysis combinations, and we find that factor analysis is not particularly helpful in classification studies.

Variable reduction techniques are motivated by statistical and behavioral reasons. The greater the difference between the number of observations and variables, the greater the confidence in results (degrees of freedom issue). For large samples, this issue is not particularly important except possibly in nonlinear (e.g., quadratic) analyses. In terms of potential practical implementation, a model that has a relatively small number of variables and satisfactory classification accuracy is seemingly attractive for its ease of application. We have found, however, that even in quadratic functions with as many as 11 discriminant variables, implementation is not hampered despite the large (97) number of individual computational operations required (Altman, 1977b). A researcher who has good reason to consider a relatively large number of variables should not be overly concerned with the final variable profile as long as it is statistically sound and economically logical.

Smith and White analyzed a number (14 and 24, respectively) of variables and then, based on several screening processes, reduced the number to 7 and 6, respectively. Two ratios, the dividend yield and total asset growth, were common to both models. White utilized two other variables, number of years of consecutive dividends and volatility of security prices, and Smith utilized one (share turnover), which are similar in their financial meaning to those used by Fisher (1959) in his well known risk premium model for corporate bonds.

Neither of the two studies demonstrate highly impressive classification accuracy, but both had respectable results, especially when one considers the number of groups involved. Smith observed 72 percent classification accuracy on his original sample of 50 securities and 56 percent accuracy on an independent holdout sample of 100 stocks. White's three-group analysis had an average accuracy of about 84 percent for a 105 stock original sample test and an average accuracy of 68 percent on an independent holdout sample.

Finally, as we have pointed out elsewhere in our discussion of fixed-income security classification by ratings (Chapter V), discriminant analysis techniques do not consider the ordinal ranking of groups, which may be implicit in rating procedures. For instance, Standard & Poor's ratings (White) implicitly assume a certain hierarchy (e.g., A, B+, B−), but the discriminant analysis technique simply attempts to separate the groups without concern for the implicit ranking. Smith's groupings (Appendix) do not connote such a hierarchy and cannot be criticized, therefore, for ignoring the ordinality aspect. The only paper thus far that attempts to highlight the ordinal ranking problem of discriminant analysis studies applied to security analysis advocated a probit analysis approach (Kaplan and Urwitz, 1979). There results, however, did not improve upon earlier linear regression study findings.

Another type of investment categorization study was performed by Farrell and Pinches (1979), who were concerned with classifying common stocks into growth and nongrowth groups with the use of a quadratic discriminant model comprising just two variables. They selected a sample of 354 stocks and measured their market return behavior over the period 1961–1977. Using a technique established by Farrell (1974), the sample was stratified into growth versus nongrowth stocks, with the latter group comprising a further breakdown of cyclical, stable, and oil companies. We find the grouping of stocks in terms of the variability patterns, i.e., cyclical and stable, with a single industrial categorization, oils, a bit awkward and wonder if the oil companies should not have been used or saved for a type of holdout sample. The two fundamental variables selected as discriminant measures were the dividend yield and a sustainable growth (retention rate × return on equity) variables.

The authors are careful to test for multivariate normality and unequal covariance matrices and to consider *a priori* probabilities of group membership. Despite their finding (not unexpected) that the model is not multivariate-normal, they feel that the results are strong enough to warrant close consideration. They caution, however, that "some discretion should be employed in assessing our classification results." Although we tend to agree with the authors that violation of the multivariate normality assumption is not critical, the authors are vague as to what they mean by "some discretion." My own feeling is that one cannot say anything about the optimality of the implied cutoff score if normality is violated. The results, however, might still be quite good and relevant—as Farrell and Pinches imply.

We are impressed by the Farrell and Pinches validation results (over 90 percent), but are a bit troubled by the almost tautological combination of discriminant variables and dependent variable groupings. Clearly, high growth companies will usually have low dividend yields because their prices are relatively high and a sustainable growth measure is likely to be consistent with a market growth measure. The authors correctly point out that using growth and yield characteristics along with exhibited price behavior should provide greater confidence that stocks can be allocated to their appropriate growth or nongrowth category and the method can provide a timely means of classifying stocks.

Growth was also the subject of the Johnson and Landes (1979) study. They separate firms into low versus high dividend growth categories within eight different industry classifications. The industries themselves were grouped into high versus low dividend growth, and separate discriminant functions were constructed for each of those two categories. Stepwise linear discriminant analysis procedures were used with the resulting low growth industries, yielding a six-variable model, one more than the high growth group. Interestingly, no specific variable appeared in both functions, indicating the sensitivity of discriminant functions to slight differences in groupings and firms within the group. Random selections and Lachenbruch validation techniques were used with classification accuracies of 60–69 percent (4 of 16 groups); 70–79 percent (5 of 16); 80–87 percent (5 of 16); and 90–99 percent (2 of 16). Firms within food products and steels (among the low growth industry groups) and computers (among the high growth groups) demonstrated the highest classification accuracies.

This study seems to be carefully executed, but one must wonder why a quantitative variable like dividend growth was analyzed within a qualitative dependent variable technique, i.e., discriminant analysis. The study is comprehensive as to growth categories and could assist the investor in choosing among high versus low dividend growth firms in specific industries. This is, however, obvious without discriminant analysis, and because the study does not test for predictive growth, one wonders whether there are any real insights to be gained.

COMMON STOCK PRICE AND EARNINGS PERFORMANCE CLASSIFICATION

Price–Earnings (P–E) Ratios

Perhaps the most frequent "first question" asked by investors with respect to a particular equity issue's performance and prospects is "what is its P–E ratio," i.e., how many dollars is the market ascribing to the stock per dollar of the firms' earnings per share. Entire investment strategies have been based on this single measure. For instance, the famous Graham and Dodd (1961) low P–E ratio-quality stock theory has been widely quoted. A companion strategy has been the purchase of out-of-favor (low P–E) quality stocks.

The P–E ratio is not a simple measure, and the complexity in its understanding encompasses all the ingredients inherent to its component parts—prices and profits. Opinion on the often disputed issue of growth or risk as the primary determinant of P–E ratios seems to swing back and forth, depending on overall stock market conditions. This controversy is not limited to investment practitioners; the work of Malkiel (1963) and the many subsequent comments on his article attest to this. In addition, certain connotations of investment quality and prospects are often linked to P–E ratios with the general feeling that high P–E firms present a greater risk–return opportunity set to investors than do lower ratio firms.

The purpose of this section is to examine studies that have attempted to discriminate between "high" and "low" P–E ratio (or its inverse, E–P ratio) firms with the use of *ex post* financial measures and statistical classification techniques. Two such studies are those by Walter (1959) and Schick and Verbrugge (1975); both studies utilized discriminant analysis for similar purposes, but were separated in time by many years. Also in this section, we will discuss studies that attempted to discriminate between firms based on one factor of the P–E ratio, namely, earnings (Haslem and Longbrake, 1971) or prices (Klemkowsky and Petty, 1973).

Walter was probably the first to apply sophisticated discrimination procedures to security analysis. He was concerned with industrial equity securities in the immediate postwar (1948–1955) period. Schick and Verbrugge (S&V) analyzed commercial bank equities in the 1967–1972 period. Both utilized published financial data and linear discriminant analysis, and both suffered from one major flaw in the group definitions. Therefore, subsequent applications must be viewed as questionable.

Walter selected the highest 50 and lowest 50 E–P ratio firms from a sample of 500 companies and proceeded to analyze the characteristics common to each of these extreme classes. S&V's groupings are a bit more complex in that the high P–E banks are defined as having ratios greater than 0.5 standard deviations above the average and low P–E banks have ratios greater than 0.5 standard deviations below the average. By definition, a proportion of the sample population in both studies is not represented. This would be fine if the analysis stopped simply with a study of the original sample and did not ascribe predictive elements. However, once holdout tests are applied, it is necessary that new observations be assigned either a high or low P–E ratio classification—even if in reality they more closely resemble some intermediate range of firms. It appears that the authors of both studies were somewhat aware of this but felt that their objectives did not require representation from a complete spectrum of observations. Walter did select holdout firms only from extreme E–P ratio classes, but this does not change our criticism that any new observation analyzed by the model must be classified in an extreme class. We will observe this methodological problem time after time in our discussion.

We do not believe that discriminant analysis is appropriate for extreme group classifications, especially when the dependent variable is quantifiable and therefore amenable to various forms of regression analysis. Both Walter and S&V were concerned with accurate discrimination and the statistical importance of the independent financial variables. Both studies state in their introductory paragraphs that certain beliefs are held about the type of firm variables coincident with various levels of P–E ratios, and set out to test this. But, in order to assess the "true" statistical importance of variables in any parametric study, certain assumptions about the independence of the explanatory variables must be made and appropriate tests on the significance of the coefficients can be applied. Regression analysis would seem to be more appropriate then.

Both Walter and S&V performed interesting, innovative procedures in their tests. Walter analyzed securities in one period (1952–1955) and then tested the results on observations from a prior period (1948–1951). Perhaps one of the reasons for the "reverse" procedure is to use the most recent data in determination of variable coefficients. Walter does speculate that either the coefficients from each of the two sample periods are not significantly different and/or that compensating variations occur in the coefficients. He observed that the signs of two of the five independent variables changed from one sample period to another and the weights of two of the other coefficients changed a great deal. We must be suspicious, therefore, about any conclusions that the two discriminant functions are similar and that reliable comparisons can be made.

S&V utilized stepwise discriminant analyses for each of the 6 (1967–1972) sample years in order to select the "best" group of independent variables. A large number of financial measures was thereby reduced to five. The resulting discriminant variable profile was utilized in each of the 6 years and results observed. There was some inconsistency in the signs of the coefficients of the five variables over the 6 years and only two of the five were perfectly consistent. This does not present a problem for analysis of the overall *Z*–scores of the individual firms but is problematic for interpretation of the informational content of the individual *variables*.

The Appendix lists the exact variables used in both P–E ratio studies, the various accuracy levels, and other comments. Walter was basically concerned with testing the effect of financial risk and dividend policy on E–P ratios. S&V's major concern was to find out the risk and growth determinants of P–E ratios; therefore, they constructed 14 growth variables and at least 9 risk characteristics out of a total of 41 candidates. The resulting discriminant functions for the two studies were not similar in the variable content, indicating that the theory and statistical measures used to explain P–E ratios are not well defined—at least in terms of statistical testing.

The observed accuracy of both studies was relatively impressive and indicates that firms are more accurately classified into their respective P–E classes than into their overall debt and equity quality ratings. It appears that firms can be classified into relatively high or low P–E classes; but keep in mind that the distinction between these two extreme classes is quite obvious, especially compared to the multigroup quality ratings of equity discussed earlier. It is conceivable that the accuracy of these two studies could have been even greater if nonlinear discriminant functions were utilized—assuming of course that the variance–covariance statistics for the groupings were significantly different. [For an excellent discussion on nonlinear discriminant functions, see Eisenbeis and Avery (1972) and Eisenbeis (1977).] Reduced accuracy would no doubt be manifest if the studies utilized a greater proportion of the entire population, involving three or more groups.

Price Volatility Classification

Implicit in questions of common stock quality ratings and price–earning ratios is the notion of risk. Risk, in terms of modern capital asset pricing theory, has come to represent an individual security's marginal contribution to existing or hypothetical portfolios and as such is concerned with covariability and/or market-related risk characteristics. For most market analysts and participants, risk still connotes price or return volatility of individual stocks, and the number of studies analyzing this firm unique aspect is numerous. An attempt to discriminate and predict relative price variability of common stocks utilizing a statistical classification technique by Klemkowsky and Petty (K&P) (1973) illustrates another application area.

Similar to most of the common stock classification studies we have discussed, K&P also have concentrated their efforts on extreme classes of stocks. From a randomly selected sample of 160 stocks, only the highest and lowest quartiles are analyzed. Hence, 50 percent of the sample—and by extension, 50 percent of the population—are not represented. The authors do admit this shortcoming, but justify it by stating that they are not interested in any predictive content of their model. The possibility of regression analysis is even mentioned (Klemkowsky and Petty, 1973:5) but dismissed due to its more *general* and *representative* features! We do not see these features as dismissible. This, in our opinion, is a limiting and unacceptable rationale. The main purpose of empirical analysis is application. Simply "explaining" what has occurred in the past is of little interest if we have no evidence of future reliability.

K&P are preoccupied with multicollinearity (discussed later) and they "drop variables that are highly correlated," but still select 11 "independent" measures. It is interesting, therefore, to observe that just two of the variables—share turnover and average price—explain the differences in price variability about as well as the entire 11-variable profile. One must assume that the information content in the remaining nine variables is nil and/or that the information is already compounded in the two most important measures.

Both ordinary and stepwise linear discriminant programs are used and the resulting model is tested on a holdout sample of upper and lower volatility quartile stocks selected in the same year of analysis. The authors are again forthright in their emphasis on the lack of predictive testing of the model. They find greater classification accuracy (86 percent) in the holdout test than in the original sample (80 percent). The authors' honesty is refreshing and the subject area interesting—unfortunately, the methodology is somewhat lacking.

Earnings Classification

The commercial bank profit analysis by Haslem and Longbrake (H&L) (1971) was similar to the S&V study in that high versus low performing banks were compared. H&L's objective, however, was to use those measures that separate *extreme* profit classes of banks to explain *all levels* of profitability in a multiple regression study. They reasoned that this was an excellent way to screen helpful measures.

The authors admit that they too were "guilty" of ignoring a significant proportion of the population in their sample selection. Their rationale was that they were interested primarily in variable selection and not discrimination accuracy. The problem, however, is that tests for determining relative importance of individual discrimination variables are not very well developed and at least six different ones have been utilized by various authors to assess this problem. These tests include stepwise (1) forward and (2) backward analysis (variables chosen or deleted by their multivariate F-tests—except for the first variable in stepwise forward analysis); (3) the scaled vector measure (coefficient $\times$ standard deviation of the pooled data matrix); (4) the Mosteller–Wallace (1963) method, which weights each discriminant coefficient by the difference in the variable's group means divided by the difference in mean discriminant scores; (5) the conditional deletion test, which measures the additional contribution of each variable to the multivariate F-statistic; and, (6) the univariate F-test, which measures group mean differences for each measure. [See Altman and Eisenbeis (1978) for a discussion of these tests.]

In most studies to date, the ranking of importance of each variable based on these tests has not been consistent and, therefore, is difficult to draw conclusions from. An exception to this lack of consistency is a recent study by Altman, Haldeman, and Narayanan (1977). Therefore, the use of discriminant analysis to select variables for further analysis via regression techniques is based on shaky assumptions. It is interesting to note that researchers have used various techniques, e.g., factor analysis for selecting helpful variables to use in a subsequent discriminant analysis. H&L have reversed the process somewhat by using discriminant analysis *first* and then regression. Although we are critical of this approach, it is innovative and worthy of analysis.

Our conclusion with respect to variable selection attempts is that successful classification still rests with the analyst and is not solely a matter of some statistical algorithm, i.e., it remains an art rather than a science.

H&L utilize the stepwise forward procedure and seemingly base their variable selection and conclusions about relative importance on the order that the variables entered the function. Unfortunately, the authors do not explicitly explain their rankings of importance. Therefore, final variable selection is based on a conditional test about which we have misgivings. If available, we prefer the conditional deletion method that begins with all variables.

From an original list of 46 candidates, 8 were selected by H&L for further regression analysis. These 8 were very accurate in classifying high versus low profit banks (86.5 percent original classification accuracy), but no holdout tests were applied. The resulting regression explained about 74 percent of the variation in bank profitability. We are more than a little concerned about the reliability and relevance of these results due to the fact that much of the same sample was used in both the discriminant and regression analyses tests. In addition, H&L conclude that expense items explain very well the profit performance of banks—hardly a revelation! Still, the analysis probably has some significance for bank management.

DISCRIMINATION BASED ON ACCOUNTING INFORMATION AND COMMON STOCK RETURNS PERFORMANCE

One of the most fascinating aspects of statistical security analysis is the attempt to predict investment returns based on historical data. For at least 40 years, various types of statistical models have been constructed to "beat the market." Recent efficient market theories and tests have presented models and evidence in direct contrast to those advocating that one can predict the future movements of common stocks based on historical data. [For an excellent review of the theory and types of empirical tests prior to 1970, see Fama (1970).] The empirical tests have taken the form of the so-called "weak-form," "semi-strong," and "strong-form" variety. The first two types of tests, based on past stock prices and all publicly available data, respectively, have repeatedly shown that markets are efficient with respect to digesting new information and it is only the random occurrence of these information sets that account for price movements that cannot be explained by overall stock market performance.

Two recent studies have attempted to examine accounting data and historical price information with respect to returns performance prior to the announcement date (Gonedes, 1974) and after the date of public availability (Altman and Brenner, 1981). These two studies have one very important similarity in that both utilized linear discriminant analysis in order to construct portfolios of stocks and to examine the information content of accounting data. While there are several other similar methodological properties of the two studies, one conspicuous difference must be noted at the outset. Gonedes started with the assumption that the capital asset market is efficient and tested for whether or not annual financial statements provide new information; Altman–Brenner (A&B) do not concede market efficiency, and in fact one of their objectives is to test for this still controversial conclusion.

Gonedes was primarily concerned with accounting information content and utilized both multivariate (several ratios based on financial statement data) and univariate discriminant analysis. His expectation was that the joint information available from several measures would be superior to individual ratios. The essence of the analysis was to identify two groups of common stocks based on their return performance and then attempt to see if the accounting numbers could discriminate effectively between these groups. The null hypothesis being that

$$\begin{matrix}\text{performance conditional}\\ \text{upon a given}\\ \text{discriminant}\\ \text{model}\end{matrix} \; - \; \begin{matrix}\text{the}\\ \text{unconditional}\\ \text{performance}\end{matrix} \; = 0$$

Performance was measured in both the Gonedes and A&B studies as the cumulative average error (CAE) from the two-factor, capital asset pricing model built upon the foundations laid by Markowitz (1959), Sharpe (1964), and Lintner (1965) and adapted to include more recent empirical development by Black (1972).

The model is clearly presented in Jensen (1972) and is of the form,

$$E(\tilde{R}_{it}|R_{zt},R_{mt}) = R_{zt} + (R_{mt} - R_{zt})\beta_{it}$$

where $E(\tilde{R}_{it})$ = *expected return of security* i in period t
R_{zt} = return on asset Z, known as the *zero-beta* variable
R_{mt} = *return on the market* (efficient) portfolio
β_{it} = *relative risk* parameter of security i

This model can be empirically estimated (Fama and McBeth, 1973) by

$$\varepsilon_{it} = R_{it} - [\gamma_{0t} - \gamma_{it} \cdot \beta_{it}]$$

where $\gamma_{ot} = R_{zt}$ is the so-called zero-beta (minimum variance–return) parameter and $\gamma_{1t} = R_{mt} - R_{zt}$ is the market risk premium parameter. Hence, for given R_z and R_m in any period t and a known "true" β_i measure of relative risk, ε_{it} is a measure of the difference between the actual return of security i in period t and the expected return. If the capital market is efficient, ε_{it} must be a fair game random variable, i.e., $E(\varepsilon_{it}) = 0$. In other words, an investor should not be able to make profits on any strategy above and beyond that which he might have been expected to receive given knowledge of the security's market related risk (β_i) and what in fact occurred in the capital markets. Gonedes and A&B construct portfolios of stocks; hence, they are interested in the portfolio return (R_{pt}), which is an average of the individual securities returns weighted evenly. Since Gonedes assumes market efficiency, he is testing for whether the stocks *classified by the discriminant model* as having superior returns did indeed manifest these above average returns. Both Gonedes and A&B assume the financial statement announcement date arrives 3 months after the year-end, i.e., April 1.

For A&B, the new information was not the basic accounting data and the associated ratios, but the actual discriminant score, i.e., score from a bankruptcy classification model developed earlier by Altman (1968). This model utilized five ratios (one of which uses capital market as well as financial statement data) in order to classify firms as having characteristics similar to past bankrupts. Whenever the resulting score, known as the Z-score, of a firm *first* dipped below the established cutoff point, the firm was selected as a member of the portfolio whose cumulative average error was to be eventually observed and tested. Gonedes and A&B utilize data from COMPUSTAT in order to calculate the ratios. This was quite important for A&B since COMPUSTAT firms are all existing going-concern entities. Gonedes (1974:34) also points out this aspect and cites that young firms and non-December 31 reporting firms are not included. Hence, all of the selections by A&B are equivalent to Type II errors in that the model predicted bankruptcy, but this event did not manifest. A&B test for whether the information-content inherent in bankruptcy prediction was digested efficiently by the market, i.e., whether the post prediction performance of the portfolio was significantly different from zero: the implied hypothesis being that the negative information implicit in the low *Z*-score is a forewarning of further deterioration, if not failure itself.

Collinearity and Multivariate Normality

Gonedes and A&B are properly *not* concerned with collinearity problems among the individual variables on an intrafirm basis. Where correlation does exist between variables of firms, it is important to remember that the information content (both the ratio itself and its coefficient) of individual measures is not independent of other variables' information. This reflects back to our earlier discussion of the difficulty in assigning relative importance statistics to each of the discriminating variables.

The effect of multicollinearity on discriminant analysis models is still subject to debate. For example, we refer the reader to the arguments made by Altman and Eisenbeis (1978), Joy and Tollefson (1975), Eisenbeis (1977), Pinches (1978), and Kshirsagar (1972). It can be argued that collinearity among the variables affects the stability of the underlying parameters and makes it difficult to isolate the impact of specific measures. We would agree that measures of individual variable importance are impossible to have confidence in when the variables are highly collinear. Variable standard errors of estimate are not calculated in discriminant analysis (nor are they advocated to be). The effect, therefore, of multicollinear variables on standard errors is irrelevant to the discriminant function. Since the ratios of the coefficients to each other, and not the coefficients themselves, are unique in discriminant analysis, the degree of association of the variables is of less concern than in regression. Of course, if the relationship between variables is unstable from one sample (e.g., original observations) to another (e.g., holdout), the coefficients will probably contribute to reduced accuracy in the holdout sample. (We would not expect high accuracy anyway if the two samples had little in common.) If collinearity is so severe as to inhibit or preclude matrix inversion, coefficients cannot be estimated. We have also observed that collinearity may cause perverse coefficient signs. However, this usually will not lead to lower classification accuracy but could be practically unacceptable in a predictive environment among nonstatisticians.

Another similarity in the two studies is their *lack* of preoccupation with the standard assumption of multivariate normality in linear discrimination analysis. They do recognize that the statistical estimation properties will be less than optimal and that the distribution theory for tests of these estimates are not available without the normality assumption. [See Altman, Haldeman, and Narayanan (1977) for an analysis of the change in optimal cutoff scores from what would be expected given multivariate normality and what actually occurred without it.]

Sample Properties and Estimation Results

Gonedes utilizes estimation and validation samples of 112 firms each covering the years 1957–1963, 1966, and 1967. Based on annual data for year-end 1960–1963, 92 firms are selected by A&B for further analysis as having bankruptcy potential. Both studies estimate the relative risk parameter of each stock (β_i) in their portfolios and utilize the market parameters γ_0, γ_1 as calculated by Fama and MacBeth (1973). Gonedes is concerned mainly with the 12-month period *prior* to the announcement date, but he also calculates portfolio returns for the 6-month period following the event.

Gonedes observes that his variables (Appendix) classified 62.3 percent of the observations in his estimation sample into the correct groupings. The variables are adjusted for cross-sectional, or market-wide, factors and only a variable's deviation from its expected value is utilized.

The classification accuracy, however, of the holdout or validation sample manifests a 46.4 percent error, which is not significantly different from the expected error rate. Gonedes concludes that the results suggest an "inconsistency with the null hypothesis of 'no information content' as applied to the joint implications of the accounting numbers" (Gonedes, 1974:46). He cautions, however, that the somewhat meager significance of his results relative to the estimated net effect of all sources of information implies that "much of the information affecting asset prices is not reflected in the accounting numbers . . . , conditional on our estimation procedures" (i.e., statistical discrimination technique). It should be noted that Gonedes' primary interest is in the accounting numbers and not the discriminant model *per se.* Therefore, we cannot conclude that a model built with a different objective in mind (e.g., profitable investment strategy) would manifest similar nonsignificant *ex post* results.

The cumulative average errors from the A&B study for the 20-month period *following* the data's announcement date declines fairly consistently after month 4 and reaches a "maximum" of −23.2 percent in month 18, which is easily significantly different from the null hypothesis expectation of zero. The implication is that the massaged publicly available data presented guidelines for investment selection that clearly outperformed (assuming a short sale strategy or a sell strategy for those who owned the securities) expectations based on market performance and systematic risk characteristics of the sample. A&B also compare the results of the 92-firm portfolio with a control sample of firms selected with the same risk (beta) estimates as the bankruptcy potential sample. These results confirm the performance of the discriminant-bankruptcy model's selection.

Both the Gonedes and Altman–Brenner studies illustrate how statistical classification techniques can be utilized to test for important aspects in finance.

We also call your attention to an unpublished study by Bear (1973) on the use of discriminant analysis to predict common stock price movements and to Renwick's (1969) study on company assignment to a portfolio category of high or low investment performance. Bear finds a discriminant model very successful in classifying firms into above versus below average stock price performers, but his results were quite poor when testing the model on holdout samples. Renwick's results are fairly obvious and of some interest but little prescriptive elements.

CAPITAL STRUCTURE DECISIONS AND CLASSIFICATION TECHNIQUES

Normative aspects of a firm's capital structure decisions revolve around the continuing debate as to the effect of leverage on valuation and cost of capital. Ultimately, the answer to this theoretical controversy lies in careful empirical observation and testing. Descriptive studies can help in a better understanding of the financing decisions made by firms, and the use of statistical classification techniques can make these descriptive analyses more credible. The purpose of this section is to review several studies that have analyzed the characteristics of corporations involved in capital structure decisions. Essentially, the approach taken by the authors of the studies described below is to observe some decision or event and then search for characteristics of the groups of firms involved in order to attempt an explanation of their behavior or the behavior of their security holders.

We will be concerned with the following paired decisions or manifestations: (1) whether to issue new debt or new equity; (2) whether convertible debt is really debt or a form of equity for the firm; and, (3) what are the characteristics of firms that repurchase their own stock—and what happens to the repurchased shares—compared with those that do not. It is clear that these questions concern the analysis of both debt and equity securities.

Debt versus Equity

Martin and Scott (M&S) (1974) are concerned with the characteristics of debt versus equity issuing firms and use linear discriminant analysis to analyze these traits both for explanation and prediction purposes.

Using year-end 1970 data for a sample of 62 industrial debt issuers and 50 industrial equity issuing firms during 1971, the authors search for separating portraits. They correctly feel that discriminant analysis is potentially helpful for this nonquantifiable decision, but several aspects of their methodology make their conclusions of somewhat limited relevance. For one thing, the two-group analysis ignores the majority of the population—firms that finance their operations neither with new debt or new equity. A new observation will necessarily be classified by their model as having characteristics more similar to debt or equity issuing firms when in reality they may have little in common with either group. Our point is that in order to make their analysis more generally applicable, at least a third group of nonissuers is called for. A fourth group might be both debt and equity issuers, and possibly *convertible* debt issuers. M&S specifically eliminate firms issuing debt and equity securities because "they belonged to both groups." Perhaps these firms "belong" to a different group altogether.

Another problem is the time element involved. It seems arbitrary to adopt a calendar year period as the basis for group differentiation. This is a tough question; should a longer time horizon be used to determine groupings? If so, how long? Oftentimes the exact timing of a financing decision is more a function of external capital market conditions than of an internal situation. It would seem appropriate to consider financial cycles as an important part of the debt or equity decision. It does seem that M&S were aware of these phenomena in their discussion of the episodic nature of financing actions, but the calendar year criterion is still adhered to.

The authors point out that several sensible intuitive procedures are followed with respect to the choice of their six measures. It is confusing to us to read that both stepwise procedures and judgment of the analysts were utilized. The former would seem to preclude the latter, except if the stepwise results were not strictly adhered to. M&S conclude that firms with larger asset bases and smaller debt ratios have a tendency to issue debt rather than equity and vice versa. An insignificant univariate liquidity measure was found to be quite important, confirming the message given by Cochran (1964).

Convertible Debt Characteristics: Debt or Equity

The potential importance on earnings dilution of debt being converted into equity is clearly considered by analysts. Still, convertible debt for some companies is less likely to be converted into equity than for other firms, and in some cases probably should not be a factor in dilution. Frank and Weygandt (1971) attempted to utilize linear discriminant analysis in order to classify and predict those firms' convertible debt that was likely to be converted over a relatively short term horizon (12 months).

Perhaps the most interesting aspect of the study was their finding that one variable by itself achieved maximum classification accuracy and there was no need to combine the information content of several variables. Of course, most of the eight variables that they analyzed were highly correlated with the single most important measure (conversion value of the debt/call price) such that the added discrimination ability of the other seven was found to be nil. In this case, collinearity precluded the addition of other variables because of the lack of additional explanatory power. What was not attempted was to try various combinations of variables that did not include the most important one on a univariate basis. The latter result is desirable whenever stepwise forward analysis is utilized. It is not likely, however, that their excellent results, 92 percent original sample and 90 percent holdout sample accuracy, could have been improved upon very easily.

One shortcoming of the study, which the authors did recognize, was the relatively short time period used to determine the *a priori* groupings. Frank and Weygandt observed a 12-month period after the point in time when the explanatory variables were noted. The study was innovative in its use of a statistical classification, qualitative variable procedure in order to present an alternative method for evaluating the debt or equity characteristics of convertible debt.

Share Repurchase

Most of the controversy in the literature concerning the repurchase of a firm's own shares has revolved around the theoretical justification of this phenomenon as an alternative to other uses of the funds. The protagonists in this controversy (i.e., Bierman and West, 1966 versus Elton and Gruber, 1968) were primarily concerned with tax considerations, transaction costs, and dividends. Several recent studies concern themselves with a different aspect of the share repurchase question, namely, what are the characteristics of firms that repurchase their own shares versus those that do not [Norgaard and Norgaard (N&N), 1974]; and the ensuing comment (White, 1974); and further, what differentiating characteristics can explain the eventual use of the repurchased shares (Spero, 1975).

Share repurchase is fairly common in the United States, and there are signs that the event may occur for the first time in other domestic environments, e.g., Brazil, where it is now legal to do so. In recent years, billions of dollars' worth of securities have been purchased by the issuing corporations in the United States and the reasons have been quite diverse. N&N (1974) sought, via linear discriminant analysis, to test the hypothesis that repurchasers in 1973 utilized share repurchase for reasons undesirable to stockholders. The authors observed that almost all firms repurchase some of their outstanding shares over time, and they decided to concentrate only on those firms repurchasing large amounts compared to those that repurchase very small numbers of shares. They categorized "large" repurchasers as holders of 8 percent or more of the issued stock in their treasury and "small" repurchasers as holders of less than 0.1 percent in their treasury. This arbitrary categorization presents the major obstacle to any meaningful conclusions from the study.

About 66 percent of their "population," and a great deal less than the theoretical population of firms, was represented in the study. N&N randomly selected 60 firms from the small repurchaser sample and found that 60 of the larger repurchaser firms had data available for testing. Since N&N were interested in quantifying the influence of firm-unique characteristics on the share repurchase question, one might logically wonder why the quantifiable share repurchase variable was not used as the dependent variable in a regression format rather than small versus large repurchasers in a discriminant structure. It is interesting to note that in his critique of the N&N paper, White (1974) concludes that discriminant analysis *was* an appropriate technique to use. We do not agree—at least not in the way that N&N utilized it. The latter technique assumes that the samples came from different populations—a rather heroic assumption for this topic.

Finally, as we have pointed out in several other instances, because a large percentage of the population is not represented, the resulting function has little applicability to new firms whose data is being applied to the model. N&N do imply that they are not interested in the predictive qualities of their model and do not even bother to test their results on a holdout sample. Because the original sample results have such obvious biases, this omission would tend to damage the credibility of results and conclusions. In choosing their final model, N&N select 15 variables and their results are mildly impressive—but keep in mind no holdout results are given. White does point out that collinearity should not have been a concern here, and both N&N and White indicate that linear analysis implies that both groups have the same dispersion. Yet, this never is tested!

The study concludes that large repurchasers have depressed stock prices, inferior operating results, lower growth in sales and earnings, and pay out less dividends than do small repurchasers. In general, they observe that in 1973, poorer performers tended to repurchase more. It would be interesting to test their conclusions under various stock market conditions instead of only during a depressed market period.

Spero (1975) argued that there are at least two distinctly different groups of repurchasers: one group composed of firms that hold the shares in their treasury for a considerable time after repurchase and another group that reissues these shares for aggressive reasons, such as stock options, conversions, and acquisitions of other firms. The latter group was hypothesized to have a relatively stronger profile of performance statistics. Using data on repurchasers from 1968 and 1969, Spero applied both linear and quadratic discriminant analysis to attempt to distinguish between firms that reissue shares repurchased within 3 years and those that do not. Spero's resulting functions also showed that the reissuers appeared to be healthier than the non-reissuers and their stock prices reflected this healthier appearance.

For the first time in any of the studies discussed in this section, various *a priori* probabilities were used to assess expected group classification. In addition, Spero varied the definition of just what is a repurchasing company and, as noted above, tried quadratic functions when he found that the covariance matrices were not equal between reissuers and non-reissuers. The latter finding leads us to believe that the covariance matrices are also dissimilar between repurchasers and non-repurchasers as well. Spero's results were fairly impressive, but also a little confusing in that he found that the quadratic function only partially outperformed the linear analysis in both the original and holdout sample tests. We feel that Spero's work is a good example of how discriminant analysis should be applied to a financial problem. He was careful about his definition of groupings, his selection of *a priori* probabilities, his holdout testing, and his functional tests.

SUMMARY AND CONCLUSION

The purpose of this paper has been to critically review statistical classification techniques applied to common stock analysis. We do find a surprisingly large number of studies of this character published in respectable financial journals despite the efficient market theories, which would all but ignore such endeavors, especially in a predictive sense. Few of the studies reviewed, however, are totally convincing due to statistical methodological problems and/or mediocre results. Still, we find that these efforts are worthwhile in that the state of the art is advanced. We can probably look forward to a continuing number of similar studies as other techniques and topics are researched; for instance, the application of logit, probit, and tobit techniques to problems involving qualitative dependent variables where ordinal rankings are important, is likely to increase. The essential problem is to identify a valid research area first and, if suitable, choose a statistical classification technique that fits the problem.

The major problem that we have found in past studies has been the elimination of an important segment of the population when choosing the *a priori* groups for analysis. It might be difficult to include all possible representative groups but every effort should be made to do so. A second problem has been the lack of a valid holdout sample and, equally important, the testing of the model after it was developed. In addition, it should now be possible for researchers to test for the homogeneity of group covariance matrices and to explore nonlinear as well as linear frameworks.

It would be difficult to itemize a complete list of topics that are related to common stock analysis and that are amenable to classification analysis, but perhaps a few can be suggested. The debt versus equity question is still of paramount interest and discussion. Methods of corporate organization and the manager versus owner viewpoint could very well be relevant. The latter concerns a popular current financial theory topic, namely, agency cost questions. Finally, option corporate and investment strategies might well be amenable to classification analysis.

ACKNOWLEDGMENT

Much of the material in this chapter is derived from the Working Paper of the same title E. Altman, (Salomon Brothers Center at NYU, 125, 1979) and later published in the *Journal of Business Research,* (1981).

APPENDIX

Review of Studies Using Statistical Classification Techniques for Common Stock Security Analysis

Author, Year, Purpose, and Group's Description	*Discriminating Variables*	*Summary of Results and Critical Comments*
1. *K.V. Smith (1965).* Classification of common stocks into five brokerage-firm determined *investment categories:* growth, stability, quality, income, and speculative. *1962* data covering 50 stock original and 100 stock holdout samples	Seven variables, including dividend yield and payout, current ratio, earnings and asset growth, P–E ratio, and share turnover. Several ad hoc but logical techniques for selection procedure. Original list of 14 variables	72 percent original and 56 percent holdout sample accuracy *first multi* (more than two) *group* security analysis discriminant model, use of univariately insignificant variables; good discussion of variable selection; small sample problem in all groups; vague group definitions; heterogeneous sample; no problem with ordinality of groups
2. *R. White (1975).* Classification of common equities into three categories of quality as determined by S & P (A, B+, B−). Original sample of 35 stocks in each group from *1965* and *1969*. Holdout samples included 68 and 69 stocks in the same 2 years	*Factor analytical* determined dimensions (10) reduced to *six* and variables include consecutive dividend years; volatility of price; dividend yield; returns (2) on assets; and *asset growth.* Original list of 24	84 percent original and 68 percent holdout sample accuracy; *poor discussion of groupings;* attempt to combine *factor analysis with linear discriminant* functions; concerned with collinearity but should not be; implicit hierarchy of ratings not considered (same as bond quality ratings studies); no explanation of why six and not ten variables selected
3. *J. Walter (1959).* Classification of *extreme low and high E/P ratio* firms; *original sample* of 50 lowest and 50 highest E–P ratios selected from 500 firms in *1952–1955*. Holdout sample of 60 firms from *earlier 1948–1951* period	Six variables including dividend payout, price stability, change (3-year) in return on assets, asset to debt ratio, interest coverage, growth in sales; all variables except size based on average of 3 years data	87 percent original and 80 percent holdout sample accuracy; *first discriminant* analysis study used for *security evaluation;* fine discussion of variables; *test* of model on data from *prior* period; problem of unrepresentative sample of the population of stocks (majority of firms not analyzed); potentially more appropriate for regression analysis; examined size and industry effects (if any) unstable signs and coefficients of variables

4. *R. Schick and J. Verbrugge (1975).* Classification of extreme high and low P–E ratio *commercial bank equities;* 0.5 standard deviations above and below the average P–E ratio were the sample selection guidelines. Original sample of 40 banks in *1967–1972* period and holdout sample of 26 banks in same period	*Stepwise discriminant analysis* used to reduce original set of 41 variables to 6; included log of outstanding shares; stability of earnings; 5 year growth in net income; return on security portfolio; loans/deposits; and 1-year growth in state income. Final model of best five variables rerun for each of the 6 years	83 percent original and 65–77 percent holdout sample accuracy; innovative variable selection, arbitrary group definitions that include only a portion of the population and is therefore *not totally representative;* no test for group homogeneity; variable significance and magnitude of coefficients were not very consistent over 6 years
5. *R. Klemkowsky and W. Petty (1973).* Classification of high and low *price variability* ($\sigma/\bar{X}$) stocks; highest and lowest quartiles of 160 stocks used for original sample (*1971*). 90 firm holdout sample also of high and low variability stocks from same period	*Stepwise discrimination* and reduction through elimination of collinear variables resulted in 11-variable model including debt/equity; interest coverage; percentage change in price; e.p.s. variability and growth; average P–E ratio and dividend yield; average price, number of shares outstanding and turnover	80 percent original and 86 percent holdout accuracy; admits problem of *no interquartile representation;* lack of predictive element or generalized results; price and share turnover found to be most important; *unnecessarily concerned* with *collinearity problem;* unclear discussion of how final variable profile was selected; greater holdout sample accuracy; no test for dispersion-similarity of groups
6. *J. Haslem and W. Longbrake (1971). Two-step* procedure of (1) classifying commercial banks into extreme high and low quartile profitability groups, and (2) using discriminant models' variables in order to explain profitability with regression analysis; *1963* cross-section of banks selected from various size categories	*Linear stepwise discriminant analysis* of 46 original variables, reduced to 8 measures, including 5 expense related items (interest, occupancy, loss on securities, furniture and all other expenses); return on loans; change in valuation reserves; securities/assets. Linear analysis of these 8 regressed on return on capital	86.5 *percent* of the original sample accurately classified by discriminant model; resulting regression had a $R^2 = 0.74$; Main problems with the *lack of full representation* (middle 2 quartiles) in discriminant model—admitted by authors, but mainly interested in search for best explanatory variables; relative importance of variables not reliable from stepwise analysis; *innovative approach* with excellent explanatory power but *results biased* due to lack of holdout sample and use of same observations in both discriminant and regression analyses

APPENDIX (Continued)

Author, Year, Purpose, and Group's Description	*Discriminating Variables*	*Summary of Results and Critical Comments*
7. *N. Gonedes (1974).* To examine the *informational content of annual accounting numbers* via capital market tests on the groups of equity securities selected by a discriminant model: model built to classify firms in periods *1957–1963, 1966, 1967* into positive and negative excess return performers for 12-month period prior to data announcement date; 112 firm estimation and 112 firm validation samples	*Stepwise linear discriminant analysis* in each of the 9 years selected from 4 to 7 variables for the model; all variables (ratios) are *transposed* to reflect the *unexpected* (different from what one would expect based on each ratio's historical association with the total sample average ratio) performance; measures include return on assets (2); earnings per share; assets (sales); cash flow to total debt + pfd; a liquidity; and a capital structure ratio	62.3 percent estimation and 53.6 percent validation accuracy; *interesting* and *innovative use of a statistical classification technique* within an empirical capital market test; *not* concerned with collinearity or normality problems; excellent variable adaptation to problem; selected groups analyzed within the *two-factor, zero-beta* model to determine information content and extraordinary performance (if any) of common stock returns; results indicate *slight information content* of joint annual financial statement items, but not much difference between joint and univariate information content in validation results; no test for dispersion matrix similarity of groups
8. *E. Altman and M. Brenner (1981).* To observe market performance of a portfolio of stocks selected based on discriminant bankruptcy prediction model; 92 firm portfolio from *1960–1963* selected based on model containing bankrupt and nonbankrupt firms; all firms selected did *not* go bankrupt; market efficiency implications; control sample tests	*Linear discriminant bankruptcy model* containing 5 variables Altman (1968) used to select bankruptcy "candidates;" *ex post* (from data declaration date) performance of equity returns based on two-factor, zero-beta model utilized for 20-month period	*Original model* had 95 percent (original) and 96 percent (holdout) accuracy of bankrupts; nonbankrupts were 94 percent (original) and 79 percent (holdout) accurate; *ex post returns* of bankrupt candidates were *significantly negative* over most of 20-month period, indicating questionable market efficiency; original nodel concerned (unnecessarily) with collinearity, subsequent tests showed quadratic model was appropriate but no difference in classification accuracy

9. *F. Bear (1973).* To distinguish between common stocks with larger than average price gains versus below average performers; groups selected from stocks in same industry (electrical equipment and electronics); 29 randomly selected firms in *1970* formed *original sample;* above average stocks had gains greater than 0.5 standard deviations above mean and less than 0.5 deviations below mean for below average, holdout tests on subsequent year data	Data from *year prior* to price performance gathered and *stepwise linear discriminant analysis* used to separate groups; original list of 28 variables reduced to just 3 including index of price stability, 5-year change in debt/equity ratio, and E–P ratio for prior year	*Excellent original* sample classification accuracy; results varied from *fair to very poor* on holdout samples; *small sample* problem in all tests; *no representation* of those observations falling within −0.5 and +0.5 standard deviations; *no adjustment* for *relative risk* of various securities or for dividend payments; *no theoretical justification* for hypothesis tests; realized that market movements were important; careful analysis of overlap area in discriminant function; model did not hold up over time
10. *J. Martin and D. Scott (1974).* To classify firms into either *new debt or new equity* issuing groups; groups selected from *security issuers* in *1971–1972;* 112 original sample observations and 58 holdout firms randomly selected	*Stepwise linear discriminant analysis* reduced original 23 variables to 6, including debt/assets; dividend payout; P–E ratio; total asset investment; current assets/total assets; cash flow/net worth; latter two ratios *scaled by industry average*	75 percent original and 78 percent holdout sample accuracy; major problems include *no representation,* in the model's development, of firms issuing *both* debt and equity or *no external financing;* also a time-series question of appropriate financing period to base original groupings on; *sensible, intuitive variable selection* process; somewhat dubious association between statistical results and theoretical debt/equity questions; no test for dispersion similarity

APPENDIX *(Continued)*

Author, Year, Purpose, and Group's Description	*Discriminating Variables*	*Summary of Results and Critical Comments*
11. *W. Frank and J. Weygandt (1971).* Classification of firms whose convertible debt is converted into equity or not; criteria for *a priori* groupings based on actual conversion over 12-month period in *1963;* original sample of 26 converted and 98 nonconverted bonds; holdout sample of 97 issues in *1966*	From original list of 8 variables *only 1* entered the *stepwise discriminant* function; the conversion value/call price ratio was the most important variable; several other variables significant by themselves but not when combined with single measure	*Single variable* yielded 92 percent accuracy of original sample and 90 percent holdout sample; suggest analysis to be done annually on outstanding convertible debt issues instead of just at time of the issue; no analysis of results with added variables or with other combinations that did not include most important one on an univariate basis; no test for homogeneity of group dispersions; *innovative use* of discriminant analysis technique; choice of 12-month period for determining group membership without justification; excellent results should be corroborated for more recent period
12. *C. Norgaard and R. Norgaard (1974).* Discrimination between large and small share repurchasing firms; 60 firms with greater than 8.0 percent of outstanding shares in treasury classified as large share repurchasers versus 60 with less than 0.1% as low share repurchasers; data from *1973* in diverse industries; interested in assessing if large share repurchasers are stronger or weaker than small repurchasers	Fifteen variables selected by authors; no test for multivariate inclusion or not of these variables; included 5 price related measures, 9 financial statement ratios, and 1 size (assets) scale measure	78 percent original sample accuracy; *no holdout* test; stated assumptions relating to multivariate normality and common dispersion but did not test for these; *no representation* for *majority of firms* that have repurchased stock but the amount in their treasury less than 8 percent; analysis *amenable* to *regression analysis* for entire population; no test for dispersion similarities in 2 groups; analysis done only in a *single down market* period, *concerned* with *collinearity unnecessarily;* concluded that large repurchasers are poorer performers; ignored subsequent reissuing activity

13. *A. Spero (1975)*. Interested in the subsequent behavior of those companies that have repurchased their own shares; classification of firm into repurchaser–reissuer versus repurchaser–nonreissuer *a priori* groups; varied definition of what constitutes the share repurchaser population; reissuer is defined as where at least 10 percent of repurchased shares reissued in following 3 years; 133 firm original sample in *1968–1969* period (1 percent definition of repurchasers) and 40 firm holdout sample in same periods. Also performed Lachenbruch test on all 173 firms	*Quadratic and linear stepwise discriminant analysis* used to reduce and examine original list of 20 financial variables; final model contained 5 variables including liquidity, profitability, prior stock price performance, leverage and dividend yield; others tried in various models include P–E ratios and growth rate measures; variables were transformed using logs where normality did not exist in original variable; tested for whether this added to discriminant model significance	Original sample results with linear model showed *excellent* classification *accuracy* for *reissuer* group but *very poor non-reissuer accuracy;* similar results in various holdout samples; *quadratic results* improved non-reissuer accuracy but reissuers' accuracy dropped; varied definition of repurchaser population from 0.1 percent repurchased shares to 1.0 percent of outstanding shares; tested model in both *up and down market* conditions; varied *a priori* probabilities of group membership as well; results examined in a type of sensitivity analysis as assumptions vary; overly concerned with variables highly correlated; *careful, thoughtful* analysis; possible to have percentage shares reissued as dependent variable in regression analysis format; finds reissuers were stronger, better performers than non-reissuers

Chapter VII

Failure-Prediction Models for Nonfinancial Firms

INTRODUCTION

When a man, a business corporation or an entire society is approaching bankruptcy, there are two courses that those involved can follow: they can evade the reality of their situation and act on a frantic, blind, range-of-the-moment expediency—not daring to look ahead, wishing no one would name the truth, yet desperately hoping that something will save them somehow—or they can identify the situation, check their premises, discover their hidden assets and start rebuilding.[1]

To prevent an impending bankruptcy requires knowledge that one is going bankrupt. Philosopher Rand suggests what to do if the approaching bankruptcy has been identified. This chapter focuses upon how to identify *nonfinancial* businesses headed for bankruptcy or failure. Failure-prediction models are designed to provide early-warning signals about approaching business failures.

MODELS FOR PREDICTING BUSINESS FAILURES: WHY, WHAT, HOW, AND FOR WHOM

Why Predict Business Failures?

In a competitive economy, market forces operate to eliminate inefficient firms. Thus, in theory at least, business failures can have a "cleansing" effect, resulting in a more efficient allocation of resources. However, business failures are not without their costs, which include hardships such as investors' loss of equity and dividends, creditors' loss of principal and interest, and employees' loss of jobs. In addition, a business failure may result in adverse spillover or ripple effects on other firms in the economy.

Business failures are important economic phenomena; they merit careful analysis. Because business failures are not costless, advance warning of future bankruptcies can reduce the burden of these costs. The significant volume of literature dealing with predicting business failures is the focal point of this chapter.

What Business Failure to Predict?

The potentially significant economic impact of large business failures suggests that predictions of bankruptcy for these businesses are the important ones. The collapse of large corporations is a recent phenomenon. As indicated in Table VII.1, the 20 largest United States bankruptcies all have occurred since June 1970, 10 of the 20 since February 1975. Because of a paucity of observations on large business failures, pre-1970 failure studies have not focused upon such firms. For example, Altman (1968) writes "the incidence of bankruptcy in the large asset-size firm is quite rare today" (Altman, 1968:593). Of course,

Table VII.1. The Twenty Largest U.S. Bankruptcies[a]

Name	*Total Liabilities (millions)*	*Date*	*Bankruptcy Chapter*
1. Penn Central Transport Co.	$3300	June, 1970	Ch. VIII, Sec. 77
2. W. T. Grant	1000	October, 1975	Ch. XI
3. United Merchants & Mfg.	552	July, 1977	Ch. XI
4. Continental Mortgage Investors	836[b]	March, 1976	Ch. XI
5. Commonwealth Oil Refining Co.	421	March, 1978	Ch. XI
6. W. Judd Kussuba	420	December, 1973	Ch. XI
7. Erie Lackawanna R.R.	404	June, 1972	Ch. VIII, Sec. 77
8. Investors Funding Corp.	379	October, 1974	Ch. X
9. Food Fair Corp.	347	October, 1978	Ch. XI
10. U.S. Financial Services	300	July, 1973	Ch. XI
11. Daylins' Department Store	250	February, 1975	Ch. XI
12. Chicago, Rock Island & Pacific	221	March, 1975	Ch. VIII, Sec. 77
13. Equity Funding Corp.	200	April, 1973	Ch. XI - X
14. Interstate Department Store	190	May, 1974	Ch. XI
15. Omega, Alpha Corp.	175	September, 1974	Ch. X
16. Reading R.R.	158	November, 1971	Ch. VIII, Sec. 77
17. Boston & Maine R.R.	148	December, 1975	Ch. VIII, Sec. 77
18. Westgage - California	144	February, 1974	Ch. XI
19. Pacific Far East Lines	132	January, 1978	Ch. XI
20. Allied Supermarkets	124	June, 1977	Ch. XI

[a]Excludes Commercial Banks.
[b]Includes $500,000 of "other liabilities" not to be deferred pursuant to Ch. XI.
Source: E. Altman, (ed.), *The Financial Handbook, 5th Edition,* Section on Bankruptcy & Reorganization, John Wiley, New York, 1981.

since then there has been a dramatic increase in the number of "large" bankrupt firms. For example, in 1968, there were only 121 business failures with liabilities greater than $1 million (1.2 percent); in 1976, there were 423 (4.4 percent).

How to Predict Business Failures?

This is the $64,000 question (in real dollars, of course). The alternative answers form the backbone of this chapter. The basic approach in the development of failure-prediction models is to analyze groups of failed and nonfailed firms to identify financial characteristics most dissimilar between the groups *prior to bankruptcy.* The second step is to reclassify the original sample using the financial characteristics. Third, a holdout sample is usually employed to test the model's predictive ability. If the model performs well, the final step is to predict future bankruptcies.

For Whom the Prediction Tolls

Predictions of future business failures provide important information for investors, creditors, auditors, accountants, government regulators, academicians, and other interested parties. In a recent issue of *Dun's Review* (October, 1975), James Loeblecke, partner and director of audit research for Touche, Ross (the Big Eight accounting firm), asserts, "We believe there is no downside risk in singling out companies possibly headed for trouble and the advantages of catching just one situation we might otherwise have missed are incalculable" (p. 63). In the same issue of *Dun's,* Ralph Verni, director of investment research at Equitable Life Assurance Society, explains, "We use mathematical forecasting for more than just sorting out good apples and bad apples. We also use them in determining how good the good apples are" (p. 63).

A DECADE OF FAILURE PREDICTION: BEAVER (1967) TO ALTMAN (1977)

Ten "major" failure-prediction studies are analyzed in detail in this chapter. The plan is to review each study using the following outline:

1. Purpose and general description
2. Definitions of groups and of "failure"
3. Sampling methods and sample characteristics
4. Selection and characteristics of variables
5. Group mean and group dispersion tests
6. Classification and validation tests
7. Major conclusion(s)
8. Critique

At the end of the chapter, a summary of the ten studies (Appendix) and a bibliography of failure-prediction studies for nonfinancial firms are presented.

Beaver (1967)

Purpose. Beaver's purpose was to test the *usefulness* of ratio analysis in the context of failure prediction. By usefulness, Beaver means *predictive ability.*

Definition of Failure. Beaver defined failure as the inability of a firm to pay its financial obligations as they mature. He claimed that failure occurs if *any* of the following events are observed:

1. Bankruptcy
2. Bond default
3. Overdrawn bank account
4. Nonpayment of a preferred stock dividend

These four events comprise an extremely *heterogeneous* failure group. An overdrawn bank account is far less serious than the other three events, especially a declaration of bankruptcy; in contrast, bond default and nonpayment of a preferred-stock dividend, while more serious than an overdrawn bank account, are less serious than bankruptcy; and, finally, bankruptcy is a far more serious failure classification than the other three events. The important point is that, in two-group classifications (i.e., failure–nonfailure), the failure group should be relatively *homogeneous* and, of course, representative of the population of failed enterprises. Beaver could have homogenized his failure group by using only observations from the bankruptcy category. Alternatively, and more interestingly, he could have considered a four-group failure classification by letting the four failure events comprise individual failure groups. Given that a bond default and nonpayment of a preferred-stock dividend are quite similar failure events, these two categories could have been combined and a three-group structure employed.

Beaver's failure group consists of 79 failed business firms. The failure events observed were: bankruptcy (59), nonpayment of a preferred-stock dividend (16), bond default (3), and overdrawn bank account (1).

Sample Selection. Beaver's sample firms "failed" during the years 1954 to 1964. Data for these firms for various years prior to failure were obtained from *Moody's Industrial Manual.* Beaver classified the failed firms according to industry [using U.S. Department of Commerce Standard Industrial Classification (SIC) codes] and asset size. He found that the 79 failed firms represented 38 different industries and the average firm had approximately $6 million in assets (based upon the most recent balance sheet prior to failure). The asset size range was $0.6 million to $45 million.

Beaver selected a sample of nonfailed firms using a *paired-sample* method. The purpose of this technique was to control for factors that otherwise might mask the relationship between financial ratios and failure. The paired or matched characteristics were industry classification code and asset size. He argued that these two factors should be controlled because across industries the same numerical value of a ratio may imply a different probability of failure and, given identical ratios, the smaller of two firms may have a higher probability of failure.

One of the shortcomings of a paired sample, which Beaver was careful to point out, is that the controlled variables may be important predictors of failure yet remain undetected because their predictive power is masked by the paired-sample technique. If a nonpaired sample is employed, the predictive power of all relevant variables can be determined. In Beaver's study, the predictive powers of industry and size were not analyzed.[2]

Data for the sample firms were obtained from *Moody's* for the 5 years prior to failure. However, since availability of data for the *full* 5-year period was not required, the number of observations decreased as the time prior to failure increased. The number of observations in the failed group, beginning with the first year prior to failure, were 79, 76, 75, 62, and 54, respectively.

The Time-Series Problem. Because business failures for which adequate data are available occur relatively infrequently within a given year, it is necessary to pool observations from different time periods to obtain workable samples. This pooling presents a time-series problem because structural change may have occurred in the *a priori* probabilities of failure and/or in the economic significance of particular financial ratios. When observations are pooled, it is assumed (usually implicitly) that the relationship among the variables has remained stationary over time.

The pooled-observations technique usually is accompanied by attempts to make failure predictions one or more periods in the future. This creates another times-series problem because the process by which a business firm fails usually is an evolutionary one. Thus, the relationships among the means and variances probably change over time. Accordingly, different failure models (i.e., parameters and/or variables) may be required for different prediction periods in the future. Although Beaver did not use discriminant analysis *per se,* both aspects of what we call the time-series problem in discriminant analysis are present.

Selection of Variables. For each of the 5 years prior to failure, Beaver computed 30 ratios. The ratios were selected on the basis of three criteria: (1) popularity in the literature, (2) performance in previous studies, and (3) definition of the ratio in terms of a "cash-flow" concept. Beaver divided his 30 ratios into the following six "common-element" groups: (1) cash flow, (2) net income, (3) debt to total assets, (4) liquid asset to total asset, (5) liquid asset to current debt, and (6) turnover. On the basis of lowest percentage prediction error (in dichotomous classification tests) for each group over the 5-year period, Beaver selected the following six variables as "best": (1) cash flow to total debt, (2) net income to total assets, (3) current plus long-term liabilities to total assets, (4) working capital to total assets, (5) current ratio, and (6) "no-credit interval."

Beaver's Empirical Findings. Beaver conducted three major empirical experiments: (1) comparison of mean values, (2) dichotomous classification tests, and (3) analysis of likelihood ratios.

Comparison of Mean Values. Beaver referred to the comparison of mean values as a profile analysis to indicate that it described the general relationships between failed and nonfailed firms. He found the anticipated differences in the mean values for each of the six ratios in all 5 years before failure. In addition, the average failed firm showed substantial deterioration as the year of failure approached. In contrast, the performance of the average nonfailed firm was relatively constant with only small deviations from trend.

Beaver's Dichotomous Classification Test. Beaver's classification test involved a dichotomous prediction or binomial response (i.e., failure or nonfailure). To make the predictions, Beaver arranged each of the 30 ratios (for both failed and nonfailed firms) in ascending order. Next, he visually inspected each pair or arrays to find the cutoff point that minimized the percentage of incorrect predictions. For example, using the profitability ratio (i.e., net income per dollar of total assets) and a cutoff point of 0.02, he found that, one year before failure, 88 percent of the firms were classified correctly. Beaver used the percentage of observations misclassified as a crude index of a ratio's predictive ability.

To validate this trial-and-error classification test and to eliminate sample bias, Beaver conducted a "holdout" experiment. He randomly divided the failed and nonfailed firms into two subsamples and conducted two experiments. In the first experiment, the firms were reclassified using the cutoff points from the *original* sample whereas in the second experiment, the cutoff points from the "holdout" sample were used. In the holdout experiment, because the firms being classified were not used in determining the cutoff points, sample bias was eliminated.

Beaver concluded that the cash flow–total debt ratio was the overall best predictor. However, its Type I error increased substantially as the number of years before failure increased. For example, the Type I error was 22 percent 1 year prior to failure and 47 percent 4 years prior to failure. In contrast, the Type II error was fairly low and stable ranging nonmonotonically between 3 and 8 percent.

In most predictions of this type, Type I errors are more costly than Type II errors and therefore a truly minimized misclassification rate should incorporate these differing costs. Beaver treated the costs of misclassification as being symmetrical and employed an *a priori* probability of failure of 0.5. In other words, a loss function incorporating the product of the ratios of *a priori* probabilities and costs of misclassification is equal to one.

Analysis of Likelihood Ratios. Likelihood ratios are useful for examining the overlap, skewness, and normality of the ratio distributions. For example, 1 year before failure the profitability distributions of the failed and nonfailed firms showed relatively little overlap between the groups. Regarding skewness, the profitability distributions of the failed firms were skewed to the left in each of the years before failure and the skewness increased as the year of failure approached. For the nonfailed firms, the skewness was in the opposite direction (i.e., to the right) and much less pronounced. Beaver found rather pronounced skewness in most of the distributions analyzed, suggesting they were not normally distributed. To test directly for normality, Beaver used cumulative density functions (cdf). On the basis of cdf tests, he concluded that the six ratios were not normally distributed. Moreover, he found that log or square-root transformations were almost as badly skewed as the original variables. Because most multivariate techniques assume normality, Beaver concluded that multivariate failure–prediction models are suspect if they use similar data.

Beaver's Major Conclusions, Qualifications, and Suggestions for Future Research. Beaver claimed that his most important contribution was to suggest a framework for the evaluation of accounting data, not merely for failure prediction, but for any purpose. His major finding was that financial ratios, or more generally, accounting data, have the ability to predict failure for at least 5 years before failure. However, he felt that there were important qualifications regarding the use of ratio analysis for failure prediction. First, not all ratios predict with the same degree of accuracy. Second, ratios have greater success predicting nonfailure rather than failure. And third, for decision-making purposes, financial ratios should be complemented by frequency distributions and likelihood ratios. As avenues for future research, Beaver suggested that (1) multiratio analysis be investigated; (2) ratios be compared with other potential predictors of failure, such as market rates of return; and (3) additional samples of failed and nonfailed firms be analyzed.[3]

Altman (1968) to (1977)

At the 1976 Conference on Financial Crisis, sponsored by Salomon Brothers Center for the Study of Financial Institutions, Altman (1977) presented a paper entitled "The Z-Score Bankruptcy Model: Past, Present, and Future." The purpose of the paper was to present a retrospective and prospective analysis of his original Z-score model (Altman, 1968) and planned extensions of the model for the future. The extension, a paper by Altman et. al. (1977) represents the state of the art in bankruptcy prediction, Altman's 1968 and 1977 papers serve as the major focus of this section.

Altman's Original Z-Score Model. Altman's (1968) purpose was to assess the quality of ratio analysis as an analytical technique using the prediction of corporate bankruptcy as an example. Altman's methodological framework and empirical tests were similar to those of Beaver (1967). However, compared to Beaver, Altman introduced two major improvements. First, his definition of failure was improved because only firms that filed a Chapter X bankruptcy petition were included in the failed group. And second, Altman used multivariate or multiratio analysis.

Definition of Failure and Sample Selection. Altman's definition of failure was simply a Chapter X bankruptcy. His sample consisted of 66 manufacturing firms with 33 observations in each group. The corporations in the failed group filed bankruptcy petitions over the years 1946–1965. Thus, Altman's data, like Beaver's, were obtained by pooling observations from different time periods.

Altman's 33 bankrupt firms ranged in asset size from $0.7 million to $25.9 million with a mean of $6.4 million. The nonbankrupt firms, as in Beaver's study, were selected on a paired basis with industry and asset size as the control variables. The selection of nonfailed firms was restricted to the $1-$25 million asset-size range; the mean for the nonbankrupt group was $9.6 million, 50 percent larger than that for the bankrupt group. Altman dismissed this difference as being slight and claimed that matching asset size exactly seems unnecessary, since ratios, by nature, tend to mitigate the effect of size. The important point is whether or not size, or in general any control variable, is a predictor of failure. The paired-sample design assumes that the variables controlled are important, otherwise they wouldn't be controlled. However, the technique simultaneously precludes making any inferences about the predictive ability of these important variables. Because of this limitation, we recommend employing random samples whenever possible. Moreover, for predictive purposes, because a random sample represents the underlying population, it is more appropriate than a paired sample. Both Altman and Beaver dismiss a random sample as being "unwise" or "inappropriate," respectively.

Data and Variables. Altman collected balance-sheet and income-statement data for the sample firms from *Moody's Industrial Manual* and selected annual reports for 1, 2, 3, 4, and 5 years before bankruptcy. The average lead time for the first year before failure was approximately 7.5 months. He analyzed 22 variables from five standard ratio categories (i.e., liquidity, profitability, leverage, solvency, and activity). The ratios were selected because of their (1) popularity in the literature and (2) potential relevancy for the research. The cash flow–total debt ratio, Beaver's best variable in terms of overall predictive ability, was not included in the set of 22 variables. Only incomplete depreciation data were available and therefore Altman was unable to construct the ratio.

Altman's Five-Variable Z-Score Model. From his original set of 22 variables, the following 5 variables, were selected as the profile with the "best" (but not optimal) predictive ability:

1. Working Capital/Total Assets (WCTA)
2. Retained Earnings/Total Assets (RETA)
3. Earnings Before Interest and Taxes/Total Assets (EBIT)
4. Market Value of Equity/Book Value of Total Debt (MEBD)
5. Sales/Total Assets (SLTA)

Altman used the following procedures to arrive at this final set of variables: (1) the statistical significance of alternative discriminant functions including the relative contribution of individual variables; (2) examination of the relevant correlation matrix; (3) predictive accuracy based upon classification tests; and (4) his own judgment as a researcher. If one's goal simply is *to predict* failure, then, of course, only the third factor (predictive ability) is relevant for selecting a set of variables.

The F-statistic for Altman's five variables taken as a set was 20.7, indicating that the null hypothesis of equality of group means was rejected. One might legitimately ask why SLTA, a statistically insignificant variable, was included in Altman's set of "best" variables (see Table

Table VII.2. Means and *F*-Statistics One Year Prior to Bankruptcy

Variable	*Bankrupt Group*	*Nonbankrupt Group*	*F-Statistic*
WCTA	−.061	.414	32.60
RETA	−.626	.355	58.86
EBIT	−.318	.153	26.56
MEBD	.401	2.477	33.26
SLTA	1.500	1.900	2.84

Data are for 1 year prior to bankruptcy with 33 observations in each group. $F(1,60).05 = 4.0$.
Source: Altman (1968, Table 1, p. 596).

VII.2). The answer is because of the *interaction* between variables. A variable that is insignificant by itself may be an important discriminator in a multivariate framework.

How did Altman determine that the sales-asset ratio is an important discriminator? There are no absolute tests for the importance of specific variables in discriminant analysis. However, several methods are available for ranking the relative contributions of specific variables to the overall discriminatory power of a variable profile. Altman used the *scaled-weighted method.* Under this technique, the *scaled* discriminant-function coefficients are *weighted* by the appropriate diagonal elements of the pooled within-group deviation sum of squares matrix. For example, for SLTA, the discriminant coefficient was 1.0 (these coefficients are discussed later) and the appropriate weight was 8.41. Thus, the scaled-weighted coefficient was 8.41.

Altman stated that a probable reason for SLTA's high rank was its strong negative correlation (−.78) with EBIT in the bankrupt group.[4] The negative correlation implied that, on average, the firms in the bankrupt group were operating in a range in which earnings per dollar of sales were declining (i.e., the range in which SLTA is greater than S^* in Figure VII.1). Because EBIT was negative for the bankrupt group, the average bankrupt firm was operating in the range beyond S_4 in Figure VII.1. The *slope* of the hypothetical curve in Figure VII.1 measures a firm's earnings per dollar of sales or its profit margin, that is,

$$\begin{aligned}\text{EBIT/SLTA} &= \text{(EARNINGS/ASSETS)/(SALES/ASSETS)}\\ &= \text{EARNINGS/SALES} = \text{PROFIT MARGIN} \quad (7.1)\end{aligned}$$

The average bankrupt firm had a profit margin of −0.21 (= −.318/1.5) compared to 0.08 (= .153/1.9) for the average healthy firm.[5]

This profit-margin interpretation of the interaction between EBIT and SLTA helps to clarify how an insignificant variable may be important in a multivariate context. It suggests that the profit-margin

Figure VII.1. The Relationship Between EBIT and SLTA

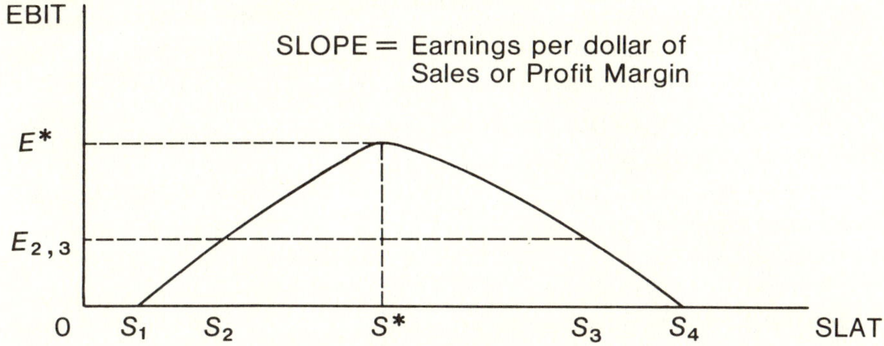

variable should be an important discriminator between healthy and unhealthy businesses because it corporates both the asset-utilization (EBIT) and asset-turnover aspects (SLTA) of a firm's performance. Referring to Figure VII.1, if a firm's goal is to maximize its asset ulitization, it does so when its marginal profit is zero. Alternatively, a firm's objective might be to maximize sales given some minimum level of asset utilization, say $E_{2,3}$. In this situation, S_3 would be preferred to S_2.

Weighting the Variables. Altman's five-variable discriminant function is:

$$Z = 1.2\,(\text{WCTA}) + 1.4\,(\text{RETA}) + 3.3\,(\text{EBIT}) + 0.6\,(\text{MEBD}) + 1.0\,(\text{SLTA}) \qquad (7.2)$$

where Z is the discriminant score (the variables on the RHS of the equation are defined in the preceding subsection).[6] Using the ratios from Table VII.2 and the coefficients from Eq. (7.2), Z-scores for the average bankrupt firm and the average nonbankrupt firm are -0.26 and 4.89, respectively.[7] These Z-scores are simply the group means or centroids of the two-group sample. The F-statistic for the group means is 20.7, indicating that the group means are significantly different.

What started as a problem with 22 dimensions (variables) was reduced to a dimensionality of 5 and then, through a linear combination of the five variables, reduced to one dimension, the Z-score. Z-scores are calculated for each firm in the sample and used to classify them into either the bankrupt or nonbankrupt group. The cutoff score that minimizes the overall misclassification was 2.675. If a firm's score was less than 2.675, it was assigned to the bankrupt group; if the score was equal to or greater than the cutoff value, it was assigned to the nonbankrupt group. Altman found that firms (from the original sample) with scores below 1.81 were classified correctly as bankrupts and that firms with scores above 2.99 were classified correctly as nonbankrupts. Because misclassifications occur in the range between 1.81 and 2.99, Altman refered to it as the "zone of ignorance" or "gray area."

Classification Results. Using the above classification rule, Altman concluded that his model is an accurate predictor of failure up to 2 years prior to bankruptcy; after the second year, the predictive ability decreases significantly. The model's decline in predictive content is illustrated by the upward trend in the Type I error: 6, 28, 52, 71, and 64 (percent). The important point is that the groups were relatively distinct (i.e., showed little overlap) in the first 2 years prior to bankruptcy; however, after the second year this distinctness became blurred. Of the 66 firms classified 1 year prior to bankruptcy, only three firms were misclassified, two of which were future bankrupts. In contrast, of the 65 firms classified 2 years prior to bankruptcy, eleven were misclassified, nine of which were future bankrupts.

Validation Tests. Altman tested his model on holdout samples of bankrupt and nonbankrupt firms. The bankrupt group consisted of a *new* sample of 25 bankrupt firms with an asset-size range similar to that of the initial sample of 33 bankrupt firms. The nonbankrupt group consisted of 66 (randomly drawn) manufacturing firms that reported net income deficits in either 1958 or 1961. Roughly 65 percent of these temporarily unhealthy firms reported negative profits for 2 or 3 years prior to 1958 or 1961. Thus, Altman's "holdout" nonbankrupt group did not consist of "completely healthy" firms; instead, it consisted of firms with temporary financial problems. Altman's objective was to test how well his model performed on firms with financial difficulties short of bankruptcy. He claimed that a bankruptcy prediction for a member of this financially ailing group is a good example of Type II classification error.

Only 15 of the 99 holdout-sample firms were misclassified and only one of these 15 was from the bankrupt group. Thus, the overall accuracy rate is 83.5 percent with a Type I error of 4.0 percent and a Type II error of 21.2 percent. Given the hybrid nature of the holdout nonbankrupt group (i.e., the firms were neither bankrupt nor nonbankrupt in terms of the original model design), The model was quite sensitive in distinguishing between permanent and temporary financial problems. This is a good illustration of the importance of multivariate analysis. Although the members of the nonbankrupt group had short-term earnings difficulties (and probably would have been classified as future bankrupts using only an operating earnings variable), they apparently had other good characteristics, such as liquidity, long-term profitability (retained earnings), and high sales turnover, to offset the short-term earnings problem. Regarding the model's sensitivity to the earnings problem of the nonbankrupt group, 10 of the 14 misclassified nonbankrupts and about one-third of the entire nonbankrupt group had *Z*-scores within the "zone of ignorance."

Application of Altman's Z-Score Model. Altman contended that his model could be used to complement (1) business loan evaluations, (2) accounts receivable management, (3) internal control procedures, and (4) investment strategies. Regarding business loan evaluations, Altman (1968, 1970) suggested using the "quantitative" model to complement the "more qualitative and intuitive" approach of loan officers. However, he was careful to point out that the model was not a credit-scoring mechanism nor a substitute for the evaluations of loan officers. He argued that the model and its generated *Z*-scores could be a valuable tool for determining the overall creditworthiness of business customers.

One of the most important tasks that a corporate manager performs is the evaluation of his or her own policies and managerial skills, factors that ultimately determine how well a company performs. Direct measurement of the effectiveness of managerial skills and policies is a difficult task. Consequently, indirect measurement (frequently via comparative ratio analysis) is employed. Ratios, of course, reflect symptoms, not causes. However, by identifying atypical or abnormal ratios, problem areas can be identified and the cause(s) of the difficulty investigated. Altman's model could be used to rate a company's overall performance (via its *Z*-score) and to pinpoint problem areas (via individual ratios). To illustrate this type of application, consider the following example derived from the article, "How To Figure Who's Going Bankrupt," *Dun's Review* (October, 1975). For this article, *Z*-scores for some 1200 publicly owned companies were computed. The companies with the 14 highest and 14 lowest *Z*-scores are listed. In this example, the four companies with the following Z-scores are analyzed: (1) highest, (2) lowest, (3) highest of the 14 lowest, and (4) lowest of the 14 highest. The *Z*-scores and ratios for these four companies (Taylor Wine, Memorex, Telex, and Data General) are presented in Table VII.3. [8]

According to Altman's classification rule, Memorex and Telex were headed for bankruptcy while Data General and especially Taylor Wine were performing very well. The managers of Memorex and Telex should have been concerned about their low *Z*-scores—and their jobs. Can Altman's model provide information to enable managers to anticipate approaching business failure and defeat it? Looking at Memorex's profile of five variables, it is clear that as of year-end 1974 the company

Table VII.3. Z-Scores: Best and Worst Performers

Company	*Z-Score*	*WCTA*	*RETA*	*EBIT*	*MEBD*	*SLTA*
		Ratios				
Taylor Wine (6/74)	304.09	0.52	0.61	0.24	501.45	0.97
Data General (9/74)	36.32	0.47	0.31	0.27	55.45	1.17
Telex (3/75)	1.78	0.22	−0.19	0.13	0.35	1.12
Memorex (12/74)	0.74	0.19	−0.49	0.04	0.25	0.92

Figures in parentheses beside company name indicate date of data, except for the MEBD data, which are as of year-end 1974. The *Z*-scores are calculated using Eq. (7.2). Going across the table, the discriminant coefficients are 1.2, 1.4, 3.3, 0.6, and 1.0, respectively.
Source: Dun's Review, (October, 1975), p. 65.

had serious profitability (both current and cumulative), liquidity, and solvency problems. The cumulative-profitability problem indicates that Memorex's financial difficulties have been longstanding ones.[9]

Since the *Z*-score for Telex (1.78) is quite close to Altman's "zone of ignorance" (i.e., 1.81 to 2.99), one has less confidence in its prediction of insolvency. However, relative to Memorex's ratios, Telex's five-variable profile is superior. In terms of contribution to *Z*-score, the cumulative-profitability variable (RETA) accounts for the greatest difference in the Memorex-Telex *Z*-score spread. For example, if Memorex had Telex's RETA ratio and vice versa, the *Z*-scores are Memorex 1.16 and Telex 1.36.

The information in Table VII.4 also can be used to illustrate another application that Altman considered for his bankruptcy model, namely, investment or stock-market strategy. Altman (1968) found that firms in his original sample whose *Z*-scores were below 1.81 experienced, on average, a decline of 45 percent in the market value of their common stock from the time the model first predicted bankruptcy until the actual failure date (about 15 months on average). Depending upon an

Table VII.4. Stock Prices: Best and Worst *Z*-Scores

Company (Exchange)	*Closing Prices* 12/31/74	10/12/76
Taylor Wine (OTC)	10 3/8	17 3/8
Data General (NYSE)	12 7/8	44 1/8
Telex (NYSE)	2 1/4	2 1/2
Memorex (OTC/PSE)	3[a]	21 1/4

[a]Indicates average of high (4 3/4) and low (1 3/8) prices for the year 1974. Telex's 1975 high was 3/4; its low was 1/4.
Sources: The Wall Street Journal and *Moody's Industrial Manual.*

investor's preferences and his confidence in Altman's model, a number of portfolio strategies are available. For example, if a company is a predicted bankrupt, a conservative investor does not buy the stock; or, if he already is holding it he sells it. In contrast, a speculator might take a short position in a company with a low *Z*-score. In general, risk-averse investors should purchase the stock of companies with high *Z*-scores and sell (or not purchase) the stock of companies with low *Z*-scores. Applying this simple rule to the four companies listed in Table VII.3 and assuming roughly a 22-month investment holding period, the investment rule is profitable in three of the four cases. The relevant data are presented in Table VII.4. Of course, neither Altman nor the authors of this book recommend that this simple *Z*-score rule be followed blindly. The important point is that *Z*-scores appear to contain information that can be relevant to guide investment decisions.

As indicated in Table VII.4, Memorex and Telex have *not* gone bankrupt. In fact, Memorex appears to have turned its operations around, while Telex, even after substantial financial assistance from Bank of America, still remains in a slump.[10]

Z-Scores and Predictions of Bankruptcy. It is important to understand in what sense Altman's *Z*-scores are predictions or forecasts. A prediction or forecast usually involves a statement at time t about some future event, at time $t + k$ (e.g., predictions about tomorrow's weather, future interest rates, or next year's GNP). Such forecasts usually incorporate *expectational* variables, such as anticipated movements of weather systems, expected rates of inflation, and anticipated consumer and investment expenditures. Because *Z*-scores are not calculated using expectational variables, in what sense are they predictive? They are predictive because the coefficients of the discriminant function are estimated *prior* to actual past bankruptcies. In effect, the coefficients provide the expectational content. For example, Memorex's *Z*-score of 0.74 (see Table VII.3) indicates that as of December 31, 1974, Memorex's five-variable profile is more similar to Altman's average bankrupt firm 1 year before failure than his average nonbankrupt firm. The predictive implication is that if Memorex's financial condition *continues* to deteriorate, in the manner of the average bankrupt firm, then 1 year hence Memorex probably will be bankrupt. It is obvious (after the fact) that Memorex's managers and their bankers were aware of their financial difficulties and took the necessary steps to prevent the company's further deterioration.

Conclusions and Extensions. Altman (1968) concluded that his model is an accurate predictor of bankruptcy up to 2 years prior to failure; beyond the second year, the accuracy of the model diminishes rapidly. Although Altman (1977) contended that his 1968 model performed well over the past 9 years, he believed that a "new" model that explicitly considers (1) recent larger bankruptcies, (2) improved statistical techniques, and (3) the new standards and guidelines for financial reporting is needed. Altman, Haldeman, and Narayanan (1977) recently completed this extension, their "ZETA" model. After a critique of Altman's 1968 model, we will examine the ZETA model.

Altman's Critics

Johnson (1970). Johnson's (1970) criticism of Altman (1968) (and also of Beaver, 1967 and Blum, 1969) focuses upon the question of whether or not models composed solely of financial ratios can predict failure. The attack concentrates upon the issues of (1) model building, (2) interpretation of financial ratios, and (3) *ex post* reasoning.

Johnson claims that Altman does not prove that ratios have predictive power but only that bankrupt and nonbankrupt firms have dissimilar ratios. Altman's *ex post* reasoning and conclusions, according to Johnson, are "largely descriptive statements devoid of predictive content" (Johnson, 1970:1168).[11] On balance, Johnson concludes that the Altman–Beaver–Blum studies do not present evidence of the ability of ratios to predict failure.

Wilcox (1973a). Wilcox reviewed Altman's (1971) book, *Corporate Bankruptcy in America,* for *The Journal of Accountancy* (February, 1973). On the subject of predicting corporate bankruptcy (Altman's Chapter 3, which is similar to his 1968 *Journal of Finance* article) Wilcox stated:[12]

> One is led to conclude that the use of a statistical dragnet, without an underlying model or a test of fresh data, is as risky here as elsewhere. Altman's attempt to improve on Beaver's results must be judged less than successful [Wilcox, 1973a:93].

On the positive side, Wilcox commended Altman for incorporating a stock market variable [the ratio of market value of equity to book value of debt (MEBD)] in his analysis, He viewed this as a radical change from using pure accounting data to predict failure. Finally, Wilcox's overall evaluation of Altman's book was: "an ambitious effort, worthy of attention by those whose work demands an appraisal of financial risk" (Wilcox, 1973a:92), but a study in which "the author's research methods do not encourage confidence in his specific results" (Wilcox, 1973a:93).

Joy and Tollefson (1975) and (1978). The most extensive critique of Altman's work (1968) is by Joy and Tollefson (1975) (hereafter J&T). Their paper, "On the Financial Applications of Discriminant Analysis," is a discussion of the methodology of discriminant analysis, with an orientation toward financial applications of the technique. J&T (1978) is a reply to a comment by Altman and Eisenbeis (1978) on J&T (1975). The articles are must readings. This section focuses upon J&T (1975).

J&T claimed that recent discriminant analysis studies have given relatively little attention to design and interpretation difficulties associated with the technique and therefore the conclusions and generalizations of these studies frequently are tenuous. Regarding Altman's work, J&T questioned: (1) the reporting of the analysis-sample results; (2) the interpretation of *ex post* discriminations as predictions; (3) the assessment of the discriminatory power of variables; and (4) the performance of Altman's classification model relative to alternative chance models. The second and fourth points are the most relevant ones.

J&T claimed that Altman's classifications are not predictions of corporate bankruptcy but merely *ex post* discriminations. They contended that Altman's holdout sample should have been drawn from a future period *completely* distinct from the original (or analysis) sample period. J&T claimed that evidence of *ex ante* predictive power requires *intertemporal* validation and not merely *cross* validation. (By cross validation, they mean verification using a time-coincident holdout sample.) J&T admitted, however, that under the assumption of *stationarity* (of the parameters and variables of the discriminant function) *ex post* discrimination (or validation) is tantamount to prediction, provided the researcher proves that stationarity indeed exists. Otherwise, according to J&T, *ex post* discriminations (or cross validations) merely are useful for making inferences about the importance of individual variables.

Eisenbeis (1977) contended that J&T incorrectly view the process of prediction as only making inferences into the future. As a result, they excluded instances when one is interested only in predicting whether or not an event will occur without reference to a particular time period (e.g., Altman's bankruptcy predictions) *and* when one is willing to assume stationarity. In such cases, Eisenbeis claimed that cross validation is not inappropriate or meaningless. Divergency in *ex ante* and *ex post* classifications, according to Eisenbeis, constitutes a crude test of the stationarity hypothesis. J&T apparently were not aware that Altman and McGough (1974) conducted an intertemporal validation of Altman's 1968 model using a sample of 34 bankrupt firms from the 1970–1973 period. Their *ex ante* findings indicated that Altman's *Z*-score model (1 year prior to bankruptcy) correctly classified 28 (82.4 percent) of the observations.

J&T's final comment dealt with the performance of Altman's classification model relative to alternative chance-classification models. J&T used the overall classificatory rate, defined as the number of observations correctly classified divided by the number of observations classified, as their measure of total classificatory efficiency. The purpose was to determine how "good" Altman's cross-validation (or holdout-sample) total efficiency rate (.835 = (24 + 52)/91) is. The standard of comparison was alternative chance models.

Assuming that *a priori* probabilities are equal to sample proportions (or frequencies) as Altman did, J&T found that Altman's model (.835) was more efficient than either a maximum-chance model (.725 = 66/91) or a proportional-chance model (.601 = (25/91)(25/91) + (66/91)(66/91). However, assuming population *a priori* probabilities of .01 for bankruptcy and .99 for nonbankruptcy, they found that Altman's efficiency rate (.835) was inferior to both the maximum-chance model (.99) and the proportional-chance model [.98 = (.01)(.01) + (.99)(.99)]. Using the population *priors* in Altman's model, the expected-correct classification rate was .789 = .01(.96) + .99(.788), which also was inferior to the chance models. Using a Bayesian approach to capture the effects of differing costs of misclassification (i.e., of Type I and Type II errors), J&T found that Altman's model was preferred to the two alternative chance models if and only if the cost of a Type I error was 21 to 22 times greater than the cost of a Type II error.

Altman (1977) contended that J&T used an inappropriate estimate of his model's Type II error, since the 21 percent figure was derived from an unusual nonrandom sample of nonbankrupt firms (i.e., the nonbankrupt group in Altman's holdout sample consisted of firms with negative earnings in either 1958 or 1961). Based upon findings by Altman and Brenner (1976), Altman claimed that a more realistic Type II error was in the 5 to 10 percent range. Using this more appropriate Type II error, Altman concluded that the cost of the Type I error only has to be in the range of 4 to 10 times greater than the cost of the Type II error for his model to be more efficient than the two alternative chance models. Since Altman (1977) estimated this cost to be in the range of 16.5 to 30, he concluded that his model "is clearly superior to either the proportional-chance or maximum-chance strategies" (Altman, 1977:13).

ZETA ANALYSIS

Altman, Haldeman, and Narayana (1977)

Purpose. The purpose of the Altman, Haldeman, and Narayanan (hereafter AH&N) study was to construct, analyze, and test a new bankruptcy classification model that explicitly considers recent methodological, accounting, statistical, and bankruptcy developments.

AH&N felt that there are at least five good reasons why a new model could improve and extend previous bankruptcy analyses. First, the average size of a bankrupt firm has increased significantly over recent years. For example, in Altman's 1968 study, the average bankrupt firm had total assets of $6.4 million. The comparable figure for AH&N's sample was approximately $100 million, roughly an 800 percent increase after adjusting for inflation. (From 1968 to 1977, the wholesale price index almost doubled.)

Second, regarding the time-series problem (i.e., stationarity), 89 percent of AH&N's bankrupt firms failed within the 6-year period, 1970–1975. This is a considerably shorter period than the 1946–1965 period used in Altman's 1968 study. However, the early 1970s were a very volatile period, perhaps, even less "stationary" than the 1946–1965 era.

Third, previous failure-prediction models focused upon either the broad classification of manufacturing firms or specific industries. AH&N's sample included retailers, a particularly vulnerable group in that period, as well as manufacturers.

Fourth, recent changes in financial reporting standards and accepted accounting principles tend to make models based upon older standards and principles obsolete. Thus, incorporation of such changes may be important for predictive purposes.

And fifth, applications of discriminant analysis have generated considerable controversy regarding the use, interpretation, and validity of the technique. AH&N proposed to test and assess several of these controversial areas of discriminant analysis.

Sample Selection and Characteristics. AH&N's sample of failed firms consisted of 53 bankrupt firms and a *paired* sample of 58 nonbankrupt firms. (Five of the failed firms did not have sufficient data for their purposes, which accounts for the unequal sample sizes.) The pairing or matching was on the basis of industry group and year of data.

Selection of Variables. AH&N analyzed 28 variables classified into the following six performance categories (figures in parentheses are the number of variables in each category):

1. Profitability (6)
2. Interest coverage and leverage (7)
3. Liquidity (4)
4. Capitalization ratios (5)
5. Earnings variability (3)
6. Miscellaneous measures (3)

The ZETA Model. Using various discriminant-analysis procedures, AH&N produced a seven-variable model that they claimed was "impressively accurate and manageable." The seven variables are:

1. *Return on Assets* (ROA): measured by the ratio of earnings before interest and taxes to total assets. ROA measures a firm's current profitability.
2. *Stability of Earnings* (SOE): measured by the inverse of the standard error of estimate around a 10-year trend in ROA. Variability of earnings is a traditional measure of business risk.
3. *Debt Service* (DS): measured by the interest–coverage ratio, i.e., EBIT/total fixed payments (including the amount imputed to capitalized leases). Coverage is a measure of leverage or riskiness, especially from creditors' point of view.
4. *Cumulative Profitability* (CP): measured by the ratio of retained earnings (from the balance sheet) to total assets. CP measures a firm's long-term profit performance.
5. *Liquidity* (LQD): measured by the current ratio, i.e., the ratio of current assets to current liabilities. LQD measures a firm's ability to meet its current obligations.
6. *Capitalization* (CAP): measured by the ratio of a 5-year average market value of the firm's common stock to total long-term capital. CAP is a proxy for a firm's future earning power. CAP is measured using market values (not book values) and preferred stock is included in the denominator.
7. *Size* (SIZE): measured by total assets, adjusted for recent financial reporting changes. A logarithmic transformation was applied to SIZE. In the past, smaller firms have been more prone to fail than larger ones.

The Relative Importance of Individual Variables. AH&N used six different tests to determine the relative importance of their variables. The "consensus" ranking is unambiguous, that is,

Variable	*Rank*
CP	1
SOE	2
CAP	3
SIZE	4
LQD	5
DS	6
ROA	7

The range of univariate *F*-statistics was from 5.5 for SIZE to 114.6 for CP. However, within the set of seven variables, SIZE was on a consensus basis, the fourth most important variable. As the least important of the seven variables, ROA still made an important relative contribution. CP, the most important single variable, can be viewed as the cumulation of ROA over time.

Covariance Matrices. The null hypothesis of equal group covariance matrices was rejected, indicating that a quadratic equation rather than a linear one should be employed. The unequal variance–covariance matrices also imply that ranking procedures that account for these differences should be used (see Karson and Martell, 1980). Thus, the rankings discussed above should be viewed as a first approximation.

The ZETA Model versus Altman's 1968 Model. In Table VII.5, the Type I errors for AH&N's 1977 linear ZETA model are compared with Altman's 1968 linear bankruptcy model. The ZETA model Type I errors clearly are superior, especially beyond the first year prior to bankruptcy. AH&N also demonstrated the superiority of the ZETA model compared to (1) the 1968 model using the ZETA sample in a holdout test and (2) the 1968 model estimated using the ZETA sample.

The Efficiency of the ZETA Model. AH&N tested the efficiency of their model by explicitly incorporating population *a priori* probabilities and costs of misclassification into their classification analyses and comparing the findings with alternative chance-classification models. They found that naive chance models were almost six times more costly (or six times less efficient) than the ZETA model.

AH&N's Conclusions. AH&N concluded that the ZETA model was a significant improvement over Altman's 1968 bankruptcy model in terms of accuracy and especially in terms of data and methodology.

Table VII.5. Type-I Errors: ZETA Model Versus Altman's 1968 Model

	Type-I Errors	
Year before Bankruptcy	*ZETA* (%)	*Altman's 1968* (%)
1	3.8	6.1
2	15.1	28.1
3	25.5	52.7
4	31.9	71.4
5	30.2	64.0

Source: Altman, Haldeman, and Narayanan (1977) and Altman (1968).

Critique of AH&N. AH&N's statistical objective was to test and assess several recent advances in discriminant analysis. In this regard, three areas are important: (1) ranking variables, (2) linear versus quadratic when holdout samples are involved and (3) consideration of population *a priori* probabilities and costs of misclassification. With respect to all three of the items, AH&N appear to have avoided pitfalls that plague previous discriminant analysis studies. However, two qualifications are necessary. First, regarding ranking variables, when the group variance–covariance matrices are not equal, a ranking procedure that accounts for these differences must be employed. Because AH&N's ranking techniques do not account for such differences, their rankings are only a first approximation. And second, with respect to the linear versus quadratic question, AH&N concluded that for *their particular sample* a linear model is relatively more efficient than a quadratic one with respect to holdout-sample tests. Given unequal covariance matrices *and* sufficient degrees of freedom, a quadratic equation will, on average, be more efficient than a linear one. Thus, it would be misleading to *generalize* from AH&N's findings in favor of a linear structure in holdout-sample tests.

Let us now focus upon AH&N's modeling strategy. The three basic modeling strategies in failure-prediction models are

1. A unique model for each year prior to bankruptcy (i.e., different variables and different estimated parameters);
2. The same model in each year but with different estimated parameters; and
3. The same model with the same parameters for each year.

The third strategy, which is appropriate in a static framework, is the one employed by AH&N. Their seven-variable model is, strictly speaking, only a one-period failure-prediction model. Analysts interested in predicting bankruptcy 2 or more years in the future would require a model based upon either strategy one or two, which are more flexible and preferable in a dynamic environment. AH&N do experiment with the second strategy but not with the first one. They conclude that "(the second strategy) is of some interest but for application purposes the analyst is left somewhat confused as to which model to apply to new data" (Altman et al., 1977:footnote 14). Are analysts that easily confused? The strategy is not complicated. The analyst interested in predicting bankruptcy t years in the future uses the model with parameters estimated t years prior to bankruptcy (t = 1, 2, 3, 4, 5 for the ZETA model). Similar remarks apply to the first strategy.

Instead of focusing upon only one strategy, alluding to another in a footnote, and not testing the third one, AH&N should test all three basic modeling strategies. They evidently feel comfortable with a static model because almost 90 percent of their bankruptcies occur within the 6-year period 1970 to 1975. This is a somewhat myopic view of stationarity that focuses mainly upon the length of the period being considered. Stationarity is a question of stability and structural changes. In general, over a long period of time, there tends to be less stability and greater change. However, relatively short periods may be extremely intense and volatile (e.g., 1928–1933). The 1970–1975 period, which comprises the kernel of AH&N's data base, is one of double-digit inflation, double-digit interest rates, high unemployment, record-size bankruptcies, the energy crisis, political scandals, etc. Employing a static model for analyzing such a period is an oversimplification.

SEVEN OTHER MODELS

Blum's Failing Company Model (1974)

Purpose. The purpose of Blum's 1974 article, "Failing-Company Discriminant Analysis," was to develop a Failing-Company Model (FCM) to aid the Antitrust Division of the Justice Department in assessing the probability of business failure. The Failing Company Doctrine [International Show v. F.T.C., 280 U.S. 291 (1930)] is one of the few acceptable defenses to a merger prosecution. According to the Doctrine, the defense applies when one of two merging companies is failing and the distressed company has not received an offer to merge from a company with which a merger would be legal. One of the difficulties in applying the Doctrine is determining the point at which a company is considered "failing." The legal jargon loosely defines failing as a "grave probability of failure." Blum's purpose was to quantify this probability by analyzing the financial and market data of failed firms.

Definition of Failure. Blum's definition of failure was based upon the criteria of the International Shoe decision. According to this case, one of the following three events constitutes failure: (1) inability to pay debts as they come due; (2) entrance into a bankruptcy proceeding; or (3) an explicit agreement with creditors to reduce debts. Ninety percent of Blum's failed firms filed federal bankruptcy petitions, whereas 10 percent entered into private debt arrangements.

Sample Selection. Blum's sample of failed firms consisted of 115 firms that failed from 1954 to 1968. Two requirements to be included in the sample were: (1) availability of data prior to failure and (2) a minimum of $1 million in liabilities at the time of failure. Since acquired firms with less than $1 million in liabilities usually are not challenged as antitrust violations, such firms were not included in Blum's analysis.

The 115 failed firms were paired with 115 nonfailed firms on the basis of industry, size, and fiscal year. Data from balance sheets, income statements, and stock market prices up to 8 fiscal years prior to failure were collected when available. The minimum number of consecutive years prior to failure for any firm was 3. Different time periods were employed to calculate the trend and variability elements used in the analysis.

Selection of Variables. Unlike most discriminant analysis studies, Blum did not search through a large set of variables to arrive at his FCM. Instead, he postulated, a la Beaver (1966), a general framework for variable selection based upon the concept of a business firm as a reservoir of financial resources with the probability of failure expressed in terms of expected cash flows. Blum's FCM was constructed with three common factors underlying the cash-flow framework: liquidity, profitability, and variability. He selected 12 variables to measure these cash-flow parameters. However, beyond the second year prior to failure, only nine variables are used.

Blum's Empirical Results. Interpreting Blum's empirical findings is somewhat difficult because of the different number of results presented. For example, regarding the classification results for 1 year prior, six sets of results corresponding to the number of years used for calculating the variability elements (ranging from 3 to 8 years) are presented. To illustrate, one of Blum's variables is the standard deviation of net income *over a period.* The period referred to is the number of years 3, 4, 5, 6, 7, or 8. Thus, for the 3-year interval, the standard deviation of net income is based upon 3 years; for the 4-year interval, it is based upon 4 years; and so on. Blum hypothesized that the ranges with periods of 4, 5, and 6 years will be more reliable for predictive purposes.

Blum's validation-sample classification results for the first 3 years prior to failure for intervals of 4, 5, and 6 years are presented in Table VII.6. The validation tests are constructed by splitting the samples in half, using one half to compute a discriminant function and the other as a validation sample for classification purposes. The overall accuracy rates for the 4-year, 5-year, and 6-year ranges are quite similar, on average, 94 percent, 80 percent, and 70 percent for 1, 2, and 3 years prior, respectively. In addition, except for the first year prior, the Type I and Type II errors have relatively stable and realistic values across the three ranges.[13]

Relative Importance of the Variables. Blum used only the relative size of the standardized discriminant-function coefficients to assess the relative importance of individual variables. The rankings vary quite a

Table VII.6. Blum's Validation-Sample Classification Results

	Interval of Years Composing the Range								
	Four			*Five*			*Six*		
Year before Failure	*Overall Accuracy* (%)	*Type-I Error* (%)	*Type-II Error* (%)	*Overall Accuracy* (%)	*Type-I Error* (%)	*Type-II Error* (%)	*Overall Accuracy* (%)	*Type-I Error* (%)	*Type-II Error* (%)
1	.95	.04	.07	.93	.12	.00	.95	.09	.00
2	.80	.16	.24	.80	.17	.23	.78	.13	.27
3	.70	.29	.32	.70	.29	.33	.70	.24	.33

Source: Blum (1974, Tables 5 and 7).

bit and, given the various ranges and years before failure, are difficult to summarize compactly.

Additional Tests. Blum conducted four additional tests that focus upon: (1) a model without financial ratios; (2) anticipation of failure by the market; (3) comparison with Altman's 1968 model; and (4) comparison with Beaver's univariate model. With respect to these four tests, Blum concluded: (1) except for the first year prior, a nonratio model is more accurate than his ratio model; (2) using a "going-to-the-market" measure, the stock market fails to anticipate the *timing* of failure; (3) Altman's model is less reliable than the FCM and Altman's model illustrates "the defects of searches for financial predictors that are selected without theoretical justification and without sound validation procedures" (Blum, 1974:13); and (4) Beaver's best ratio, cash flow to total debt, is as accurate as his FCM. Regarding the last point, Blum added that the Antitrust Division prefers his FCM over Beaver's because the FCM has a lower Type II error in the first year prior to failure and because the FCM is less susceptible to manipulation due to its multivariate character.

Blum's Suggestions for Future Research. Blum concluded that further research is needed and suggests four potential approaches: (1) develop a nonratio model with pairing precisely calibrated according to size and introduce age as an explicit variable; (2) consider alternative ratios or combinations of ratios beyond the traditional ones; (3) incorporate decision-tree analysis into the experimental design by splitting the sample using such criteria as delay in publishing financial statements or presence of preferred stock; and (4) retain the FCM design and try to improve the variables that appeared to be suboptimal.

Critique. Motivated by the Failing Company Doctrine, Blum's research is theoretically sound and technically competent for a 1969 MDA study.[14] A modernized version would require the covariance matrices to be tested for equality and alternative ranking procedures to be considered for determining a "consensus" ranking.

Blum, like Wilcox, criticized Altman for "searching" to establish his 1968 model. Yet, in his suggestions for future research, Blum proposed that alternative ratios be considered. How does a researcher determine which theoretically justified variables are the important ones? He or she searches.

Deakin (1972)

Purpose. The purpose of Deakin's 1972 study was to propose an alternative business-failure model to the ones developed by either Beaver or Altman. In his 1977 study, Deakin used his 1972 model, as modified by Libby [1975], to assess the impact, frequency, and nature of bankruptcy misclassification. The plan of this section is to examine Deakin's 1972 model, followed by Libby's 1975 modification, and conclude with Deakin's 1977 extension.

Deakin's 1972 Framework. Deakin liked Beaver's empirical results for their predictive accuracy *and* Altman's multivariate approach because of its intuitive appeal. His plan was to capture the best of both of these studies by employing the 14 ratios Beaver used and to search for the linear combination of these ratios with greatest predictive accuracy.

Definition of Failure and Sample Selection. Deakin analyzed 32 firms that failed between 1964 and 1970. His definition of failure included bankrupt, insolvent, or liquidated firms. Each firm was matched with a nonfailed firm on the basis of industry classification, asset size, and year of financial data.

Replication of Beaver's Dichotomous Classification Tests. Using the 14 ratios from Beaver's (1968) study, Deakin replicated Beaver's dichotomous classification tests.[15] Deakin's and Beaver's classification results for the overall most accurate predictor, the cash flow to total debt ratio, are quite similar. However, for the first 3 years prior to failure, Beaver found that the ratio of net income to total assets had the same overall accuracy as the cash flow to total debt ratio. In contrast, except for the third year prior when the ratio of total debt to total assets was the most accurate predictor (78 percent), Deakin's results favored the cash flow to total debt ratio.

To gain some operational insight into what is happening in these firms as they approach failure, consider the components of the cash flow to total debt ratio. Cash flow is defined as net income plus depreciation, depletion, and amortization; total debt is total liabilities plus preferred stock. The means for cash flow, net income, and total debt for both Beaver's and Deakin's sample firms are presented in Table VII.7. Both data sets reveal a similar pattern with respect to cash flow and net income. As failure approaches, negative net income seriously impairs the average failed firm's cash flow. The failed firms analyzed by Deakin show highly volatile movements in total debt compared to the monotonic upward trend observed by Beaver. The nonfailed firms in both samples have relatively stable movements in cash flow, net income, and total debt.

Deakin's Discriminant Analysis Results Deakin hoped to improve upon the univariate classification results by linearly combining the 14 variables for each of the 5 years prior to failure. The discriminant-function was *not* derived using Deakin's paired sample. Instead, the 32

Table VII.7. Failed and Nonfailed Firms: Means of Cash Flow, Net Income, and Total Debt[a]

Year before Failure	Deakin (1972)						Beaver (1968)					
	Cash Flow		*Net Income*		*Total Debt*		*Cash Flow*		*Net Income*		*Total Debt*	
	Failed	*Nonfailed*	*Failed*	*Nonfailed*	*Failed*	*Nonfailed*	*Failed*	*Nonfailed*	*Failed*	*Nonfailed*	*Failed*	*Nonfailed*
5	145	523	65	206	5929	4192	230	680	50	500	3140	2260
4	308	381	−29	46	13327	4683	260	750	70	550	3400	2730
3	−244	557	−664	211	19876	5568	−20	780	−220	570	3430	2640
2	−518	867	−858	426	9639	6573	−250	840	−450	500	4520	2910
1	−909	941	−1309	480	10268	7105	−770	830	−950	570	5050	3080

[a]Data are in thousands of dollars.
Source: Beaver (1968, Table 5, p. 120) and Deakin (1972, Table 3, pp. 170–171).

failed firms were combined with a random sample of 32 nonfailed firms, drawn from *Moody's Industrial Manual* for the years 1962–1966. Because random samples tend to be more representative of the underlying population, they are more relevant for predictive purposes.

Given the potential interrelatedness of the data, it is somewhat surprising that the pooled variance–covariance matrices were nonsingular and that Deakin was able to derive linear combinations for each 14-variable set. The *F*-statistics indicated that the mean vectors were significantly different in each of the 5 years prior to failure. Deakin classified the original sample and a holdout sample. The original sample consisted of 64 firms—the 32 failed ones and the 32 randomly selected, nonfailed ones. The holdout sample consists of 11 failed firms and 23 nonfailed firms selected at random from *Moody's Industrial Manual* (1963, 1964).

Deakin's total misclassification rates for the original sample for the first 3 years prior were all less than 5 percent. These *descriptive* classifications indicated that the two groups are quite distinct, i.e., there is little group overlap. In the fourth and fifth years prior, however, the groups were less distinct and the error rates, according to Deakin, "probably were too high for decision-making purposes" (Deakin, 1972:176).

To test the *predictive* ability of his failure model, Deakin employed the holdout sample described above. The results indicated the presence of some sample bias, as expected. The most interesting result was the substantial deterioration in the error rates for the first year prior, a result that Deakin contended "cannot be explained by the presence of any unusual events peculiar to the sample used" (Deakin, 1972:176).

Deakin's 14-variable set produced his most accurate classification results. When he tried to reduce the number of variables the "classification error increased substantially" (Deakin, 1972:173).[16]

Deakin's Conclusions. Deakin concluded that discriminant analysis can be used to predict business failures "as far as three years in advance with a fairly high accuracy" (Deakin, 1972:178). Given the relatively small size of his samples, he suggested that further testing is required before a conclusive judgment about his model can be rendered.

Libby (1975)

Purpose. Libby's study was designed to determine whether accounting ratios provide useful information to loan offices trying to predict business failures. Using a subset of Deakin's 14-variable set, commercial bank loan officers were asked to analyze the ratios and then to predict either "failure" or "nonfailure." The usefulness of the information was judged on the basis of the accuracy of the loan officers' predictions.

Sample Firms and Data. Libby's sample consisted of 60 of the 64 firms from Deakin's derivation sample. Thirty failed firms and thirty nonfailed firms drawn at random are used. Next, the 14 ratios are computed for 1 of the 3 years prior to failure (chosen at random), to result in an equal number of firms for each of the 3 years before failure (10 failed and 10 nonfailed).

Dimensionality Reduction

Using principal-components analysis, Libby identified five independent sources of variation within the 14-variable set. The five dimensions and the five ratios derived from the rotated factor matrix are

Dimension	*Ratio*
1. Profitability	Net Income/Total Assets
2. Activity	Current Assets/Sales
3. Liquidity	Current Assets/Current Liabilities
4. Asset Balance	Current Assets/Total Assets
5. Cash Position	Cash/Total Assets

Classification Results

Libby's reduced-set classifications compared favorably with the entire 14-variable set. The reduced set correctly reclassified 51 of the 60 firms based upon the derivation sample and 43 of 60 using a "double, cross-validation" sample. The classifications using all 14 variables were slightly better for the derivation sample (54 correctly identified) but slightly worse for the holdout sample (41 correctly identified). Given these results and the greater manageability of the five-variable set for his test purposes, Libby used the reduced set for his experiment.

The Loan Officers

Forty-three commercial loan officers participated in Libby's experiment. Sixteen of the officers were from seven small banks located in Champaign-Urbana (CU), Illinois with each bank providing one to four participants. Twenty-seven of the officers were from five large banks located in Philadelphia, Pennsylvania, with each bank providing two to eight participants. The typical loan officer was 39 years old with 16.2 years of formal education and nine years of experience as a loan officer, processing between 51 and 250+ loan applications annually. For the CU bankers, the average client's total assets were $127,000, whereas for the Philadelphia bankers, they were $146,198,000. Libby reported that the CU bankers thought the Philadelphia bankers would "win" because they had greater experience in analyzing audited financial statements associated with the larger client-asset size of the Philadelphia market.

The Experiment. Each loan officer was given 70 ratio data sets of five ratios each. (There were ten repeat firms to check for consistency.) To set the *a priori* probabilities, they were told that one-half of the firms experienced failure within 3 years of the statement date. The loan officers were instructed to work independently and to complete the cases within 1 week. They were told that a correct prediction was worth one point and that an incorrect prediction cost one point. The loan officers were given the definition of failure and told that the sample firms were large industrial ones with independently audited financial statements.

Empirical Results. Libby found that the loan officers' predictive accuracy was superior to random assignment (i.e., fail–nonfail) and concluded that the ratio information was utilized correctly by the loan officers. The results, based upon the analysis of the sixty-firm sample, are summarized in Table VII.8.

On the basis of other tests, Libby concluded that (1) there was no significant difference between the mean predictive accuracy of the CU bankers and the Philadelphia bankers, in spite of the CU bankers' inferiority complex; (2) there were no significant correlations between predictive accuracy and loan officer characteristics, such as age and experience; (3) there were no differences in short-term, test–retest reliability between user subgroups; and (4) there was a relatively uniform interpretation of the accounting data across bankers.

Table VII.8. Loan Officers' Predictive Accuracy (60 firms)

Frequency Interval (Correct Classifications)	*Number of Loan Officers*
49–51	9
46–48	8
43–45	14
40–42	8
37–39	1
34–36	2
31–33	0
28–30	0
25–27	1
Total	43
Mean	44.4
Standard Deviation	4.5
Maximum	50.0
Minimum	27.0

Source: Libby (1975, Figure 1, p. 156).

Libby's Conclusion

Libby concluded that his reduced set of accounting ratios permits bankers with diverse backgrounds to make accurate predictions of business failures.

Libby's Contribution

From a statistical perspective, Libby's contribution was to show that factor analysis can be an important first step in multiple discriminant analysis. Identifying independent sources of variation is useful for reducing the number of variables, removing superfluousness, and highlighting the prominent financial characteristics of a data set.

Deakin (1977)

Purpose. Building upon Libby's factor analysis contribution, Deakin extended his 1972 analysis in a 1977 study. The purpose of the extension was twofold: (1) to provide an indication of the frequency and nature of misclassification of nonfailing companies and (2) to compare auditors' opinions with the model's predictive ability.

Sample Firms and Data. Deakin's failed group consisted of 63 firms: the 32 companies from his 1972 study and 31 firms (from a 1972 study by Altman) that failed in 1970 and 1971. The nonfailed group consisted of 80 firms randomly selected from *Moody's Industrial Manual* and matched *only* by year of data. Data 2 years prior to failure are employed spanning the years 1964 to 1969. For each of the 143 firms, the five-ratio set derived by Libby is computed.

Classification Results. Deakin's linear and quadratic classification results using the Lachenbruch holdout technique are presented in Table VII.9. Since the Type I and Type II errors were so different between the linear and quadratic equations, Deakin adopted the following

Table VII.9. Deakin's Classification Results (Two Years Prior to Failure)

Model	*Type-I Error* (%)	*Type-II Error* (%)	*Overall Accuracy* (%)
Quadratic	1.59	27.50	83.92
Linear	11.11	1.25	94.41

The Lachenbruch holdout technique is used to classify the sample firms. There are 63 failed firms and 80 nonfailed firms. Deakin does not specify whether he used equal *priors* (.50/.50) or sample proportions (.44/.56) as the *a priori* probabilities. Costs of misclassification are not included.
Source: Derived from Deakin (1977, Table 5, p. 80).

fail–nonfail decision rule for his validation tests: (1) classify as failing, if *both* the linear and quadratic functions classify as failing; (2) classify as nonfailing, if *both* the linear and quadratic functions classify as nonfailing; and (3) investigate further, if the functions produce conflicting results. Deakin contends that this eclectic rule tends to minimize the overall misclassification rate, if the "investigate-further" group is excluded.

Deakin's validation test for the five-variable model was applied to 1780 firms on the COMPUSTAT 1800 file for fiscal year 1971. The linear *and* quadratic models agreed that 290 firms (16.29 percent) had characteristics (i.e., five ratios) that were more similar to the failed group than the nonfailed group, 2 years prior to failure. The corresponding figure for the nonfailed group was 1317 firms (73.99 percent). One hundred and seventy-three firms (9.72 percent) were assigned to the "investigate-further" category.

To determine the accuracy of these predictions, Deakin scrutinized the financial performances of the 290 firms predicted to fail and of 100 of the 1317 firms predicted not to fail. However, he did not follow up on any of the firms in the "investigate-further" group. This is unfortunate because such analysis might have been useful in assessing the predictability of linear versus quadratic.

Deakin's follow-up analysis was for the 3.5-year period from 1972 until June 30, 1975. The findings are summarized in Table VII.10. Interpreting these findings critically depends upon the definition of failure employed. Because Deakin's model was developed with failure defined as bankruptcy, liquidation, or reorganization, this would appear to be the appropriate criterion for judging the predictive accuracy of the model. On this basis, only 18 (6.2 percent) of the 290 predicted

Table VII.10. Deakin's Follow-Up Analysis

Future Event (1972–June 30, 1975)	*Predicted Failures* (1971)	*Predicted Nonfailures* (1971)
1. Merger	7	2
2. No Adverse Event	66	68
3. Dividend Cut or Omitted	124	15
4. Major Disposal of Assets	123	20
5. Loan Default or Pf. Div. Omitted	46	0
6. Bankruptcy, Liquidation, Reorganization	18	0
Total Events	388	105
Number of Firms	290	100
Total Events 3–6	315	35
Firms (Events 3–6)	217	30

Source: Deakin (1977, Table 6, p. 82).

failures were accurately classified. If the seven mergers that occurred were arranged under distressed conditions (Deakin does not indicate whether they were), the number of failures correctly identified is 25 (8.6 percent). Regarding the firms predicted not to fail, none of the 100 sample firms failed. However, two firms were acquired via mergers by other firms.

Using a weaker definition of failure (i.e., to exclude only event (2) in Table 10), Deakin's model correctly identified 224 firms (77.2 percent) as failures. However, based upon the sample of 100 predicted nonfailures, 35 firms that eventually "failed" (i.e., 15 cut or omitted dividends while 20 had major disposal of assets) were not identified as failures, a 35 percent error rate.

As an alternative test of his model, Deakin analyzed 47 companies that went bankrupt from 1972 to 1974. The purpose of the test is to assess the model's accuracy with respect to a holdout sample of "hard-core" failures. Two years prior to failure, the five-variable model with the combined linear–quadratic decision rule correctly identified 39 of the failures, misclassified 1 firm, and identified 7 companies as in need of further investigation.

Comparison with Auditors' Reports. Like Altman and McGough (1974), Deakin analyzed the auditors' opinions for the 47 bankrupt companies. The purpose of the analysis was to determine whether the auditors had "predicted" the impending failures and to compare their accuracy rate with the model's predictability. Altman and McGough (1974) discovered that auditors did not perform as well as the Altman-McGough model in classifying companies as failures.

Deakin claimed that an auditor was considered to have predicted failure if the opinion rendered was "qualified" instead of "clean." Qualified was defined to include: (1) inability to continue profitable operations; (2) inability to meet existing debts as they come due; (3) a going-concern exception; or (4) a disclaimed opinion for going-concern related reasons. A clean opinion indicated an unqualified opinion or a qualified one in which specific contingencies or minor exceptions were noted (e.g., changes in accounting practices).

Auditors' reports for fiscal year 1971 for the 47 bankrupt firms and 116 nonfailed firms were analyzed. Of the 8 firms given qualified opinions, 7 of them eventually failed. However, of the 155 firms given clean bills of health, 40 firms (25.81 percent) went bankrupt within 2 years. The findings suggest that auditors' qualified opinions should be taken seriously, whereas their unqualified ones require further investigation. With respect to the more costly Type I error, Deakin's model clearly is superior to the auditors' implicit predictions.

Deakin's Conclusions. Deakin concluded that (1) using financial ratios in a discriminant analysis model can predict failure with a "high degree of accuracy"; (2) because the model's estimate of the number of failing firms overstates the actual number of failures, the model has limited usefulness when misclassification of *nonfailing* companies is costly; and (3) auditors "predictions" have a lower Type II error but a higher Type I error compared to the MDA model.

Critique. Deakin regarded the Type I error of his linear model (11.1 percent) and the Type II error of his quadratic model (27.5 percent) as too high. (The overall accuracies were 5.6 percent for the linear model and 16.1 percent for the quadratic one.) Rather than address the task of measuring the costs of these errors, he adopted a compromise classification rule: classify a firm as failing (nonfailing) if both models classify as failing (nonfailing); investigate further, if the classifications conflict. Unless a failing–nonfailing decision is made for the firms in the investigate-further group, the model's accuracy cannot be determined. Because the cost of a Type II error usually is much lower than the cost of a Type I error, Deakin should not be overly concerned about a high Type II error. Because the actual failure rate tends to be quite low (1 to 3 percent, depending on the definition of failure), a naive model predicting zero failures has an accuracy rate of at least 97 percent. Thus, unless the costs of misclassification are considered explicitly, a statistical model must be highly accurate to beat the most naive alternative. The important point is that the cost of *not* identifying failure is extremely high. This suggests that the firms in Deakin's investigate-further group should be classified as failing to attempt to reduce the cost of not identifying failure.

Edmister (1972)

Purpose. Edmister's purpose was to develop and test a number of methods of analyzing financial ratios to predict the failure of *small* businesses. A small business was defined as one with a loan from the Small Business Administration (SBA).

Definition of Failure and Sample Firms. The sample firms employed by Edmister were borrowers and guarantee recipients from the SBA for the period 1954 to 1969. Loss borrowers were designated as failures and nonloss borrowers were considered to be nonfailures. Under the stipulation that three consecutive annual financial statements be available from the period prior to the date when the loan was granted, Edmister's sample of loss borrowers consisted of 42 firms. Under the less restrictive requirement that only one annual statement be available from the period prior to the loan, 562 firms were analyzed. An equal number of nonloss borrowers were used with each sample. For the 42-firm sample, the average total asset size was $164,940.

Selection of Variables and Methodology. Edmister analyzed 19 financial ratios, including most of those found to be important in previous failure-prediction studies such as Beaver (1966), Altman (1968), and Blum (1969). His methodological framework focused upon testing four hypotheses: (1) a ratio's level is a predictor of small business failure; (2) the 3-year trend of a ratio is a predictor of small business failure; (3) the 3-year average of a ratio is a predictor of small business failure; and (4) the combination of the industry relative trend for each ratio and the industry level for each ratio is a predictor of small business failure.

Zero–One Regression Analysis. Edmister employed a zero–one regression technique. The relationship between discriminant and regression coefficients is a proportional one in the two-group case. Edmister chose to use zero–one regression because he believed that the regression computer programs were somewhat better developed.

Edmister was intent upon limiting multicollinearity in his regression equation. Accordingly, he employed an *arbitrary* stepwise procedure in which a variable was not permitted to enter the regression equation if its simple correlation coefficient with an included variable was greater than .31.[17] Edmister contended that the maintenance of pairwise independence among his regressors outweighed the arbitrariness of the method. A major shortcoming with this approach is that important explanatory power may be excluded from the regression equation because of the arbitrary, correlation coefficient cutoff point.

Another element of arbitrariness in Edmister's statistical methodology was his treatment of the regressors or independent variables. Rather than have the independent variables enter in their raw ratio form, he transformed each ratio into qualitative zero–one variables based upon *arbitrary* cutoff points. For example, if the ratio of annual funds flow (defined as net profit before taxes plus depreciation) to current liabilities was less than .05, the ratio was assigned a value of one; otherwise it was assigned a value of zero. Such a transformation *gives up information* and should be avoided. Edmister's rationale for the transformations was (1) to prevent extreme values from unduly affecting estimated parameters and (2) to permit level and trend variables to be combined into a single dichotomous variable.

Regression Results. Using his smaller sample of 42 failed firms and 42 nonfailed firms, Edmister developed a seven-variable, zero–one linear regression equation:

$$Z = .951 - \underset{(4.24)}{.423X_1} - \underset{(2.82)}{.293X_2} - \underset{(4.51)}{.482X_3} + \underset{(2.61)}{.277X_4}$$
$$- \underset{(2.60)}{.452X_5} - \underset{(1.68)}{.352X_6} - \underset{(7.11)}{.924X_7}$$

with $R^2 = .74$, $F = 14.02$, and $N = 84$. (Figures in parentheses are *t*-statistics.) The variables are

- Z = zero–one dependent variable; one for nonfailure (nonloss borrower) and zero for failure (loss borrower)
- X_1 = ratio of annual funds flow to current liabilities; equals one if the ratio is less than .05, zero otherwise
- X_2 = ratio of equity to sales; equals one if the ratio is less than .07, zero otherwise
- X_3 = ratio of net working capital to sales divided by the corresponding RMA ratios; equals one if the ratio is less than −.02, zero otherwise
- X_4 = ratio of current liabilities to equity divided by the corresponding SBA ratio; equals one if less than .48, zero otherwise
- X_5 = ratio of inventory to sales divided by the corresponding RMA ratio; equals one if the ratio has shown an upward trend, zero otherwise
- X_6 = the quick ratio divided by the trend in RMA quick ratio; equals one if trend is downward *and* level just prior to the loan is less than .34, zero otherwise
- X_7 = the quick ratio divided by RMA quick ratio; equals one if the ratio has shown an upward trend, zero otherwise

Classification Accuracy. The classification results reported by Edmister all have an overall accuracy of at least 90 percent. For example, using $Z \geqslant .530$ to determine nonfailure and $Z < .530$ for failure, all of the failed firms and 86 percent of the nonfailed firms were classified correctly for an overall accuracy rate of 93 percent. Thus, a zero Type I error is achieved while still maintaining a high overall accuracy.

The actual Z-score cutoff point, of course, is a product of the minimized loss function, which depends upon the population *priors,* Type I and Type II errors, and costs of misclassification. Edmister argued that, because many lenders do not know the costs of misclassification, a practical alternative for setting up Z-score decision rules is a "black–gray–white" method. "Gray" refers to firms subject to classification error, Altman's "zone of ignorance." White refers to the unambiguous nonloss borrowers and black to the unambiquous loss borrowers. Edmister's method called for accepting the "white," rejecting the "black," and further investigating the "gray." He suggested that nonfinancial statement information regarding management, markets, plant and equipment, and other factors should be considered.

Edmister's Conclusions. Edmister concluded that the predictive power of ratio analysis depends upon both the choice of analytical method and the selection of ratios. Two of the methods he found useful are: (1) dividing a ratio by its respective industry average and (2) classifying ratios by quartiles. In addition, Edmister stated that no single ratio predicts as well as a small group; independent predictors are superior to nonindependent predictors; and some ratios that are insignificant by themselves add important information when combined with other variables. However, unlike Altman, Beaver, and Blum who found that one financial statement is sufficient for accurate classification, Edmister concluded that three consecutive statements are required for effective analysis of *small* businesses.

Critique. The large number of small-business failures and recent interest in business-development centers to assist small businesses indicate a need for identifying the financial characteristics of distressed small businesses. Although Edmister's classification results are quite good, they may be due in part at least to his data transformations (e.g., converting ratios into zero-one variables). However, since the financial ratios for small businesses usually are dispersed widely, it is difficult to obtain a meaningful data set without some sort of adjustment.

Elam (1975)

Purpose. Elam's purpose was to determine if capitalization of (nonpurchase) leases enhanced the accuracy of a failure-prediction model. Given the significant increase in leasing as a means of financing, especially over the last decade, the effect of lease data on the predictive ability of financial ratios is a timely and important question. Elam's focus was upon the predictive power of capitalization versus footnote disclosure of long-term leases.

Definition of Failure and Sample Firms. Elam's definition of failure included at least one of the following actions: (1) filed for reorganization under Chapter X or XI of the Federal Bankruptcy Act; (2) stockholders voted to file either under Chapter X or XI; and (3) reached agreement with creditors to reduce the firm's liabilities at a loss to creditors. Using the *Wall Street Journal Index* and Dun and Bradstreet failure information, Elam compiled a list of firms that failed from 1966 to 1972. This list was reduced on the basis of data availability (at least one financial statement prior to failure was required) and reporting of lease information in the footnotes of the financial statements. Elam was left with

48 firms, 9 of which failed in 1972, 19 in 1971, 14 in 1970, 1 in 1969, 2 each in 1968 and 1967, and 1 in 1966. Because some firms did not report lease data for a particular year, only 48 failed firms were available for the first year prior to failure. The number of failed firms available for the second through fifth years prior were 44, 37, 29, and 25, respectively.

Each bankrupt firm was matched with a nonbankrupt firm according to (1) fiscal year, (2) Enterprise Standard Industry classification, (3) net sales in the fifth year prior to bankruptcy within the industry class, and (4) reporting of uncapitalized long-term leases.

Long-Term Lease Data, Conversions, and Capitalization. Lease information was obtained from footnotes to the sample firm's original financial statements. The information, which was presented in four different formats, then was converted into annual lease payments. The method of conversion depended upon the type of footnote disclosure. For example, in the most straightforward case, the footnote disclosed the lease obligations on an annual basis, including the life of the lease. At the other extreme, significantly less information was provided and lease payments and maturities had to be estimated.

Given the annual lease payments and lease life, Elam capitalized the future lease commitments for each firm using an interest rate of 6 percent, that is,

$$CL = \sum_{t=1}^{N} \frac{L_t}{(1.06)^t}$$

where CL = capitalized lease; L_t = annual lease payment in year t; and N = lease life in years. The value of the capitalized leases and the ratio of capitalized leases to total assets (excluding leases) for Elam's bankrupt and nonbankrupt groups are presented in Table VII.11.

The lease patterns in Table VII.11 are quite interesting. Five years prior to failure, the average bankrupt firm was leasing quite heavily.

Table VII.11. Capitalized Leases: Bankrupt and Nonbankrupt Firms

	Bankrupt Group		*Nonbankrupt Group*	
Year Prior to Bankruptcy	*\$ Amount (millions)*	*%of Assets*	*\$ Amount (millions)*	*% of Assets*
1	6.53	19.7	7.06	15.4
2	5.92	17.3	5.76	16.7
3	5.50	20.0	3.05	9.0
4	5.85	31.1	2.18	8.0
5	3.95	26.9	1.06	8.2

Leases were capitalized at 6 percent.
Source: Elam (1975, Tables 2 and 3, pp. 31–32).

The lease indebtedness increases over the next year and then declines, remaining fairly constant over the last 3 years prior to bankruptcy. In contrast, the average nonbankrupt firm gets into leasing much more gradually and not to the extent of the average bankrupt firm. "Fools rush in . . ."

Selection of Variables and the Effects of Capitalization. Elam selected 28 ratios commonly discussed in the financial literature and in textbooks for analysis in his study. The categories and individual ratios are presented in Table VII.12. The capitalized leases were added to

Table VII.12. Elam's Financial Ratios

SHORT-TERM LIQUIDITY RATIOS
1. Cash to current liabilities
2. Current assets to current liabilities
3. Current assets minus inventories to current liabilities

CASH-FLOW RATIOS
4. Cash flow to sales
5. Cash flow to total assets
6. Cash flow to net worth
7. Cash flow to total liabilities

LONG-TERM SOLVENCY RATIOS
8. Net worth to total liabilities
9. Net worth to long-term liabilities
10. Net worth to fixed assets
11. Net operating profit to interest

SHORT-TERM CAPITAL PRODUCTIVITY RATIOS
12. Sales to inventory
13. Sales to accounts receivable
14. Sales to working capital
15. Sales to current assets minus inventories
16. Sales to cash

PROFIT MARGIN RATIOS
17. Net operating profit to sales
18. Net profits to sales

LONG-TERM CAPITAL PRODUCTIVITY RATIOS
19. Sales to fixed assets
20. Sales to total assets
21. Sales to net worth

RETURN ON INVESTMENT RATIOS
22. Net income to net worth
23. Net operating profit to total assets
24. Net operating profit to total debt

DEBT COVERAGE RATIOS
25. Current liabilities to total assets
26. Long-term liabilities to current assets
27. Current plus long-term liabilities to total assets
28. Current plus long-term liabilities plus preferred stock to total assets

Source: Elam (1975, Table 1, p. 26).

each firm's (1) net plant and equipment (fixed assets), (2) long-term liabilities, and (3) total assets. This affects 13 of the 28 ratios in Table VII.12 (i.e., ratios 5, 7, 8–10, 19–20, 23–28).

Major Hypothesis. Elam's null hypothesis was that inclusion of lease data does not improve the accuracy of a failure-prediction model. The alternative hypothesis is that the accuracy is improved. Single- and multivariable models were tested.

Empirical Findings. Based upon either single-ratio or multiple-ratio tests, Elam found that the addition of capitalized-lease data did not significantly improve the overall classification accuracies of the models tested. Moreover, in some cases the classifications were less accurate when lease data were included. The tests were straightforward: the classification accuracies of models with lease data were compared with those without lease data. A "*T*" test statistic was used to determine if the classification rates were significantly different.

On a single-ratio basis, the 13 ratios affected by the lease data were analyzed individually. On a multiple-ratio basis, a 25-variable discriminant model was tested for each of the 5 years prior to failure. The 25 variables are the 28 ratios listed in Table VII.12, except for ratios 9, 10, and 27. Given the potential interrelatedness of these data, it is quite surprising that the variance–covariance matrices are nonsingular and that Elam was able to compute the discriminant coefficients.[18] Be that as it may, Elam found no evidence that the addition of lease data enhanced bankruptcy prediction.

Critique. Elam stated that his purpose was "not to demonstrate or optimize predictive power but rather to analyze an effect [lease capitalization] on predictive power" (Elam, 1973:38, insert mine). Elam did not attempt to reduce the number of variables below 25. Accordingly, it is possible that potential predictive power is deliberately masked by the large number of variables. For example, Edmister concluded that "when ratios are added without consideration of independence to an analysis with ratios already included, the real predictive power of the analysis does not increase" (Edmister, 1972:1490). Thus, when lease data are added to 10 of the 25 ratios, its potential contribution may be obscured by the overabundant and redundant information already contained in the model. Similar to Altman's (1976) conclusion on Elam's article, we conclude that the leasing issue (with respect to bankruptcy prediction) is unresolved.

Wilcox (1971a), (1971b), (1973), and (1976)

Purpose. Wilcox's research focused upon applications of the gambler's-ruin model to business risk or financial failure. The 1971 articles stressed the theoretical development of the model whereas the 1973 and 1976 papers dealt with empirical tests to assess the probability of a firm's ultimate failure.

The purpose of the 1971 articles (1971a is a watered-down version of 1971b) was to develop a theoretical model to better explain Beaver's results and to generate hypotheses leading to potentially better predictors of failure. Wilcox was critical of Beaver, Altman, et. al. because the studies lacked a conceptual framework. Consequently, scarce bankruptcy information was statistically "used up" by searching procedures. Wilcox's plan was to develop a useful generalization or model *first* and *then* to test it. Using the gambler's-ruin approach, the 1973 and 1976 articles focused upon (1) quantifying the risk of financial failure; (2) presenting empirical evidence, and (3) describing potential remedial action for the management of distressed firms.

The Model

Wilcox's adaptation of the classic gambler's-ruin problem (Feller, 1968) to measuring business risk focused upon net liquidation value (NLV) and the factors that cause it to fluctuate. NLV is simply a dollar *level* determined by liquidity inflow and outflow rates. For a given period Wilcox defined the inflow rate as net income minus dividends and the outflow rate as the increase in the book value of assets minus the increase in the liquidation value of those assets. The inflow rate is a function of a firm's profitability and divident policy, whereas the outflow rate is determined by capital-budgeting decisions and current-asset controls.

Using the familiar bathtub analogy, NLV is the water level in a tub with *both* its spigot *and* drain *open*. When the inflow rate exceeds the outflow rate, NLV increases; when the opposite occurs, NLV decreases. When the flows are equal, the level remains constant. Combining the inflow and outflow variables, Wilcox refered to this net flow as the "adjusted cash flow," the period-to-period change in NLV, excluding stock issues, accounting changes, and other *noncontinuing* processes.

Alternatively, Wilcox defined NLV as asset liquidation value less total liabilities. For test purposes, Wilcox (1976) used the following weights to determine liquidation values:

Cash Equivalents	1.00
Other Current Assets	0.70
Long-Term Assets	0.45+

The plus sign (+) on the weight for long-term assets indicates an adjustment for inflation using the GNP deflator for the past 4 years (e.g., in 1975 the adjustment factor is 0.30 and the weight 0.75). Wilcox intended his weights to be representative and not definitive.

The main concern of the model was, of course, with predicting when NLV will be negative, which often portends bankruptcy. Assuming a "stable process," Wilcox postulated that the *probability* of NLV being reduced to zero (interpreted as bankruptcy or ultimate failure) is a function of (1) the current NLV or current wealth, (2) the *average* adjusted cash flow μ, and (3) the variability of the adjusted cash flow, measured by its variance, σ^2. To summarize,

$$\Pr(\text{NLV} < 0) = f(\overset{+}{\text{NLV}}, \overset{+}{\mu}, \overset{-}{\sigma^2}).$$

In words, the chance of failure is greater (other things being equal), the smaller the NLV, the smaller the adjusted cash flow, and the larger the variation of the adjusted cash flow.

To determine how much NLV and average adjusted cash flow are needed for a given degree of safety, Wilcox (1976) introduced a concept called the "size of bet" (S). He interprets S as the adjusted cash flow at risk each year or as the simplest probabilistic process underlying the NLV cash flows.

In terms of the gambler's-ruin model, NLV $= NS$ (where N *is* the number of states away from failure and S the size of bet) $= \hat{\mu}^2 + \hat{\sigma}^2$. As an approximation, Wilcox measured S^2 as the average of the squared annual charges in NLV. The firm was viewed, at time t, as being in state N with wealth of NLV $= NS$. In period $t + 1$, the firm (the gambler) moves either to state $N - 1$ with wealth of (NLV $- S$) or to state $N + 1$ with wealth of (NLV $+ S$). In period $t + 2$, the firm moves from its *new* initial state to a new state with a change in wealth of either $+S$ or $-S$ depending upon whether it "wins" or "loses." If the probability of winning is denoted by P and the probability of losing by Q (with $P + Q = 1$ and $P > Q$), the probability of failure (or ruin) is

$$\Pr(F) = (Q/P)^N$$

If $P \leqslant Q$, then failure or ruin is inevitable.

A firm's average winnings per period, μ, is equal to $S(P - Q)$. Defining μ/S as X, the ratio Q/P is equal to $(1 - X)/(1 + X)$. Thus,[19]

$$\Pr(F) = \left(\frac{1 - X}{1 - X}\right)^N \cong 1 - 2XN.$$

While Wilcox conceded that the gambler's-ruin model (in this business-failure context) is an extreme over-simplification, he argued, however, that the parameters X and N are fundamental indicators of relative financial risk, especially if they are based upon 5 years of adjusted cash flow.

Definition of Failure and Sample Firms

Wilcox's [1973] definition of failure was a Chapter X or XI bankruptcy petition. The date of failure was taken as the date of the petition. A sample of 52 firms that failed between 1955 and 1971 was selected. Each firm was required to have at least six annual balance sheets and five annual income statements prior to its bankruptcy. Each failed firm is matched with a nonfailed firm on the basis of (1) industry group (5 years prior); (2) size (within 20 percent of total assets 5 years prior); and (3) availability of data for the same years as the failed firm up to 9 years prior.

On an annual basis, data were collected for each of the 104 firms for at least 5 years prior and in some cases up to 9 years prior. The data items collected were

1. Net Income (including special or extraordinary)
2. Cash Dividends
3. Stock Issued (in merger or acquisition)
4. Cash plus Marketable Securities
5. Current Assets
6. Total Assets
7. Total Liabilities (including reserves)

Using these data, NLV, μ, and σ^2 were calculated for each firm, with μ and σ^2 based upon five observations (i.e., the current and four preceding ones). Then, $X(= \mu/S)$ and N were calculated.

Empirical Results

Wilcox's 1976 empirical tests updated his 1973 experiment (i.e., incorporated additional data not available for the 1973 study). The 1976 findings are emphasized in this section.

Wilcox's original classifications (1973) were based upon a paired test of the formula $[(1 - X)/(1 + X)]^N$, with a complicated set of tie-breaking rules when either X or N was negative for both firms.[20] These results are presented in Table VII.13 along with Beaver's (1966) and Altman's (1968) classification findings. Wilcox's (1976) updated results were based upon a linear gambler's-ruin score defined by $10X + N$, which indicated a firm's distance from the best diagonal line in X N space.

Wilcox contended that his gambler's-ruin approach compared "very favorably" with Beaver's and Altman's models, especially since (1) his model did not represent the result of statistical searching; (2) his model was tested over a long time period, during which inflation had altered typical financial ratios; and (3) his model was derived from a conceptual framework with implications for the managerial process. Wilcox claimed that the effect of statistical searching was often misunderstood. Such

Table VII.13. Wilcox's Classification Results

Model	Overall Accuracy Rate (%) Year Before Failure 1	2	3	4	5
Original Gambler's-Ruin Rules (paired)	94	89	89	91	76
Linear Gambler's-Ruin Score (paired)	94	93	83	84	78
Linear Gambler's-Ruin Score (unpaired)	91	86	78	77	76
Beaver: Cash flow/total assets (paired)	90	80	76	72	72
Beaver: Cash flow/total debt (unpaired)	90	82	79	76	78
Altman (1968) *Z*-Score	95	72	48	29	36

Source: Wilcox 1976, (Table 1, p. 41).

searching *may* result in a model that is unique to the data set from which it is derived and hence be unreliable if applied to new data.

A Holdout-Sample Test. The gambler's-ruin score ($10X + N$) was calculated for 26 major firms for 1973 to 1975. The firm with the lowest score in 1973 and 1974, W. T. Grant, went bankrupt in 1975. W. T. Grant's performance from 1966 to 1975 in terms of the gambler's-ruin model is summarized in Table VII.14. These data indicate that W. T. Grant was in a position of high risk since 1970 and in a position similar to that of failed firms 1 year prior to failure since 1972. In 1966, W.

Table VII.14. W. T. Grant's Gambler's-Ruin Score

Year	*Net Liquidation Value Size of Bet (N)*	*Average Adjusted Cash Flow Size of Bet (X)*	*Gambler's Ruin Score (N + 10X)*	*Risk Position*
1966	9.0	−0.45	4.50	High
1967	11.5	0.05	11.00	OK
1968	13.0	0.19	11.10	OK
1969	16.0	0.25	13.50	OK
1970	5.0	−0.30	2.00	High
1971	3.5	−0.29	0.60	High
1972	3.8	−0.55	−1.70	Very High
1973	0.1	−0.71	−7.00	Very High
1974	−1.0	−0.93	−10.30	Very High
1975	−3.0	−0.75	−10.75	Very High

Source: Derived from Wilcox (1976, Figure 6, p. 44).

T. Grant already was in a high risk position. However, over the next 3 years, both its solvency and cash positions improved. This upward trend was only temporary, however, as 1970 was a financially devastating year for W. T. Grant. Over the next 5 years, the firm's financial position continued to deteriorate, and it petitioned for a Chapter XI bankruptcy in October of 1975.

Remedial Attention. Within the context of the gambler's-ruin model, Wilcox focused upon three means for reducing the risk of ruin: (1) increase NLV directly, (2) increase μ, and/or (3) reduce S. NLV can be increased directly via one-time changes such as mergers, acquisitions, and stock issues. Increasing the average adjusted cash flow requires increasing the inflow rate and/or reducing the outflow rate. Significant changes in cash flow usually cannot be made over night, although disinvestment of unprofitable ventures is an exception. Some of the important factors in determining cash flow are effective capital budgeting, controlled growth, careful profit planning and analysis, and effective overall planning. The size of bet S is governed by the variability of liquidity flows, which is influenced by such factors as dividend policy, earnings and investment stability, and the covariation between investments and profits.

Wilcox's Conclusions. Wilcox concluded that most bankruptcies can be avoided. However, such prevention requires more than the superficial attempts to reduce risk that have characterized most bankruptcies over the past three decades.

Critique. Wilcox's application of the classic gambler's-ruin model to predicting business failure is straightforward and it has intuitive appeal. Moreover, his empirical findings indicate that his model is at least as accurate as those of other researchers. For example, comparing Wilcox's best results with those of AH&N (1977), the overall accuracy rates for years 1 through 5 prior are 94, 93, 83, 84, and 78 percent, respectively, for Wilcox's model and 93, 89, 84, 80, and 78 percent, respectively, for AH&N's linear model. Both theory and evidence tend to support Wilcox's approach. More importantly, perhaps, Wilcox's analytical framework requires the reader to focus upon the dynamic factors that determine a firm's financial risk and hence its success or failure. In addition, such a foundation highlights the controllable factors that financial managers should focus upon when trying to remedy financial difficulties.

EPILOGUE

This completes the review of failure-prediction studies for nonfinancial corporations. The common elements in most of the studies are (1) a paired-sample approach; (2) use of accounting data in the form of ratios and/or trends; (3) a binomial-response statistical technique; (4) "searching" for the failure model rather than building it; (5) holdout-sample tests to determine predictive ability; and (6) a conclusion that accounting data contains useful information for discriminating between failed and nonfailed firms and that future business failures can be predicted. Potential pitfalls in failure-prediction studies are (1) the time-series or stationarity problem; (2) unequal group covariance matrices; (3) attempting to rank variables, especially if covariance matrices are unequal; (4) estimating and incorporating *a priori* probabilities and costs of misclassification into the analysis; and (5) developing appropriate hold-out sample tests. Avenues for future research include the aforementioned pitfall areas plus (1) the development of *ex ante* failure models; (2) keeping failure-prediction models up to date with respect to structural changes (e.g., in accounting standards and practices); (3) the development of models based upon market data or a combination of accounting and market data; and (4) applying alternative statistical methods to the failure-prediction problem.

NOTES

1. Rand, Ayn, *For the New Intellectual: The Philosophy of Ayn Rand,* New York: The New American Library (1961), p. 10.
2. Since his pairings do not control completely for size, Beaver does test for its effect. He concludes that size is not an important predictor of failure.
3. For a critique of Beaver's study, see Mears (1967) and Neter (1967).
4. Cochran (1964) has shown that negative correlations are more important than positive ones in adding new information to discriminant functions.
5. The profit margins (i.e., earnings per dollar of sales) are calculated from the figures in Table VII.2.
6. The weights or coefficients in Eq. (7.2) are from Altman's 1977 paper and not from his 1968 article or 1971 book. The coefficients are not the same in these various sources because the input data (ratios) were not reported correctly until 1974. The problem is that SLTA is entered in decimal form whereas the other four variables are entered in percentage form. Thus, to calculate a correct *Z*-score, the original weights required data with decimal and percentage formats. In presenting the group means in his 1968 article, Altman expressed all of the variables in percentage form but did not simultaneously adjust the coefficient of SLTA in the discriminant function to reflect this change. In his 1971 book, Altman clarified this oversight by telling his readers to express SLTA in decimal or straight ratio form. Thus, a turnover ratio of 2-to-1 should be expressed as 2.0 (and not 200 percent) for calculating a firm's *Z*-score. However, in presenting the group means in his book, the turnover ratio of 2.0 (200 percent) is expressed as 2.0 percent (0.02) to be consistent with the other four variables expressed in percentage form. Altman's 1974 paper has the decimals where they belong, that is, the ratios in decimal form (see Table VII.2) and the coefficients adjusted to reflect the decimal format [see Eq. (7.2)].
7. Because of rounding, the *Z*-scores are slightly different from those reported by Altman. He reports −0.29 and 5.02.
8. Note the MEBD used in the *Dun's Review* calculations does not include short-term debt, whereas Altman's MEBD is the book value of *total* debt.

9. During 1972, Memorex sold at a high of 38½ on the NYSE. On August 8, 1973, when Memorex was selling at 2¼, the NYSE halted trading in the stock in a move for delisting it from the exchange. On March 16, 1978, Memorex closed on the NYSE at 29¼.

10. Altman (1970:1169) cautioned analysts against using his model for predicting the bankruptcy of individual firms. As indicated in his 1968 article, a low *Z*-score is intended to be an "early-warning" signal for more detailed analysis of a firm's viability. On March 16, 1978, Telex closed at 3⅞.

11. As a technical point, since Altman's classification rule does not incorporate population *a priori* probabilities of failure or costs of misclassifications, his results are more "descriptive" than "predictive." Johnson's criticism, however, is of a broader nature and not on this finer point.

12. Since Altman (1968) did conduct validation tests using holdout samples, the model is tested on "fresh" data. Altman and McGough (1974) also test the model using fresh data.

13. Blum [pp. 10–11] also estimates what he called "moving discriminant functions" by using an "updating procedure." Although he regards the tests as being inferior, he suggests that an updating procedure may be important to allow for structural changes that could influence the character of business failures over the long run.

14. Blum's 1974 article is an outgrowth of his 1969 Ph.D. dissertation, "The Failing Company Doctrine," Columbia University.

15. Beaver (1968a) is an extension of Beaver (1967).

16. Using factor analysis, Libby (1975) finds a subset of five ratios that is almost as accurate as Deakin's set of 14 variables. Libby's research is discussed below.

17. It is not clear how Edmister handles variables that have a strong negative correlation.

18. Two plausible explanations come to mind: (1) the matrices truly are nonsingular or (2) the computer program's inversion routine is not very sensitive at identifying singular matrices.

19. For proof of the approximation, see Wilcox, 1971b:392–393.

20. The tie-breaking rules are described in Wilcox 1973:165–166. Wilcox (1976) changed notation from his 1973 article, substituting *Y* for *N*. The 1973 notation is used in this report.

APPENDIX

Summary of Major Studies Using Statistical Classification Techniques for Predicting the Failure of Nonfinancial Firms

Purpose and Sample Characteristics	*Statistical Method and Important Variables*	*Contribution and Critique*
1. *W. Beaver (1967).* To test the usefulness of ratio analysis in the context of failure prediction. Analyzes 79 firms that "failed" from 1954 to 1964 and a paired sample of nonfailed firms. Matching characteristics: industry classification code and asset size	Does *not* use a multivariable approach. Empirical tests focus upon comparison of means, dichotomous classification tests, and analysis of likelihood ratios. Of 30 ratios tested, cash flow to total debt is key variable	One of the first and most extensive failure-prediction studies. Concludes that accounting data (i.e., financial ratios) can predict failure at least 5 years in advance. Cautions against using ratio analysis indiscriminately because different ratios have different predictive abilities and because it is easier to predict nonfailure than failure. Major shortcomings: definition of failure and lack of multiple-variable analysis
2. *E. Altman (1968).* To assess the quality of ratio analysis as an analytical technique using the prediction of corporate bankruptcy as an example. Thirty-three failed manufacturing firms from the period 1946 to 1965 and a paired sample of nonfailed firms are analyzed. Pairings made on the basis of industry and asset size	Uses multiple discriminant analysis to analyze 22 variables. Develops a five-variable *linear* model consisting of (1) working capital/total assets, (2) retained earnings/total assets, (3) ' earnings before interest and taxes/total assets, (4) market value of equity/book value of total debt, (5) sales/total assets	Reconfirms usefulness of ratio analysis and demonstrates importance of multiple-variable analysis. To date, most widely referenced failure-prediction model. Shortcomings: model doesn't have predictive ability beyond 2 years prior to failure; doesn't develop a theoretical framework for failure prediction; fails to avoid several MDA pitfalls
3. *E. Deakin (1972).* To develop an alternative to the Beaver and Altman models. Analyzes 32 firms that fail between 1964 and 1970 and a paired sample of nonfailed firms matched by industry classification, asset size, and year of data	Uses *linear* multiple discriminant analysis and 14 of Beaver's ratios to find combination of variables with greatest predictive accuracy (see Note 16 and Table 7.2 for the 14 variables). Ratio of cash flow-to-total debt is an important variable	Model predicts failure as far as 3 years in advance with fairly high accuracy. Only minor extension of Beaver and Altman. Shortcomings: small-sample problems; doesn't attempt to find a subset of 14-variable set; pitfalls in application of MDA not avoided

Purpose and Sample Characteristics	*Statistical Method and Important Variables*	*Contribution and Critique*
4. *R. Edmister (1972).* To test the usefulness of financial ratio analysis for predicting *small* business failure. Works with two different samples of loss and nonloss SBA borrowers. Each sample contains an equal number of loss and nonloss cases (42 and 562). The large sample only has data for 1 year prior to loss (failure); the small sample has 3 years of data	Uses stepwise, zero–one, linear, multiple regression analysis. Nineteen ratios are tested and a 7-variable regression equation developed. The independent variables (regressors) are transformed to dichotomous zero–one variables	First failure-prediction model for small businesses. Finds that at least three consecutive financial statements are required for accurate discrimination between loss and nonloss borrowers. Shortcomings: transformation of independent variables to zero–one form gives up information and is arbitrary; selection of "less than .31" as the correlation–coefficient cutoff point for an included regression variable (in the stepwise procedure of the regression) may exclude important variables and also is arbitrary
5. *M. Blum (1974).* To aid in assessing the probability of business failure, where failure is defined in accordance with the meaning the courts have given to it in the context of antitrust defense (i.e., The Failing Company Doctrine). Paired sample of 115 failed firms (1954 to 1968) and 115 nonfailed firms. Matching characteristics: industry, sales, employees, and fiscal year	Uses *linear* multiple discriminant analysis. A 12-variable model with emphasis upon liquidity, profitability, and variability is developed. One year before, failure model is 93–95 percent accurate, 80 percent two years before, and 70 percent thereafter up to 5 years before	Application of MDA using accounting and financial market data to Failing Company Doctrine. Stresses the importance of a failure-prediction model to have theoretical justification and sound validation procedures. Shortcoming: doesn't test for equality of group dispersion matrices

6. *R. Libby (1975)*. To jointly evaluate (1) the predictive power of ratio information and (2) the ability of loan officers to evaluate ratio information in a failure-prediction framework. Employs Deakin's (1972) sample	Uses principal-components analysis to identify five independent sources of variation in the Beaver–Deakin 14-variable set and MDA to test classification accuracy. The five dimensions are labeled (1) profitability, (2) activity, (3) liquidity, (4) asset balance, and (5) cash position. The 5-variable set is only slightly less accurate than the 14-variable set	Illustrates the usefulness of principal-components analysis in reducing the dimensionality of a data set and shows that accounting ratios enable bankers to make highly accurate and reliable predictions of business failures
7. *R. Elam (1975)*. To determine if capitalization of nonpurchase leases enables financial-statement users to predict bankruptcy more accurately than without such an adjustment. Analyzes 48 bankrupt firms (1966–1972) with reported lease information and a matched sample of nonbankrupt firms. Matching characteristics: data year, industry, sales, and reported leases	Uses MDA to test a set of 28 ratios. Single-ratio and multiratio predictions are made. Models with lease data are not more accurate than ones without lease data	First researcher to incorporate and test the effect of lease data on the accuracy of bankruptcy predictions. Rejects hypothesis that lease data enhances ability to predict bankruptcy. Shortcomings: doesn't attempt to find "best" model, simply tests 25-variable model; several misconceptions about theory and application of MDA. Altman (1976) concludes that the effect of leasing or failure prediction is not yet resolved
8. *J. Wilcox (1976)*. To show how to usefully quantify the risk of financial failure through the gambler's-ruin approach. (Study builds upon Wilcox's (1971a,b) and (1973b) articles.) Uses matched samples of 52 bankrupt firms and 52 nonbankrupt firms from Wilcox (1973b)	Uses gambler's-ruin model to discriminate between bankrupt and nonbankrupt firms. Important variables are net liquidation value, average adjusted cash flow, and the concept of "size of bet." Model's accuracy is comparable to other failure-prediction studies	Develops a strong conceptual framework with implications for the management process and prevention of bankruptcy. No major shortcomings. Seems to be overly concerned about "evils" of statistical searching

APPENDIX (*Continued*)

Purpose and Sample Characteristics	*Statistical Method and Important Variables*	*Contribution and Critique*
9. *E. Deakin (1977).* To assess the impact, frequency, and nature of bankruptcy *misclassification* using his 1972 model as modified by Libby (1975). A sample of 63 bankrupt firms (1966–1971) and a *nonmatched* sample of 80 nonfailing companies are analyzed. Data are from the period 1964 to 1969	Uses both linear and quadratic MDA. The five ratios from Libby (1975) are: (1) net income/total assets, (2) current assets/total assets, (3) cash/total assets, (4) current assets/current liabilities, and (5) sales/current assets	Focuses upon the concepts of fail*ing* and nonfail*ing* rather than fail*ed* and nonfail*ed* to emphasize that a company may enter the failing state and still avoid the failed state. Adopts a unique classification rule based upon both linear and quadratic equations. Compares model's predictions with auditors' opinions. Shortcomings: doesn't attempt to measure costs of misclassification; overly concerned about size of Type-II error; to reduce costs of the Type-I error, the firms in the "investigate-further" group could be classified as failing
10. *E. Altman, R. Haldeman, and P. Narayanan (1977).* To construct, analyze, and test a new bankruptcy classification model that explicitly considers recent developments with respect to business failures. A sample of 53 bankrupt firms (1969–1975) and a matched sample of nonbankrupt firms are analyzed	Both linear and quadratic classification equations are employed. Their "ZETA" model is a seven-variable one consisting of (1) return of assets, (2) stability of earnings, (3) debt service, (4) cumulative profitability, (5) liquidity, (6) capitalization, and (7) size. ZETA model outperforms Altman's 1968 model	Most sophisticated and up-to-date MDA model of corporate bankruptcy. Employs linear and quadratic equations; tests for model efficiency; explicitly considers cost of misclassification and *a priori* probabilities; among others. No major shortcomings.

Chapter VIII

Early-Warning Systems for Financial Institutions

INTRODUCTION

The 1970s and the early 1980s have been an extremely uneasy period for financial institutions, not only in the United States but throughout the world. As a result, there has been a proliferation of research attempting to measure the risk exposure of financial institutions. A substantial portion of the analysis has focused upon the financial difficulties of United States commercial banks, the most important components of the United States financial system. The bulk of the work has been done by the U.S. Federal banking agencies, either internally through their research staffs (e.g., at the FDIC and Federal Reserve Bank of New York) or externally via outside consultants (e.g., at the office of the Comptroller of the Currency). In addition, but to a lesser extent, researchers at academic institutions have investigated this question. Given their congressional mandate to "maintain the safety and soundness of the banking system," it is not surprising that the banking authorities have been the front runners in this research area.[1]

In addition to commercial banks, savings and loans associations (SLAs), over-the-counter broker-dealers, and credit unions have been the subject of "early-warning" or failure-prediction research. Major early-warning or surveillance studies of financial institutions are analyzed in detail in this chapter. All of the studies are of recent vintage (since 1970) and a few of them still are considered to be on-going projects. The studies will be analyzed (if applicable) according to the criteria used in the previous chapter. The order of presentation is

1. FDIC studies
2. Federal Reserve Bank of New York studies

3. The National Bank Surveillance System (Comptroller of the Currency)
4. Board of Governors (Federal Reserve System) studies
5. Other studies

At the end of the chapter, a summary of the major studies (Appendix) and a comprehensive bibliography of early-warning research for financial institutions are presented.

THE FINANCIAL ENVIRONMENT IN THE 1980s

The Depository Institutions Deregulation and Monetary Control Act of 1980 (DIDMCA), inflation, and competition from retailers (e.g., Sears), money-market funds, foreign banks, and others have made the environment for U.S. depository institutions a highly competitive one. Moreover, with the demise of geographic restrictions on depository institutions anticipated in the 1980s, the environment is expected to become even more competitive. Thus, the need for early-warning systems for financial institutions, especially depository ones, is a critical one. Thrift institutions (SLAs and MSBs) currently are in the deepest trouble. Some analysts are predicting that 200 thrifts will be forced to close their doors in 1981. In addition, with the relaxation of geographic barriers, a substantial consolidation of the commercial-banking system is anticipated in the 1980s. Accordingly, the material in this chapter is extremely current and should be of keen interest to researchers in the financial-institutions area.

THE CONCEPT OF AN EARLY-WARNING SYSTEM

This section focuses upon the concept of an early-warning system from the bank regulator's perspective. Surveillance mechanisms also would be of interest, but for different reasons, to investors, uninsured depositors, creditors, auditors, accountants, and brokers, to mention a few.

The rationale for an early-warning or surveillance system (from the bank regulator's viewpoint) is grounded in the fundamental economic tenet of efficient resource allocation. The banking agencies have scarce examination resources with which to determine (on an annual basis) the "safety and soundness" of over 14,000 commercial banks. Any type of mechanism, such as a computer-based, early-warning system, that can identify banks with financial difficulties should be a useful *tool* for scheduling the timing, intensity, and extent of a particular bank's examination and for focusing upon potential remedial attention. Such a tool, of course, is not intended to be a replacement for the human skills or judgments needed in solving problems of bank supervision.

INFORMATION AVAILABLE FOR IDENTIFYING BANKS WITH FINANCIAL DIFFICULTIES

One of the ways the banking authorities attempt to carry out their safety-and-soundness mandate is to prevent existing banks from failing. Because the failure path tends to be a decaying one rather than an explosive one, identifying banks with financial difficulties is the first step toward achieving the failure-prevention goal.

The major weapon in the banking authorities' identification arsenal has been and still is the on-site bank examination. This inspection technique mainly focuses upon evaluating the quality of a bank's loan portfolio relative to its capital and reserves. It results in a *de facto* definition of a "problem bank" as one with a large volume of "substandard loans" relative to its capital and reserves (Sinkey, 1978b).

Four decades ago Secrist (1938) suggested that bank accounting data be used to distinguish sound from unsound banking. However, only recently have the banking agencies attempted to make more efficient use of these data in the form of early-warning or surveillance systems. These systems can be used to assist in scheduling on-site bank examinations and allocating more efficiently the banking agencies' scarce resources.

To date, the banking agencies have not seriously attempted to use market information to estimate banks' risk exposure. The strongest form of the "efficient-market hypothesis" insists that all relevant information on the future performance of any asset is included and properly discounted in its current price. If the market for bank stocks is efficient, investors' required rates of return are adjusted for risk, including risk of bankruptcy.

If markets are efficient, they provide a continuous surveillance mechanism. However, accounting data only are available on a quarterly basis and examination data even less frequently, roughly once a year. Because there is evidence that the three alternative information sources have basically the same content and because, in the past at least, bank examinations have *not* been scheduled on the basis of banks' potential risk exposure, market data should provide the *earliest* warning signal followed by the accounting and examination data. Market data, if available, and accounting data can be used to increase the efficiency of the bank-examination process.

If markets are efficient and market data available, aren't the accounting and examination information superfluous? In theory, yes; in practice, no. The major cause of bank failures has been some form of managerial dishonesty or misconduct [Hill (1975), e.g., embezzlement, fraud, excessive insider transactions]. This type of activity tends to be deliberately masked and therefore harder to uncover, even by bank examiners (e.g., C. Arnholt Smith's wheeling and dealing with USNB). When both market and accounting data are available, the accounting data probably are redundant. However, because the marginal cost of massaging the accounting data is minimal, the redundancy is not expensive and can serve as a safety check. When market data are not available, accounting data can be used to complement the bank-examination process.

The greatest threat to the solvency of the Federal deposit-insurance fund and to the safety and soundness of the U. S. commercial-banking system comes from large commercial banks. As of December 31, 1978, there were only 181 commercial banks with total assets greater than $1.0 billion. However, these giant banks, which are only 1.23 percent of the population of commercial banks, control 58.13 percent of the banking system's total assets.[2] To monitor the riskiness of large commercial banks, the banking agencies should employ as efficiently as possible all available information: examination, accounting, and market. For banks without actively traded securities, the efficient-market hypothesis cannot be tested. Thus, surveillance mechanisms for such banks must concentrate on examination and accounting data.

To summarize, examination, accounting, and market information are available for identifying financial difficulties in commercial banks. To effectively monitor the risk exposure of individual banks and the banking system, the banking authorities should employ as efficiently as possible all of these information sources.

EARLY WARNING AND BANK SUPERVISORY ISSUES

Early warning is an identification task, that is, it is the task of identifying banks with undue or excessive risk exposure (see Sinkey, 1979: 27–32). What are bank supervisors supposed to do with early-warning information? Given the limited objective of using early warning as a tool for scheduling on-site bank examinations, early-warning information simply can be used to rank banks according to their degree of risk exposure so that an examination schedule can be established. Thus, high-risk banks are examined first, medium-risk banks second, etc.

A more critical supervisory issue has to do with the connection between early warning and the treatment of problem and failing banks. What is suppose to happen in cases where there is conflict between early-warning tests and on-site examinations? Suppose that a bank flagged by early warning as "high risk" is given a clean bill of health by the examination team; what happens to this bank? One approach to this conflict is to view early warning as attempting to detect "smoke" with the on-site inspection designed to determine if there is "fire." If the signal clearly is a false alarm, the bank should be considered to be "safe and sound." However, remembering the adage, "Where there is smoke, there is fire," unresolved conflict situations should be appropriately monitored for signs of trouble.

The opposite case, that of an undetected failing bank, is, of course, the critical one. An early-warning system with high error rates, especially of the latter kind, could not be tolerated and such constitutional weaknesses would have to be corrected or the system scrapped.

Despite solid statistical research and evidence, the banking agencies have been slow to make use of early-warning systems. One of the major drawbacks in implementing such systems is their complexity, because they usually are grounded in a multivariate statistical technique. Thus, a prerequisite for implementation is that the system and its information be digestible by the prospective users, namely, bank examiners.

Finally, there is the difficult problem of what to do with a bank that is failing (i.e., a bank whose early-warning signal has been confirmed by the examination team). This becomes what Sinkey (1979) has described as the "enforcement" problem, as distinct from the "identification" problem that we have been discussing. Whereas a complete answer to this question goes beyond the scope of this book, we present a brief answer focusing upon the issues involved. First, there is the issue of the goal of bank regulation and the number of bank failures that can be tolerated without loss of confidence in the banking system. Since the inception of the FDIC, the goal appears to have been one of limited failure prevention. A second issue has to do with the distinction between bank failures that are costly to the FDIC (e.g., USNB of San Diego at a cost of roughly $150 million) versus those that are zero-loss failures to the FDIC (e.g., the much-publicized failure of Franklin National Bank of New York). The arrangements for the deposit assumptions in the USNB and Franklin cases both took roughly 1 year to complete. However, USNB's workout was a financial disaster to the FDIC whereas Franklin's case resulted in a zero nominal loss to the insurance fund. (Considering opportunity costs, there was, of course, a loss to the FDIC from Franklin's failure.) What is the lesson for the handling of large failing banks? Slow resolution of a problem situation does not appear to be the answer, since USNB's workout took roughly 5 months longer than Franklin's transaction. Looking at the cause of failure, however, may provide a clue. USNB's demise was due to misuse of funds and other illegal activity whereas Franklin's failure was due to economic and financial mismanagement. The implication is that for cases in which pervasive dishonesty has occurred it may be difficult for the FDIC to avoid a loss (e.g., Sharpstown State Bank, Texas). In contrast, in Franklin-type situations, lengthy workouts may be critical in avoiding losses. An important question for early-warning research is whether or not any early-warning system can distinguish between a Franklin and a USNB. Because the answer would appear to be negative, it is up to the on-site inspection team to determine whether the early-warning symptoms are due to dishonest or inept management or some combination of both. Finally, since dishonest actions tend to be deliberately masked, they are, of course, more difficult to detect. Thus, while the potential for early warning in USNB and Sharpstown-type cases is indeed limited, this shortcoming should not detract from the potential overall usefulness of such systems.

FDIC STUDIES

Meyer and Pifer (1970)

One of the first failure-prediction studies sponsored by the Federal banking agencies was by Meyer and Pifer (1970), hereafter M&P. The purpose of the study was to attempt to discriminate between failed and nonfailed banks that faced similar local and national market conditions. The approach of the study was to select a set of financial variables, reflecting managerial ability and employee honesty, and to determine statistically the "best" subset of variables for distinguishing between failed and nonfailed banks one or more years prior to failure.

Definition of Failure. M&P defined failure in the strict legal sense, that is, as a declaration of insolvency (negative net worth) either by the Comptroller of the Currency in the case of a nationally chartered bank or by the respective state banking agency in the case of a state-chartered bank. This definition of failure avoids the problem of identifying mergers that occurred because the acquired bank was in a financially distressed condition. Such mergers are important, however, because to ignore them could result in groups that are not completely discrete and identifiable. That is, usually the acquired bank in a distressed merger is treated as if it had failed. Thus, to include such a bank in the nonfailed group would be a misspecification of the true group membership. In contrast, it is possible that without the merger the bank could have survived; in which case it would have been inappropriate to identify the bank as a failure. Thus, the mere existence of such mergers creates an "identification" problem.

Sample Groups. M&P's failed-bank group consisted of 39 banks that closed between 1948 and 1965. Each failed bank was matched with a nonfailed bank on the basis of location, size, age, and regulatory agency. These 39 pairs then were divided into an original sample of 30 pairs and a holdout sample of 9 pairs.

Data and Variables. Data for 6 years prior to failure were collected from balance sheets, income statements, and examination reports. This information was summarized into 28 operating ratios and 4 balance-sheet levels. Each of the 32 variables was expressed in five different forms: (1) current period value, (2) lagged value, (3) trend or growth value, (4) coefficient of variation, and (5) unexpected deviation. Thus, the total number of variables was 160 (= 32 × 5).

Regression Model. M&P employed a zero–one regression model with the dependent variable equal to one for a failed bank and zero for a nonfailed bank. The independent variables were selected using a stepwise-regression technique that combined forward selection and backward reduction at each step. The forward-selection criterion required that the *entering* variable, combined with the previously selected variables, minimize the residual sum of squares and satisfy a prespecified minimum F-value. The backward-reduction criterion deleted a variable if on a later iteration its contribution fell below a minimum F-value.

Empirical Results. M&P found that with a lead time of 1 or 2 years they could correctly reclassify about 80 percent of their sample banks. Beyond the second year, however, their regression equations were not significant and their classifications were not better than chance.

M&P's nine-variable regression results for 1 year prior are presented in Table VIII.1. The results for 2 years prior are not presented here but are summarized below.

Using the nine-variable equation presented in Table VIII.1 and a cutoff value of 0.5 for the dependent variable, only 7 of the 60 original-sample banks were misclassified (88.33 percent overall accuracy, see the notes to Table VIII.1). Three failed banks and four nonfailed banks were misclassified. Using the paired holdout sample of 18 banks, two failed banks and one nonfailed bank were misidentified: an overall accuracy of 83.33 percent. Employing a six-variable model and a 0.4 cutoff value, the overall accuracy rates were 78.5 percent (original) and 94.5 percent (holdout)—a somewhat surprising result since accuracy usually *decreases* with a holdout sample.

For 2 years prior to failure, M&P's best results (in terms of overall classification accuracy) were 85 percent (original) and 78 percent (hold-

Table VIII.1. Meyer and Pifer's Zero–One Regression Results: One Year Prior to Failure

Variable	*Estimated Coefficient*	*t-statistic*
1. Error in predicting cash and securities/total assets	.016	2.53
2. Coefficient of variation in rate of interest on time deposits	.005	4.23
3. Lagged ratio of time deposits to demand deposits	.002	3.76
4. Operating income/total assets (lagged)	−.328	2.37
5. Growth of consumer loans/total assets	−.128	2.77
6. Growth of cash and securities/total assets	−.084	3.80
7. Coefficient of variation of total loans	−.025	3.10
8. Real estate loans/total assets	−.022	3.01
9. Fixed assets/total assets	.168	2.44
10. Constant term	.871	—

R^2 = .741 and F-statistic = 6.77. With a cutoff point of 0.5 for the dependent variable, the Type I error was 10 percent whereas the Type II error was 13 percent (for the original sample). For the holdout sample, the error rates were 22 percent and 11 percent, respectively.
Source: Meyer and Pifer (1970, Tables 1 and 3)

out). These results were obtained with two *different* models. The original-sample results were based upon a nine-variable model with a 0.4 cutoff value. The holdout-sample accuracy for *this* model was 61 percent. The "best" holdout-sample results (78 percent) were based upon a six-variable model with a 0.6 cutoff score. The original-sample accuracy for *this* model was 66.5 percent, another case of "accuracy reversal" going from original to holdout.

M&P's Conclusions. M&P stated two main conclusions. First, although most of the banks they analyzed failed because of embezzlement and other financial irregularities, M&P found that ordinary balance-sheet and income–expense data still were fairly accurate in distinguishing between failed and nonfailed banks for up to 2 years prior to failure. Beyond the second year, however, the models were ineffective. And second, since their nine-variable model consisted of only one *current* variable and eight variables based upon trends, variation, unexpected changes, and values 2 years prior to failure, M&P concluded that more than current financial information was needed to discriminate between failed and nonfailed banks. Finally, M&P felt that their models could be useful as screening devices to aid in scheduling bank examinations and thus lead to a more efficient allocation of examination resources.

Sinkey (1974–1979)

According to Guttentag (1977), Sinkey's research "must comprise at least two-thirds of the citable items on early-warning systems" (p. 56). These items are listed in the comprehensive bibliography at the end of this chapter. A convenient summary of Sinkey's work is his 1979 book, *Problem and Failed Institutions in the Commercial Banking Industry*.

Overview. Sinkey's early-warning research has focused upon three different types of models or mechanisms: (1) failure-prediction models, (2) problem-prediction models, and (3) outlier or peer-group models. The concept of a failure-prediction model already has been discussed thoroughly and does not require further explanation. A problem-prediction model is one designed to replicate *and* predict bank examiners' "problem-bank" classifications (i.e., problem versus nonproblem). This type of model requires an understanding of what is a "problem bank," which will be discussed later. Finally, an outlier model is simply one that focuses upon statistical atypicalness. Sinkey's retrospective analyses of the downfalls of Franklin National Bank of New York, United States National Bank of San Diego, and Security National Bank of Long Island are examples of *ex post* outlier or peer-group analyses. In addition, the Comptroller's National Bank Surveillance System (via Haskins & Sells) was based entirely upon the outlier approach, quite surprisingly without any empirical validation. The idea behind the outlier model is to establish benchmark measures of a bank's vulnerability or "safety and soundness" and then to flag banks with outlier characteristics as being in need of supervisory attention. Martin (1977) has referred to the outlier model as an *a priori undefined* approach because the concept of vulnerability is made without references to failure or problem status. In essence, this approach simply measures a bank's deviation from peer-group averages.

Problem Prediction and the Concept of a Problem Bank. Although banks with financial difficulties (i.e., problem institutions) have existed for centuries, the term "problem bank" only recently was made popular by the U.S. banking authorities because of their so-called problem-bank lists. Accordingly, every financial reporter is looking for a "deep vault" so that he or she can provide his or her newspaper with a headline like "Citibank, Chase Manhattan on U.S. 'Problem' List" (*The Washington Post*, January 11, 1976).

The banking agencies have interpreted their "safety and soundness" mandate as one of failure prevention.[3] By identifying banks with the highest failure risks as "problem banks," the banking agencies hope to achieve this goal. The FDIC's Division of Bank Supervision identifies three classes of problem banks, separated according to examiners' perception of failure (or insolvency) risks. Banks perceived as having at least a 50 percent chance of requiring FDIC financial assistance in the near future are classified as "potential payoffs" (PPOs). Banks that appear to be headed for PPO status unless drastic changes occur are referred to as "serious problems" (SPs). And finally, banks with significant weaknesses, but a lesser degree of vulnerability than PPO or SP banks, are called "other problems" (OPs). The FDIC usually lumps the PPO and SP banks together, referring to them as "serious problem" banks. As of June 30, 1976, there were 365 banks on the FDIC's problem-bank list, consisting of 121 serious problem banks (PPO + SP) and 244 other problem banks (see Table VIII.2). On average, over the period 1968 IV–1976 II, the figures were 226 (59), 55 (28), and 171 (38), respectively (figures in parentheses are standard deviations).

The problem-bank identification procedure is rooted in the bank-examination process. The purposes of a bank examination are:

1. To determine asset quality
2. To determine the nature of liabilities
3. To ascertain compliance with laws and regulations
4. To evaluate controls, procedures, accounting practices, and insurance
5. To evaluate management and its policies
6. To determine capital adequacy

Table VIII.2. Problem Banks, 1968 IV–1976 II

		Serious Problems	*Other Problems*	*Total*
1968	IV	35	250	240
1969	I	32	190	222
	II	30	181	211
	III	39	175	214
	IV	39	177	216
1970	I	45	181	226
	II	53	190	243
	III	57	189	246
	IV	57	194	251
1971	I	60	185	245
	II	60	182	242
	III	58	185	243
	IV	53	186	239
1972	I	47	179	226
	II	42	175	217
	III	35	178	213
	IV	28	162	190
1973	I	30	133	163
	II	29	129	158
	III	33	115	148
	IV	36	119	155
1974	I	42	102	144
	II	47	103	150
	III	49	113	162
	IV	52	129	181
1975	I	61	144	205
	II	95	176	271
	III	109	201	310
	IV	115	232	347
1976	I	124	235	359
	II	121	244	365
Mean		55	171	226
(sd)		(28)	(38)	(59)

Source: Problem-Bank Lists, Division of Bank Supervision, FDIC.

Sinkey (1978b) has shown that the multidimensionality of this process can be reduced to a single ratio that combines the asset-quality and capital-adequacy factors, the FDIC's net capital ratio.[4] Thus, he has concluded that a problem bank mainly is one with a large volume of substandard loans relative to its capital and reserves. Unless there is a clear understanding of what a substandard loan is and the subjective process by which a loan is determined to be substandard, knowledge that a financial institution is considered to be a problem bank can be subject to serious misinterpretation. Thus, in most cases, the fact that a bank is flagged as a problem does not mean that it is about to fail. Basically, it means that such a bank has a large volume of substandard loans, which are examiners' *least* risky loan-classification category (in a loan-evaluation process that is described by the banking agencies as an "art" and not a "science," i.e., an examiner's judgment is the primary determining factor). If the quality of these substandard loans continues to deteriorate, the bank *could* be in danger of failing; otherwise, it is simply a bank that should be watched closely and given remedial attention.

Using the problem-bank data in Table VIII.2, Sinkey (1979) has estimated that there is about a five-quarter lag and an inverse relationship between the state of the economy (as measured by quarterly changes in real GNP) and the number of problem banks. Thus, the fact that a bank is on one of the agencies' problem-bank lists does not necessarily mean that it is still a problem today.

To summarize, a "problem bank" basically is one with a "high" risk loan portfolio as perceived by bank examiners. There are, of course, other reasons why banks have financial difficulties, but they appear to be of secondary importance. Problem-prediction models have focused upon trying to identify balance-sheet and income-expense items that could replicate and forecast these examination ratings.

Problem-Prediction Models. A problem-prediction model employs examiners' judgments regarding problem–nonproblem status for identifying group membership. The major potential shortcoming of this approach is that the *true* groups may not be discrete and identifiable because of (1) examiners' identification errors and/or (2) lags in the decentralized bureaucratic process of maintaining up-to-date problem-bank lists.

Whether the *modus operandi* is failed–nonfailed or problem–nonproblem, the methodological and statistical approaches tend to be the same. That is, the groups are selected (with the nonfailed or nonproblem group constructed either by pairing or random sampling), data collected, and statistical discrimination attempted using balance-sheet and income–expense data. Sinkey has employed both the paired-sample and random-sample approaches in his research. Since random samples are more appropriate for predictive purposes, they should be employed, unless the pairing factors are deemed to be critical and cannot be controlled directly.

Sample Banks. In the *Journal of Finance* (March, 1975), Sinkey analyzed the financial characteristics of 110 "new" problem banks. The group consisted of 90 insured commercial banks identified by the FDIC as problem institutions during 1972 and 20 additional banks that were added to the problem-bank list during the first few months of 1973. "New" problem banks were chosen to minimize the supervisory effects of remedial attention on the data and to provide for relative homogeneity between the problem and nonproblem groups in the years prior to 1972.

Each problem bank was matched with a nonproblem (control) bank on the basis of (1) geographic market area, (2) total deposits, (3) number of banking offices, and (4) Federal Reserve membership.

Data and Variables. Balance sheets and income statements for the years 1969–1972 were collected for each of the sample banks. Because the sample problem banks were not identified as distressed institutions until 1972–1973, both groups of banks, technically, were nonproblems during the years 1969–1971. Thus, Sinkey was attempting to discover if there were any indicators of the impending problem status from routinely collected accounting data.

On a univariate basis, Sinkey tested over 100 variables. However, most of the MDA computer runs [using Eisenbeis and Avery's (1972) computer program MULDIS] were drawn from a pool of 30 variables with the average run consisting of 10 variables, which was most efficient in terms of the MDA results and use of computer time.

Tests for the Equality of Group Covariance Matrices and Group Mean Vectors. Sinkey found (for the various sets of variables tested) that in almost all instances the null hypotheses of equal covariances and equal means were rejected. For example, consider the following ten-variable profile, which is representative of the types of variables Sinkey analyzed:

Category	*Variable(s)*
1. Liquidity	1. [Cash + U.S. Treasury Sec.]/Assets
2. Loan Volume	2. Loans/Assets
3. Loan Quality	3. Provision for Loan Losses/Oper. Expense
4. Capital Adequacy	4. Loans/[Capital + Reserves]
5. Efficiency	5. Operating Expense/Operating Income
6. Source of Revenue	6 a. Loan Revenue/Oper. Income
	6 b. U.S. Treas. Sec. Revenue/Oper. Income
	6 c. State & Loc. Oblig. Rev./Oper. Income
7. Use of Revenue	7 a. Interest paid on Deposits/Oper. Income
	7 b. Other Expenses/Oper. Income

Both the group dispersions and group means for this set of variables were unequal in each of the 4 years tested (1969 to 1972). In addition, the differences became more pronounced as the date of problem detection approached.

The Importance of Individual Variables. Although there are no absolute tests for the importance of specific variables in discriminant analysis, there are a number of methods for ranking the relative contribution of individual variables. Regardless of the method used, Sinkey found that for 1969 the loan-revenue, efficiency, and other-expenses variables were the more important ones. In general, the efficiency and other-expenses variables appear to be important early-warning signals (1969–1971) whereas the loan-volume and loan-quality variables were more important in 1972, after the majority of the banks were identified as problems. The data presented in Table VIII.3 illustrate these phenomena.

Classification Results. Since the covariance matrices were unequal, Sinkey used a quadratic discriminant function to reclassify his sample banks. In addition, a validation test using the Lachenbruch holdout technique was performed. The classification results using the ten-variable profile described above are presented in Table VIII.4.

From a *descriptive* point of view, classification results should be viewed as a way of examining group overlap. Accordingly, the simple reclassification of the sample banks suggests that as of year-end 1969 the groups were relatively distinct such that 73.18 percent of the banks could be reassigned correctly. Unfortunately, the Type I error (38.18 percent) was more than twice as large as the Type II error (15.45 percent).

The Lachenbruch results, which adjust for sample bias, can be interpreted from a *predictive* perspective. On average, these classifications are less accurate by 5–10 percentage points in each year, including both the Type I and Type II errors. Like the reclassified sample, the accuracy of the classifications improves over time.

The implications for problem prediction are mixed. That is, on the one hand, although the mean vectors are significantly different, the distributions of the two groups overlap in each of the 4 years. On the other hand, the groups are relatively distinct even in 1969 and they overlap less and less over the next 3 years. Thus, Sinkey's findings suggest that any sort of early-warning mechanism designed to predict problem status will be fairly accurate over the short run (say with a year or less lead time); however, if greater lead time is required, the error rates, especially the Type I error rate, tend to increase quickly.

The Cost of a Bank Failure versus the Cost of Policing a Problem Bank. The probability of an insured commercial bank becoming a problem bank is quite low, less than 3 percent based on recent history.

Table VIII.3. Means and Standard Deviations of Selected Variables for Problem and Nonproblem Banks

Variable	1969		1970		1971		1972	
	Problem	*Nonproblem*	*Problem*	*Nonproblem*	*Problem*	*Nonproblem*	*Problem*	*Nonproblem*
1. Loan/assets	53.9*	49.3	55.4*	48.9	56.9*	47.8	56.0*	47.8
	(11.1)	(10.2)	(9.6)	(11.0)	(9.1)	(11.5)	(9.8)	(11.5)
2. Provision for loan losses/	3.9	3.2	4.4*	2.8	5.3*	2.8	7.9*	2.5
operating expenses	(4.7)	(4.2)	(4.9)	(3.2)	(5.2)	(3.9)	(8.6)	(3.4)
3. Loans/(Capital + reserves)	648.3*	564.5	692.2*	562.5	768.9*	562.4	838.6*	577.5
	(199.7)	(182.6)	(196.1)	(184.6)	(244.6)	(185.3)	(240.6)	(188.5)
4. Operating expense/operating	83.9*	78.5	85.5*	78.6	89.3*	81.8	94.1*	82.4
income	(10.9)	(10.1)	(8.7)	(9.4)	(11.1)	(9.5)	(15.2)	(9.3)
5. Loan revenue/operating	64.7*	59.3	65.8*	59.2	68.8*	59.9	69.8*	59.6
income	(12.7)	(10.1)	(11.1)	(10.5)	(8.9)	(11.1)	(8.3)	(11.6)
6. Other expenses/operating	15.8*	12.3	16.0*	13.0	16.3*	13.2	16.4*	13.7
income	(7.1)	(4.7)	(6.7)	(5.1)	(6.4)	(5.4)	(5.2)	(5.2)

Variables are expressed as percentages and figures in parentheses are standard deviations. An asterisk (*) indicates that the variables within a given year are significantly different at the 5 percent level.
Source: Sinkey, (1975a, Table 3, p. 27).

Table VIII.4. Quadratic Classification Results

	Reclassified Sample			*Lachenbruch Validation Test*		
Year	*Type-I Error* (%)	*Type-II Error* (%)	*Misclassification Rate* (%)	*Type-I Error* (%)	*Type-II Error* (%)	*Misclassification Rate* (%)
1969	38.18	15.45	26.82	46.36	25.45	35.91
1970	35.45	20.00	27.73	42.73	27.27	35.00
1971	28.18	20.00	24.09	38.18	24.55	31.36
1972	22.33	13.59	17.96	28.15	21.36	24.76

These classifications are based upon the ten-variable profile described in the text; the number of banks in each group was 110, except in 1972 when the number was 103, since seven banks had been removed from the problem-bank list by year-end 1972.
Source: Sinkey (1975a, Table 5, p. 32).

However, since bank regulators are more concerned about misclassifying a problem bank (i.e., making a Type I error) than about misclassifying a nonproblem bank (i.e., making a Type II error), the costs of misclassification are significantly greater for the former than the latter. If an incorrectly classified bank actually fails (e.g., USNB or Franklin), it presumably is more costly for the FDIC to liquidate the bank than it would have been for the supervising banking agency to police the bank as a problem bank.

From 1934 to 1975, 519 insured banks have failed with total losses to the FDIC of approximately $237 million.[5] Thus, the average bank failure has cost the FDIC approximately $457,000. In contrast, during 1975, the FDIC incurred *total* administrative and operating expenses of approximately $68 million. Given the 8595 insured nonmember banks in existence as of December 31, 1975, the FDIC spent approximately $7900 per bank. Alternatively, given the 28,254 field examinations and investigations conducted by the FDIC during 1975, the average cost of such a field operation was approximately $2400. Note that both of these figures reflect average costs and not the more relevant marginal costs. In addition, both of the figures could be viewed as overestimates, since supervisory costs were lumped together with other FDIC costs. However, if the activities of the FDIC's division of supervision are viewed as not being independent of the activities of other divisions (e.g., legal, research), the degree of overestimation would be much smaller. Whatever the actual nominal costs are, the important point is that a bank's failure would appear to be more costly than trying to prevent (over some reasonable period of time) the bank's collapse.[6]

Using the average cost of a bank failure of $457,000 and the "supervisory" expense-per-bank figure of $7900, a conservative estimate of the cost ratio is approximately 58:1. Weighting this ratio by the *a priori* probabilities of a bank becoming a problem or nonproblem, respectively, the true cost ratio is in the range of 1.8:1 to 0.6:1 (using 3 and 1 percent as the chances of a bank becoming a problem).

In discriminant analysis classification procedures, it is common practice (although not always appropriate for predictive purposes) to use the sample proportions as *a priori* probabilities. Thus, when a paired sample is employed, the sample proportions are simply .5 and .5. When such a procedure is used, the costs of misclassification usually are ignored. Since .5 does not fall between .55 and 1.67 (the inverses of the ratios 1.8:1 and 0.6:1, respectively), the sample-proportions technique is only a first approximation of the estimated misclassification-cost ratio. Finally, note that to minimize the number of Type I errors within the specified cost range, the most costly ratio of misclassifying a problem bank (1.67) should be employed.

Alternative Variables. In his contribution to the book *Financial Crises* (1977b), Sinkey stated that there was nothing magical about any of the particular sets of variables he analyzed. "If certain dimensionalities are captured, the form that the individual variables take is relatively unimportant (p. 37)." In banking, the important dimensions appear to be such factors as profitability, liquidity, capital adequacy, loan quality, expense control, and the aggressiveness of liability management.

An alternative model that Sinkey found to be relatively effective as an early-warning mechanism consisted of the following seven variables:

1. LRI = interest and fees on loans as a percentage of total operating income (measures revenue concentration).
2. OEOI = total operating expense as a percentage of total operating income (measures operating efficiency).
3. USA = U.S. Government securities as a percentage of total assets (measures liquidity and asset composition).
4. SLA = state and local securities as a percentage of total assets (measures asset composition).
5. LA = total loans as a percentage of total assets (measures loan volume).
6. NFA = net federal funds (sales minus purchases) as a percentage of total assets (measures federal-funds activity and aggressiveness of liability management).
7. KRA = capital and reserve for bad debt losses on loans as a percentage of total assets (measures capital adequacy).

The seven-variable model was developed using various groups of problem and nonproblem banks. Using year-end 1974 data, the classification results for the FDIC's March 31, 1975 problem-bank list (204 banks) and 208 randomly selected nonproblem banks are presented in Table VIII.5. The 95 percent confidence interval for a Type I error is 33.16 ± 6.39; for a Type II error it is 16.95 ± 5.02.

While these statistical tests give some idea as to how this model will perform, there still is substantial overlap between the problem and nonproblem banks. This implies that there is no substitute for the judgment and analysis of the examination staff, particularly with respect to the "close" cases. Thus, the real usefulness of such early-warning systems will not be as a substitute for bank examination, but rather as a means to direct the examination talents to those areas where judgment and further analysis can have the highest payoff. The next section illustrates how such a system could be used.

Table VIII.5. Classification Results[a]

Actual	*Total*	*Predicted Group Membership* *Problem*	*Nonproblem*
Problem	204	137	67
	(100.00)	(67.16)	(32.84)
Nonproblem	208	34	174
	(100.00)	(16.35)	(83.65)
Total	412	171	241
	(100.00)	(41.50)	(58.50)

[a]Figures in parentheses are percentages. The misclassification rate is 24.51 percent. A quadratic equation and the Lachenbruch holdout technique were used to reclassify the groups.
Source: Sinkey (1977c, p. 37).

Population Predictions: National Banks

Using the seven-variable model described above and data from year-end 1974 Reports of Condition and Income, Sinkey made predictions of *future* problem national banks.[7] To allow for a period of start-up experience, the screenings were for all banks established prior to December 31, 1972. The problem-bank group consisted of the 30 *national* banks on the FDIC's December 31, 1974 problem-bank list whereas the nonproblem-bank group contained *all nonproblem national banks* in existence for at least 2 years. The predictions are summarized in Table VIII.6 and the means for the problem- and nonproblem-bank groups are presented in Table VIII.7.

Of the 4465 banks screened, 126 banks were predicted to have characteristics more similar to the average problem national bank than the average nonproblem national bank. Of these 126 banks, 19 of them were on the December 31, 1974 problem-bank list. Over the first 9 months of 1975, 30 national banks were added to the problem list. The model identified eight of these banks as problem institutions (25.81 percent). However, and this is the important part, the model identified 66 banks, with characteristics more similar to problem national banks than nonproblem ones, that were not on the FDIC's problem-bank list by September 30, 1975. The scheduling of these banks for priority examinations illustrates the role of a computer-based, early-warning system.

An additional feature of the seven-variable model was the computation of three statistics indicating how similar each predicted problem bank was with all national banks in (1) the United States, (2) the bank's FDIC region, and (3) the bank's state. These "outlier" tests indicate how similar a bank is to all other national banks in the nation, region, and state.

Table VIII.6.

Panel A: Predictions of Problem National Banks

	Number of Banks
1. National banks screened	4465
2. Predicted problem banks	126
3. Actual problems (12/74)	30
4. Additional problems (3/75)	6
5. " " (6/75)	13
6. " " (9/75)	11
7. Total problems (12/74–9/75)	60
8. Banks from (7) predicted as problems[a]	27

Panel B: Predictions by Problem Class

Date	*Actual Problems*				*Predicted*			
	OP	*SP*	*PPO*	*Total*	*OP*	*SP*	*PPO*	*Total*
12/74	20	8	2	30	11	6	2	19
3/75[b]	6	0	0	6	3	0	0	3
6/75[b]	10	2	1	13	3	0	0	3
9/75[b]	10	1	0	11	1	1	0	2
Total	46	11	3	60	18	7	2	27

[a](8) as a percentage of (2) = 21.4 percent; as a percentage of (7) = 45 percent.
[b]Indicates additional or new problem banks as of that date.
Source: Sinkey seminar at the OCC, November 6, 1975.

The Outlier Approach

The high degree of group overlap between examiner-determined problem and nonproblem banks suggests that (1) models based upon balance-sheet and income–expense data alone may not be very effective in distinguishing between such banks and/or (2) examiner identification

Table VIII.7. Group Means

Variable	*Average Problem National Bank*	*Average Nonproblem National Bank*
LRI	65.4	60.4
OEOI	104.0	82.2
USA	13.6	14.6
SLA	7.4	13.4
LA	55.1	50.4
NFA	2.3	4.6
KRA	6.3	8.6

Sources: Reports of Income and Condition, FDIC. Figures are percentages.

error exists. The latter, if it exists, probably is due to a tendency on the part of the banking authorities to be overcautious regarding their "safety-and-soundness" mandate, rather than to any sort of malperformance on their part. The inability of the models to discriminate with a higher degree of accuracy could be due to improper specification. Thus, an early-warning system based upon examiners' definitions and groups may not provide an appropriate foundation.

An alternative approach explored by Sinkey and others is to abandon the examiner-determined groups and to work with peer groups (e.g., all banks with deposits greater than $100 million in some particular location). In this peer-group or "outlier" analysis, each bank in the group (which may include both problem and nonproblem banks) is compared with the average performance of the group. The Eisenbeis and Avery multiple discriminant analysis program (MULDIS) can be adapted to handle this one-group outlier technique. A chi-square score, which serves as a measure of resemblance between a particular bank and the group average, provides an approximation of the percentage of the population of peer-group banks that can be expected to lie farther from the peer-group's center (in either direction from the mean vector) than a particular bank.

Sinkey has experimented with the outlier technique in the cases of the failures of Franklin National Bank of New York and United States National Bank of San Diego and the emergency merger of Security National Bank of Long Island. In addition, he has conducted various outlier tests using alternative peer groups for the FDIC. A simple but effective outlier (or ranking) variable is a bottom-line or operating-efficiency measure (such as OEOI described above). For example, Keefe Management Service of New York City attempted to evaluate the riskiness of the FDIC's largest banks. They came up with a 35-variable measure of riskiness and ranked the banks on this basis. The rank correlation coefficient between their 35-variable ranking and a 1-variable ranking (net operating income, before taxes and securities gains or losses, as a percentage of total assets) was 89.1 percent. This should not be interpreted to mean that 1 variable can supply as much information as 35. It simply serves to highlight the potential usefulness of a simple outlier or ranking technique.

Martin (1977) has described the outlier technique as an *a priori undefined* approach. That is, an approach that abstracts from the definition of bank failure or problem status and instead focuses upon the general concept of financial weakness or vulnerability. The major shortcoming of this approach, according to Martin, is that financial weakness is undefined or defined ambiguously. As a result, the concept of financial weakness cannot be expressed as a probability of any specific event. There is, of course, a counterexample. If financial weakness is defined as the state of negative profits, then the probability of that event occurring can be studied just as the probability of negative net worth or failure can be analyzed. With other measures of financial weakness such as illiquidity, poor loan quality, or capital inadequacy, defining vulnerability becomes somewhat arbitrary and is difficult to express as the probability of any specific event. Moreover, if the event negative profits is combined with these other measures, the probability concept becomes blurred. Thus, there is little argument against Martin's label of "a priori undefined" from a probability perspective.

The outlier or peer-group approach is popular (as evident by its use in NBSS and JAWS, the acronym for the FDIC's Just A Warning System) because it is understood by examination and supervision personnel (i.e., it does not depend upon some esoteric statistical technique). The approach simply involves ratio or trend comparisons between a bank and its peer group. The group's average or historically developed norms are used to rate a bank's "safety and soundness." This type of analysis, uncluttered with probabilities, coefficients, etc., is something that the banking authorities can relate to and handle on an operational basis. It is imperative that future early-warning researchers produce systems that are palatable for users' consumption.

The Failed-Bank Approach

Given the conceptual difficulties encountered with problem-prediction and outlier models, let us consider the failed-bank or failure-prediction approach. The majority of failure-prediction studies follow what Martin (1977) refers to as an *ex post empirical* approach. That is, a group of actual failures is identified [with failure defined either narrowly (i.e., in a strict legal sense) or broadly to include supervisory mergers] and the financial characteristics of the failed banks compared with a group of nonfailed banks 1 or more years prior to failure. The major advantage of the failure approach is the elimination of supervisory judgment regarding problem status. Thus, failed and nonfailed groups should be more discrete and identifiable than problem and nonproblem groups. However, because of the existence of supervisory mergers, a potential "identification" problem still exists. Martin contends that to include banks merged under distressed conditions in the nonfailed group is a misspecification.

Two additional problems encountered in commercial bank, failure-prediction studies are (1) the time-series (or pooling) problem presented by too few bank failures within a given time period and (2) the cause-of-failure problem, that is, most bank failures have been caused by insider misconduct such as insider transactions, embezzlement, and manipulation. The first problem is one that researchers should recognize; however, it is one about which they can do very little. The second problem suggests that balance-sheet and income–expense information may not be very effective in identifying future bank failures. For example, of the 84 banks that failed between 1960 and April 30, 1976, 45 of the failures were due to improper loans to officers, directors, or owners or loans to out-of-territory borrowers (there was misuse of brokered funds in 22 of these cases); 25 of the cases could be traced to embezzlement or manipulation; and, finally, 14 of the failures were due to managerial weaknesses in loan-portfolio administration.[8] On the surface, these findings would appear to be ominous for any sort of failure-prediction mechanism. However, most researchers' findings tend to confirm Meyer and Pifer's (1970) conclusion that "even when failure frequently results from embezzlement and other financial irregularities, financial measures can evaluate the relative strengths of firms" (p. 867).

Regarding specific failure-prediction studies, Meyer and Pifer's model was discussed earlier and Martin's paper will be discussed later in the section dealing with the Federal Reserve Bank of New York studies.

In completing this section on FDIC studies, we now turn to Sinkey's (1978b) analysis of problem banks *using bank-examination data.*

Replication of Examiners' Problem-Bank Classifications Using Bank-Examination Data. Sinkey has shown that (1) for all practical purposes banks classified by the FDIC as "problem" institutions are those with low "net capital ratios" (NCR); (2) the most important component of the NCR is the volume of examiner-determined "substandard" loans; and (3) banks that failed in recent years almost invariably had low NCRs months before failure, although most banks with low NCRs did not fail.

Examination Data. Except for examiners' loan classifications, examination data are not much different from ordinary accounting data. The way the FDIC uses examination data in its problem-bank analyses is to adjust a bank's total capital account for various subgroups of adversely classified assets, mainly consisting of "substandard" loans.

The FDIC's *Analysis of Examination Reports* (Form 96) provides a statistical summary of a bank examiner's report. The information on this form is condensed further into a ratings vector that consists of two capital ratios, an earnings ratio, and a managerial rating. The two capital ratios critically depend upon the loan-evaluation process, the most important and subjective part of the traditional, on-site bank examination.

Regarding the capital ratios, the first one is the *adjusted capital ratio* (ACR). It is constructed by subtracting from a bank's total capital accounts those assets classified as "loss" and *50 percent* of those classified as "doubtful." This adjusted capital position becomes the numerator of the ACR with the denominator defined as the bank's quarterly average of gross assets for the calendar year. Using 1973 examination data and a group of 143 problem banks and a random sample of 163 nonproblem banks, the average ACRs were 6.4 percent (2.6 percent) and 8.8 percent (2.5 percent), respectively. (Figures in parentheses are standard deviations.)

The NCR has a numerator with all of the loss, doubtful, and substandard classifications netted out against a bank's capital. Thus, the difference between ACR and NCR is the remaining 50 percent of the doubtful and all of the substandard. The 1973 NCR data for the groups described above were −2.3 percent (5.2 percent) and 7.6 percent (3.0 percent), respectively.

The FDIC's *Manual of Examination Policies* states:

> One of the most important aspects of the examination process is the evaluation of loans, for, in large measure, it is the quality of a bank's loans which determines the risk to depositors. To a great extent, conclusions regarding the condition of the bank, the quality of its management, and its service to the community are weighted heavily by the examination's findings with regard to loans (8, Section H, p. 1).

Adversely classified assets (mainly low quality loans) are listed as "loss," "doubtful," or "substandard" based upon examiners' estimation of probable default. Moreover, it is widely recognized that the classification of assets is an "art" and not a "science," that is, an examiner's judgment is the primary determining factor.

The end result of an examiner's loan evaluations is a list of loans that is subject to criticism and/or comment in the report of examination. Ranked according to increasing risk of nonpayment, adversely classified loans are assigned to "substandard," "doubtful," or "loss" categories.

> The Substandard category includes loans which have *positive* and *well defined weaknesses* which jeopardize the orderly liquidation of the debt. Such loans are inadequately protected by the current sound worth and paying capacity of the obligor, or pledged collateral, if any. They are characterized by a degree of risk which poses the distinct possibility that the bank will likely sustain some loss if the deficiencies are not corrected (8, Section H, p. 5).

The important words in this passage are the last thirteen. They clearly indicate that only a *portion* of a bank's "substandard" loans are relevant for estimating its true risk exposure. Moreover, if bank examiners do their job (i.e., see to it that the loan deficiencies are corrected), the implication is that losses from the "substandard" category will be quite small. However, on the same page as the previously mentioned passage, the FDIC's *Manual* also states:

> It will be apparent that there is a close relationship between the several classifications, and no classification category should be viewed as more important than another. The uncollectibility aspect of Doubtful and Loss classifications makes their

> segregation of obvious importance. On the other hand, it is the function of the Substandard classification to indicate those loans which are unduly risky and which may be a future hazard to the bank's solvency. No bank can safely hold a large amount of low quality loans, even though they are not presently subject to either a Doubtful or Loss classification (8, Section H, p. 5).

This passage suggests a more conservative treatment of "substandard" loans and, based upon the empirical findings presented later, best describes the way the banking agencies treat such loans in determining their lists of "problem banks."

Problem-Bank Replication. Sinkey found, based upon either univariate or multivariate discriminant analysis tests and using the examination data and groups described earlier, that NCR had the most accurate reclassification rate of any variable or set of variables. The NCR accuracy rates were quite impressive, that is, 95.4 percent overall (306 banks), 95.1 percent for the 143 problem banks, and 95.7 percent for the 163 nonproblem banks. The corresponding rates for ACR were 73.2, 65.0, and 80.4. Recalling the construction of ACR and NCR, it is clear that a bank's volume of "substandard" loans is the kicker in the NCR formula, since, on average, substandard loans account for about 80 percent of a problem bank's classified loans. Thus, the present procedure for identifying problem banks depends largely on the amount of loans designated substandard.

NCR and Distressed Banks. Let us consider NCR's record with respect to the financial difficulties of the following large banks: (1) the three largest bank failures (Franklin National of New York, USNB of San Diego, and Hamilton National of Chattanooga), (2) the emergency merger of Security National of Long Island, and (3) the distressed Bank of the Commonwealth of Detroit. All five of these banks had net capital ratios low enough to warrant classification as FDIC problem banks *prior* to their collapses. The relevant NCR information is contained in Table VIII.8.

Regarding NCR forecasts, as of December 21, 1975, there were two billion-dollar banks on the FDIC's problem-bank list. Thus, their NCR lead times already have been substantial. Perforce, both of these banks had low net capital ratios (i.e., 0.0 and −1.0) and large volumes of "substandard" loans. Of course, given their goal of failure prevention, the banking authorities try to correct a bank's financial difficulties and thus NCR predictions will be biased toward becoming Type II errors (i.e., problem banks that do not fail or require financial assistance).

During 1975 and the first 5 months of 1976, 18 commercial banks were declared insolvent (13 in 1975). Excluding Hamilton National, which was discussed earlier, the remaining 17 banks (each with total

Table VIII.8. Large Banks and the Predictability of NCR

Bank	*Date of exam that led to FDIC problem classification*	*NCR (1)/(2)*[a]	*Date of failure, merger, or bailout*	*NCR lead time (months)*
1. USNB	6-26-72	−16/−12	10-18-73	16
2. Franklin	11-14-73	2/0	10-18-74	11
3. Hamilton	9-30-74	−3/−8	2-16-76	16
4. Security	6-24-74	0/0[b]	1-19-75	6
5. Commonwealth	3-07-69	2/−2	1-18-72[c]	34

[a](1) The NCR as of the exam date that led to FDIC problem classification and (2) the NCR on the last exam before closing or financial aid.
[b]Indicates same exam date for both NCRs. As of 1-29-73 and 10-23-73, Security's NCRs were 2.0 and 0.0, respectively; however, the bank was not listed by the FDIC as a "problem" bank during 1973.
[c]Commonwealth's second bailout occurred on 5-22-76. As of 6-30-75, Commonwealth's NCR was −1.0.
Source: Sinkey (1978b, Table 2, p. 190).

deposits less than $100 million) had an average NCR (or problem-bank list) lead time of approximately 22 months (the median lead time was 20 months). The range of lead times was from 2 weeks to 70 months. The $16-million Bank of Picayune (Mississippi) with a lead time of 2 weeks was the only "surprise" failure. The cause of Picayune's closing was "irregularities" (among other things, the chief executive office of the bank withheld about $600,000 in cash). During 1975, the FDIC's problem-bank list contained, on average, 283 banks.

To summarize, most "problem" banks do not fail and most failed banks are classified as "problem" banks prior to their closing. The banking agencies recognize (in words at least) that identification of banks experiencing financial difficulty is a multidimensional problem. However, in practice, bank capital and examiners' "substandard" loan classifications (as manifested in the FDIC's net capital ratio) are the important variables.

Critique of FDIC Research

The latest (February 7, 1978) FDIC surveillance mechanism, called Integrated Monitoring System (IMS), is a patchwork of ratio, trend, and critical-level analyses. It is a peer-group or outlier approach. Although it is a multiple-variable system, interaction among variables is not considered. In a nutshell, IMS is more of an NBSS-type system (NBSS is discussed later) than a statistical classification model.

The FDIC's research efforts have been successful in identifying financial characteristics of problem and/or failed banks. However, the MDA techniques and specific models have not been adopted by supervisory personnel. If researchers expect to have an impact upon operational activities, they must produce nontechnical products and be able to sell them to the ultimate users. Since the designers and users (examiners) usually have diverse backgrounds and skills, the technical aspects of developing and implementing early-warning systems present a major stumbling block. Getting the users involved on the ground level reduces the salability problem, but usually results in a basic one-variable-at-a-time approach with some arbitrary weighting scheme, which in most instances is inferior to a multivariate approach. A basic dilemma exists in which tradeoffs and political considerations must be weighed carefully.

Future FDIC early-warning research should focus upon several broad areas. First, although the on-site examination is still the cornerstone of the bank supervisory process, its focus should be redirected toward overall portfolio behavior and performance and away from asset quality and capital adequacy. Second, since the greatest risk to the financial system and the FDIC insurance fund comes from the largest banks, they are the institutions to be watched closely. Moreover, the giant banks must be evaluated in terms of their holding-company structures and not in isolation. Finally, since some form of misconduct has been the major cause of bank failures, alternative ways of uncovering and dealing with these irregularities should be addressed.

FEDERAL RESERVE BANK OF NEW YORK STUDIES

Introduction: Martin (1977)

This section focuses upon the most recent and what appears to be the "best" of the studies completed at the Federal Reserve Bank of New York (FRBNY), namely Martin's (1977) "Early Warning of Bank Failure: A Logit Regression Approach." Referring to Martin's paper as the "best" should not detract from the contributions made by Stuhr and Van Wicklen (1974), Korobow and Stuhr (1975), or Korobow, Stuhr, and Martin (1976 and 1977). In any ongoing research such as the FRBNY's early-warning project, the latest output benefits from the accomplishments and mistakes of the previous researchers—a fact that we are sure Martin would be the first to acknowledge.

Martin's approach differs from the previous FRBNY's studies in two important ways. First, Martin employs the failure concept (broadly defined) in his analysis, as opposed to the concepts of "resistant" and "vulnerable" (for defining group membership) used in the previous studies. And second, Martin uses a logit regression model as opposed to MDA or arctangent regression.

Definition of Failure. Martin defines failure as the occurrence of (1) negative net worth, (2) supervisory merger, or (3) an emergency measure to resolve an imminent failure situation. To identify failure, Martin scrutinizes publicly available sources such as merger decisions of the Federal banking agencies, newspaper articles, and balance sheets (for banks whose net worth declined significantly within a year). Martin conjectures that his method of identifying failure probably understates the true occurrence of failure since emergency financial rescues and the motivations for mergers frequently are kept secret.

Sample Banks. Martin identified 58 Federal Reserve Member banks that "failed" between 1970 and 1976. These firms constituted Martin's failed-bank group. Since only 12 member banks were declared insolvent by their respective chartering authorities during this period, 46 (79.31 percent) of Martin's failed banks were "noninsolvency" failures.

By restricting his failed-bank group to member banks only, Martin precluded 42 insured nonmember banks (that were declared insolvent by their state banking commissions during the period 1970–1976) from membership in his failed-bank sample. Except for his FRBNY affiliation, one must conjecture why Martin eliminated these banks from his analysis. Because the failure rate for member banks is about one half of the failure rate for nonmember banks, it would seem that Martin passed up a chance to investigate some interesting questions. For example, is the higher failure rate for nonmember banks due to their smaller size? Or, does membership in the Federal Reserve system promote greater "safety and soundness" and hence fewer failures? If the latter is true, then perhaps Federal Reserve membership should be mandatory; alternatively, for those who think that the bank-failure rate is too low, nonmembership should be mandatory.

Martin's nonfailed group consisted of the population of nonfailed member banks. Apparently, Martin did not allow for any start-up experience, as Sinkey did in some of his FDIC experiments, and lumped newly chartered banks in with more mature ones.

Data and Variables. Martin's independent variables are selected from a set of 25 financial ratios from the FRBNY's data base for research on bank-surveillance programs. Variables are selected because of their usefulness in previous early-warning studies and are grouped into four broad categories: (1) asset risk, (2) liquidity, (3) capital adequacy, and (4) earnings.

Martin's Logit Model. Since logit analysis and its relationship to various other classification techniques are discussed in Chapter I, only a brief summary of Martin's logit model is presented here.

Assuming a logistic functional form, Martin expresses his logit model as

$$\Pr(Y_i = 1) = P_i = \frac{1}{1 + e^{-W_i}} \quad i = 1,2,\ldots,N \tag{8.1}$$

where $W_i = b_0 + \Sigma_{j=1}^{M} b_j x_{ij}$ is a linear combination of the independent variables with the b's estimated from the data. The dependent variable Y_i equals one for a failed bank and zero for a nonfailed bank. The probability that $Y_i = 1$ is a function of the observed data (the x_{ij}), the estimated coefficients (the b's), and the assumed logistic functional form. W can be viewed as an index of a bank's propensity to fail; the higher the value of W_i, the higher the probability of failure for the ith bank.

Martin postulates that a bank can be viewed as having a "tolerance for vulnerability" (or failure), call it $\bar{W}_i$. If $W_i \geq \bar{W}_i$, the bank fails; otherwise, it does not fail. $\bar{W}_i$ is, of course, unobservable and only known *ex post.* It is a function of excluded variables such as the "true" quality of a bank's loan portfolio; attitudes and prejudices of regulators, uninsured depositors, major stockholders, etc.; and purely random events.

On an *ex ante* basis and assuming W is a random variable with a cumulative distribution function, $G(W)$, the probability of failure is:

$$\Pr(Y_i = 1) = \Pr(W_i \geq \bar{W}_i) = \Pr(\bar{W}_i \leq W_i) = G(W_i) \tag{8.2}$$

According to Martin, Eq. (8.2) does not by itself determine the *a priori* probability of failure, since that probability is equal to $G(W^*)$, where W^* is the sample mean of W and where W^* can be set at any level by adjusting the constant term.

If $G(W)$ is the cumulative normal distribution, the estimation of the coefficients of W_i is known as *probit* analysis. If $G(W)$ is the logistic distribution (an approximation of the normal distribution), the estimation is known as logit analysis. Thus, the basic equation of the logit model, Eq. (8.1), can be rewritten as

$$\Pr(Y_i = 1) = G(W_i) = \frac{1}{1 + e^{-W_i}}. \tag{8.3}$$

If the data from each group arise from multivariate normal populations with equal (sample) covariance matrices, then, in this special case, the logit model reduces to the linear discriminant function.

In nontechnical language, the purpose of Martin's logit analysis is to generate a set of probability estimates such that failed banks are assigned high *ex ante* probabilities of failure and nonfailed banks are assigned low probabilities. A "good fit" is a set of estimated coefficients that approximates this objective. To fit his logit model, Martin uses the maximum-likelihood estimation technique. In general, the solution is obtained using an iterative procedure in which an initial set of coefficients is converged to the maximum-likelihood solution. For computational purposes and for convenience in applying tests of significance, Martin restates the likelihood problem as the equivalent one of minimizing -2 log likelihood:

$$-2 \ln L(Y,B) = -2 \sum_{i=1}^{N} [Y_i \ln P_i + (1 - Y_i) \ln(1 - P_i)]. \qquad (8.4)$$

The logit estimates are compared with the null hypothesis that all banks have equal probability of failure equal to N_1/N, where N_1 = number of failures and N = population.

Empirical Findings. Martin's logit-regression models are estimated for various periods between 1970–1976 and with various combinations of financial ratios as independent variables. In this section, the focus is upon Martin's "best" model. To determine his "best" model, Martin uses an *Information Criterion* (IC) which is equal to -2 log likelihood (for the estimated model) plus two times the number of coefficients. Since Martin's null hypothesis is stated in the form of equal to or less than, the model with the *minimum* IC is judged "best," provided the signs of the estimated regression coefficients conform with *a priori* expectations.

Martin's "best" model is a four-variable one with an IC = 166.99. This model is estimated using 1974 data to construct the independent variables and 1975–1976 failures and nonfailures to determine the dependent variables. There are 5598 observations consisting of 23 failed banks and 5575 nonfailed banks. The estimated linear combination W is:

$$\begin{aligned} W = \; & -5.33 - 120.86X_1 + 2.20X_2 + 7.89X_3 - 33.63X_4 \\ & (1.00) \quad (1.00) \qquad (.99) \qquad (1.00) \qquad (1.00) \end{aligned}$$

The figures in parentheses are significance levels and the independent variables are

X_1 = Net Income/Total Assets
X_2 = Gross Charge-Offs/Net Operating Income
X_3 = Commercial Loans/Total Loans
X_4 = Gross Capital/Risk Assets

The *ith bank's probability of failure* is calculated using Eq. (8.3) and a model's -2 log likelihood is calculated using Eq. (8.4). For example, the null hypothesis of -2 log likelihood is

$$-2 \ln L(N_1/N) = -2[23 \ln N_1/N + 5575 \ln(1 - N_1/N)].$$

With $N_1 = 23$ and $N = 5598$, the null-hypothesis critical value is 298.66. If an estimated model's -2 log likelihood is equal to or less than 298.66, then the null hypothesis that all member banks have equal probability of failure of .0041 (= 23/5598) is rejected. Martin's four-variable logit model had a -2 log likelihood = 156.99. In contrast, the corresponding linear and quadratic MDA models had -2 log likelihood values equal to 699.88 and 698.38, respectively. In other words, the logit model rejects the equal probability-of-failure hypothesis, whereas the two MDA models accept it. Alternatively, the discriminant functions are rejected as probability estimates.

Whereas the logit and discriminant functions Martin estimated are different with respect to their acceptability as probability estimates, their classification accuracies are almost identical. The accuracy rates for the logit, linear MDA, and quadratic MDA models for failed and nonfailed banks are (91.3 and 91.1 percent), (82.6 and 96.2 percent), and (91.3 and 92.0 percent), respectively. Because the hypothesis of equal covariance matrices is rejected, the quadratic MDA results are preferred over the linear ones and technically (by 0.9 percent) they are preferred over the logit results.

As Martin points out, the relative merits of logit versus MDA would appear to depend upon the intended use of the results. If simple dichotomization into "examine *now*" and "examine *later*" is the goal, either approach would appear to be appropriate. However, if finer distinctions are desired (e.g., setting deposit-insurance premiums, determining federal-funds or large CD risk premiums), then logit analysis, because of the *quality* of its probability estimates, would be preferred.

A very important aspect of any type of early-warning system is the *lead time* given by the alarm mechanism. Martin's 1974 logit model correctly predicted 20 out of 23 1975–1976 member-bank failures. Of these 23 failures, only 6 of them were explicitly recognized as failures (i.e., declarations of insolvency by the banking authorities). These declarations were made on the following dates: (1) January 3, 1975, (2) July 12, 1975, (3) October 21, 1975, (4) February 16, 1976, (5) June 25, 1976, and (6) September 15, 1976. Assuming that the data for the logit model would have been available by March 31, 1975 and assuming that the six insolvencies were flagged by the model, the lead times ranged from a negative 3 months to 18 months, with five of the six lead times greater than zero.

How much lead time do the banking authorities need to prevent failure or to minimize adverse externalities? The *examination* lead times for Franklin and USNB were roughly 6 months and 13 months, respectively. Both of these banks subsequently failed. However, neither failure jeopardized the "safety and soundness" of the banking system, although Franklin's collapse generated more adverse publicity and uneasiness than USNB's downfall. In contrast, from the FDIC's perspective, since USNB's failure cost the FDIC about $150 million whereas Franklin's demise was a zero-loss failure, USNB's outcome was very *unsatisfactory* whereas Franklin's closing was *satisfactory*.

To diffuse potential adverse effects, common sense suggests that a large, money-market bank will require greater lead time than any other type of bank. The banking authorities can prevent *any* bank from failing if they want to spend the time and resources (e.g., the bail out of First Pennsylvania Bank in 1980). However, except to prevent a full-scale financial panic, this is not an appropriate goal for bank supervision and normally the banking authorities avoid such operations.

Alternative Models. Martin tested various models using data as of period t and failures from periods $t + 1$ and $t + 2$, $t = 1969, 1970, \ldots, 1974$. He did not test lead times greater than 2 years. There were significant differences in the overall quality of the estimated logit equations with the earlier years clearly inferior to the later ones. Martin interprets the stronger relationship between failure and financial ratios in the later years as mainly due to the 1973–1974 recession and the accompanying asset-quality problems, especially the increase in loan losses relative to earnings and capital.

Martin's Conclusions. Martin states two major conclusions. First, the importance of financial data for measuring the "safety and soundness" of individual banks will vary with the business cycle. The implication for early-warning research is that systems developed during recessionary periods (such as 1974–1976) will tend to overpredict failure in future nonrecessionary periods and vice versa. And second, in contrast with the studies of bank failure in the 1930s, the "adequacy" of a bank's capital is found to have a significant relationship with the incidence of failure. Martin suggests that a reinvestigation of the failures of the 1930s on a multivariate basis might show that a higher capital ratio made banks less likely to fail. On the other hand, he suggests that such ratio tests may be ineffective during periods of *extreme* financial crisis, implying that early-warning models would be of limited usefulness during such periods.

Critique. Martin's paper makes significant contributions in three areas. First, in the area of early-warning research, he catalogs and explains various types of early-warning models (e.g., failure-prediction, problem-prediction, and outlier or peer-group models). Second, in the statistical area, Martin shows the relationship between logit analysis and MDA and presents an example of logit analysis applied to Federal

Reserve member banks that failed between 1970 and 1976. And third, in the banking area, Martin's empirical tests suggest, in contrast to some earlier bank-failure studies, that bank capital is an important explanatory variable in failure models, especially during recessionary periods such as 1974–1976.

The criticisms of Martin's paper are relatively minor and some of them already have been anticipated in his qualifying remarks. One criticism, however, which Martin acknowledges, deserves mention, that is, the small number of banks in his failed-bank group for the years 1969–1972 (i.e., 12, 12, 10, and 13, respectively). Martin's empirical results improve as the U. S. economy deteriorates, but at the same time his *sample of failed banks increases.* Martin bemoans his small sample sizes as "a fortunate fact from a real-world point of view, however inconvenient for statistical work." With a wider view of the real world to include insured *nonmember* bank failures (for which data are readily available), Martin could have easily increased the size of his samples (to 24, 18, 14, and 19 for the suspect years 1969–1972, respectively, and to 31 and 46 for the nonsuspect years 1973 and 1974) and removed some of the question of the reliability of his estimates. According to Martin, Jones (1975) contends that a sample size of about 15 in the smallest group seems to be the minimum required. By including nonmember banks, Martin's samples would have passed Jones' test. In addition, he could have investigated the interesting question of why the nonmember-bank failure rate is higher than the member-bank failure rate.

THE NATIONAL BANK SURVEILLANCE SYSTEM

Introduction

The National Bank Surveillance System (NBSS) (see Haskins & Sells, 1975 and Mullin, 1977) does not contain any sort of statistical classification model, which, of course, is the focus of this book. However, it is an early-warning system designed to "alert it [the Office of the Comptroller of the Currency (OCC)] on a more timely basis to deteriorating conditions in individual banks or in the national banking system as a whole."[9] Accordingly, a review of what NBSS is and how it operates is appropriate.

The Components of NBSS

NBSS consists of four basic components: (1) a data-collection system; (2) a computed-based monitoring system designed to identify unusual or significant changes or circumstances within a bank or within the national banking system; (3) an evaluation and analysis by experienced personnel (NBSS specialists) of the impact of the symptoms (identified by the computer in step 2) on bank soundness; and (4) a review process to provide administrative controls over all proposed OCC remedial actions by either a regional or Washington office. *The NBSS Bank Performance Report: A Users Guide for Bankers and Examiners* (September, 1977) refers to the four components of NBSS as

1. A computer based data collection and calculation system
2. An Anomaly Severity Ranking System (ASRS)
3. An Evaluation by an NBSS Specialist
4. An Action Control System

The second component of NBSS is the outlier or peer-group model part of the system and thus we will focus upon it. The first component of NBSS provides the data, the second component provides a screening mechanism, and the third and fourth components provide evaluation and review, respectively.

The NBSS Outlier or Peer-Group Approach

The important elements of the NBSS monitoring system are the key indicators, the peer groups, and the action-oriented reports. Key-indicator statistics (ratios and trends) are used to make time-series, cross-section (or peer-group), and combined time-series–cross-section comparisons. Banks whose statistics either fall outside acceptable ranges or vary significantly within acceptable ranges receive action-oriented reports.

The Key Indicators. Haskins & Sells and OCC personnel jointly developed a set of key indicators, which they contend are *leading* indicators of potential banking problems. Data from the years 1968 through 1974 were used to establish the key indicators. The test group consisted of banks with assets between $100 million and $500 million. According to Mullin (1977:51), this group was selected as a test base because it was "relatively clean," i.e., not characterized by the sharp seasonal swings of smaller banks or the foreign activities of larger banks.

Since the financial difficulties of a large bank (over $500 million) can have a significant impact on public confidence in the banking system and since these banks tend to engage in activities (e.g., extensive foreign-exchange trading or heavy reliance on purchased funds such as CDs, federal funds, or Eurodollars) that can lead to a rapid deterioration in a bank's soundness, NBSS includes a special emphasis on monitoring the performance of banks with assets in excess of $500 million.

The Haskins & Sells report recommends 22 indicators for initial adoption by the OCC to apply to *all* national banks. The indicators are designed to measure the performance of both banking departments *and* trust departments. The banking-department indicators focus upon the financial condition, results of operations, and the quality of management whereas the trust-department indicators focus upon the quality of account administration and the results of operations. The 22 indicators are

I. Banking Departments

A. Financial Condition

1. Nonincome-Producing Loans.
2. Ratio of Loans to Adjusted Capital Funds.
3. Volume of Key Earning Assets.
4. Indirect Loans, including Loans to Affiliates.
5. Ratio of Discounted Loans to Unearned Income.
6. Borrowed Funds.
7. Foreign Deposits.
8. Deposit Mix.

B. Results of Operations

9. Net Interest Earnings.
10. Sources of Total Revenues.
11. Other Revenues.
12. Provision for Loan Losses.
13. Interest Paid on Out-of-Area Deposits.
14. Other Operating Expenses.
15. Return on Total Assets.

C. Quality of Management

16. High-Risk, Middle-Management Experience.
17. Audit Expenditures.
18. Banking-Department Salaries.

II. Trust Departments

D. Quality of Account Administration

19. Number of Active Accounts Administered per Trust Officer.
20. Trust Personnel Experience.
21. Trust-Department Salaries.

E. Results of Operations

22. Trust Income.

The large-bank key indicators (17) suggested by Haskins & Sells are

I. Banking Departments

A. Financial Condition

1. Asset Growth Rate.
2. Unrealized Losses in Investment Portfolio.
3. Level of Out-of-Area Loans or Deposits.
4. Portfolio Concentrations.
5. Ratings of Capital Notes or Other Indebtedness.

B. Results of Operations

6. Yield from Securities Portfolios.
7. Charge-Offs of Loans to Particular Industries.
8. Losses on Securities Transactions.

C. Quality of Management

9. Recovery of Charge-Offs.
10. Loans per Credit Officer.
11. Violations of Laws and Regulations.
12. Consumer Complaints.

D. Other

13. Stock-Price Fluctuations.
14. Debt of Affiliates.
15. Number of Internal Auditors.

II. Trust Departments

E. Quality of Account Administration

16. Number of Debt and Equity Issues Held per Decision-Making Employee.
17. Legal Suits.

It should be noted that Haskins & Sells do not regard any of these indicators as "absolutes." That is, as new and better indicators are developed or as changing conditions in the banking industry require new indicators, they should be submitted into the system. Haskins & Sells tried to design NBSS with such substitutions in mind.

Peer Groups. Given the key indicators, a bank's performance should be compared with that of its peers, i.e., banks with similar characteristics. In selecting peer groups for *banks,* some of the factors Haskins & Sells considered are (1) competitive environment; (2) branching status; (3) types of services offered; (4) types of lending performed; (5) geographic distribution; and (6) size.

Regarding peer groups for *trust* departments, size, as measured by the market value of assets held in trust, was considered the most important factor. Accordingly, trust departments simply are classified as small, medium, or large.

The banking-department peer groups that Haskins & Sells considered most relevant for NBSS are

Peer-Group Description	*Approximate Number of National Banks*
Banks with total assets greater than $1 million	55
Banks with total assets of $500 million to $1 billion	60
Banks with total assets of $100 million to $500 million:	
In states permitting branch banking	200
In states that do not permit branch banking	150
Banks with total assets of $25 million to $100 million:	
Banks with principal offices in an SMSA:	
In states that permit branch banking	200
In states that do not permit branch banking	400
Banks with principal offices outside an SMSA:	
In states that permit branch banking	200
In states that do not permit branch banking	500
Banks with assets of less than $25 million:	
Banks with principal offices in an SMSA:	
In states that permit branch banking	200
In states that do not permit branch banking	400
Banks with principal offices outside an SMSA:	
In states that permit branch banking	300
In states that do not permit branch banking	2000
Total Banks	4665

Similar to the key indicators, Haskins & Sells regard their peer-group structure not as a rigid classification scheme but as a flexible system to be modified by experience and changing banking conditions.

Action-Oriented Reports. According to Mullin (1977:53–55), NBSS produces (among others) three important computerized reports: (1) a fifteen-page performance report based upon a bank's financial statements for the past 5 years; (2) an "anomaly-severity ranking" that singles out atypical banks (on the basis of the key indicators) for attention by NBSS specialists; and (3) an "action-control system" that records and monitors the results of all segments of NBSS. These reports are analyzed by NBSS specialists, whose primary task is to convert the computerized output into a form that will help bank managers make decisions and correct deficiencies before they become serious problems. The performance and anomaly-severity reports are by-products of the peer-group analyses, whereas the action-control report gives an overview of NBSS operations.

The NBSS performance report focuses upon a bank's ratios, percentages, and percentiles relative to the bank's peer group. The NBSS specialists or analysts are suppose to look for atypical percentile rankings, short-term changes, and long-term trends that may be *leading* indicators of impending financial difficulties. The NBSS specialists are not expected to make "judgments" on their findings, but simply to report them and request an investigation of the observed phenomena.

The purpose of the (quarterly) anomaly-severity report is to determine which banks should be given a priority review. Key leading indicators are employed in these reports. With respect to each indicator, the focus is upon the bank's current position, short-term changes, and long-term trends. Each leading indicator is ranked and then all of the rankings are added together to determine a bank's total score relative to its peers. Thus, a bank receives individual relative scores with respect to factors such as profitability and growth and an overall relative score.

Summary and Conclusions

According to Mullin (1977:55), NBSS, although still an infant system, has been successful in its initial applications because of the interaction of personnel, computer, and attitudes. The system combines surveillance, control, and remedial action into one integrated unit. Moreover, NBSS is viewed as being flexible enough to adjust to changing conditions in the banking industry. Finally, NBSS also is considered to be a service instrument since its data (in summary form) is available on a quarterly basis to national bankers.

Critique

From the MDA, arctangent, or logit "scientist's" point of view, NBSS is a high-priced (over $3 million was paid to Haskins & Sells), quick-and-dirty attempt to build an early-warning system. The system was implemented in a relatively short time because (1) it was imposed from the top down (i.e., Comptroller Smith committed himself to a functional reorganization of the office and NBSS was one of the newly created functions); (2) big money was spent on the reorganization, making it difficult not to accept any of the reform proposals; and (3) the future users of NBSS had a voice in its construction, eliminating the possibility of an esoteric, statistical system being developed.

NBSS's " dirtiness" can be viewed in light of Guttentag's (1977:58) criticism of the statistical outlier approach. He sees three major weaknesses. First, the statistical indicators frequently are chosen on the basis of informed judgment instead of empirical testing. Second, because the indicators are measured relative to peer groups, the outlier technique provides little information about the vulnerability of the banking system as a whole.[10] And third, the outlier approach is inadequate for identifying the problems of multibillion dollar banks. Because of the great diversity of giant banks, Guttentag contends that statistical comparisons of specific activities have limited value, because, relative to its peers, every large bank is bound to be atypical in some area. Whether or not these large banks are so characterized is, of course, an empirical question, one that Guttentag does not answer. Guttentag believes that none of the proposed early-warning systems are capable of dealing effectively with the giant banks. His solution is to build a custom-fitted, simulation model for each multibillion dollar bank. Then, for various economic environments, each bank's financial statements could be simulated and its soundness or vulnerability evaluated. Emphasis would be placed upon a bank's net-worth position under "worst-case" circumstances.

NBSS, despite its shortcomings, is an operational system that apparently has satisfied its users. In fact, former Comptroller Smith was so pleased with the system that he proclaimed that his office could prevent national banks from failing—*except in extreme circumstances.* However, because failure rarely occurs except in extreme situations, this statement has little meaning.

FEDERAL RESERVE STUDIES

Hanweck (1977a,b) literature review

The Board of Governors of the Federal Reserve System was the last of the federal banking agencies to hop on the early-warning/surveillance bandwagon. In two separate studies (both in 1977), Hanweck attempted to develop (1) a simulation model for identifying and monitoring problem banks and (2) a failure-prediction model for commercial banks.

The Simulation Model

This model employs a "statement-projection approach" with behavioral yield-adjustment elasticities specified for the bank to guide its portfolio adjustment as relative yields change. The purpose of the model is to provide a tool for identifying problem situations *and* a tool for analyzing alternative remedial policies to improve the situation.

Balance-sheet, income-expense, and equity-loan loss reserve adjustment algorithms form the kernel of the model. To illustrate, for the ith balance-sheet item (excluding equity capital) in period t, $X(i,t)$, the typical equation is

$$X(i,t) = X(i,t-1)\,(1 + \sum_{j=1}^{n} E(i,j)GRI(j,t))GR(i,t) \qquad (8.5)$$

where

$E(i,j)$ = the interest-rate elasticity of the ith balance-sheet item with the jth item. (The summation of the $E(i,j)$ for all i is constrained to be zero.)

$GRI(j,t)$ = the projected proportional change in interest rate j from $t-1$ to t.

$GR(i,t)$ = the projected proportional change in the ith balance-sheet item in the absence of any interest-rate change from $t-1$ to t.

Employing alternative scenarios with respect to interest rates, loan-loss performance, and economic growth, Hanweck focuses upon the effects of these simulation scenarios on the "capital adequacy and soundness" of a large money-center bank. The model is run for two annual periods and the following ratios analyzed:

1. Capital-to-assets
2. Loans-to-capital
3. Net income-to-assets
4. Loan-loss provision-to-net income
5. Required new equity-to-net income

Even under the worst-case scenario (constructed to characterize the early to mid-1974 period), the bank does not at anytime reach a state of failure (e.g., at the end of the second period capital-to-assets = 4.5 percent and net income-to-assets = 0.51 percent). These artificially generated findings are consistent with the recent failure experience of large banks, that is, it takes widespread misconduct (e.g., USNB) and/or gross and pervasive mismanagement (e.g., Franklin) for a billion-dollar bank to fail.

Hanweck contends, a la Guttentag (1975), that simulation models can be useful to both analysts and examiners in formulating bank monitoring policies. However, since the simulation approach has yet to be tested under real world circumstances, its true usefulness is not known.

The Failure-Prediction Model

The purpose of Hanweck's failure-prediction study is to provide an empirical analysis of recent (1973 to 1976) bank failures to serve as a foundation for a successful bank "screening" program. A failed bank is defined as one that was either closed by the chartering authority or merged for recognized financial difficulties. The failed group consists of 20 banks and a holdout sample of 12 banks to test the model's predictability. The nonfailed group consists of a random sample of 177 banks in continuous operation from December 31, 1971 to October 21, 1976. Publicly available Reports of Condition and Income for 1 and 2 years before failure for the failed group and for the year 1974 for the nonfailed group comprise the data base. Confidential bank-examination data are not analyzed.

Hanweck's model, which is stated in terms of the probability of failure in period t, $PF(t)$, can be summarized as

$$PF(t) = f[\overset{(-)}{NOA(t-1)}, \overset{(-)}{KA(t-1)}, \overset{(+)}{\Delta NOA(t-1)/NOA(t-2)}, \overset{(+)}{\Delta A(t-1)/A(t}, \overset{(+)}{LK(t-1)}, \overset{(-)}{LNA(t-1)}] \tag{8.6}$$

where

$$\begin{aligned} NOA &= \text{ratio of net operating income to assets} \\ KA &= \text{capital-to-asset ratio (book value)} \\ \Delta NOA/NOA &= \text{rate of change of } NOA \\ \Delta A/A &= \text{rate of change of total assets (book value)} \\ LK &= \text{loan-to-capital ratio (book value)} \\ LNA &= \text{natural logarithm (base } e\text{) of total assets (book value)} \\ t &= \text{time} \end{aligned}$$

The signs above the variables indicate the expected relationship between an independent variable and the probability of failure. For example, the greater the rate of change of NOA (a proxy for the variance of income), the greater the probability of failure. The group means and t-statistics for this model are presented in Table VIII.9.

To determine the separate influence of the independent variables and to establish a classification equation, Hanweck uses multivariate probit analysis. The estimated probit function is presented in Table VIII.10. Only *NOA* and *LK* are statistically significant in this multiple-variable test. To test the classification power of his model, Hanweck employs 12 banks (withheld from the original sample) that failed in 1976 and the 177 nonfailed banks. For both groups, 1975 data are used. Eight of the 12 failed banks and 176 of the 177 nonfailed banks are classified correctly; an overall accuracy of 97 percent with a Type I error of 33 percent. Hanweck considered the performance of the estimated probit function to be "remarkable" and of potential use in early-warning applications. While the Type I error is less than re-

Table VIII.9. Hanweck's Group Means and *t*-Statistics One Year Before Failure

Variable	*Means* Nonfailed Group (177 banks)	Failed Group (20 banks)	*t-Statistics*
NOA	.0124	−.0122	−7.85**
KA	.0862	.0728	−2.49**
ΔNOA/NOA	.1863	−8.4406	−4.43**
ΔA/A	.4605	−.0071	−1.20
LK	6.2284	13.9850	4.12**
LNA	9.6947	10.1430	1.67*

*Indicates significance at the 5 percent level.
**Indicates significance at the 1 percent level or smaller. Data for the nonfailed group are for 1973 and 1974, whereas data for the failed group are 1 and 2 years before failure, for failures from 1973 to 1975.
Source: Hanweck (1977a, Table 1, p. 15).

markable, Hanweck's findings are similar to those obtained by Martin (1977) and Sinkey (1979).

OTHER STUDIES

Introduction

This chapter concludes with (1) another look at the probability of failure for commercial banks; (2) a screening technique to detect potential bank failure using accounting and market data; (3) a savings-and-loan, performance-prediction model; and (4) an early-warning

Table VIII.10. Hanweck's Estimated Probit Function

Variable	*Estimated Coefficient*	*Estimated Standard Error*
Constant Term	−4.1326*	2.0319
NOA	−69.4948**	17.8184
KA	14.8583	10.6791
ΔNOA/NOA	−.0109	.0962
ΔA/A	−1.1835	.7381
LK	.2640**	.1099
LNA	.0246	.1318

*Indicates significance at the 5 percent level.
**Indicates significance at the 1 percent level or smaller. The test statistic for the goodness of fit of the probit function (approximately distributed as a chi square) was highly significant with a value of 62.57 (6 degrees of freedom).
Source: Hanweck (1977a, Table 2, p. 17).

model for over-the-counter broker-dealers. The last two papers, by Altman (1975) and Altman and Lorris (1976), are similar in approach to Altman's bankruptcy studies. Thus, they are analyzed because of their unique applications and not because of any new methodology or statistical technique (MDA). The commercial-bank paper, by Santomero and Vinso (1977), examines the cross-section riskiness of the banking structure and its sensitivity to variations in bank capital. Santomero and Vinso develop a "problem-bank" screen to be used as a first approximation for identifying outlier banks. The market-data papers by Pettway (1980), Shick (1980), and Pettway and Sinkey (1980), focus upon the efficiency of bank capital markets and a screening technique using accounting *and* market information.

Santomero and Vinso (1977)

Santomero and Vinso's (S&V's) paper focuses upon estimating the *cross-section riskiness* of the present banking structure and its sensitivity to variations in bank capital. To attack these two issues, S&V first develop a theoretical framework for evaluating cross-section risk (i.e., probability of failure) in the banking system. This model is estimated using a sample of 224 weekly reporting Federal Reserve banks for the period February, 1965 to January, 1974. Next, they analyze the sensitivity of the probability distribution to changes in the capital account. Finally, S&V develop a screening mechanism to flag potential "problem banks."

Theoretical Framework. S&V's theoretical foundation is similar to Wilcox's adaptation of the classical ruin problem to measure risk (presented in the previous chapter). S&V focus upon a bank's total capital account (Wilcox's net liquidation value) and the factors that cause it to fluctuate. Bank capital, which is perceived as a stochastic time series that must be specified, is the pool of resources available to prevent a bank's ruin.[11] As the bank operates, additions to and subtractions from its capital account occur. Because the size of the capital account depends upon the number and size of these changes, the value of the account can be viewed as a stochastic process involving changes of random size. Given this stochastic process, two time-series techniques, first-passage time (or expected time to ruin) and maximum-risk exposure, are used to estimate the risk or failure exposure of the commercial-banking industry.

Failure is defined as $\Pr(K_t < 0)$, where K = bank capital and $K_t = K_0 + \Delta K_t$. The focus is upon the risk or probability that $K_t = (K_0 + \Delta K_t) < 0$, the probability of failure. Alternatively, the probability of failure can be expressed as $\Pr(\Delta K_t < -K_0)$.

Some complicated and tedious manipulations (not presented here) are required to arrive at S&V's final expression for the probability of failure and at their so-called "safety index at the riskiest time." The latter is a function of the initial capital endowment, K_0, the moments of the change-size distribution, (assumed to be stationary), and the expected-change arrival rate.[12] (S&V determine the change-size distribution using first differences of the capital accounts.) Given their safety index [see their Eq. (11)], a value for the probability of failure at the riskiest point can be derived from the tables for the standard normal distribution.

Capital-Account Data. To test their model, S&V need information on the variability of the capital account. The data are obtained from the Weekly Report of Condition (Form 416) supplied to the Federal Reserve System by a sample of member banks. The pool of resources (or buffer stock) to prevent failure is defined as total capital accounts (including both debt and equity capital) plus reserves for bad debt and security losses. The weekly data (from February, 1965 to January, 1974) are transformed into monthly averages and first differences taken to generate the changes in the capital account. The data are available for 224 member banks.

In determining the moments of the change-size distribution, S&V exclude any positive change size greater than 10 percent of total capital. They contend that such large changes probably are due to mergers or infusions of external capital and hence not representative of capital variations due to ordinary banking business.

Depending upon the sample autocorrelations for each bank, an appropriate model for that series is determined. The results of the Box and Jenkins fitting process indicate that the change size for most of the banks followed a random walk (or white-noise series).[13] The parameters of the fitted model are used to determine the mean of the change-size distribution whereas the other moments are derived from the moments of the residual distribution. These moments then are used to determine the risk of failure for a given bank at the riskiest point in that bank's expected, future time path.

Empirical Findings. Each bank's "safety index" is calculated using K_0 (capital + reserves) as of January, 1974 and the moments of the change-size distribution. The risk exposure of the entire banking system is found by aggregating the results for the individual banks. The kernel of S&V's stochastic-process approach is a frequency distribution of the safety index. Individual banks fall into this distribution based upon their relative riskiness—the lower the safety index, the greater the relative risk.

The distribution of safety-index values for S&V's 224 sample member banks is presented in Figure VIII.1. The distribution is approximately normal with a mean of 23.4 and a median of 16.6.[14] The safety index at its riskiest point (23.4) translates into a probability of capital inadequacy or failure for the *banking system* of 1×10^{-99}, a very low average risk exposure for the *system*. The occurrence of the riskiest point has a future median time of approximately 36 years for most banks. S&V interpret these results as indicating that, for most banks, capital is "quite large" and that expected capital changes and the variance of these changes are "so small" that there is little danger of capital inadequacy, or failure for the system. S&V's findings, of course, depend upon the historical nature of their 1965–1974 generating distribution, which they acknowledge. It would be interesting to know how the 1974–1977 distribution compares with the earlier one.

To promote bank "safety and soundness," bank regulators traditionally have argued for more bank capital. In contrast, free marketeers such as Vojta (1973) contend that the market should decide whether or not a bank's capital is "adequate," implicitly implying that less stringent capital standards are needed. To test these alternative capital strategies, S&V assess the impact of changes in capital upon the distribution of the safety index. Their findings for various initial capital accounts are presented in Table VIII.11.

Regarding increases in bank capital (cases 2–5 in Table VIII.11), S&V conclude that such increases have a negligible impact on the safety

Figure VIII.1. The Distribution of S&V's Safety Index

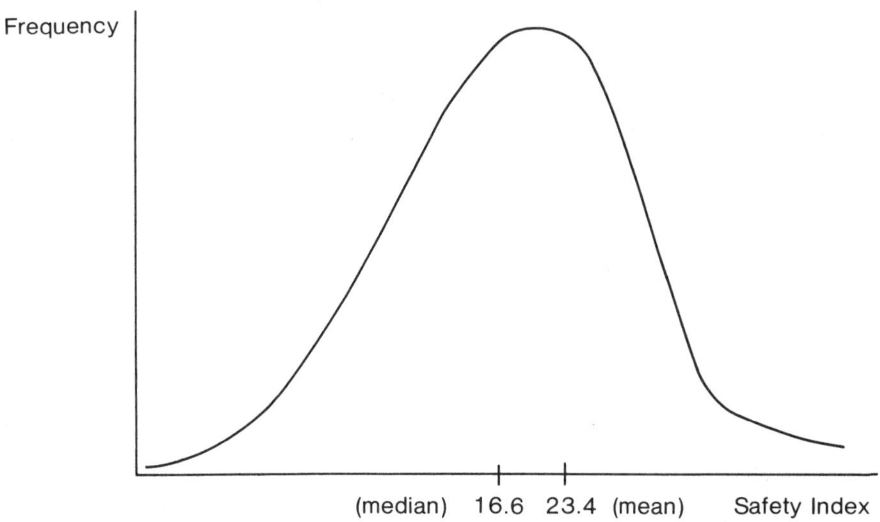

Table VIII.11. Bank Capital: More or Less?

Initial Capital Account	*Safety Index* *Mean*	*Median*
1. Original Capital, K_0	23.4	16.6
2. K_0 + \$1,000,000	23.7	16.7
3. K_0 + .01 Assets	24.8	17.7
4. Max (K_0, .06 Assets)	23.4	16.6
5. Max (K_0, .10 Assets)	26.2	19.8
6. K_0 − \$1,000,000	23.2	16.5
7. K_0 − .01 Assets	21.9	15.3

Source: Santomero and Vinso, (1977, Table 2, p. 198).

index. In addition, arbitrarily defining banks with a safety index less than 11.0 as risky or problem banks, S&V find very little movement between the groups as capital is increased. For example, in case 5 with capital equal to the maximum of K_0 or 10 percent of assets (the most stringent of the capital requirements tested), only eight banks (3.6 percent of the sample of 244) move from the problem to the nonproblem group as a result of the increase.[15] Moreover, the eight banks that shift to the nonproblem group barely exceed the critical value of 11.0.

Regarding less stringent capital requirements (cases 6 and 7 in Table VIII.11), S&V find that decreases in capital have little impact on risk and that, for the entire safety-index distribution, the findings are symmetrical with those for increases in capital. while the impact of less capital is negligible and symmetrical from a statistical point of view, an increase in the number of problem banks by approximately 2 percent of the population (case 7), or almost 300 banks, probably would be unacceptable to the banking authorities. This observation prompts S&V to examine the characteristics of *their* problem banks and to construct a problem-bank screen or early-warning mechanism.

A Problem-Bank Screen. S&V want to determine if their so-called problem banks (those to the left of the basic safety-index distribution in Figure VIII.1 are significantly different from the remaining sample banks. And, if they are, can an effective problem-bank screen be developed?

S&V have a dilemma, however. They have only one group of 224 banks, not two discrete and identifiable groups. *Any* dichotomization on their part has to be an *arbitrary, ad hoc procedure.* To divide their sample, S&V choose the first value of the safety index that results in over 30 banks in the "problem" group.[16] The cutoff value is 11.0, leading to 37 "problem" banks and 187 "nonproblem" banks.

These two groups are analyzed using the following five variables:[17]

1. The capital-asset ratio
2. Total assets
3. Total capital
4. The variance of the capital-jump size
5. The coefficient of variation for the jump size

The distribution of these five variables are computed for both groups and tested for differences. Only the capital-asset ratio and the coefficient of variation of the jump size are significantly different between the two groups. The groups means for these two variables are .076 versus .082 and 16.01 versus 1.86, respectively. S&V's so-called problem banks have significantly lower capital per dollar of assets and significantly higher variation in capital normalized for bank size.

Using the two significant variables, S&V develop the following discriminant-analysis screen:

$$Z = .0028(K/A) + .00158(CVJS), \tag{8.7}$$

where K/A = capital-asset ratio and $CVJS$ = coefficient of variation of the jump size. Equation (8.7) is found by varying the safety-index cutoff point and searching for the highest F-statistic associated with the screen. The cutoff point corresponding to Eq. (8.7) is 5.0, which results in a problem-bank group of only *ten* banks and a nonproblem-bank group of 214 banks.

Rather than let the data determine the *Z-score* cutoff value for reclassifying their sample, S&V use the following two alternative decision rules:

1. The Z-score associated with the least risky bank in the problem group is the critical value, Z_c. If $Z_i > Z_c$, assign to the problem group.
2. The Z-score associated with the first safe bank is the critical value. If $Z_i > Z_c$, assign to the problem group.

Rule 1 does not permit a Type I error to be made, whereas rule 2 does not permit a Type II error to be made. Using rule 1, the critical Z-score is .01197 and the Type II error is 2.8 percent (six banks). Using rule 2, the weaker decision rule, the critical Z-value is .02309 with a Type I error of 40 percent (four banks).[18] The range of Z-scores for the total sample is .26303 to .00307.

S&V interpret their problem-bank screen and the corresponding classification results as supporting the much-maligned, traditional capital-asset ratio as an important indicator of bank soundness. However, they caution that the variability of a bank's capital account is of equal importance. Both elements must be considered to obtain accurate classifications.

S&V Conclusions. Based upon 1965–1974 banking experience, S&V conclude that the banking *industry* is confronted with, on average, a very low probability of capital inadequacy. In addition, variations in bank capital appear to have little effect on this probability of failure. These conclusions, of course, do not apply to all banks on an individual basis. High-risk banks can be explained by their relatively low capital-asset ratios *and* by the variability of their capital accounts.

Critique. S&V's failure model can be described as an *a priori defined* approach.[19] That is, their model employs a measure of risk that is independent of actual bank failures or examiners' ratings of bank soundness. Failure risk is defined as zero or negative net worth. S&V estimate the probability of this event occurring using average monthly changes in capital for 224 *large* weekly reporting member banks for the period February, 1965 to January, 1974. Their average sample bank has total capital of *$137 million* and total assets of *$1761 million.* The typical commercial bank's *asset size* is significantly less than the total capital of S&V's average sample bank. Clearly, their sample is not representative of the population of U. S. commercial banks. In addition, their sample has been purged of any banks that did not report continuously over the period or that changed their identification number over the period.[20] Thus, S&V have a very "clean and stable" sample that excludes any outliers such as Franklin and USNB. It would seem that S&V have "stacked the deck" against finding a high probability of failure. S&V's empirical findings must be interpreted with these qualifications in mind. Moreover, the arbitrariness that S&V are forced to adopt to define their problem- and nonproblem-bank groups makes their early-warning device and related tests suspect. Finally, S&V contend that the traditional capital-asset ratio is important for determining bank soundness. Their problem-bank screen [Eq. (8.7)] implies that this ratio is positively related to membership in *their* problem-bank group.

Pettway (1980)

Pettway uses the so-called market model and a three-stage procedure to generate residuals (of actual return less expected return) for a small sample of failed banks with actively traded securities (see Table VIII.12). Stage one involves regressing the *weekly* holding period return for the Keefe Bank Index (see Table VIII.12) against the weekly yield on the S&P 500 Composite Index for the period preceding *each* bank's demise. In stage two, the estimated α_j and β_j for the jth bank (from the market model) are used to generate corresponding expected returns for the Keefe index. In stage three, the *actual* return on the ith failed bank less the *estimated* return on the Keefe index in the *same* period is calculated. To focus upon the timing of any changes in failure risk, the

Table VIII.12.
Pettway's Sample of Failed Banks

1. Franklin National Bank, N.Y.
2. United States National Bank, San Diego
3. Hamilton National Bank, Chattanooga
4. International City Bank & Trust, New Orleans
5. American City Bank & Trust, Milwaukee
6. Commonwealth Bank, Detroit[a]
7. Security National Bank, Long Island, N.Y.[b]

Keefe Bank Index
Bank or Bank Holding Company

1. Bankers Trust N. Y. Corp.
2. Charter New York Corp.
3. Chase Manhattan Corp.
4. Chemical New York Corp.
5. Citicorp
6. Manufacturers Hanover
7. J. P. Morgan & Co.
8. First National Boston Corp.
9. Mellon National Corp.
10. Philadelphia National Corp.
11. Continental Illinois Corp.
12. First Chicago Corp.
13. National Detroit Corp.
14. Northwest Bancorporation
15. Cleve Trust Corp.
16. National City Corp.
17. Wachovia Corporation
18. Citizens & Southern N.B.
19. First International Banc Shares
20. Valley National Bank
21. BankAmerica Corporation
22. Security Pacific Corporation
23. Wells Fargo & Company
24. Seafirst Corp.

[a]Received financial assistance from the FDIC on 1-18-72 and on 5-22-76.
[b]Emergency merger with Chemical Bank on 1-19-75.

residuals are averaged and cumulated. Three critical dates are analyzed: (1) the starting date of the examination that led to the bank being classified as a problem bank; (2) the date the bank was placed on the FDIC's problem-bank list; and (3) the bank's failure date. A pattern of negative cumulative residuals is interpreted as adverse information about the failed banks that did not affect the Keefe index.

Pettway finds that *both* the individual and cumulative average residuals indicate adverse information prior to each of the three critical dates.

He concludes that the market for banks with actively traded securities is efficient and that employing market returns for such banks could aid in identifying potential bankruptcy.

Shick and Sherman (1980)

One of the large-bank key indicators recommended to the OCC by Haskins & Sells is to monitor stock-price fluctuations. In a recent study for the OCC, Shick and Sherman (1980) focus upon the behavior of bank stock prices as a potential early-warning device. Their basic hypothesis is that significant deterioration in a bank's financial condition will be reflected by a decline in the price of the bank's common stock.

Shick and Sherman, like Pettway, employ the market model. Their sample consists of 25 banks (with reliable stock-price information) that experienced a major change in their examination rating over the period 1967 and 1976. The critical date in their analysis is the date of the rating change. If the market for bank stocks is efficient, forecasted and actual returns will differ and negative residuals will be observed. They find that a negative residual pattern leads the examination-rating change by at least 15 months. Although they regard their findings as preliminary, Shick and Sherman conclude that stock-price behavior has potential as an early-warning device and recommend further investigation.

Pettway and Sinkey (1980)

Pettway and Sinkey (hereafter P&S) have developed an early-warning technique using accounting and market information, designed to serve as an aid in scheduling on-site bank examinations. They combine their early-warning research based upon market data, Pettway (1980), and accounting data, Sinkey (1979), to establish a dual-screening mechanism. If a bank is flagged as a potential failure by either the market or the accounting screen, it is considered to be in immediate need of an on-site inspection to determine whether or not the early-warning signal is correct. If a bank is flagged by both systems, the early-warning signal is considered to be doubly urgent. Banks that are not flagged by either system and that have "clean" histories are placed at the end of the examination queue.

It is important to note that P&S's proposed dual-screening technique applies only to banks with actively traded securities, such banks are the largest ones and present the greatest risk to the Federal deposit-insurance fund and to the stability of the banking system. For banks without active markets for their securities, P&S propose a single screen based solely upon accounting data.

P&S's dual-screening technique is tested against a sample of failed and nonfailed banks. In addition, the model also is applied to a holdout sample of large nonfailed banks to assess the Type II error of the system.

The dual-screening mechanism constructed by P&S consists of an accounting screen and a market screen. The accounting filter is a two-variable MDA classification model. The two variables are

1. OEOI = Total operating expenses as a percentage of total operating income.
2. IA = Investments as a percentage of total assets, where investments include *all* securities plus federal funds sold.

OEOI is a measure of a bank's operating efficiency and IA is a measure of safety (or risk). Failed banks tend to be less efficient and make fewer investments (i.e., make more loans, especially bad ones) than nonfailed banks.[21] The market filter focuses upon a bank's cumulative firm-specific error generated via a capital asset pricing model (CAPM). To detect significant trends in a bank's cumulative firm-specific error, P&S develop two heuristic filters: a runs test and an appropriate *t*-test.

P&S's test sample consists of a failed-bank group containing only six institutions (the number of large-bank failures with actively traded securities has been relatively small) and a nonfailed group represented by the Keefe Bank-Stock Index (24 banks). A validation test focusing upon the model's potential Type II error also was conducted using a sample of six large nonfailed banks.

P&S conclude that their dual-screening technique would have scheduled examinations for six of the largest banks that subsequently failed at least 1 full year before the beginning of the on-site examination that led to classification as an FDIC "problem bank." Based upon the sample of six nonfailed banks, the dual-screening technique did not flag any of these banks as problem banks during the 3-year test period, 1974–1976. Because the dual-screening system did provide an earlier classification of problem banks that subsequently failed and did not have an excessive Type II error, P&S conclude that the technique should be useful in scheduling bank examinations and providing regulators with more time to prevent bank failure.

Altman (1977)

Altman's purpose is to develop a performance-predictor system (i.e., early-warning mechanism) for identifying savings and loan associations (SLAs) with severe financial problems. [Altman was invited to do this study by the Federal Home Loan Bank Board (FHLBB).]

Definition of Groups. Altman analyzes three groups of SLAs separated according to degree of financial weakness. They are identified as "serious problem" (SP), "temporary problem" (TP), and "no problem" (NP) associations and defined as follows:

1. The SP agroup consists of 56 SLAs whose condition at some time during the period 1966–1974 was deemed "serious." A serious condition includes the following events: (1) receivership, (2) financial assistance (e.g., loans, purchase of assets), and (3) supervisory merger.
2. Each SP SLA is closely matched, if possible, with a TP SLA, where a TP SLA is defined as one that had fairly serious financial problems (at the same time as the SP), but did not require any of the treatment that the SP associations received. The judgment as to whether or not an SLA was a TP was made by the supervisory authorities (FSLIC). Forty-nine SLAs are included in the TP group.
3. The NP group consists of SLAs considered by examiners to be virtually free from problems. Except for time and SMSA location, the NP associations were selected randomly from the NP pool. The NP group consists of 107 associations.

Data and Variables. Balance-sheet, income-expense, and examination data are collected for each of the 212 SLAs for five semiannual periods prior to the critical date for the SP group. Thus, lead times of 6, 12, 18, 24, and 30 months are tested and referred to as periods 1–5, respectively. The data collection period ranges from June, 1966 to December, 1973. Because of data constraints, the sample size (212) drops to 164 in period 3 and to 144 in period 5. Seven different financial schedules are used to obtain the raw data, which are transformed into 32 financial ratios and 22 trends.

A Twelve-Variable Discriminant Model. After intensive searching of the 54-variable data set and consideration of alternative modeling strategies, Altman arrives at the following 12-variable model:

1. Net Operating Income/Gross Operating Income
2. Net Worth/Total Assets
3. Real Estate Owned/Total Assets
4. Earned Surplus/Total Assets
5. Total Loans/Total Savings
6. Borrowed Money/Total Savings
7. FHLB Advances/Net Worth
8. One-Year Trend in #1

9. One-Year Trend in #2
10. One-Year Trend in #3
11. One-Year Trend in #6
12. One-Year Trend in Real Estate Owned (SI)/Total Assets.

Regarding the last variable, SI refers to scheduled items (i.e., loans that are delinquent or worse). Since the data are semiannual observations, the 1-year trend refers to a two-period change. Using alternative ranking procedures, Altman concludes that variables 1, 2, 3, and 8 consistently had high rankings, especially variables 2 and 3. Thus, profit margin (both the level and trend), capital adequacy, and operating leverage (i.e., fixed assets in the form of real estate owned) appear to be the more important discriminators of SLA performance.

Altman's testing procedure is to estimate the model in period 1 (6 months prior) and then to use data from earlier periods (2–5) in a form of holdout test. Altman finds that this type of model (with the same variables and the same coefficients) outperforms an alternative one employing the same variables but different coefficients. In testing the models, emphasis is placed upon the TP–SP group and the three-group alignment.

Classification Results. Altman's classification equations are quadratic ones because the variance-covariance matrices are found to be unequal. The overall classification accuracy for alternative pairs of SLAs are presented in Table VIII.13. Recall that each period represents a 6-month interval. The basic 12-variable model (discussed above) is used only in the first three periods (see the notes to Table VIII.13). This

Table VIII.13. Altman's Lachenbruch Validation Tests for SLAs

Period	*Overall Accuracy for Listed Groups* *NP-SP*	*TP-SP*	*NP-TP*
1	94.5	80.9	85.3
2	89.3	66.3	80.3
	(89.9)	(74.0)	
3	86.6	62.1	73.0
	(88.9)	(65.8)	
4 (with 6-month trends)	83.9	58.0	74.2
5 (with no trends)	82.8	65.2	73.2

The models for periods 1–3 contain the 12 variables listed in the text. The period-4 model substitutes 6-month trends for the 12-month trends and the period-5 model has no trends, only 12 ratios. The weights for each model are unique for those groups and that particular period. The figures in parentheses are classification rates for the period-1 model using the data from periods 2 and 3 in a holdout test.

Source: Altman (1975, Tables 12, 15, and 17).

model is fairly accurate up to 18 months before the critical problem date. Across the alternative pairings, the greatest separation is between the NP–SP groups; the least separation is between TP and SP; and NP–TP group separation is in the middle.

Implementation: An SLA Early-Warning System. To make his findings operational, Altman suggests that each of the three models (e.g., NP–SP, TP–SP, and NP–TP) be used for rating an SLA's performance. Thus, each SLA would be assigned three classifications, one from each model. Based upon these classifications, a composite rating, as illustrated in Table VIII.14, would be assigned [i.e., Very Good (VG), Good (G), Poor (P), and Very Poor (VP)].[22] For supervisory purposes, the VP-rated SLAs would be given immediate remedial attention; the P-rated ones would be next in the examination queue; etc.

Critique. We have three general comments about Altman's SLA paper. First, the paper is strictly a technique-oriented one. There is little rationale provided for the groupings used *vis-à-vis* the supervisory concerns of the FSLIC or for the variables used. Second, it would appear that the three-group model (NP–TP–SP) should be the proper focus of the paper. And finally, there is the time-series problem associated with studies of this type. The problem would seem to be particularly acute in this application, since the period 1966–1973 was an extremely unstable period for the SLA industry with binding Regulation Q ceilings and disintermediation occurring in 1966 and 1969–1970. Thus, combining data across these years may distort the true underlying SLA performance relationship and produce unstable parameter estimates.

Table VIII.14. Altman's Composite-Rating Scheme for SLAs

	Model		
NP-SP	*NP-TP*	*TP-SP*	*Composite[a] Rating*
NP	NP	TP	VG
NP	NP	SP	—
NP	TP	TP	G
NP	TP	SP	—
SP	NP	TP	—
SP	NP	SP	—
SP	TP	TP	P
SP	TP	SP	VP

[a]VG, Very good; G, good; P, poor; VP, very poor; —, not realistic.
Source: Altman (1975, Table 21).

Collins (1980)

In a study of credit union liquidations, Collins compares the static, one-period type variables (ratios) found in Altman (1968) with the trend-type variables found in Meyer and Pifer (1970).

Definition of Failure. Collins defines failure to include all federally chartered credit unions that closed with negative net worth over the period 1960 through 1971. To be included in the failed group, the credit union had to be in operation for more than 4 years prior to failure.

Data and Variables. Collins' data are obtained from the National Credit Union Administration (NCUA). His final sample consists of 162 failed credit unions and a random sample of 162 nonfailed credit unions established prior to 1956 and still in existence at the end of 1971. For each institution, Altman-type and Meyer and Pifer-type variables are calculated. These variables are designed to measure such factors as liquidity, profitability, loan quality, dividend rate and asset size. Using an Altman-type model, Collins finds that the probability of credit union failure in period t *decreases* with *increases* in the dividend rate, liquidity, total assets, and total reserves in period $t - 1$, whereas it *increases* with *increases* in delinquent loans and loan activity in period $t - 1$.

Classification Results. Using a linear-probability model and a hold-out sample, Collins achieves highly accurate overall classification results for both an Altman-type model (94.4 percent) and a Meyer and Pifer-type model (93.2 percent). The critical Type I errors for the models are 3.73 percent and 4.35 percent, respectively.

Conclusion and Critique. Collins is surprised that the Meyer and Pifer-type model does not outperform the Altman-type model. However, his results are consistent with those found by Altman (1977) and Sinkey (1979) for SLAs and commercial banks, respectively, findings that Collins does not seem to be aware of. Because the variables for an Altman-type model are easier to construct and maintain, he favors that type of model for a credit-union, early-warning system. Collins attempts to make too much about the "substantial computational burden" of a Meyer and Pifer-type model, especially for regulatory agencies with abundant computer resources.

Altman and Loris (1976)

A few years ago the National Association of Securities Dealers (NASD) commissioned a study to develop a system for identifying broker-dealers that might be failure prone. The resulting system, called Financial Early Warning System (FEWS), was developed by Altman and Loris (1976, hereafter A&L).

Definition of Failure. A failed broker-dealer is defined as a firm that has been placed in trusteeship by the Securities Investor Protection Corporation (SICP). A&L's failed group consists of 40 broker-dealers placed in trusteeship during the period 1971–1973. To develop their failure-prediction model, A&L select at random 113 healthy or active broker-dealers to form a nonfailed group. In terms of age and asset size, the nonfailed firms are representative of the population of NASD companies. The typical failed broker-dealer is less than 5 years old and has total assets of about $700,000. The typical nonfailed broker-dealer has been in existence for more than 5 years (55 percent of these firms are more than 10 years old) and has total assets of about $860,000.

Data and Variables. Each of the sample firm's Annual Financial Report is used to construct a data set. For the failed firms, the most recent report filed before bankruptcy is used. The financial-statement lead times range from 7 to 29 months with a mean of 13.7 months (median 12 months). A&L regard their model as a 1-year predictive mechanism.

A&L's data set consists of 24 variables. A final profile of six variables is selected as the "best" set for distinguishing between the failed and nonfailed broker-dealers. The six variables are

1. Net Income After Taxes/Total Assets
2. (Total Liabilities + Subordinated Loans)/Owners Equity
3. Total Assets/Adjusted Net Capital
4. (Ending Capital − Capital Additions)/Beginning Capital
5. Scaled Age
6. Composite

The first five variables attempt to measure profitability, leverage, liquidity, capital structure, and experience. The so-called composite variable consists of ten elements that are selected by NASD personnel and that in their judgment are indicators of a problem situation. The ten elements of the composite and their quantification are

1. Organizational Form: Incorporated = 1, All Others = 0.
2. Age: Less than Five = 1, Greater than Five = 0.
3. Profit or Loss from Principal Transactions in OTC Trading Accounts: Loss = 1, Profit (or Breakeven) = 0.
4. Net Income Before Taxes: Negative = 1, Positive (or Zero) = 0.

5. Profit or Loss on Principal Transactions and Net Income before Taxes: Negative (or Zero) = 1, Positive = 0.
6. Subordinated Loans: Positive = 1, Negative (or Zero) = 0.
7. Subordinated Loans: Greater than 1/3 of Capital = 1, Otherwise = 0.
8. Beginning Capital: Negative (or Zero) = 1, Positive = 0.
9. Net Income after Taxes/Beginning Capital: (Equal to or Less than −.25) = 1, Otherwise = 0.
10. Filing of Report: Late = 1, On Time = 0.

The scores (0 or 1) for these ten elements are summed to produce a composite score, 0 = "good" whereas 10 = "bad."

A&L do not attempt to defend the use of the composite variable. Perhaps, it was imposed from above by NASD. Whatever the reason for its inclusion in the analysis, it is an important discriminator on both a univariate and a multivariate basis. It has the highest univariate *F*-statistic (118.7) and it consistently is the number one variable in various ranking tests. The average composite score for the failed group is 5.46 versus 2.05 for the nonfailed group.

Classification Results. Since the null hypothesis of equal covariance matrices is rejected, A&L employ a quadratic classification equation. Although the classification results presented below are obtained using the sample proportions (.26 and .74) as *a priori* probabilities, A&L indicate that more realistic *priors* (e.g., .10 and .90) do not significantly alter the findings. The Lachenbruch classification results are: overall accuracy = 86.2 percent with a Type I error of 17.5 percent and a Type II error of 12.4 percent. The original classification results are 90.1, 10.0, and 9.7 percent, respectively.

In addition to the Lachenbruch validation test presented above, A&L conduct another holdout test using 12 firms that failed in 1973, which were not included in the original failed group, and 12 broker-dealers that were considered to be "problems" by NASD. The FEWS model correctly identifies 8 of the 12 failures; however, the Type I error (33.3 percent) is almost double the Lachenbruch Type I error (17.5 percent). Regarding the "problem" firms, FEWS predicts that 7 of the 12 firms would fail. Determining the accuracy of "problem-firm" predictors is difficult, because managers, owners, and NASD officials are working to save these firms from failure.

Because NASD officials would prefer more frequent evaluation of their member firms, A&L also experiment with a quarterly model. Because of the lack of some data, the quarterly model is not exactly the same as the annual one; however, it still is quite similar (i.e., the first variable and two of the composite elements are not included). The five-variable quarterly model is only slightly less accurate than the annual one.

Conclusion and Critique. A&L conclude that their models could be extremely useful as early-warning mechanisms to complement NASD surveillance activities. Except for their *ad hoc* composite variable, A&L's application of MDA to the broker-dealer industry is an excellent paper.

EPILOGUE ON EARLY-WARNING SYSTEMS

As evidenced by the number of studies reviewed in this chapter, failure prediction and financial early-warning systems are popular research topics. The majority of these undertakings have been technique-oriented studies focusing upon classification problems. Consequently, most of the authors have avoided the difficult assignment of trying to *define and quantify risk.* Thus, in many cases, the research efforts have generated more problems and questions than they have answered. Future researchers should attempt to maintain a better *balance* between the *concept of risk* and the *statistical technique.*

Proposed surveillance mechanisms should make efficient use of all available information sources: accounting, market, and examination (or audit). For example, in banking, with the OCC's NBSS and the FDIC's IMS, the banking authorities have potential accounting screens already in place. Moreover, because the on-site examination is the cornerstone of the bank supervisory process, the only missing link is a screening mechanism based upon market data. In the past, the banking authorities (see Wille, 1973 and Sheehan, 1973) have pooh-poohed the concept of market discipline in banking. However, recent evidence suggests that bank capital markets are efficient and that large banks are subject to the same market discipline that other major firms face. The efficient-market hypothesis even has surfaced in the banking bureaucracy. Former Governor Jackson (1978:6) of the Federal Reserve recently stated:

> I think the industry as a whole has become overregulated by the way its supervisors set standards for a bank's capital and assets. We need to stop treating banks like public utilities and allow the market place by its own risk analysis to make a determination between the successful and the unsuccessful bank. No government official, regardless of how competent or well intentioned, can manage an individual bank or the industry as a whole as well as the collective efforts of bank stockholders, directors and officers.

Because it took the banking authorities roughly four decades to heed Secrists' (1938) advice regarding the potential usefulness of accounting data for distinguishing sound from unsound banking, don't expect a screening mechanism based upon market information to appear before the year 2018.

NOTES

1. During his recent Senate confirmation hearing, John G. Heimann, Comptroller of the Currency, indicated that he felt that the Comptroller's principal responsibility was "the safety and soundness of the banking system." In addition, he stated that the Comptroller also should insure that "those that use the system are protected" and that the "capital needs of society are met." *American Banker*, June 10, 1977, pp. 1 and 8.

2. As of December 31, 1978, there were 1487 banks with total assets greater than $100 million. These banks are only 10.09 percent of the population but they control 79.03 percent of bank assets. FDIC, *Annual Report*, (1978), Table 105.

3. Congressional oversight and recent hearings on problem and failed banks have reinforced this interpretation. The concept of a problem bank is basically the same across the three federal banking agencies.

4. These concepts and tests will be explained in detail later in this chapter.

5. Includes estimated losses in 61 cases that still are active. Losses are calculated as disbursements minus recoveries minus estimated additional recoveries (*FDIC Annual Report 1975*). As of March 15, 1975, the FDIC's revised estimate of its eventual loss in USNB's receivership is $150 million, the original estimate was $84.3 million. Thus, the FDIC could lose more money because of USNB's failure than it has on all previous bank closings.

6. In the cases of a large problem bank, such as Frankln, the lender of last resort, the Fed, may be reluctant to subsidize it for very long—Franklin got about 6 months.

7. This illustration is based upon a seminar given by Sinkey to the Research Division, Comptroller of the Currency, November 6, 1975.

8. George W. Hill, "Why 67 Insured Banks Failed—1960–1974," Washington, D.C.: Federal Deposit Insurance Corporation, 1975. Updated through 1976 using FDIC Division of Liquidation reports.

9. Haskins & Sells (1975, p. C-60, parentheses added).

10. This would appear to be somewhat of an overstatement because the deterioration in a profitability measure (say to zero or negative profits or to a level not sufficient to cover current dividend payments) for all groups would be a clear indication of vulnerability.

11. Actually S&V define the pool of resources as total capital accounts (including debt capital) *plus* reserves on loans and securities.

12. The stationarity assumption does not imply that a bank's capital account is constant over time but simply that the probability of a given change occurring is the same over time.

13. A white-noise series is a random sequence that is independent, normally distributed with zero mean and constant variance. A positive drift process is a white-noise series around a positive mean (e.g., capital account).

14. The mean was greater than the median because a few banks had very high safety indexes. S&V verified the symmetry of the distribution by calculating a skewness coefficient.

15. From 1968 IV to 1976 II (see Table VIII.2), the average number of FDIC problem banks was 226. Thus, S&V's findings suggest that abouı eight banks (= 226 × .036) would be removed from the list as a result of the capital increase.

16. The number 30 was chosen to minimize small-sample problems.

17. Capital-jump size (or change size) refers to the first difference in the total capital accounts.

18. The error rates for S&V's problem-bank screen with "acceptable" sample sizes of 37 and 187 (by their definition) were 89.30 percent (167 banks, rule 1) and 64.86 percent (24 banks, rule 2). This screen does worse than a simple chance model. Recall that the safety-index value to establish the 37/187 sample was 11.0.

19. The terminology is due to Martin (1977).

20. Changing home-office location for branching purposes cost S&V over 100 banks, because as a result, the banks changed ID number.

21. For example, Franklin's 1971 data are 91.99 and 27.55 percent, respectively. Both linear and quadratic functions based upon these two variables classify Franklin as a future failure. See Sinkey (1979, Chapter V).

22. Regarding the "not realistic" rating in Table VIII.14. Altman indicates that only two of the 212 SLAs in period 1 had such a rating. Unless data errors are responsible for a "not realistic" rating, such institutions should be examined closely.

APPENDIX

Summary of Major Failure-Prediction and Early-Warning Studies for Financial Institutions

Purpose and Sample Characteristics	*Statistical Method and Important Variables*	*Contribution and Critique*
I. *FDIC Studies*		
A. *Meyer and Pifer (1970)*. To develop a failure-prediction model for commercial banks. Analyzes 39 banks that failed between 1948 and 1965. Employs a paired sample based upon location, size, age, and regulatory agency	Uses a zero–one regression model and stepwise procedures to search a 160-variable data set. A nine-variable regression model is developed. Eight of the nine variables are noncurrent ones, e.g., trends, lagged values	One or two years before failure, the model correctly classifies about 80 percent of the sample banks. However, beyond the second year, the classifications are not better than chance. Shortcomings: narrow definition of failure, zero–one regression technique, time-series or stationarity problem, and lack of predictive ability beyond 2 years prior to failure
B. *Sinkey (1974–1979)*. Studies have focused upon the financial characteristics of problem and failed banks; the bank-examination process; and the development of so-called early-warning systems. The ultimate purpose has been to develop screening models to identify existing or potential financial difficulties and thus aid in scheduling on-site examinations. Both paired- and random-sample techniques have been applied to examiner-determined problem banks or failed banks	MDA has been the statistical method, either in standard or "outlier" form. In general, income–expense ratios are more important than balance-sheet ratios and two or three ratios classify about as well as seven or eight ratios	Main contribution has been to serve as a catalyst on the early-warning frontier. First research in banking to use quadratic classification technique. Shortcomings: use of examiner-determined groups; exclusive use of MDA and ratios; and lack of a directional element in the outlier technique
II. *Federal Reserve Bank of New York Studies*		
A. *Martin (1977)*. To analyze alterna-	Uses logit analysis and MDA. Four-vari-	Catalogs and explains alternative early-

APPENDIX (Continued)

Purpose and Sample Characteristics	*Statistical Method and Important Variables*	*Contribution and Critique*
tive types of early-warning models; to compare logit analysis with discriminant analysis; and to apply logit analysis to the case of commercial bank failure. Uses a broad definition of failure to include supervisory merger and other emergency measures. A sample of 58 Fed member failures are compared with the population of nonfailed member banks	able logit model consists of net income/total assets, gross charge-offs/net operating income, commercial loans/total loans, and gross capital/risk assets	warning models; shows relationship between logit analysis and MDA; and applies logit analysis to study of bank failures. Shortcomings: small sample size and excludes nonmember bank failures
B. *Korobow, Stuhr et al. (1974–1977).* To investigate statistical techniques to assist in the supervision of banks in the Second Federal Reserve District. Sample banks restricted to "vulnerable" member banks in the Second District	MDA and arctangent regression employed. Latest (five-variable arctangent) probability function consists of loans and leases/total sources of funds, equity capital/adjusted risk assets, operating expenses/operating revenues, gross charge-offs/net income + provision for loan losses, and commercial and industrial loans/total loans	Along with the FDIC's research, the N.Y. Fed's efforts constitute the seminal work on statistical early-warning systems for banks. Shortcomings: small samples and use of the concept of vulnerability
III. *Office of the Comptroller of the Currency*		
A. *National Bank Surveillance System*	One-variable-at-a-time analysis based	Shows that if top management wants a

(Haskins & Sells). NBSS is a device for the early detection of problem banks *and* a management tool based upon peer-group analysis of leading bank indicators. National banks with resources of $100 million to $500 million were used as a test base	upon percentile rankings. Fifteen significant ratios and other variables are analyzed	surveillance mechanism in a hurry and is willing to pay big dollars, an operational system can be achieved. Shortcomings: limited empirical testing and exclusive use of the outlier or peer-group approach
IV. *Board of Governors of the Federal Reserve System*		
A. *Hanweck (1977)*. To develop a simulation model for monitoring so-called problem banks *and* to develop a failure-prediction model for commercial banks. The failure study has a sample of 32 failed banks and a random sample of 177 nonfailed banks	Uses multivariate probit analysis and develops a six-variable failure model. Ratios of net operating income to assets and loans to capital are the only significant variables	Adds probit analysis to the MDA, arctangent, logit analysis arsenal. Attempts to implement Guttentag's suggestion regarding a simulation model for the largest banks. Shortcomings: simulation model requires real world testing whereas failure-prediction model is based upon an esoteric technique that will probably prohibit its implementation
V. *Other Studies (Commercial Banking)*		
A. *Santomero and Vinso (1977)*. To estimate the cross-section riskiness of the banking system and its sensitivity to variations in bank capital. Sample consists of 224 weekly reporting Federal Reserve banks for the period February, 1965 to January, 1974	Use MDA to develop a problem-bank screen for their safety-index distribution. The capital-asset ratio and the coefficient of variation of the capital-jump size are important variables	Sound theoretical foundation with a measure of risk that is independent of actual bank failures or examiners' ratings of bank soundness. Failure risk is defined as zero or negative net worth. Shortcomings: sample banks not representative of the population and arbitrary definition of a problem bank

APPENDIX (Continued)

Purpose and Sample Characteristics	*Statistical Method and Important Variables*	*Contribution and Critique*
B. *Pettway (1980).* To determine if the returns on actively traded bank equities are sensitive to increased potential for bankruptcy. Seven failed, merged, or reorganized large banks are analyzed. The control group consists of the 24 banks that make up the Keefe Bank Stock Index	Uses asset-pricing model and standard regression model to analyze informational impact on cumulative average residuals. Methodological approach does not permit testing of alternative ariables	Shows that the market for large bank stocks exhibits characteristics of efficiency and that market information may be useful as an early-warning mechanism. Shortcomings: standard criticisms of the market model apply (e.g., definition of relevant holding period, stationarity of Beta); small sample; and lack of a rigorous test for the decline of the residuals
C. *Shick & Sherman (1980).* To determine if significant deterioration in a bank's (examiner-determined) financial condition is reflected by a decline in the price of the bank's common stock. Analyzes 25 banks that experienced a major change in their examination rating over the period 1967 to 1976. Control group is S&P's index of banks outside NYC	Like Pettway, uses the so-called market model. Alternative variables not tested because of the model employed	Concludes that stock-price behavior has potential as an early-warning device and recommends further investigation. Shortcomings: problem group may be subject to examiners' identification error; market-model problem; and test of significance of cumulative average residual may be suspect
D. *Pettway and Sinkey (1980).* To develop a screening technique to identify potential bank failure using accounting and market information. Sample banks are from Pettway (1980).	See Pettway (1980) and Sinkey (1979)	Shows that both accounting and market information lead examiners' identification of problem status. Shortcomings: see previous criticisms of Pettway and Sinkey

VI. *Other Studies (Nonbanking)*		
A. *Altman (1977)*. To develop a performance-predictor system to identify SLAs with severe financial problems. Sample consists of 212 SLAs. The 105 problem institutions are separated according to degree of financial weakness and a random sample of 107 nonproblem institutions comprise the control group	Uses quadratic MDA and develops a 12-variable model that is fairly accurate up to 18 months before the critical date	First MDA classification model applied to SLAs. Shortcomings: strictly a technique-oriented approach; lack of justification for problem groups *vis-à-vis* FSLIC's supervisory concerns; and the time-series problem, especially since the period 1966 to 1973 was an unstable one for the SLA industry
B. *Altman and Loris (1976)*. To develop a mechanism for identifying broker-dealers that might be failure prone. Failed group consists of 40 broker-dealers placed in trusteeship during the period 1971–1973. Nonfailed group consists of 113 randomly selected nonfailed broker-dealers	Uses quadratic MDA and develops a six-variable discriminant function. A composite variable consisting of ten elements selected by NASD personnel as indicative of problem status is the most important variable	First MDA classification model applied to broker-dealers. Further confirmation of the usefulness of accounting data for early-warning purposes. Shortcomings: the *ad hoc* composite variable
C. *Collins (1980)*. To compare an Altman-type model with a Meyer and Pifer-type model for 162 failed credit unions and a random sample of 162 nonfailed credit unions	Uses a linear probability model and develops a six-variable function. Important variables are those that measure dividend rate, liquidity, loan quality, asset size, reserve strength, and loan activity	First classification model applied to credit unions. Further confirmation of the usefulness of accounting data for the development of early-warning systems for depository institutions.

References

Chapter I

Anderson, T.W. (1958), *An Introduction to Multivariate Statistical Analysis,* Wiley, New York.

Berkson, J. (1944), "Application of the Logistic Function to Bio-Assay," *Journal of the American Statistical Association* **39,** 357–365.

——— (1951), "Why I Prefer Logits to Probits," *Biometrika* **7,** 327–329.

——— (1955), "Maximum Likelihood and Minimum Chi-Square Estimations of the Logistic Function," *Journal of the American Statistical Association* **50,** 130–161.

Bliss, C.I. (1934), "The Method of Probits," *Science* **79,** 38–39.

Box, G.E.P. (1949), "A General Distribution Theory for a Class of Likelihood Criteria," *Biometrika* **36,** 317–346.

Cooley, W.W. and P.R. Lohnes (1971), *Multivariate Data Analysis,* Wiley, New York.

Cox, D. (1970), *Analysis of Binary Data,* Methuen, London.

DeGroot, M.H. (1970), *Optimal Statistical Decisions,* McGraw-Hill, New York.

Domencich, T. and D. McFadden (1975), *Urban Travel Demand: A Behavioral Analysis,* North Holland, Amsterdam.

Eisenbeis, R.A. and R.B. Avery (1972), *Discriminant Analysis and Classification Procedures: Theory and Applications,* D.C. Heath, Lexington, Mass.

Eisenbeis, R.A. and A.S. McCall (1971), "Some Effects of Affiliations Among Mutual Savings and Commercial Banks," *Journal of Finance* **27,** 865–877.

——— (1978), "The Impact of Legislation Prohibiting Director-Interlocks Among Depository Financial Institutions," *Journal of Banking and Finance* **2,** 323–337.

Finney, D. (1971) *Probit Analysis,* 3rd Edition, Cambridge University Press, Cambridge.

Fisher, R.A. (1936), "The Use of Multiple Measures in Taxonomic Problems," *Annals of Eugenics* **7,** 179–188.

Fletcher, R. and M.J.D. Powell (1963), "A Rapidly Convergent Descent Method for Minimization," *The Computer Journal* **6,** 163–168.

Goldberger, A.S. (1964), *Econometric Theory,* Wiley, New York.

Goldfeld, S. and R. Quant (1972), *Non-Linear Methods in Econometrics,* North Holland, Amsterdam.

Goodman, J.L. (1976), "Is Ordinary Least Squares Estimation with a Dichotomous Dependent Variable Really that Bad," Working Paper, Urban Institute.

Green, P. (1978), *Analyzing Multivariate Data,* Dryden Press, Hinsdale, IL.

Haberman, S. (1974), *The Analysis of Frequency Data,* University of Chicago Press, Chicago.

Hausman, J.A. and D.A. Wise (1978), "A Conditional Probit Model For Qualitative Choice: Discrete Decisions Recognizing Interdependence and Heterogeneous Preferences," *Econometrica* **46,** 403–426.

Hotelling, H. (1931), "The Generalization of Student's Ratio," *Annals of Mathematical Statistics* **2,** 360–378.

Hotz, V.J. (1980), *A Theoretical and Empirical Analysis of Fertility and Married Women's Allocation of Time Over the Life Cycle,* unpublished Ph.D. Dissertation, University of Wisconsin, Madison.

Kohn, M.C. Manski and D. Mundel (1976), "An Empirical Investigation of Factors which Influence College Going Behavior," *Annals of Economic and Social Measurements* **5,** 391–419.

Ladd, G.W. (1966), "Linear Probability Functions and Discriminant Functions," *Econometrica* **34,** 873–885.

Luce, R.D. (1959), *Individual Choice Behavior,* Wiley, New York.

Maddala, G.S. (1977), *Econometrics,* McGraw-Hill, New York.

Martin, D. (1977), "Early Warning of Bank Failure: A Logit Regression Approach," *Journal of Banking and Finance* **1,** 249–276.

McFadden, D. (1974a), "Conditional Logit Analysis of Qualitative Choice Behavior," in P. Zarembka, ed., *Frontiers in Econometrics,* Academic Press, New York.

——— (1974b), "The Measurement of Urban Travel Demand," *Journal of Public Economics* **3,** 303–328.

——— (1976), "Quantal Choice Analysis: A Survey," *Annals of Economic and Social Measurement* **5,** 363–390.

——— (1978), "On the Use of Probabilistic Choice Models in Economics," presented at the 1978 meetings of the American Economic Association.

——— (1980a), "Econometric Models for Probabilistic Choice Among Products," *Journal of Business* **53,** S13–S29.

——— (1980b), "Structural Discrete Probability Models Derived from Theories of Choice," in C.F. Manski and D. McFadden, eds., *Structural Analysis of Discrete Data with Econometric Applications,* M.I.T. Press, Cambridge, Mass.

McGillivray, R. (1970), "Estimating the Linear Probability Function," *Econometrica* **38,** 775–776.

Nerlove, M. and S. Press (1973), *Univariate and Multivariate Log-Linear and Logistic Models,* Rand Report No. R-1306-EDANIH.

Overall, J.E. and C.J. Klett (1972), *Applied Multivariate Analysis,* McGraw-Hill, New York.

Pindyck, R.S. and O.L. Rubinfeld (1976), *Econometric Models and Economic Forecasts,* McGraw-Hill, New York.

Poirier, D.J. (1977), "The Determinants of Home Buying," in H.W. Watts and A. Rees, eds., *The New Jersey Income-Maintenance Experiment,* Vol. 3, *Expenditures, Health and Social Behavior; and the Quality of the Evidence,* Academic Press, New York.

Porebski, O.R. (1966), "On the Interrelated Nature of the Multivariate Statistics Used in Discriminatory Analysis," *British Journal of Mathematical and Statistical Psychology* **19,** 197–214.

Rao, C.R. (1952), *Advanced Statistical Methods in Biometric Research,* Wiley, New York.

——— (1965), *Linear Statistical Inference and its Applications,* Wiley, New York.

Smith, V.K. and C.J. Cicchetti (1972), "Regression Analysis with Dichotomous Dependent Variables," paper presented at the Third World Congress of the Econometric Society, Toronto, Canada.

Tatsuoka, M.M. (1971), *Multivariate Analysis: Techniques for Educational and Psychological Research,* Wiley, New York.

Theil, H. (1969), "A Multinomial Extension of the Linear Logit Model," *International Economic Review* **10,** 251–259.

——— (1970), "On the Estimation of Relationships Involving Qualitative Variables," *American Journal of Sociology* **76,** 103–154.

——— (1971), *Principles of Econometrics,* Wiley, New York.

Tobin, J. (1955), "The Application of Multivariate Probit Analysis to Economic Survey Data," Cowles Foundation Discussion Paper No. 1.

Tryon, R.C. and D.E. Bailey (1970), *Cluster Analysis,* McGraw-Hill, New York.

Walker, S. and D. Duncan (1967), "Estimation of the Probability of an Event as a Function of Several Independent Variables," *Biometrika* **54,** 167–179.

Warner, S.L. (1963), "Multivariate Regression of Dummy Variates under Normality Assumptions," *Journal of the American Statistical Association* **58,** 1054–1063.

Zellner, A. and T. Lee (1965), "Joint Estimation of Relationships Involving Discrete Random Variables," *Econometrica* **33,** 382–394.

Chapter II

Aitchison, J. and S. Silvey (1957), "The Generalization of Probit Analysis to the case of Multiple Responses," *Biometrika* **13,** 131–140.

Albright, R.L., S.R. Lerman and C.F. Manski (1977), "Report on the Development of an Estimation Program for the Multinomial Probit Model," Cambridge Systematics Working Paper.

Amemiya, T. (1975), "Qualitative Response Models," *Annals of Economic and Social Measurement* **4,** 363–372.

——— (1976), "The Maximum Likelihood Estimator vs. the Minimum Chi-Square Estimator in the General Qualitative Response Model," *Journal of the American Statistical Association* **7,** 347–351.

Anderson, T.W. (1958), *An Introduction to Multivariate Statistical Analysis,* Wiley, New York.

Avery, R.B. (1977), "Credit Scoring Models with Discriminant Analysis and Truncated Samples," Working Paper #5-77-78, Carnegie-Mellon University.

Bartlett, M.S. (1947), "Multivariate Analysis," *Journal of the Royal Statistical Association, Series B* **9,** 176–197.

Ben-Akiva, M. and T. Watanatada (1980), "Application of a Continuous Spatial Choice Logit Model," in C.F. Manski and D. McFadden, eds., *Structural Analysis of Discrete Data with Econometric Applications,* M.I.T. Press, Cambridge, Mass.

Box, G.E.P. (1949), "A General Distribution Theory for a Class of Likelihood Criteria," *Biometrika* **36,** 317–346.

Cooley, W.W. and P.R. Lohnes (1971), *Multivariate Data Analysis,* Wiley, New York.

Cosslett, S.R. (1980), "Efficient Estimation of Discrete Choice Models," in C.F. Manski and D. McFadden, eds., *Structural Analysis of Discrete Data with Econometric Applications,* M.I.T. Press, Cambridge, Mass.

Domencich, T. and D. McFadden (1975), *Urban Travel Demand: A Behavioral Analysis,* North Holland, Amsterdam.

Fisher, R.A. (1936), "The Use of Multiple Measures in Taxonomic Problems," *Annals of Eugenics* **7,** 179–188.

Goldberger, A.S. (1973), "Correlations Between Binary Outcomes and Probabilistic Predictions," *Journal of the American Statistical Association* **68,** 84.

Gunderson, M. (1974), "Retention of Trainees," *Journal of Econometrics* **2,** 79–93.

Gurland, J., I. Lee and P. Dahm (1960), "Polychotomous Quantal Response in Biological Assay," *Biometrics* **16,** 382–398.

Hausman, J.A. and D.A. Wise (1978), "A Conditional Probit Model for Qualitative Choice: Discrete Decisions Recognizing Interdependence and Heterogeneous Preferences," *Econometrica* **46,** 403–426.

Heckman, J.J. (1979), "Sample Selection Bias as a Specification Error," *Econometrica* **47,** 153–161.

Horrigan, J.O. (1966), "The Determination of Long-Term Credit Standing with Financial Ratios," *Empirical Research in Accounting 1966, Journal of Accounting Research* **4,** 44–62.

Hotelling, H. (1951), "A Generalized T-test and Measure of Multivariate Dispersion," *Proceedings of the Second Berkeley Symposium of Mathematical Statistics and Probability* **2,** 23–41.

Kaplan, R. and G. Urwitz (1979), "Statistical Models of Bond Ratings: A Methodological Inquiry Inquiry," *Journal of Business* **52,** 231–261.

Lachenbruch, P.A. and M.R. Mickey (1968), "Estimation of Error Rates in Discriminant Analysis," *Technometrics* **10,** 1–11.

Lachenbruch, P.A. (1967), "An Almost Unbiased Method of Obtaining Confidence Intervals for the Probability of Misclassification in Discriminant Analysis," *Biometrics* **23,** 639–645.

Ladd, G.W. (1966), "Linear Probability Functions and Discriminant Functions," *Econometrica* **34,** 873–885.

Lohnes, P.R. (1961), "Test Space and Discriminant Space Classification Models and Related Significant Tests," *Educational and Psychological Measurement* **21,** 559–574.

Luce, R.D. (1959), *Individual Choice Behavior,* Wiley, New York.

Manski, C.F. and S.R. Lerman (1977), "The Estimation of Choice Probabilities from Choice Based Samples," *Econometrica* **45,** 1977–1988.

Manski, C.F. and D. McFadden (1980), "Statistical Analysis of Discrete Probability Models," in C.F. Manski and D. McFadden, eds., *Structural Analysis of Discrete Data with Econometric Applications,* M.I.T. Press, Cambridge, Mass.

McFadden, D. (1974), "Conditional Logit Analysis of Qualitative Choice Behavior," in P. Zarembka, ed., *Frontiers in Econometrics,* Academic Press, New York.

——— (1976a), "Quantal Choice Analysis: A Survey," *Annals of Economic and Social Measurement* **5,** 363–390.

——— (1976b), "A Comment on Discriminant Analysis 'Versus' Logit Analysis," *Annals of Economic and Social Measurement* **5,** 511–523.

——— (1980), "Econometric Models for Probabilistic Choice Among Products," *Journal of Business* **53,** S13–S29.

McKelvey, R., and W. Zavoina (1975), "A Statistical Model for the Analysis of Ordinal Level Dependent Variables," *Journal of Mathematical Sociology* **4,** 103–120.

Moore, D.H. (1973), "Evaluation of Five Discrimination Procedures for Binary Variables," *Journal of the American Statistical Association* **68,** 399–404.

Morrison, D. (1972), "Upper Bounds for Correlation between Outcomes and Probabilistic Predictions," *Journal of the American Statistical Association* **67,** 68–70.

Nerlove, M. and S. Press (1973), *Univariate and Multivariate Log-Linear and Logistic Models,* Rand Report No. R-1306-EDA/NIH.

Pindyck, R.S. and O.L. Rubinfeld (1976), *Econometric Models and Economic Forecasts,* McGraw-Hill, New York.

Poirier, D.J. (1975), "Aggregate Prediction and Goodness-of-Fit in Models with Qualitative Dependent Variables," Institute for Policy Analysis, Working Paper No. 7510, University of Toronto.

Rao, C.R. (1952), *Advanced Statistical Methods in Biometric Research,* Wiley, New York.

Schatzoff, M. (1966), "Sensitivity Comparisons Among Tests of the General Linear Hypothesis," *Journal of the American Statistical Association* **61,** 415–435.

Simon, F.H. (1971), *Prediction Methods in Criminology,* Her Majesty's Stationary Office, London.

Tatsuoka, M.M. (1971), *Multivariate Analysis: Techniques for Educational and Psychological Research,* Wiley, New York.

Theil, H. (1969), "A Multinomial Extension of the Linear Logit Model," *International Economic Review* **10,** 251–259.

——— (1970), "On the Estimation of Relationships Involving Qualitative Variables," *American Journal of Sociology* **76,** 103–154.

Thurstone, L. (1927), "A Law of Comparative Judgement," *Psychological Review* **34,** 273–286.

Timm, N.H. (1975), *Multivariate Analysis with Applications in Education and Psychology,* Brooks/Cole, Belmont, Calif.

Tversky, A. (1972), "Elimination by Aspects: A Theory of Choice," *Psychological Review* **79,** 281–299.

Tversky, A. and S. Sattath (1979), "Preference Trees," *Psychological Review* **86,** 542–573.

Walker, S. and D. Duncan (1967), "Estimation of the Probability of an Event as a Function of Several Independent Variables," *Biometrika* **54,** 167–179.

Westin, R. (1974), "Predictions from Binary Choice Models," *Journal of Econometrics* **2,** 1–16.

Zellner, A. and T. Lee (1965), "Joint Estimation of Relationships Involving Discrete Random Variables," *Econometrica* **33,** 382–394.

Chapter III

Adelman, I. and C.T. Morris (1968), "Performance Criteria for Evaluating Economic Development Potential: An Operational Approach," *Quarterly Journal of Economics* **82,** 260–280.

Altman, E.I. (1968), "Financial Ratios, Discriminant Analysis and the Prediction of Corporate Bankruptcy," *Journal of Finance* **23,** 589–609.

——— (1977), "Some Estimates of the Cost of Lending Errors for Commercial Banks," *Journal of Commercial Bank Lending* **60,** 51–58.

Altman, E.I. and R.A. Eisenbeis (1978), "Financial Applications of Discriminant Analysis: A Clarification," *Journal of Financial and Quantitative Analysis* **13,** 185–195.

Altman, E.I., R. Haldeman and P. Narayanan (1977), "Zeta Analysis: A New Model for Identifying Bankruptcy Risk," *Journal of Banking and Finance,* **1,** 29–54.

Altman, E.I. and S. Katz (1975), "An Analysis of Bond Ratings in the Electric Public Utility Industry," in M. Schiff and G. Sorter, eds. *Relevant Research in Accounting,* NYU Press, New York.

Altman, E.I. and S. Katz (1976), "Statistical Bond Rating Classification Using Financial and Accounting Data," NYU Working Paper, Fall 1974 and in M. Schiff and G. Sorter, eds., *Topical Research in Accounting,* NYU Press, New York.

Anderson, T.W. (1958), *An Introduction to Multivariate Statistical Analysis,* Wiley, New York.

Anderson, T.W. and R.R. Bahadur (1962), "Classification into Two Multivariate Normal Distributions with Different Covariance Matrices," *Annals of Mathematical Statistics* **33,** 420–431.

Andrews, D.F., R. Gnandesikan and J.L. Warner (1973), "Methods for Assessing Multivariate Normality," in P.R. Krishnaiah, ed., Multivariate Analysis-III, Academic Press, New York, pp. 95–116.

Arnold, H.J. (1964), "Permutation Support for Multivariate Techniques," *Biometrika* **51,** 65–70.

Aspin, A.A. (1948), "An Examination and Further Development of a Formula Arising from the Problem of Comparing Two Mean Values," *Biometrika* **35,** 88–96.

Avery, R.B. (1977), "Credit Scoring Models with Discriminant Analysis and Truncated Samples," unpublished paper.

Banerjee, S.K. (1960), "Approximate Confidence Interval for Linear Function of Means of R Populations When the Population Variances Are Not Equal," *Sankhyā* **22,** 357–358.

Banerjee, S.K. (1961), "On Confidence Interval for Two-Means Population Based of Separate Estimates of Variances and Tabulated Values of t-Table," *Sankhyā,* Ser. A., **23,** 359–378.

Bartlett, M.S. (1939), "The Standard Errors of Discriminant Function

Coefficients," Supplement to the *Journal of the Royal Statistical Society (Industrial and Agricultural Research Section),* Vol. VI, No. 2, issued with Part IV, Vol. 102.

Bates, T. (1973), "An Econometric Analysis of Lending to Black Businessmen," *Review of Economics and Statistics* **55,** 272–283.

Bennett, B.M. (1951), "Note on a Solution of Generalized Behrens - Fisher Problem," *Annals of Institute of Statistical Mathematics* **2,** 87–90.

Box, G.E.P. (1949), "A General Distribution Theory for a Class of Likelihood Criteria," *Biometrika* **36,** 317–346.

Broffit, J.D. (1969), *Estimating the Probability of Misclassification Based on Discriminant Function Techniques,* Ph.D. dissertation, Colorado State University, Fort Collins.

Carleton, W.T. and E.M. Lerner (1969), "Statistical Credit Scoring of Municipal Bonds," *Journal of Money, Credit, and Banking* **1,** 750–764.

Chang, P.C. and A.A. Afifi (1974), "Classification Based on Dichotomous and Continuous Variables," *Journal of the American Statistical Association* **69,** 336–339.

Chase, G.R. and W.G. Bulgren (1971), "A Monte Carlo Investigation of the Robustness of T^2", *Journal of the American Statistical Association* **66,** 499–502.

Clumies-Ross, C.W. and R.H. Riffenburgh (1960), "Geometry and Linear Discrimination," *Biometrika* **47,** 185–189.

Cochran, W.G. (1964), "On the Performance of the Linear Discriminant Function," *Technometrics* **6,** 179–190.

——— (1968), "Commentary on 'Estimation of Error Rates in Discriminant Analysis,' " *Technometrics* **10,** 204.

Cochran, W.G. and C.E. Hopkins (1961), "Some Classification Problems with Multivariate Qualitative Data," *Biometrics* **17,** 10–32.

Cooley, W.W. and P.R. Lohnes (1962), *Multivariate Procedures for the Behavioral Sciences,* Wiley, New York.

——— (1971) *Multivariate Data Analysis,* Wiley, New York.

D'Agostino, R.B. (1973), "Monte Carlo Power Comparison of W' and D Tests of Normality for $n = 100$," *Communications in Statistics* **1,** 545–551.

Dillon, W.R. and M. Goldstein (1978), "On the Performance of Some Multinomial Classification Rules," *Journal of the American Statistical Association* **73,** 305–313.

Dince, R.R. and J.C. Fortson (1972), "The Use of Discriminant Analysis to Predict the Capital Adequacy of Commercial Banks," *Journal of Bank Research* **3,** 54–62.

Dunn, O.J. (1971), "Some Expected Values for Probabilities of Correct Classification in Discriminant Analysis," *Technometrics* **13,** 345–353.

Dunn, O.J. and P.D. Varady (1966), "Probabilities of Correct Classification in Discriminant Analysis," *Biometrics* **22,** 908–924.

Edmister, R.O. (1972), "An Empirical Test of Financial Ratio Analysis for Small Business Prediction," *Journal of Financial and Quantitative Analysis* **7,** 335–356.

Eisenbeis, R.A. (1977), "Pitfalls in the Application of Discriminant Analysis in Business, Finance, and Economics," *Journal of Finance* **32,** 875–900.

——— (1978), " 'A Multivariate Analysis of Industrial Bond Ratings' and the Role of Subordination: A Comment," *Journal of Finance* **33,** 325–335.

Eisenbeis, R.A. and R.B. Avery (1972), *Discriminant Analysis and Classification Procedures: Theory and Applications,* D.C. Heath, Lexington, Mass.

——— (1973), "Two Aspects of Investigating Group Differences in Discriminant Anlysis," *Decision Sciences,* **4,** 487–493.

Eisenbeis, R.A., G.G. Gilbert and R.B. Avery (1973), "Investigating the Relative Importance of Individual Variables and Variable Subsets in Discriminant Analysis," *Communications in Statistics* **2,** 205–219.

Eisenbeis, R.A. and A.S. McCall (1971), "Some Effects of Affiliations Among Mutual Savings and Commercial Banks," *Journal of Finance* **27,** 865–877.

Eisenbeis, R.A. and N.B. Murphy (1974), "Interest Rate Ceilings and Consumer Credit Rationing: A Multivariate Analysis of a Survey of Borrowers," *Southern Economic Journal* **41,** 115–123.

Elashoff, J.D., R.M. Elashoff and G.E. Goldman, "On the Choice of Variables in Classification Problems with Dichotomous Variables," *Biometrika* **54,** 668–670.

Fisher, R.A. (1935), "The Fiducial Argument in Statistical Inference," *Annals of Eugenics* **6,** 391–398.

——— (1936), "The Use of Multiple Measurement in Taxonomic Problems," *Annals of Eugenics* **7,** 179–188.

Frank, R.E., W.F. Massy and D.G. Morrison (1965), "Bias in Multiple Discriminant Analysis," *Journal of Marketing Research* **2,** 250–258.

Ghosh, B.K. (1972), "Oh Lehmann's Test for Homogeneity of Variances," *Journal of the Royal Statistical Society* **B34,** 221–234.

Gilbert, E.S. (1968), "On Discrimination Using Qualitative Variables," *Journal of the American Statistical Association* **63,** 1399–1412.

——— (1969), "The Effect of Unequal Variance–Covariance Matrices on Fisher's Linear Discriminant Function," *Biometrics* **25,** 505–515.

Gilbert, G.G. (1974), "Predicting *de novo* Expansion in Bank Merger Cases," *Journal of Finance* **29,** 151–162.

——— (1975), "An Analysis of Federal Regulatory Decisions on Market Extension Bank Mergers," *Journal of Money, Credit, and Banking* **7,** 81–92.

Glick, N. (1973), "Sample-based Multinomial Classification," *Biometrics* **29,** 241–256.

Goldstein, M. and W.R. Dillon (1977), "A Stepwise Discrete Variable Selection Procedure," *Communications in Statistics, Theory and Methods, A6,* **14,** 1423–1436.

Goldstein, M. and M. Robinowitz (1975), "Selection of Variates for the Two-Group Multinomial Classification Problem," *Journal of the American Statistical Association* **70,** 776–781.

Habbema, J.D.F. and J. Hermans (1977), "Selection of Variables in Discriminant Analysis by F-Statistic and Error Rate," *Technometrics* **19,** 487–493.

Harter, T.R. (1973), "Measuring Risk on Mortgage Credit," *Mortgage Banker* **34,** 71–80.

Hartley, H.O. (1940), "Testing the Homogeneity of a Set of Variances," *Biometrika* **31,** 249–255.

Haslem, J.A. and W.A. Longbrake (1971), "A Discriminant Analysis of Commercial Bank Profitability," *Quarterly Review of Economics and Business* **2,** 39–46.

Hills, M. (1966), "Allocation Rules and their Error Rates," *Journal of the Royal Statistical Society* **28,** 1–20.

——— (1967), "Discrimination and Allocation with Discrete Data," *Applied Statistics* **16,** 237–250.

Holloway, L.N. and O.J. Dunn (1967), "The Robustness of Hotelling's T^2," *Journal of the American Statistical Association* **62,** 124–136.

Hopkins, J.W. and P.P.F. Clay (1963), "Some Empirical Distributions of Bivariate T^2 and Homoskedasticity Criterion M under Unequal Variance and Leptokurtosis," *Journal of the American Statistical Association* **58,** 1048–1053.

Horton, J.J., Jr. (1970), "Statistical Classification of Municipal Bonds," *Journal of Bank Research* **1,** 29–40.

Ito, K. and W.J. Schull (1964), "On the Robustness of the T^2_0 Test in Multivariate Analysis of Variance When Variance–Covariance Matrices are Not Equal," *Biometrika* **51,** 71–82.

James, G.S. (1951), "The Comparison of Several Groups of Observations When the Ratios of the Population Variances Are Unknown," *Biometrika* **38,** 324–329.

——— (1954), "Tests of Linear Hypotheses in Univariate and Multivariate Analysis When the Ratios of the Population Variances Are Unknown, *Biometrika* **41,** 19–43.

Joy, M.O. and J.O. Tollefson (1975), "On the Financial Applications of Discriminant Analysis," *Journal of Financial and Quantitative Analysis* **10,** 723–739.

Karson, M.J. and T.F. Martell (1977), "A Procedure for Ranking Variables in Quadratic Discriminant Analysis," unpublished paper, University of Alabama.

Katz, S. (1974), "The Price Adjustment Process of Bonds to Rating Reclassifications," *Journal of Finance* **29,** 551–559.

Klemkowsky, R.C. and J.W. Petty (1970), "A Multivariate Analysis of Stock Price Variability," *Journal of Business Research* **1,** 1–10.

Kmenta, J. (1971), *Elements of Econometrics,* Macmillan, New York.

Krzanowski, W.J. (1975), "Discrimination and Classification Using Both Binary and Continuous Variables," *Journal of the American Statistical Association* **70,** 782–790.

——— (1977), "The Performance of Fisher's Linear Discriminant Function under Non-Optimal Conditions," *Technometrics* **19,** 191–200.

Kshirsagar, A.M. (1972), *Multivariate Analysis,* Marcel Dekker, New York.

Lachenbruch, P.A. (1966), "Discriminant Analysis When the Initial Samples Are Misclassified," *Technometrics* **8,** 657–662.

——— (1967), "An Almost Unbiased Method of Obtaining Confidence Intervals for the Probability of Misclassification in Discriminant Analysis," *Biometrics* **23,** 639–645.

——— (1968), "On Expected Probabilities of Misclassification in Discriminant Analysis, Necessary Sample Size, and a Relation with Multiple Correlation Coefficient," *Biometrics* **24,** 823–834.

——— (1974), "Discriminant Analysis When the Initial Samples Are Misclassified II: Non-Random Misclassification Models," *Technometrics* **16,** 419–424.

——— (1975), *Discriminant Analysis,* Macmillan, New York.

——— (1979), "Note on Initial Misclassification Effects on the Quadratic Discriminant Function," *Technometrics* **21,** 129–132.

——— and M.R. Mickey (1968), "Estimation of Error Rates in Discriminant Analysis," *Technometrics* **10,** 1–11.

——— C. Snuringer and L.T. Revo (1973), "Robustness of the Linear and Quadratic Discriminant Function to Certain Types of Non-Normality," *Communications in Statistics* **1,** 39–56.

Ladd, G.W. (1966), "Linear Probability Functions and Discriminant Functions," *Econometrica* **34,** 873–885.

Lane, S. (1972), "Submarginal Credit Risk Classification," *Journal of Financial and Quantitative Analysis* **7,** 1379–1386.

Lee, A.F.S. and J. Gurland (1975), "Size and Power Tests for Equality of Means of Two Normal Populations with Unequal Variances," *Journal of the American Statistical Association* **70,** 933–941.

Lehman, E.L. (1959), *Testing Statistical Hypotheses,* Wiley, New York.

Linhart, H. (1959), "Techniques for Discriminant Analysis with Discrete Variables," *Metrika* **2,** 138–149.

Lohnes, P.R. (1961), "Test Space and Discriminant Space Classification Models and Related Significance Tests," *Educational and Psychological Measurement* **21,** 559–574.

Mardia, K.V. (1970), "Measures of Multivariate Skewness and Kurtosis with Applications," *Biometrika* **57,** 519–530.

——— (1971), "The Effect of Nonnormality on Some Multivariate Tests and Robustness to Nonnormality in the Linear Model," *Biometrika* **58,** 105–121.

——— (1975a), "Assessment of Multinormality and the Robustness of Hotelling's T^2 Test," *Applied Statistics* **24,** 163–171.

——— (1975b), "Measures of Multivariate Skewness and Kurtosis," *Applied Statistics* **24,** 262–265.

Mardia, K.V. and P.J. Zemrock (1975), "Measures of Multivariate Skewness and Kurtosis," *Applied Statistics* **24,** 262–265.

Marks, S. and O.J. Dunn, "Discriminant Functions When Covariance Matrices Are Unequal," *Journal of the American Statistical Association* **69,** 555–559.

Martell, T.F. and R.L. Fitts (1978), "Determinants of Bank Trust Department Usage," *Journal of Bank Research* **9,** No. 1, 8–14.

Matuseta, K. (1954), "On the Estimation by the Minimum Distance Method," *Annals of the Institute of Statistical Mathematics* **7,** 67–77.

McCabe, G.P., Jr. (1975), "Computations for Variable Selection in Discriminant Analysis," *Technometrics* **17,** 103–109.

McDonald, L.L., V.W. Lowe, R.K. Smidt and K.A. Meister (1976), "A Preliminary Test for Discriminant Analysis Based on Small Samples, *Biometrics* **32,** 417–423.

McFadden, D. (1976), "Quantal Choice Analysis: A Survey," *Annals of Economic and Social Measurement* **5,** 363–390.

McHenry, C.E. (1978), "Computation of a Best Subset in Multivariate Analysis," *Applied Statistics* **27,** 291–296.

McKay, R.J. (1976), "Simultaneous Procedures in Discriminant Analysis Involving Two Groups," *Technometrics* **18,** 47–53.

——— (1978), "A Graphical Aid to Selection of Variables in Two-Grays Discriminant Analysis," *Applied Statistics* **27,** 259–263.

McLachlan, G.J. (1972), "Asymptotic Results for Discriminant Analysis When the Initial Samples are Misclassified," *Technometrics* **14,** 415–422.

——— (1974a), "Estimation of the Errors of Misclassification on the Criterion of Asymptotic Mean Square Error," *Technometrics* **16,** 255–260.

——— (1974b), "An Asymptotic Unbiased Technique for Estimating the Error Rates in Discriminant Analysis," *Biometrics* **30,** 239–249.

——— (1974c), "The Relationship In Terms of Asymptotic Mean Square Error Between the Separate Problems of Estimating Each of the Three Types of Error Rate of the Linear Discriminant Function," *Technometrics* **16,** 569–575.

——— (1975), "Confidence Intervals for the Conditional Probability of Misallocation in Discriminant Analysis," *Biometrics* **31,** 161–167.

——— (1976), "A Criterion for Selecting Variables for the Linear Discriminant Function," *Biometrics* **32,** 529–534.

——— (1977), "Estimating the Linear Discriminant Function From Initial Samples Containing a Small Number of Unclassified Observations," *Journal of the American Statistical Association* **72,** 403–406.

Meyer, P.A. and H.W. Pifer (1970), "Prediction of Bank Failures," *Journal of Finance* **25,** 853–868.

Michaelis, J. (1973), "Simulation Experiments with Multiple Group Linear and Quadratic Discriminant Analysis," in Theophilos Cacoullos, ed., *Discriminant Analysis and Applications,* Academic Press, 225–238.

Moore, D.H., II (1973), "Evaluation of Five Discrimination Procedures for Binary Variables," *Journal of the American Statistical Association* **68,** 339–404.

Moran, M.A. (1975), "On the Expectation of Errors of Allocation Associated with a Linear Discriminant Function," *Biometrika* **62,** 141–148.

Morrison, Donald F. (1976), *Multivariate Statistical Methods,* 2nd edition, McGraw-Hill, New York.

Mosteller, F. and D.F. Wallace (1963), "Inference in the Authorship Problem," *Journal of the American Statistical Association* **58,** 275–305.

Murray, G.D. (1977), "A Cautionary Note on Selection of Variables in Discriminant Analysis," *Applied Statistics* **26,** 246–250.

Nerlove, M. and S.J. Press (1973), *Univariate and Multivariate Log-Linear and Logistic Models,* Santa Monica, The Rand Corporation: R-1306-EDA/NIH.

——— (1976), *Multivariate Log-Linear Probability Models for Analysis of Qualitative Data,* Discussion Paper No. 1, Center for Statistics and Probability, Northwestern University.

Neyman, J. and E.S. Pearson (1931), "On the Problem of R Samples," *Bulletin, Acad. Polon. Sci. Lett. A,* pp. 460–481.

Norgaard, R. and C. Norgaard (1974), "A Critical Examination of Share Repurchase," *Financial Management* **3,** 44–49.

Okamoto, M. (1963), "An Asymptotic Expansion for the Distribution of the Linear Discriminant Function," *Annals of Mathematical Statistics* **34,** 1286–1301.

Pagurova, V.I. (1968), "On A Comparison of Means of Two Normal Samples," *Theory of Probability and Its Applications* **13,** 527–534.

Pinches, G. (1975), "The Role of Subordination and Industrial Bond Ratings," *Journal of Finance* **30,** 201–206.

——— (1978), "Classification Results and Multiple Discriminant Analysis," Working Paper No. 116, School of Business Working Paper Series, The University of Kansas.

Pinches, G. and K.A. Mingo (1973), "A Multivariate Analysis of Industrial Bond Ratings," *Journal of Finance* **28,** 1–18.

Pinches, G. and J.S. Trieschmann (1974), "The Efficiency of Alternative Models for Solvency Surveillance in the Insurance Industry," *Journal of Risk and Insurance* **41,** 563–577.

Plackett, R.L. (1947), "An Exact Test for the Equality of Variances," *Biometrika* **34,** 311–319.

Pogue, T.F. and R.M. Soldofsky (1969), "What's in a Bond Rating," *Journal of Financial and Quantitative Analysis* **4,** 201–228.

Porebski, O.R. (1966), "On the Interrelated Nature of the Multivariate Statistics Used in Discriminatory Analysis," *British Journal of Mathematical and Statistical Psychology* **19,** 197–214.

Rao, C.R. (1952), *Advanced Statistical Methods in Biometric Research,* Wiley, New York.

——— (1965), *Linear Statistical Inference,* Wiley, New York.

Roy, J. (1958), "Step-Down Procedure in Multivariate Analysis," *Annals of Mathematical Statistics* **29,** 177–87.

Rulon, P.J., D.V. Tiedeman, M.M. Tatsuoka and C.R. Langmuir (1967), *Multivariate Statistics for Personnel Classification,* Wiley, New York.

Samiuiddin, M. and M. Atiqullah (1975), "A Test for Equality of Variances," *Biometrics* **31,** 206–208.

Scheffé, H. (1959), *The Analysis of Variance,* Wiley, New York.

Schick, R.A. and J.A. Verbrugge (1975), "An Analysis of Bank Price–Earnings Ratios," *Journal of Bank Research* **6,** 140–149.

Sedransk, N. and M. Okamoto (1971), "Estimation of the Probabilities of Misclassification for a Linear Discriminant Function in the Univariate Normal Case," *Annals of Institute of Statistical Mathematics* **23,** 219–436.

Shapiro, S.S. and R.S. Francia (1942), Mathematics "Approximate Analysis of Variance Test for Normality," *Journal of the American Statistical Association* **67,** 215–216.

———, Wilk, M.B. and H.J. Chen (1968), "A Comparative Study of Tests of Normality," *Journal of the American Statistical Association* **63,** 1343–1372.

Sinkey, J.F., Jr. (1975), "A Multivariate Statistical Analysis of the Characteristics of Problem Banks," *Journal of Finance* **30,** 21–36.

Smith, C.A.B. (1947), "Some Examples of Discrimination," *Annals of Eugenics* **13,** 272–282.

Smith, K.V. (1965), *Classification of Investment Securities Using Multiple Discriminant Analysis.* Institute Paper No. 101, Purdue University Institute for Research in the Behavioral, Economic and Management Sciences.

Sorum, M. J. (1971), "Estimating the Conditional Probability of Misclassification," *Technometrics* **13,** 333–343.

——— (1972), "Estimating the Expected and the Optimal Probabilities of Misclassification," *Technometrics* **14,** 935–943.

——— (1973), "Estimating the Expected Probability of Misclassification for a Rule Based on the Linear Discriminant Function: Univariate Normal Case," *Technometrics* **15,** 329–339.

Stevens, J.P. (1973), "Step-Down Analysis and Simultaneous Confidence Intervals in MANOVA," *Multivariate Behavioral Research* 391–402.

Stuhr, D. and R. Van Wicklen (1974), "Rating the Financial Condition of Banks: A Statistical Approach to Aid Bank Supervision," *Monthly Review* (Federal Reserve Bank of New York), **56,** 233–238.

Subrahmaniam, K. and E.F. Chinganda (1978), "Robustness of the Linear Discriminant Function to Nonnormality: Edgeworth Series," *Journal of Statistical Planning and Inference* **2,** 79–91.

———, Subrahmaniam, K. and K. Subrahmaniam (1973), "On the Multivariate Behrens–Fisher Problem," *Biometrika* **60,** 107–111.

Tatsuoka, M.M. (1971), *Multivariate Analysis: Techniques for Educational and Psychological Research,* Wiley, New York.

Urbakh, V. Yu (1971), "Linear Discriminant Analysis: Loss of Discriminating Power When a Variate Is Omitted," *Biometrics* **27,** 531–534.

Van Ness, J. (1979), "On the Effects of Dimension in Discriminant Analysis for Unequal Covariance Populations," *Technometrics* **21,** 119–127.

Van Ness, J. and C. Simpson (1976), "On the Effects of Dimension in Discriminant Analysis," *Technometrics* **18,** 175–187.

Wahl, P.W. and R.A. Kronmal (1977), "Discriminant Functions When Covariances are Unequal and Sample Sizes Are Moderate," *Biometrics* **33,** 479–484.

Wald, A. (1955), "Testing the Difference Between the Means of Two Normal Populations with Unknown Standard Deviations," in T.W. Anderson et al., eds. *Selected Papers in Statistics by Abraham Wald,* McGraw-Hill, New York.

Walter, J.E. (1959), "A Discriminant Function for Earnings Price Ratios of Industrial Corporations," *Review of Economics and Statistics* **41,** 44–52.

Weiner, J.M. and O.J. Dunn (1966), "Elimination of Variates in Linear Discrimination Problems," *Biometrics* **22,** 268–275.

Welch, B.L. (1947), "The Generalization of 'Students' Problems When Different Population Variances are Involved," *Biometrika* **34,** 28–35.

——— (1949), "Further Note on Mrs. Aspin's Tables on Certain Approximations to the Tabled Functions," *Biometrika* **36,** 293–296.

Yao, Y. (1965), "An Approximate Degrees of Freedom Solution to the Multivariate Behrens–Fisher Problem" *Biometrika* **52,** 139–147.

Zumwalt, J.K. (1975), "A Multivariate Analysis of the Preferred Stock Ratings of Electric Utilities," presented at the 1975 Midwest Finance Association Meetings.

Chapter IV

Abate, R.P. (1969), "Numerical Scoring Systems for Commercial Loans," *Journal of Commercial Bank Lending* **51,** No. 11, 32–36.

Altman, E.I., M. Margaine, M. Schlosser, and P. Vernimmen (1974), "Financial and Statistical Analysis for Commercial Loan Evaluation: A French Experience," *Journal of Financial and Quantitative Analysis* **9,** 195–214.

Altman, E.I. and R.A. Eisenbeis (1978), "Financial Applications of Discriminant Analysis: A Clarification," *Journal of Financial and Quantitative Analysis* **13,** 185–195.

Amstutz, A.E. and L.H. Liebman (1966), "Micro-Analytic Customer Account Review," *Industrial Management Review* **8,** 25–35.

Apilado, V.P., D.C. Warner, and J.J. Dauten (1974), "Evaluative Techniques in Consumer Finance—Experimental Results and Policy Implications," *Journal of Financial and Quantitative Analysis* **9,** 275–286.

Avery, R.B. (1977), "Credit Scoring Models with Discriminant Analysis and Truncated Samples," unpublished paper.

Bates, T. (1973), "An Econometric Analysis of Lending to Black Businessmen," *Review of Economics and Statistics* **55,** 272–283.

Biborosch, R.A. (1965), "Numerical Credit Scoring," *Credit World* **53,** 6–9.

——— (1967), "Credit Scoring Systems Have Built-In Bonuses," *Bankers Monthly Magazine* **84,** 40–44.

Bierman, H. and W.H. Hausman (1970), "The Credit Granting Decision," *Management Science* **16,** 519–532.

Boggess, W.P. (1967), "Screen-test Your Credit Risks," *Harvard Business Review* **46,** 113–123.

Cannellys, N. (1967), "Automation and Computers in Commercial Lending," *Journal of Commercial Bank Lending* **49,** No. 9, 21–27.

Chandler, G.G. and J.Y. Coffman (1977), "Using Credit Scoring to Improve the Quality of Consumer Receivables: Legal and Statistical Implications," presented at the Financial Management Association Meetings, Seattle, Wash.

Chandler, G.G. and D.C. Ewert (1975), "The Value of Credit Reports Versus Their Costs," Proceedings of the Eastern Finance Association Meetings.

Chang, P.C. and A.A. Afifi (1974), "Classification Based on Dichotomous and Continuous Variables," *Journal of the American Statistical Association* **69,** 336–339.

Chatterjee, S. and S. Barcun (1970), "An Nonparametric Approach to Credit Screening," *Journal of the American Statistical Association* **65,** 150–154.

Chesser, D. (1974), "Predicting Loan Noncompliance," *Journal of Commercial Bank Lending* **56,** No. 8, 28–38.

Coakley, W.D. (1970), "Points for Small Loan Credit Scoring," Burroughs Clearing House **55,** 28–29, 54 f.

Cohen, K.J., T.G. Gilmore, and F.A. Singer (1966), "Bank Procedures for Analyzing Business Loan Applications," in F.F. Hammer and K.J. Cohen, eds., *Analytical Methods in Banking,* Irwin, Homewood, Ill. 281–351.

Cooley, W.W. and P.R. Lohnes (1962), *Multivariate Procedures for Behavioral Sciences* Wiley, New York.

——— (1971), *Multivariate Data Analysis* Wiley, New York.

Dirickx, Y.M. and L. Wakeman (1976), "An Extension of the Bierman–Hausman Model for Credit Granting," *Management Science* **22,** 1229–1237.

Durand, D. (1941), *Risk Elements in Consumer Installment Lending,* Studies in Consumer Installment Financing, No. 8, National Bureau of Economic Research, Inc., New York, N.Y.

Edelstein, R.H. (1975), "Improving the Selection of Credit Risks: An Analysis of A Commercial Bank Minority Lending Program," *Journal of Finance* **30,** 37–55.

Edmister, R.O. (1971), "Financial Ratios and Credit Scoring for Small Business Loans," *Journal of Commercial Bank Lending* **53,** 10–23.

Edmister, R.O. and G.G. Schlarbaum (1974), "Credit Policy in Lending Institutions," *Journal of Financial and Quantitative Analysis* **9,** 335–355.

Eisenbeis, R.A. (1977), "Pitfalls in the Application of Discriminant Analysis in Business, Finance, and Economics," *Journal of Finance* **32,** 887–893.

——— (1978), "Problems in Applying Discriminant Analysis in Credit Scoring Models," *Journal of Banking and Finance* **2,** 205–219.

Eisenbeis, R.A. and R.B. Avery (1972), *Discriminant Analysis and Classification Procedures: Theory and Applications,* D.C. Heath, Lexington, Mass.

Eisenbeis, R.A., G.C. Gilbert and R.B. Avery (1973), "Investigating the Relative Importance of Individual Variables and Variable Subsets in Discriminant Analysis," *Communications in Statistics* **2,** 205–219.

Evans, C.D. (1971), "An Analysis of Successful and Unsuccessful Farm Loans in South Dakota," U.S. Department of Agriculture, Economic Research Section.

Ewert, D.C. (1969), "Trade Credit Manager: Selection of Accounts Receivable Using A Statistical Model," Institute for Research in the Behavioral, Economic and Management Sciences, Krannert Graduate School of Industrial Administration, Purdue University, Paper No. 236.

Ewert, D.C. and G.G. Chandler (1974a), "Credit Formulas for Loan Extension," *Atlanta Economic Review* **24,** No. 4, 34–37.

Ewert, D.C. and G.G. Chandler (1974b), "Monitoring Slow-paying Credit Card Accounts to Improve Collection Efficiency," Proceedings of the Eastern Finance Association Meetings.

Gau, G.W. (1978), "A Taxanomic Model for Risk-Rating of Residential Mortgages," *Journal of Business* **51,** 687–707.

Gooch, L.L., G.R. Wagner, and D.W. Statham (1973), "A Method for Obtaining Personalized Credit Scoring Systems," *Credit World* **61,** 12–15.

Greer, C.C. (1967a), "The Optimal Credit Acceptance Policy," *Journal of Financial and Quantitative Analysis* **2,** 399–415.

——— (1967b), "Measuring the Value of Information in Consumer Credit Screening," *Management Services* **4,** 44–54.

Hammer, F.S. and Y.E. Orgler (1969), "Developments in Credit Scoring for Commercial Loans," *Journal of Commercial Bank Lending* **51,** No. 11, 25–31.

——— (1973), "Measuring Risk on Mortgage Credit," *Mortgage Banker* 71–80.

Harter, T.R. (1974), "Potentials of Credit Scoring: Myth or Fact," *Credit and Financial Management* **76,** 27–28.

Hester, D.C. (1962), "An Empirical Examination of a Commercial Bank Loan Offer Function," *Yale Economic Essays* **2,** 2–57.

——— and J.C. Pierce (1975), *Bank Management and Portfolio Behavior,* Yale University Press, New Haven and London.

Hettenhouse, G.W. and J.R. Wentworth (1971), "Credit Analysis Model—A New Look for Credit Scoring," *Journal of Commercial Bank Lending* 54, 26.

Hills, M. (1966), "Allocation Rules and their Error Rates," *Journal of the Royal Statistical Society, Series B,* **28,** 1–21.

——— (1967), "Discrimination and Allocation with Discrete Data," *Applied Statistics* **16,** 1–20.

Hsia, D.C. (1978), "Credit Scoring and the Equal Credit Opportunity Act," *Hastings Law Journal* **30,** 371–448.

James, G.S. (1954), "Tests of Linear Hypotheses in Univariate and Multivariate Analysis When the Ratios of the Population Variances are Unknown," *Biometrika* **41,** 19–43.

Lachenbruch, P.A. (1975), *Discriminant Analysis,* Hafner Press, New York.

Lane, S. (1972), "Submarginal Credit Risk Classification," *Journal of Financial and Quantitative Analysis* **7,** 1379–1386.

Linhart, H. (1959), "Techniques for Discrimination with Discrete Variables," *Metrica* **2,** 138–149.

——— (1973), *Credit Scoring Development for Optimal Credit Extension and Management Control,* Ph.D. dissertation, Purdue University.

Long, M.S. (1976), "Credit Screening System Selection," *Journal of Financial and Quantitative Analysis* **11,** 313–328.

McGarth, J.L. (1960), "Improving Credit Evaluation with a Weighted Application Blank," *Journal of Applied Psychology* **44,** 325–328.

Marks, S. and O.J. Dunn (1974), "Discriminant Functions When Covariance Matrix are Unequal," *Journal of the American Statistical Association* **69,** 555–559.

Martell, T. and R.L. Fitts (1977), "Determinants of Bank Trust Department Usage," unpublished paper, University of Alabama.

Mehta, D. (1968), "The Formulation of Credit Policy Models," *Management Science* **15,** B30–B50.

——— (1970), "Optimal Credit Policy Selection: A Dynamic Approach," *Journal of Financial and Quantative Analysis* **5,** 421–444.

Mitchner, M. and R.P. Peterson (1957), "An Operations-Research Study of the Collection of Defaulted Loans," *Operations Research* **5,** 522–545.

Myers, J.H. and E.W. Forgy (1963), "The Development of Numerical Credit Evaluation Systems," *Journal of the American Statistical Association* **58,** 799–806.

Orgler, Yair E. (1970), "A Credit Scoring Model for Commercial Loans," *Journal of Money Credit and Banking* **2,** 435–445.

——— (1971), "Evaluation of Consumer Loan Portfolios with Credit Scoring Models," *Journal of Bank Research* **2,** 31–37.

Pinches, G.E. (1978), "Classification Results and Multiple Discriminant Analysis," Working Paper No. 116, School of Business Working Paper Series, The University of Kansas.

Pratt, R.J.A. and W.P. McGhee (1967), "An Application of Multivariate Statistical Techniques As an Aid in Decision Making with Regard to Applications for Credit," Investigation of Corporate Credit and Risk Policies Working Paper No. 2, Graduate School of Business, University of Pittsburgh.

Pye, G. and A. Tezel (1974), "Optimal Foreclosure Policies," *Management Science* **21,** 141–147.

Reinsel, E. and J. Brake (1966), "Borrower Characteristics Related to Farm Loan Repayment," Research Report #59, Agricultural Experiment Station, Michigan State University.

Roy, H.J.H. and E.M. Lewis (1970), "Overcoming Obstacles in Using Credit Scoring Systems," *Credit World* **58,** 16–18.

——— and R.D. Sanderson (1972), "Human Judgment vs. Credit Scoring," *Credit World* **60.**

Rulon, P.J., D.V. Tiedeman, M.M. Tatsuka, and C.R. Longmuir (1967), *Multivariate Statistics for Personnel Classification,* Wiley, New York.

Sexton, D.E., Jr. (1977), "Determining Good and Bad Credit Risks Among High- and Low-Income Families," *The Journal of Business* **50,** 236–239.

Shinkel, B.A. (1977), "Alternative Methodologies to Reduce Selection Bias in Credit Scoring," paper presented at the 1977 Financial Management Association Meetings, Seattle, Wash.

Smith, P.F. (1964), "Measuring Risks on Consumer Installment Credit," *Management Science* **11,** 327–340.

Weingartner, H.M. (1966), "Concepts and Utilization of Credit-Scoring Techniques," *Banking* **58,** 51–53.

Work, G.R. (1967), "Loan Decision Market and the Critical Assumption," *Journal of Commercial Bank Lending* **49,** No. 10, 16–23.

Chapter V

Altman, E. (1968), "Financial Ratios, Discriminant Analysis and the Prediction of Corporate Bankruptcy, *Journal of Finance* **23,** 589–619.

Altman, E., M. Margaine, M. Schlosser and P. Vernimmen (1974), "Financial and Statistical Analysis for Commercial Loan Evaluation: A French Experience, *Journal of Financial and Quantitative Analysis* **9,** 195–212.

Altman, E. and S. Katz (1976), "Statistical Bond Rating Classification Using Financial and Accounting Data," *NYU Working Paper,* Fall 1974; and in M. Schiff and G. Sorter, eds., *Topical Research in Accounting,* NYU Press.

Alves, J. and I. Dambolena (1979), "Industry Relative Information and Corporate Failure," *Eastern Finance Association.*

Ang, J. and K. Patel (1975), "Bond Rating Methods: Comparison and Validation," *Journal of Finance* **30,** 631–640.

Atkinson, T. and E. Simpson (1967), *Trends in Corporate Bond Quality,* New York, National Bureau of Economic Research.

Bhandari, S., R. Soldofsky, and J. Boe (1979), "Discriminant Analysis Model For Predicting Rating Changes of Industrial Bonds," *Financial Management* **8,** 74–81.

Burke, R. (1974), "Remarks" made before the *New York Society of Security Analysts, Computer Application Section,* New York City.

Cochran, W.G. (1964), "On the Performance of the Linear Discriminant Function," *Technometrics,* May.

——— (1977), "Pitfalls in the Application of Discriminant Analysis in Business, Finance and Economics," *Journal of Finance* **32,** 875–900.

Edmister, R.O. (1972), "An Empirical Test of Financial Ratio Analysis For Small Business Prediction," *Journal of Financial and Quantitative Analysis* **VII,** No. 1.

Eisenbeis, R. (1978), "A Comment on a Multivariate Analysis of Industrial Bond Ratings and the Role of Subordination," *Journal of Finance* **33,** 325–335.

Fisher, L. (1959), "Determinants of Risk Premiums on Corporate Bonds," *The Journal of Political Economy,* 217–237.

Forster, G. (1978), *Financial Statement Analysis,* Prentice Hall, New York.

Fraser, R. (1976), Comment on Altman–Katz (above), in M. Schiff and G. Sorter, eds., *Topical Research in Accounting,* NYU Press.

Grier, P. and S. Katz (1976), "The Differential Effects of Bond Rating Changes Among Industrial and Public Utility Bonds By Maturity," *Journal of Business* **49,** 226–239.

Harold, G. (1938), *Bond Rating as an Investment Guide,* Ronald Press, New York.

Hettenhouse, G. and W. Sartoris (1976), "An Analysis of the Informational Value of Bond Rating Changes," *Quarterly Review of Economics and Business* **16.**

Hickman, W.B. (1958), *Corporate Bonds: Quality and Investment,* National Bureau of Economic Research, Princeton University Press.

Horrigan, J. (1966), "The Determination of Long Term Credit Standing with Financial Ratios," Empirical Research in Accounting: Selected Studies, Supplement to Volume 4, *Journal of Accounting Research,* **4** Suppl.

Kaplan, R. and G. Urwitz (1979), "Statistical Models of Bond Ratings: A Methodological Inquiry," *Journal of Business* **52,** 231–262.

Katz, S. (1974), "The Price Adjustment Process of Bonds to Rating Reclassifications," *Journal of Finance* **29,** May. 551–559

Lachenbruch, P. (1967), "An Almost Unbiased Method of Obtaining

Confidence Intervals for the Probability of Misclassification in Discriminant Analysis," *Biometrics* December.

Lev, B. (1974), *Financial Statement Analysis: A New Approach,* Prentice-Hall, Englewood Cliffs, New Jersey.

Long, H. (1974), "An Analysis of the Determinants and Predictability of Agency Ratings of Domestic Utility Bond Quality," *Journal of Finance* **29,** December.

McKelvey, R. and W. Zavolina (1975), "A Statistical Model for the Analysis of Ordinal Level Dependent Variables," *Journal of Mathematical Sociology* Summer.

Martin, D. (1977), "Logit Analysis and Early Warning Systems for Bank Supervision," *Journal of Banking and Finance* **1,** 249–276.

Melicher, R. and D. Rush (1974), "Systematic Risk, Financial Data, and Bond Rating Relationships in a Regulated Industry Environment," *Journal of Finance* **29,** May.

Morton, T.G. and D. McLeavey (1976), "A Cluster Analysis of Industrial Bond Rating" Working Paper, University of Connecticut.

Pinches, G. and K. Mingo (1973), "A Multivariate Analysis of Industrial Bond Ratings," *Journal of Finance* **28,** 1–18.

——— (1975), "A Note on the Role of Subordination in Determining Industrial Bond Ratings, *Journal of Finance* **33,** 336–344.

Pinches, George and J.C. Singleton (1978), "The Adjustment of Stock Prices To Bond Rating Changes," *Journal of Finance* **33,** 29–44.

Pogue, T. and R. Soldofsky (1969), "What's in a Bond Rating?" *Journal of Financial and Quantitative Analysis* **4,** June.

——— and D. Wert (1978), "An Examination of Factors Influencing Bond Ratings," Midwest Finance Association Meeting.

Rappaport, A., J. Murphy and A. Parr (1979), "A Discriminant Analysis of the Commercial Paper Ratings of Industrial Companies," paper presented at the Financial Management Association Meeting.

Reilly, F. and M. Joehnx (1976), "The Association Between Market Determined Risk Measures for Bonds and Bond Ratings," *Journal of Finance* **5.**

Sinkey, J. (1979), *Problem and Failed Institutions in the Commercial Banking Industry,* JAI Press, Greenwich, Conn.

Standard & Poor's Rating Guide, McGraw-Hill, 1979.

Tambini, L. (1969), "Financial Policy and the Corporate Income Tax," in A.C. Harberger and M.J. Bailey, eds., *The Taxation of Income,* from Capital, Brookings Institution, Washington, D.C.

Weinstein, M. (1977), "The Effect of a Rating Change Announcement on Bond Price," *Journal of Financial Economics,* **5.**

——— (1978), "The Seasoning Process of New Corporate Bond Issues," *Journal of Finance* **33,** 1343–1357.

West, R.R. (1970), "An Alternative Approach to Predicting Corporate Bond Ratings," *Journal of Accounting Research* **8,** 118–125.

——— (1973), "Bond Ratings, Bond Yields, and Financial Regulation: Some Findings," *Journal of Law and Economics* **16,** 158–168.

Chapter VI

Altman, E. (1968), "Financial Ratios, Discriminant Analysis and the Prediction of Corporate Bankruptcy," *Journal of Finance* **23,** 589–619.

Altman, E. (1977a), "Statistical Replication of Bond Quality Ratings: A Worthwhile or Futile Exercise," *Salomon Brothers Center for the Study of Financial Institutions,* Working Paper No. 121.

Altman, E. (1977b), "Predicting Performance In the Savings & Loan Industry," *Journal of Monetary Economics* **3,** 443–466.

——— (1981), "Statistical Classification Models Applied to Common Stock Analysis," *Journal of Business Research,* forthcoming.

Altman, E. and M. Brenner (1981), "Information Effects and Stock Market Response to Signs of Firm Deterioration," *Journal of Financial and Quantitative Analysis* **16,** forthcoming.

Altman, E. and R. Eisenbeis (1978), "Financial Applications of Discriminant Analysis: A Clarification," *Journal of Financial and Quantitative Analysis* **13,** 185–196.

Altman, E., Haldeman, R., and P. Narayanan (1977), "ZETA Analysis: A New Model for the Identification of Bankruptcy Risk," *Journal of Banking and Finance* **1,** 29–54.

Altman, E. and S. Katz, (1976), "An Analysis of Bond Ratings in the Electric Public Utility Industry," Proceedings of the *Conference on "Topical Research in Accounting,"* G. Sorter and M. Schiff, eds., Ross Institute at N.Y.U.

Bear, F. (1973), *The Use of Multiple Discriminant Analysis to Predict Common Stock Price Movements,* Ph.D. dissertation, University of Georgia.

Bierman, H. and R. West (1966), "The Acquisition of Common Stock by the Corporate Issuer," *Journal of Finance* **21,** December.

Black, F. (1972), "Capital Market Equilibrium with Restricted Borrowing," *Journal of Business* **45,** 444–455.

Cochran, W.G. (1964), "On the Performance of the Linear Discriminant Function," *Technometrics* May.

Eisenbeis, R. (1977), "Pitfalls in the Application of Discriminant Analysis," *Journal of Finance* **32,** 875–900.

Eisenbeis, R. and R. Avery (1972), *Discriminant Analysis and Classification Procedures,* Lexington Books, Lexington, Mass.

Elton, E. and M. Gruber (1968), "The Effects of Share Repurchase on the Value of the Firm," *Journal of Finance* **23,** March.

Fama, E. (1970), "Efficient Capital Markets: A Review of Theory and Empirical Work," *Journal of Finance* **25,** May.

Fama, E. and J. MacBeth (1973), "Risk, Return and Equilibrium: Empirical Tests," *Journal of Political Economy* **81,** 607–636.

Farrell, J. (1974), "Analyzing Covariation of Returns to Determine Homogeneous Stock Groupings," *Journal of Business* **47,** 186–207.

Farrell, J. and G. Pinches (1979), "Using the Dividend Capitalization Model to Analyze Differences in 'Growth' or 'Non-Growth' Stocks," Working Paper.

Fisher, L. (1959), "Determinants of Risk Premiums on Corporate Bonds," *Journal of Political Economy* **67,** June.

Frank, W. and J. Weygandt (1971), "A Prediction Model of Convertible Debentures," *Journal of Accounting Research* **9,** 116–126.

Gonedes, N. (1974), "Capital Market Equilibrium and Annual Accounting Numbers: Empirical Evidence," *Journal of Accounting Research* **12,** 36–62.

Graham, B. and D. Dodd (1961), *Security Analysis,* McGraw-Hill, New York.

Haslem, J. and W. Longbrake (1971), "A Discriminant Analysis of Commercial Bank Profitability," *Quarterly Review of Economics and Business* **3,** Fall.

Horrigan, J. (1966), "The Determination of the Long Term Credit Standing with Financial Ratios," *Journal of Accounting Research* **4,** 44–62.

Jensen, M. (1972), "Capital Markets: Theory and Evidence," *Bell Journal of Economics and Management Science* **3,** 357–398.

Johnson, T. and W. Landes (1979), "Financial Position and the Ability To Discriminate Firms Into Dividend Growth Groups," *FMA* Meetings, Boston, Mass.

Joy, O.M. and J. Tollefson (1975), "On the Financial Applications of Discriminant Analysis," *Journal of Financial & Quantitative Analysis* **10,** 723–739.

Kaplan, R. and G. Urwitz (1979), "Statistical Models of Bond Ratings: A Methodological Inquiry," *Journal of Business* **52,** 231–262.

Klemkowsky, R. and J.W. Petty (1973), "A Multivariate Analysis of Stock Price Variability," *Journal of Business Research* Summer.

Kshirsagar, A.M. (1972), *Multi-variate Analysis,* Marcel Dekker, N.Y.

Lintner, J. (1965), "The Valuation of Risky Assets and the Selection of Risky Investments in Stock Portfolios and Capital Budgets," *Review of Economics and Statistics* February.

Malkiel, B. (1963), "Equity Yields, Growth and the Structure of Share Prices," *American Economic Review* **53**.

Markowitz, H. (1959), *Portfolio Selection: Efficient Diversification of Investments,* Wiley, New York.

Martin, J. and D. Scott, Jr. (1974), "A Discriminant Analysis of the Corporate Debt-Equity Decision," *Financial Management* **3,** 71–79.

Mosteller, F. and D. Wallace (1963), "Inference in the Authorship Problem," *Journal of the American Statistical Association,* June.

Norgaard, C. and R. Norgaard (1974), "A Critical Examination of Share Repurchase," *Financial Management* **3,** 44–51.

Pinches, G. (1975a), "Classification Results and Multiple Discriminant Analysis," Working Paper No. 116, University of Missouri-Columbia.

Pinches, G. (1978), "Classification Results and Multiple Discriminant Analysis," Working Paper No. 116, School of Business, University of Kansas.

Pinches, G. and K. Mingo (1975), "A Note On the Role of Subordination in Determining Industrial Bond Ratings," *Journal of Finance* **33,** 336–344.

Pinches, G. and M. Mingo (1973), "A Multivariate Analysis of Industrial Bond Ratings," *Journal of Finance* **28,** 1–18.

Pogue, T. and R. Soldofsky (1969), "What's in a Bond Rating?" *Journal of Financial and Quantitative Analysis* **4,** June.

Renwick, F. (1969), "Asset Management and Investor Portfolio Behavior: Theory and Practice," *Journal of Finance* **24,** pp. 181–206.

Schick, R. and J. Verbrugge (1975), "An Analysis of Bank Price-Earnings Ratios," *Journal of Bank Research* **5,** Summer.

Sharpe, W. (1964), "Capital Asset Prices: A Theory of Market Equilibrium Under Conditions of Risk," *Journal of Finance* September.

Smith, K.V. (1965), *Classification of Investment Securities Using MDA,* Institute Paper No. 101, Purdue University, Institute for Research in Behavioral, Economic and Management Sciences.

Spero, A. (1975), *A Financial Profile of Firms Repurchasing Their Own Stoct,* Ph.D. dissertation, NYU.

Walter, J. (1959), "A Discriminant Function for Earnings-Price Ratios of Large Industrial Corporations," *Review of Economics and Statistics* February.

West, R. (1970), "An Alternative Approach to Predicting Corporate Bond Ratings," *Journal of Accounting Research* **8,** 118–125.

White, R. (1974), "A Critical Examination of Share Repurchase," *Financial Management* **3,** 68–72.

White, R. (1975), "A Multivariate Analysis of Common Stock Quality Ratings," *Financial Management Association Meetings.*

Chapter VII

Altman, E.I. (1968), "Financial Ratios, Discriminant Analysis and the Prediction of Corporate Bankruptcy," *Journal of Finance* **23,** No. 4, 589–609.

——— (1969), "Bankrupt Firms' Equity Securities As an Investment Alternative," *Financial Analysts Journal* **25,** No. 4, 129–133.

——— (1970), "Corporate Bankruptcy Prediction and Its Implications For Commercial Loan Evaluation," *The Journal of Commercial Bank Lending* **53,** No. 4, 8–22.

——— (1971), *Corporate Bankruptcy in America,* Heath Lexington Books, New York.

——— (1973), "Predicting Railroad Bankruptcies in America," *The Bell Journal of Economics and Management Science* **4,** 184–211.

——— (1976), "Capitalization of Leases and the Predictability of Financial Ratios: A Comment," *The Accounting Review* **2,** 408–412.

——— (1977), "The Z-Score Bankruptcy Model: Past, Present, and Future," in E.I. Altman and A.W. Sametz, ed., *Financial Crises,* Wiley, New York, pp. 89–129.

——— (1978), "Examining Moyer's Re-examination of Forecasting Financial Failure," *Financial Management* **7,** 76–79

Altman, E.I. and M. Brenner (1977), "Information Effects and Stock Market Response to Signs of Firm Deterioration," Salomon Brothers Center for the Study of Financial Institutions Working Paper Number Seventy-Seven.

Altman, E.I. and R. A. Eisenbeis (1978), "Financial Applications of Discriminant Analysis: A Clarification," *Journal of Financial and Quantitative Analysis* **13,** No. 1, 185–195.

Altman, E.I., R.G. Haldeman and P. Narayanan (1977), "ZETA Analysis: A New Model to Identify Bankruptcy Risk of Corporations," *Journal of Banking and Finance* **1,** 29–54.

Altman, E.I., M. Margaine, M. Schlosser and P. Vernimmen (1974), "Financial and Statistical Analysis for Commercial Loan Evaluation: A French Experience," *Journal of Financial and Quantitative Analysis* **9,** No. 2, 195–214.

Altman, E.I. and T.P. McGough (1974), "Evaluation of A Company As A Going Concern," *The Journal of Accountancy* **138,** No. 6, 50–57.

Beaver, W.H. (1967), "Financial Ratios As Predictors of Failure," *Empirical Research in Accounting: Selected Studies 1966, Journal of Accounting Research,* Supplement to Volume **4,** 71–111.

——— (1968a), "Alternative Accounting Measures As Predictors of Failure," *The Accounting Review* **43,** No. 1, 113–122.

——— (1968b), "Market Prices, Financial Ratios, and the Prediction of Failure," *Journal of Accounting Research* **6,** No. 2, 179–192.

———, J.W. Kennelly and W.M. Voss (1968), "Predictive Ability as a Criterion for the Evaluation of Accounting Data," *The Accounting Review* **43,** No. 4, 675–683.

Blum, M. (1969), "The Failing Company Doctrine," Ph.D. dissertation, Columbia University.

——— (1974), "Failing Company Discriminant Analysis." *Journal of Accounting Research* **12,** No. 1, 1–25.

——— (1977), "Discussion of the Z-Score Bankruptcy Model," in E. Altman and A. Sametz, eds., *Financial Crises,* Wiley, New York, pp. 120–129.

Cochran, W.G. (1964), "On the Performance of the Linear Discriminant Function," *Technometrics* **6,** 179–190.

Deakin, E.B. (1972), "A Discriminant Analysis of Predictors of Business Failure," *Journal of Accounting Research* **10,** No. 1, 167–179.

——— (1976), "Distributions of Financial Accounting Ratios: Some Empirical Evidence," *The Accounting Review* **51,** No. 1, 90–96.

——— (1977), "Business Failure Prediction: An Empirical Analysis," in E.I. Altman and A.W. Sametz, eds., *Financial Crises,* Wiley, New York, pp. 72–88.

Edmister, R.O. (1972), "An Empirical Test of Financial Ratio Analysis for Small Business Failure Prediction," *Journal of Financial and Quantitative Analysis* **7,** No. 2, 1477–1493.

Eisenbeis, R.A. (1977), "Pitfalls in the Application of Discriminant Analysis in Business, Finance, and Economics," *Journal of Finance* **32,** No. 3, 875–900.

Elam, R. (1975), "The Effect of Lease Data on the Predictive Ability of Financial Ratios," *The Accounting Review* **50,** No. 1, 25–43.

Gupta, M.C. and R.J. Huefner (1972), "A Cluster Analysis Study of Financial Ratios and Industry Characteristics," *Journal of Accounting Research* **10,** No. 1, 77–95.

"How to Figure Who's Going Bankrupt," *Dun's Review,* October, 1975, pp. 63, 64, 107, 108.

Johnson, C.G. (1970), "Ratio Analysis and the Prediction of Firm Failure," *Journal of Finance* **251,** 1116–1172.

Joy, O.M. and J.O. Tollefson (1975), "On the Financial Applications of Discriminant Analysis," *Journal of Financial and Quantitative Analysis* **101,** 723–739.

——— (1978), "Some Clarifying Comments on Discriminant Analysis," *Journal of Financial and Quantitative Analysis* **13,** 197–200.

Karson, M.J and T.F. Martell (1980), "On the Interpretation of Individual Variables in Multiple Discriminant Analysis," *Journal of Financial and Quantitative Analysis* **15,** No. 1, 219–236.

Kennedy, H.A. (1975), "A Behavioral Study of the Usefulness of Four Financial Ratios," *Journal of Accounting Research* **13,** No. 1, 97–116.

Kristy, J.E. (1977), "Sidestepping Those Big Bankruptcies," *Credit and Financial Management* **79,** No. 7, 16, 17, 38.

Libby, R. (1975), "Accounting Ratios and the Prediction of Failure: Some Behavioral Evidence," *Journal of Accounting Research* **13,** No. 1, 150–161.

Mears, P.K. (1967), "Discussion of Financial Ratios as Predictors of Failure," *Empirical Research in Accounting: Selected Studies 1966, Journal of Accounting Research,* Supplement to Volume **4,** 119–122.

Moyer, C.R. (1977), "Forecasting Financial Failure: A Re-Examination," *Financial Management* **6,** 11–17.

Moyer, C.R. (1978), "Reply to 'Examining Moyer's Re-Examination of Forecasting Financial Failure,' " *Financial Management* **7,** 80–81.

Nash, N.C. (1976), "Recessions Legacy: A Rise in Bankruptcies," *The New York Times,* October 12, Section 3, 1, 16.

Neter, J. (1967), "Discussion of Financial Ratios as Predictors of Failure," *Empirical Research in Accounting: Selected Studies 1966, Journal of Accounting Research,* Supplement to Volume **4,** 112–118.

Rand, A. (1961), *For the New Intellectual: The Philosophy of Ayn Rand,* The New American Library, New York, p. 10.

Scott, E. (1978), "On the Financial Applications of Discriminant Analysis: Comment," *Journal of Financial and Quantitative Analysis* **13,** 201–205.

Scott, J. (1981), "The Probability of Bankruptcy: A Comparison of Empirical Predictions and Theoretical Models," *Journal of Banking and Finance,* forthcoming.

Wilcox, J.W. (1971a), "A Gambler's Ruin Prediction of Business Failure Using Accounting Data," *Sloan Management Review* **12,** No. 3, 1–10.

——— (1971b), "A Simple Theory of Financial Ratios as Predictors of Failure," *Journal of Accounting Research* **9,** No. 2, 389–395.

——— (1973a), "Review of Corporate Bankruptcy in America," *The Journal of Accountancy* **135,** No. 2, 92–93.

——— (1973b), "A Prediction of Business Failure Using Accounting Data," *Journal of Accounting Research* (Supplement) **11,** 163–171.

——— (1976), "The Gambler's Ruin Approach to Business Risk," *Sloan Management Review* **18,** No. 1, 33–46.

Chapter VIII

Altman, E.I. (1968), "Financial Ratios, Discriminant Analysis and the Prediction of Corporate Bankruptcy," *Journal of Finance* **23,** No. 4, 589–609.

——— (1975, 1977), "The Development of a Performance-Prediction System for Savings and Loan Associations," Invited Research Working Paper No. 10, Federal Home Loan Bank Board, Washington, D.C. and *Journal of Monetary Economics* **3,** 443–466.

——— and B. Loris (1976), "A Financial Early-Warning System for Over-The-Counter Broker-Dealers," *Journal of Finance* **31,** No. 4, 1201–1217.

Beighley, H.P. (1977), "The Risk Perceptions of Bank Holding Company Debtholders," *Journal of Bank Research* **7,** No. 2, 85–93.

Collins, R.A. (1980), "An Empirical Comparison of Bankruptcy Prediction Models," *Financial Management* **9,** No. 2, 52–57.

Eisenbeis, R.A. and R.B. Avery (1972), *Discriminant Analysis and Classification Procedures: Theory and Applications,* D.C. Heath, Lexington, Mass.

Fraser, D.R. and J.P. McCormack (1977), "Bank Failures, Bank Capital, and Risk Premiums on Bank Debt Capital," paper presented at 1977 FMA Annual Meeting.

Guttentag, J.M. (1975), "Reflections on Bank Regulatory Structure and Large Bank Failures," *Proceedings of a Conference on Bank Structure and Competition,* Federal Reserve Bank of Chicago.

——— (1977), "Discussion on Identifying Financial Problems of Institutions in Today's Economy," in E.I. Altman and A.W. Sametz, eds., *Financial Crises,* Wiley, New York, pp. 56–58.

Hanweck, G.A. (1977a), "Predicting Bank Failure," Research Papers in Banking and Financial Economics, Financial Studies Section, Board of Governors of the Federal Reserve System.

——— (1977b), "Using a Simulation Model Approach for the Identification and Monitoring of Problem Banks," Research Papers in Banking and Financial Economics, Financial Studies Section, Board of Governors of the Federal Reserve System.

Haskins & Sells Study 1974–75, Haskins & Sells, New York, 1975.

Herzig-Marx, C. (1977), "Comparing Market and Regulatory Assessments of Bank Condition," paper presented at the Southern Finance Association Annual Meeting.

Hill, G.W. (1975), "Why 67 Insured Banks Failed: 1960–1974," Division of Liquidation, FDIC, Washington, D.C.

Ho, T. and A. Saunders (1980), "A Catastrophe Model of Bank Failure," *Journal of Finance* **35,** No. 5, 1189–1207.

Jackson, P.C. (1978), Remarks before the Alabama Bankers Association, May 11, 1978, Board of Governors of the Federal Reserve System.

Jones, R.H. (1975), "Probability Estimation Using a Multinomial Logistic Function," *Journal of Statistics and Computer Simulation* **3,** 315–329.

Korobow, L. and D.P. Stuhr (1975), "Toward Early Warnings of Changes in Banks' Financial Condition: A Progress Report." *Monthly Review* **57,** No. 7, 157–165.

Korobow, L., D.P. Stuhr and D. Martin (1976), "A Probabilistic Approach to Early Warning of Changes in Bank Financial Condition," *Monthly Review* **58,** No. 7, 187–194.

Manual of Examination Policies, FDIC, Washington, D.C., 1976.

Martin, D. (1977), "Early Warning of Bank Failure: A Logit Regression Approach," *Journal of Banking and Finance* **1,** No. 3, 249–276.

Meyer, P.A. and H.W. Pifer (1970), "Prediction of Bank Failures," *Journal of Finance* **25,** No. 4, 853–868.

Mullin, R.A. (1977), "The National Bank Surveillance System," in E. Altman and A. Sametz, eds., *Financial Crises,* Wiley, New York, pp. 49–55.

NBSS Bank Performance Report: A User's Guide for Bankers and Examiners (1977), Comptroller of the Currency, Washington, D.C.

Pettway, R.H. (1980), "Potential Insolvency, Market Efficiency, and Bank Regulation of Large Commercial Banks," *Journal of Financial and Quantitative Analysis* XV, No. 1, 219–236.

Pettway, R.H. and J.F. Sinkey, Jr. (1980), "Establishing On-Site Bank Examination Priorities: An Early-Warning System Using Accounting and Market Information," *Journal of Finance* **35,** No. 1, 137–150.

Rose, P.S. and W. L. Scott (1976), "Risk in Commercial Banking: Theory and Evidence from Postwar Bank Failures," paper presented at the Southern Finance Association Annual Meeting.

Santomero, A.M. and J.D. Vinso (1977), "Estimating the Probability of Failure for Commercial Banks and the Banking System." *Journal of Banking and Finance* **1,** 185–206.

Secrist, H. (1938), *National Bank Failures and Nonfailures,* The Principia Press, Bloomington, Indiana.

Sheehan, J.E. (1973), "Bank Capital Adequacy—Time to Pause and Reflect," ABA Correspondent Banking Conference Speech, November 6, 1973. Board of Governors, Washington, D.C.

Shick, R.A. and L.F. Sherman (1980), "Bank Stock Prices as an Early-Warning System for Changes in Condition," *Journal of Bank Research* **11,** No. 3, 136–146.

Sinkey, J.F., Jr. (1974), "The Way Problem Banks Perform," *The Bankers Magazine* **157,** No. 4, 40–51.

——— (1975a), "A Multivariate Statistical Analysis of the Characteristics of Problem Banks," *Journal of Finance* **30,** No. 1, 21–36.

——— (1975b), "The Failure of United States National Bank of San Diego: A Portfolio and Performance Analysis," *Journal of Bank Research* **6,** No. 1, 8–24.

——— (1975c), "Early-Warning System: Some Preliminary Predictions of Problem Commercial Banks," *Proceedings of a Conference on Bank Structure and Competition,* 85–91.

——— (1977a), Statement on the Condition of the U.S. Banking System and the Effectiveness of Bank Supervision, Committee on Banking,

Housing and Urban Affairs, United States Senate, March 11, 1977. Reprinted in the *Congressional Record.*

——— (1977b), "The Collapse of Franklin National Bank of New York," *Journal of Bank Research* **7,** No. 2, 113–122.

——— (1977c), "Problem and Failed Banks, Bank Examinations, and Early-Warning Systems: A Summary," in E.I. Altman and A.W. Sametz, eds., *Financial Crises,* Wiley, New York, pp. 24–47.

——— (1977d), "Identifying Large Problem/Failed Banks: The Case of Franklin National Bank of New York," *Journal of Financial and Quantitative Analysis* **12,** No. 5, 779–800.

——— (1978a), "The Bank-Examination Process and Major Issues in Banking: A Survey," *The Bankers Magazine* **161,** No. 3, 43–45.

——— (1978b), "Identifying 'Problem' Banks: How do the Banking Authorities Measure a Bank's Risk Exposure." *Journal of Money, Credit and Banking* **10,** No. 2, 184–193.

——— (1979), *Problem and Failed Institutions in the Commercial Banking Industry,* JAI Press, Greenwich, Conn.

——— and D.A. Walker (1975), "Problem Banks: Identification and Characteristics," *Journal of Bank Research* **5,** No. 4, 208–217.

Stuhr, D.P. and R. Van Wicklen (1974), "Rating the Financial Condition of Banks: A Statistical Approach to Bank Supervision," *Monthly Review* **56,** No. 9, 233–238.

Talmor, E. (1980), "A Normative Approach to Bank Capital Adequacy," *Journal of Financial and Quantitative Analysis* **15,** No. 4, 785–812.

Vojta, G.J. (1973), *Bank Capital Adequacy,* Citicorp, New York.

Wille, F. (1973), "The FDIC Views the Questions of Capital Adequacy," FDIC PR-82-73, (November 6, 1973 Speech), Washington, D.C.

Author Index

Abate, R. P. 196
Adelman, I. 134
Afifi, A.A. 122, 150
Aitchison, J. 62
Albright, R.L. 82
Altman, E.I. 125, 132, 134, 153, 158, 159, 160, 162, 164, 185, 194, 197, 198, 206–209, 211, 213, 214, 216–221, 228–230, 236–242, 250, 262–277, 288, 295, 320–303, 306, 357–364, 371
Amemiya, T. 78, 83
Amstutz, A.E. 196
Anderson, T.W. 34, 36, 40, 41, 43, 44, 88, 89, 93, 94, 126, 127, 147, 163, 164
Andrews, D.F. 161
Ang, J. 212, 214, 222
Apilado, V.P. 179, 188, 194, 197
Arnold, H.J. 161
Aspin, A.A. 162
Atiqullah, M. 162
Atkinson, T. 199
Avery, R.B. 34, 102, 129, 133, 137, 138, 139, 146, 148, 162, 163, 164, 165, 192, 194, 195, 198, 235, 319, 327

Bahadur, R.R. 127, 147
Bailey, D.E. 35
Banerjee, S.K. 162
Barcun, S. 176, 188, 189, 190, 191, 192, 193, 197, 198
Bartlett, M.S. 92, 139, 141, 162, 164
Bates, T. 125, 162, 184, 187, 192, 194, 197
Bear, F. 242, 251
Beaver, W. 257–262, 281, 302–303
Ben-Akiva, M. 71
Bennett, B.M. 162
Berborosch, R.A. 196
Berkson, J. 16, 23, 24, 25, 27
Bhandari, S. 209, 210, 223
Bierman, H. 168, 169, 170, 171, 172, 197, 244
Black, F. 238
Bliss, C.I. 14
Blum, M. 277–280, 302, 304
Boe, J. 209, 210, 223

Boggess, W.P. 176, 188, 197, 198
Box, G.E.P. 45, 93, 94, 162
Brake, J. 174, 188, 197
Brenner, M. 238–242, 250, 272
Broffit, J.D. 156, 165
Bulgrew, W.G. 161
Burke, R. 200

Cannellys, N. 196
Carleton, W.T. 125, 134, 163
Chandler, G.G. 167, 180, 187, 189, 191, 193, 194, 195, 197, 180, 187, 191, 193, 194, 195, 197, 198
Chang, P.C. 122, 190
Chase, G.R. 161
Chatterjee, S. 176, 188, 189, 190, 191, 192, 193, 197, 198
Chen, H.J. 161
Chinganda, E.F. 125
Chesser, D. 184, 187, 189, 192, 193, 197
Cicchetti, C.J. 8
Cloy, P.P.F. 126, 161, 162
Clumies-Ross, C.W. 127
Cookley, W.D. 196
Cochran, W.G. 122, 123, 142, 154, 164, 207, 229, 243, 301, 400
Coffman, J.Y. 167, 189, 191, 194, 195, 197
Cohen, K.J. 182, 197, 198
Collins, R. 361, 371
Cooley, W.W. 34, 86, 126, 146, 162, 163, 198
Cosslett, S.R. 104
Cox, D. 15, 24

D'Agostino, R.B. 161
Dahm, P. 62
Dauten, J.J. 179, 188, 194, 197
Deakin, E. 280–283, 286–289, 303
DeGroot, M.H. 36
Dillon, W.R. 123, 164
Dirickx, Y.M. 168, 170, 172, 197
Dodd, D. 232
Domeneich, T. 7, 9, 24, 26, 70, 108, 109, 116
Duncan, D. 28, 78
Dunn, O.J. 126, 127, 218, 219, 137, 138, 145, 163, 164, 165, 191
Durand, D. 173, 188, 191, 193, 195, 197

Edelstein, R.H. 186, 187, 193, 197, 198
Edmister, R.O. 132, 142, 168, 170, 171, 172, 183; 194, 197, 198, 289–292, 304
Eisenbeis, R.A. 11, 34, 112, 122, 129, 133, 137, 138, 139, 146, 147, 148, 153, 158, 159, 160, 162, 163, 164, 165, 192, 196, 198, 235–236, 240, 271, 319, 327
Elam, R. 292–295, 305
Elashoff, J.D. 164
Elton, E. 244
Evans, C.D. 176, 187, 188, 197, 198
Evert, D.C. 180, 182, 187, 191, 193, 194, 197, 198

Fama, E. 237, 239, 241
Farrell, J. 231
Finney, D. 14, 30
Fisher, L. 202–204, 216, 230
Fisher, R.A. 33, 38, 48, 87, 97, 120, 127, 129, 162
Fitts, R.L. 162, 198
Fletcher, R. 55
Forgy, E.W. 174, 187, 188, 189, 192, 197, 198
Fortson, J.C. 134, 153

Francia, R.S. 161
Frank, R.E. 154, 155, 164, 165
Frank, W. 243, 244, 252
Fraser, R. 200

Gau, G.W. 181, 197
Ghosh, B.K. 162
Gilbert, E.S. 122, 123, 127, 129, 162
Gilbert, G.G. 137, 138, 139, 146, 147, 159, 162, 163, 164, 192
Gilmore, T.G. 182, 197
Glick, N. 122
Gnandesikan, J.I. 161
Goldberger, A.S. 6, 109
Goldfeld, S. 30, 31, 55
Goldman, G.E. 164
Goldstein, M. 123, 164, 165
Gonedes, N. 238–242, 250
Gooch, L.L. 197
Goodman, J.L. 7
Graham, B. 232
Green, P. 34
Greer, C.C. 168, 169, 171, 172, 197
Grier, P. 202
Gruber, M. 244
Gurland, J. 62, 162
Guttentag, J. 315, 344–346

Habbema, J.D.F. 139, 143, 146, 150
Haberman, S. 31
Haldeman, R. 215, 153, 237, 241, 272–277, 306
Hammu, F.S. 196
Hanweck, G. 345–348, 369
Harold, G. 199
Harter, T.R. 153, 179, 188, 193, 194, 197
Hartley, H.O. 162
Haslem, J.N. 163, 233, 236, 237, 249
Hausman, J.A. 20, 82
Hausman, W.H. 168, 169, 170, 171, 172, 197
Heckman, J.J. 104
Hermans, J. 139, 143, 146, 150
Hester, D.C. 171
Hettenhouse, G.W. 177, 193, 194, 197, 202
Hickman, W.B. 199
Hill, G. 310
Hills, M. 121, 122, 123, 162, 165, 190
Holloway, L.N. 126
Hopkins, C.E. 122, 123
Hopkins, J.W. 126, 161, 162
Horrigan, J.O. 62, 203–206, 208, 210–213, 216, 220, 228
Hotelling, H. 46, 93
Horton, Jr., J.J. 125
Hotz, V.J. 19
Hsia, D.C. 167

Ito, K. 126

Jackson, P. 364
James, G.S. 144, 162, 198
Jensen, M. 238
Johnson, C. 270, 302
Johnson, T. 231
Jones, R. 339
Joy, M.O. 132, 139, 153, 158, 159, 160, 163, 164, 240, 270–272

Kaplan, R. 64, 205, 210–213, 222, 228, 231
Karson, M. 144, 275
Katz, S. 134, 164, 202, 206, 208, 209, 211, 213, 214, 216, 221, 228
Klemkowsky, R. 163, 233, 235, 249
Klett, C.J. 34

Kmenta, J. 143
Kohn, M. 19
Korobow, L. 333, 368
Kronmal, R.A. 128, 129
Krzanowski, W.J. 122, 123
Kshirsagar, A.M. 139, 141, 142, 163, 164, 240

Lachenbruch, P.A. 106, 123, 125, 134, 135, 154, 163, 155, 156, 157, 158, 164, 165, 198, 208
Ladd, G.W. 49, 163, 164
Landes, W. 231
Lane, S. 162, 178, 187, 188, 191, 194, 197
Langmuir, C.R. 126, 196
Lee, A.F.S. 162
Lee, T. 27, 69
Lehman, E.L. 162
Lerman, S.R. 82, 103, 104
Lerner, E.M. 125, 134, 163
Lewis, E.M. 196
Lev, B. 200
Libby, R. 283–286, 305
Liebman, L.H. 196
Linhart, H. 122, 190
Lintner, J. 238
Loeblecke, J. 257
Long, M.S. 168, 170, 171, 172, 195
Longbrake, W. 233, 236, 237, 249, 163
Lohnes, P. R. 126, 127, 146, 162, 163, 198
Loris, B. 361–364, 371
Lowe, V.W. 134
Luce, R.D. 20, 70, 75

Maddala, G.S. 54
Malkiel, B. 232
Manski, C. 19, 82, 103, 104
Mardia, K.N. 121, 161, 162
Margaine, M. 185, 194, 197, 198, 207
Markowitz, H. 238
Marks, S. 127, 128, 129, 191
Martell, T.F. 144, 162, 198, 275
Martin, D. 19, 316, 327–328, 333–339, 368
Martin, J. 242, 243, 251
Massy, W.F. 154, 156, 164, 165
Matuseta, K. 123
MacBeth, J. 239, 241
McCabe, G.P. 146, 164, 165
McCall, A.S. 11, 112, 162
McDonald, L.I. 134
McFadden, D. 7, 9, 18, 19, 21, 24, 26, 70, 71, 73, 74, 75, 78, 104, 108, 109, 111, 116, 121, 143
McGarth, J.C. 196
McGhee, W.P. 175, 188, 193, 197, 198
McGillivray, R. 6
McGough, T. 271, 288
McHenry, C.F. 164, 165
McKay, R.J. 163, 164, 165
McKelvey, R. 63, 204
McLeavey, D. 207, 218, 222
McLochlau, G.J. 134, 139, 147, 154, 155, 156, 157, 158, 163, 164, 165
Mears, P. 301, 400
Mehta, D. 168, 169, 172, 197
Meister, K.A. 134
Meyer, P. 151, 153, 163, 312–315, 329, 367
Michaelis, J. 162
Mickey, M.R. 106, 154, 155, 156, 157, 158, 164, 165
Mingo, K. 125, 134, 142, 159, 206–208, 213, 221, 228, 229
Mitchner, J.H. 174, 187, 188, 189, 192, 197, 198
Moore, D.H. 105, 123, 124

Moran, M.A. 156, 165
Morris, C.T. 134
Morrison, D.G. 109, 154, 155, 164, 165
Mortson, T.G. 207, 218, 222
Mosteller, F. 136, 139, 236
Moyer, C. 400
Mullin, R. 339
Mundel, D. 19
Murphy, J. 209, 223
Murphy, N.B. 162, 165
Murray, G.D. 164

Narayanan, P. 125, 153, 237, 241, 272–277, 306
Nerlove, M. 27, 38, 70, 72, 73, 121
Neter, J. 301, 400
Neymon, J. 162
Norgaard, C. 163, 244, 245, 252
Norgard, R. 163, 245, 252

Okamota, M. 165
Orgler, Y.E. 178, 183, 187, 194, 197, 196, 198
Overall, J.E. 34

Pagurova, V.I. 162
Parr, A. 209, 223
Patel, K. 212, 214, 222
Pearson, E.S. 162
Peterson, R.P. 197
Pettway, R. 354–357, 370
Petty, J.W. 163, 233, 235, 249
Pierce, J.C. 171
Pifer, H.W. 151, 153, 163, 312–315, 329, 367
Pinches, G. 206–208, 213, 221, 228, 231, 240
Pindyck, R.S. 19, 69
Plackett, R.L. 162
Pogue, T.F. 134, 205, 212, 213, 214, 216, 220, 228, 229
Poirier, D.J. 19
Porebski, O.R. 44, 161, 164
Powell, M.J.D. 55
Pratt, R.J.A. 175, 188, 193, 197, 198
Press, S. 27, 38, 70, 72, 73, 121
Pye, G. 197

Quant, R. 30, 31, 55

Rand, A. 255, 301
Rao, C.R. 46, 54, 92, 95, 99, 133, 147, 148, 163
Rappaport, A. 209, 223
Remsel, E. 174, 188, 197
Reno, L.T. 123, 125
Renwick, F. 242
Riffenburgh, R.H. 127
Robinowitz, M. 164, 165
Roy, H.J.H. 196, 197
Roy, J. 145, 164, 165
Rubinfeld, O.L. 19, 69
Rulon, P.J. 126, 196

Samiuiddin, M. 162
Sanderson, R.D. 197
Santomero, A. 349–354, 369
Sartoris, W. 202
Sattath, S. 83
Schatzoff, M. 93
Scheffé, H. 126
Schick, R.A. 131, 233, 234, 249
Schlarbaum, G.G. 168, 170, 171, 172
Schlosser, M. 185, 194, 197, 198, 207
Schull, W.J. 126
Scott, Jr., D. 242, 243, 251
Scott, E. 400
Scott, J. 400
Secrist, H. 309, 364
Sedransk, N. 165

Sexton, D.E. 181, 188, 192, 197, 198
Shapiro, S.S. 161
Sharpe, W. 238
Sheehan, J. 364
Sherman, L. 356, 370
Shick, R. 356, 370
Shinkel, B.A. 195
Simpson, E. 199
Silvey, S. 62
Simon, F.H. 107
Simpson, C. 162, 164, 165
Singer, F.A. 182, 198
Sinkey, Jr., J.F. 134, 151, 153, 159, 162, 309, 315–334, 356–359, 367, 370
Smidt, R.K. 134
Smith, C.A.B. 165, 310, 311
Smith, K.V. 148, 228, 229, 230, 248
Smith, P.F. 173, 188, 189, 192, 197, 198
Smith, V.K. 8
Soldofsky, R. 134, 205, 209, 212–214, 216, 220, 223, 228
Sorum, M.J. 154, 157, 165
Spero, A. 244, 246, 253
Statham, D.W. 197
Stevens, J.P. 145, 164
Stuhr, D. 134, 333, 368
Subrahmaniam, K. 125, 162

Tambini, L. 202
Tatsuoka, M.M. 34, 100, 126, 196
Tezel, A. 197
Theil, H. 23, 26, 54, 56, 64, 70, 73, 76
Thurstone, L. 82
Tiedeman, D.V. 126, 196
Timm, N.H. 93, 94
Tobin, J. 15, 30
Tollefson, J.O. 132, 139, 153, 158, 159, 160, 163, 164, 240, 270–272
Trieschmann, J.S. 161
Tryon, R.C. 35
Tversky, A. 75, 83

Urbakh, V.Y. 139, 143, 163
Urwitz, G. 64, 205, 210, 211, 212, 213, 222, 228, 231

Van Ness, J. 162, 164, 165
Van Wicklen, R. 134, 333, 368
Varady, P.D. 165
Verbrugge, J.A. 131, 233, 234, 249
Verni, R. 257
Vernimmen, P. 185, 194, 197, 198, 207
Vinso, J. 349–354, 369
Vojta, G. 351

Wagner, G.R. 197
Wahl, P.W. 128, 129
Wakeman, L. 168, 170, 172, 197
Wald, A. 162
Walker, S. 28, 78
Wallace, D.F. 136, 139, 163, 236
Walter, J.F. 131, 133, 163, 233, 234, 248
Warner, D.C. 179, 188, 194, 197
Warner, J. 161
Warner, S.L. 7
Watanatada, T. 71
Wiener, J.M. 137, 138, 145, 163, 164, 165
Weingartner, H.M. 196
Weinstein, M. 202
Welch, B.I. 162
Wenhvoth, J.R. 177, 193, 194, 197

Weston, R. 109
West, R. 199, 202, 204–206, 210, 211, 212, 213, 216, 220, 228, 244
Weygandt, J. 243, 244, 252
White, R. 228, 229, 230, 244, 245, 248
Wilcox, J. 270, 295–300, 302–305
Wilk, M.B. 161
Wille, F. 364
Wise, D.A. 20, 82
Work, G.R. 196

Yao, Y. 162

Zavoina, W. 63
Zellner, A. 27, 69
Zemrock, P.J. 161
Zumwalt, J.K. 142

Subject Index

Altman Z-score 239–240, 262–270
A priori probabilities 36, 38, 39, 41, 54, 68, 85, 88, 89, 90, 103, 104, 107, 111, 120, 150, 151, 153, 159, 165, 173–175, 178, 179, 181, 183, 190, 193–194, 261, 272, 275, 285, 291, 301, 320, 323, 335, 363
Angular transformations 13
Arctangent model 13, 14, 27
Auditor's reports 288
Axiom of independence of irrelevant alternatives 22, 75, 80, 82, 88, 90, 111

Bankruptcy:
- model 2, 3, 4, 5, 13, 18, 22, 26, 28, 34, 35, 36, 42, 63, 101, 102, 104, 107, 255–306
- problems 182, 255–257

Bank:
- capital 309, 317, 329–331, 336, 346, 350–353
- examination 308–312, 316–318, 323, 329–331, 339–345, 356–357
- Franklin National 311, 327, 331–332, 355
- USNB of San Diego 310–312, 327, 331–332, 355

Banks:
- failed 19, 307–312, 320, 323, 328–329, 336, 338, 346–347, 355–357, 364–365
- problem, 307–312, 316–318, 320, 323, 325–332, 352–353, 357, 364–365

Bayes procedure 36, 40, 85, 172
Behrens-Fisher problem 44, 93
Berkson-Theil method 23–27, 64, 67, 76–78, 82
Board of Governors of the FRS 308, 345–348, 364
Bond rating 2, 61, 62, 64
Bonds and bond ratings:
- accuracy-of-rating studies 199–219
- "announcement effect" 211–214
- changes in ratings 202–203, 209–210

definition of ratings 201–202
industry effects 205, 215–216
"mixed (split) ratings" 217–218
municipal bonds 218
Broker-dealers, 307, 361–364

Canonical correlation 100–101, 164
Cardinal ranking 2, 59–62, 64
Causality 12, 33, 35, 36, 46, 110–112, 145
Chi-square tests 25–27, 57, 78, 86, 92–94, 99, 109, 133, 148, 327
Choice-based sampling 102–103
Choice-set size 70, 76, 77
Classification 127, 150, 154, 257, 260–261, 266–267, 270–272, 275, 278–279, 281, 284, 286–288, 291–292, 295, 298–300, 313–315, 320, 322, 325–326, 331, 336–338, 347–348, 353, 357, 359–361, 363–364
Classification:
group (choice) assignment 12, 31, 32, 39–42, 53–54, 88–90, 98, 106–108, 113–117
Lachenbruch 106, 154, 156, 208, 212, 232, 320, 322
linear 38, 40, 41, 87, 89, 90, 98, 121–126, 275, 286, 337
quadratic 37, 40, 41, 86, 89, 90, 98, 121–126, 128–129, 200, 206, 208, 230, 231, 246, 286, 320, 322, 337, 359, 363
probabilities 34–39, 85–88, 108–109, 154, 361
Cluster analysis 35, 134, 181, 200, 207
Common-stock analysis:
capital-structure decisions 227, 242–246
common-stock returns 227, 237–242
convertible debt 243–244
debt vs. equity 242–243
earnings classification 236–237
investment-category classification 227, 228–232
price-earnings ratios 131–132, 227, 232–235
price-volatility classification 235–236
share repurchase 244–246
Commercial paper 209
Comptroller of the Currency: 307, 339–345, 364
COMPUSTAT 239, 287
Conditioning methods 145, 146
Conference on Financial Crises 242
Consistent 4–6, 8–10, 24, 25, 28, 30, 56, 61, 101–103, 111
Costs of Misclassification 40, 42, 88, 89, 150, 153, 179, 180, 193, 194, 271–272, 275, 320, 323
Covariance:
coefficients 30, 56
equal group matrices 37, 38, 40, 43, 49, 87, 89, 92, 93, 98
error 3, 35, 65, 67, 77, 78, 81
unequal group matrices 37, 40, 44, 86, 89, 93, 126–127, 129, 133, 144, 189, 191, 319–320
Credit scoring:
methodology 2, 168–172
models 173–189
problems, 189–196
Credit unions 307–308, 361

Data General 267–269
DIDMCA 307
Director-interlock problem 11–12, 31–33, 52–54, 112–117

Discrete groups 120, 131, 315–316, 318
Discrete variables 122, 123, 174, 175, 180, 290, 362–363
Discriminant analysis
  discriminant functions 38, 41, 47–52, 96–102, 123, 125, 144, 148
  multigroup classification 85–90, 98
  multigroup significance tests 91–96, 98
  relation to linear probability model 33, 34, 41, 44, 46–47, 50, 54, 99, 105, 110–117
  relation to logit model 33, 34, 38, 46, 84, 88, 90, 105, 110–117
  relation to probit model 33, 34, 36, 84, 105, 110–117
  stratification 101–104, 194–195
  two-group classification 34–42, 49, 53–54, 134
  two-group significance tests 42–49, 53
Discriminant criterion 52, 99–100
Discriminant score 41, 48, 54
Dispersion (see covariance or variance)
Distribution:
  Bernoulli 5, 7
  Cauchy 14
  extreme value 21, 22, 74
  logistic 14, 16, 17, 19, 21, 23, 63, 64, 66, 71, 74
  normal 7, 14, 16, 17, 19–22, 24, 28, 30, 34, 36, 42, 56, 63, 64, 66, 74, 80, 84, 120, 121–126, 161, 189–191
Dun and Bradstreet 292
Dun's Review 257, 267
Dynamic programming models 170

Early-warning systems:
  and bank supervision 310–312
  concept of 255–257, 308–309
  information available 309–310
Efficient 4–6, 24, 28, 30, 56, 65
Efficient-market theory 216, 237–239
Eigenvalues 96, 98, 99, 126, 148
Eigenvectors 97, 100, 135, 148, 162
Elimination-by-aspects model 83
Equal credit opportunity 136, 167, 188

Factor analysis 200, 206–207, 209, 229–230, 237
Failure:
  bank 312–357
  corporate 255–306
  definition 258, 262, 277, 281, 288–290, 292–293, 298, 321, 328, 334, 346–347, 349, 362
  modeling strategies 276–277
  small business 289–292
FDIC 307, 310, 312, 323–324, 329–333, 364
Federal Reserve 345–347
FRB of New York 307, 333–339
Fitch (ratings) 199

Gambler's-ruin model 296–297
Gompit model 13
Group means 260, 264, 282, 321, 326

Haskins & Sells 339–345, 369
Heteroskedastic 5–8, 10, 12, 24–27, 69, 77, 108
Holdout sample (see classification: Lachenbruch) 106, 154, 155, 194
Hypothesis tests 6, 7, 25–27, 30–31, 42–49, 53, 56–57, 78, 91–96, 98, 99, 109

Index function 18–19, 21
Information criterion 336

Jackknife error estimates 154, 176

Keefe Bank Index 354–355

Lachenbruch (see classification)
Leases, 292–295
Least squares 2–7, 9–10, 12, 24–29, 44, 46, 47, 50, 52, 61, 65, 69, 77, 78, 99, 108, 202, 203–206, 210–212, 233–237
Likelihood ratio 37, 40, 85, 86, 89, 122–123, 261
Likelihood-ratio tests 56–57, 109, 261
Linear probability model:
  binary 2–13, 15, 16, 33, 41, 44, 50, 54, 99, 135
  ordered multiple choice 61–62, 64
  relation to discriminant analysis 33, 34, 41, 44, 46–67, 50, 54, 99, 105, 110–117
  relation to probit/logit 13, 62, 70, 105, 110–117
  stratification 101–104
  unordered multiple choice 69–70
Loan officers 284–286
Loan-review models 133
Logit (log odds) 24, 25, 26, 64, 67, 71, 76, 77
Logit model
  binary 2, 11, 16–19, 21, 23–26, 27–30, 31–33, 38, 63, 64, 66, 84, 121, 123–124, 184, 189, 190, 192, 200, 205, 210–212, 246, 234, 239
  estimation binary 23–30
  estimation multinomial 76–80
  estimation ordered multichoice 64–66
  multinomial 70–80, 82, 88
  multiple-data 71, 72, 74, 76–80, 82, 88
  multiple-weighting 71–74, 76–80, 82
  ordered multichoice 62–66, 68, 72
  relation to discriminant analysis 33, 34, 38, 46, 84, 88, 90, 105, 110, 117
  relation to linear probability model 13, 62, 70, 105, 110–117
  sequential 83–84
  stratification 101–104
Log-likelihood function 28–32, 55, 57, 65, 68, 78, 103, 109

Markow process 169
Maximum likelihood 24, 28–32, 54–57, 65–68, 78–80, 82
Measures of fit 105–109, 113–117
Memorex 267–269, 302
Minimum chi-square estimation 25–26
Misclassification rates 106–108, 113, 132, 134, 135, 154, 159, 275
Model misspecification 7, 9, 25, 70, 102
Model selection 104–117
Monte Carlo tests 8, 26, 93, 105, 124, 127
Moody's 199, 201, 207, 208, 209, 213, 214, 217–219, 228
MULDIS 319, 327
Multicollinearity 29, 80, 123–124, 142–144, 162, 164, 290
Multivariate normality (see distribution: normal)

National Bank Surveillance System (NBSS) 308, 328, 332, 339–345, 364
Nearest-neighbor procedures 122, 189, 190, 191
Net capital ratio (FDIC) 329–332
Net liquidation value 296–300
Non-linear least squares 28, 78
Nonnormality 123, 124
Non-random sampling 2, 101–104, 133, 194–195
Normal (see distribution)
Normit model 14, 27, 150

Omitted groups 132, 133
Ordinal ranking 2, 59–62, 64
Outlier approach 326–329, 340–345

Paired-sample method 151, 205, 259, 262–263, 273, 278, 281, 293, 313, 319, 358
Partial derivatives 12, 15, 16, 18, 33
Principal-components analysis 207, 284
Probabilistic choice 19–21, 73–76, 80
Probit 26, 27, 67
Probit model:
- binary 2, 11, 14–16, 18, 19, 21, 23–28, 30–32, 33, 74, 84
- estimation binary 26–27, 30–31, 121, 190, 192, 211, 212, 231, 246
- estimation ordered multichoice 67–68
- multinomial 74, 80–82
- ordered multichoice 63, 66–68
- relation to discriminant analysis 33, 34, 46, 84, 105, 110–117
- relation to linear probability model 13, 62, 70, 105, 110–117
- sequential 83, 84
- stratification 101–104

Problem banks (see banks)

Quadratic programming 9–11

R^2 measures of fit 108–109, 117
Random-coefficients model 20
Ratios:
- cash flow 260, 278, 281, 290–291, 294, 296–298
- capital 274, 329–332, 337, 346–354
- leverage 260, 263, 273–275, 290–291, 294, 319
- liquidity 260, 263, 273–275, 278, 290–291, 294, 319
- profitability 260, 263, 273–275, 278, 294, 319
- turnover 263–265, 294

Reduced-space transformations 50–52, 87, 97–99, 126
Regulation B 167, 189
Regression (see linear probability model or least squares)
Residuals 25, 108

Sample selection 258–259, 262, 273, 277, 281, 284, 286, 289, 292, 298, 313, 318–319, 334, 358, 362
Savings-and-loan associations 307–308, 357–360
Selection of variables, 145–148, 260, 263, 273–274, 278, 284, 290, 294–295, 314, 319, 324, 334, 341, 358, 362
Sequential-decision methods 169, 182
Size of bet 297
Standards & Poors 199, 201,

208–209, 213, 214, 217–219, 228, 230
Standard error (see variance)
Stationarity 160, 259
Stepwise methods 136, 137–139, 145, 146, 209, 232, 236, 237, 264, 274–275, 278, 280, 301, 320, 324, 358–359
Stock prices 268, 309–310
Substandard loans 329–332

Taylor Wine 267–269
Telex 267–269, 302
Tests:
  holdout 155, 194, 260–261, 266, 275, 278, 298–299, 320
  validation 260–261, 266, 270–272, 278–279, 287
Tests of equality of group:
  covariance matrices 45, 53, 93, 94, 126–127, 129, 133, 144, 162, 189, 191, 275, 319–320, 359, 363
  means 42–44, 46–49, 53, 91–93, 98, 121, 126, 190, 319
Tests of individual variables (see variables: ranking)
Time-series problems 158–160, 174, 186, 190, 192, 196, 259, 273
Tobit analysis 190, 246
Transformations 125, 127, 184

Unbiased 4, 5, 8–10, 12, 102, 103
Utility function 19–22, 73–76, 80, 83, 111

Variables:
  cash flow 260, 278, 281–282, 296–298
  dispersion 275, 278, 313–314
  net income 282
  ranking or tests of 46–47, 94–96, 135–144, 191–192, 229–230, 236
  total debt 282
Variance:
  coefficient 4–7, 12, 30–32, 103
  error 3, 5, 6, 8, 16–18, 20, 24, 25, 32, 62, 65, 77

Wall Street Journal Index 292
Weighted least squares 6, 7, 12, 24–27, 65, 67, 69, 77
W.T. Grant 256, 299–300

Zeta model 274–275
Z-Score model 262–270
Zone of ignorance 266